AIRFRAME & POWERPLANT MECHANICS

AIRFRAME TEST GUIDE

Written, Oral & Practical FAA Exam Prep with Practical Test Standards

FOR USE WITH

FAA-H-8083-31A & FAA-H-8083-31A-ATB

Airframe & Powerplant Mechanics Handbook

2023 EDITION

AIRCRAFT
TECHNICAL
BOOK COMPANY

Printed and Published by
Aircraft Technical Book Company
72413 US Hwy 40 - Tabernash, CO 80478-0270 USA
1.970.726.5111
www.actechbooks.com

If you purchased this Test Guide with the Skyprep option, your activation code is located on the inside front cover of this book.

LOOK FOR THIS STICKER ON THE INSIDE FRONT COVER TO FIND YOUR ACTIVATION CODE	**SKYPREP ACTIVATION CODE** **XXXXX-XXXXX**

Enhance your test preparation with Skyprep online exam practice. With Skyprep, you can take practice exams in the same format as you will take your FAA written tests. Skyprep allows you to practice your exams in three useful ways:

1. Practice all questions in all topics in random order.
2. Practice only those questions in a particular topic.
3. Take a simulated timed practice exam just as you would for the FAA.

After completing any of the above formats, Skyprep will give you your score for that session including corrections, explanations, and references within the 8083-ATB Handbooks for any questions answered incorrectly. Skyprep keeps track of your progress so you can see your improvements over multiple testing sessions. Your unlimited Skyprep subscription remains valid for two years from when you first sign in.

How To Access Skyprep
Access Skyprep through any online device by scanning the QR code or visit the following URL https://actechbooks.skyprepapp.com/users/enrol?course_id=137784
Complete the registration process along with your activation code.

DON'T HAVE SKYPREP YET?

If you purchased this Test Guide without Skyprep, you may add Skyprep at any time for this version of Test Guide for $21.95. To order Skyprep visit this URL https://www.actechbooks.com/skyprep.html and place your order. Your activation code will be emailed to you within one business day.

2 YEARS OF UNLIMITED SKYPREP PRACTICE EXAMS FOR $21.95

TABLE OF CONTENTS

Chapter 01 - Aircraft Structures
Written questions, answers, explanations, oral question samples, practical test and sample projects.

Chapter 02 - Aerodynamics, Assembly, Rigging
Written questions, answers, explanations, oral question samples, practical test and sample projects.

Chapter 03 - Fabric Covering
Written questions, answers, explanations, oral question samples, practical test and sample projects.

Chapter 04 - Metal Structural Repair
Written questions, answers, explanations, oral question samples, practical test and sample projects.

Chapter 05 - Aircraft Welding
Written questions, answers, explanations, oral question samples, practical test and sample projects.

Chapter 06 - Aircraft Wood
Written questions, answers, explanations, oral question samples, practical test and sample projects.

Chapter 07 - Composite Materials
Written questions, answers, explanations, oral question samples, practical test and sample projects.

Chapter 08 - Painting & Finishing
Written questions, answers, explanations, oral question samples, practical test and sample projects.

Chapter 09 - Electrical Systems
Written questions, answers, explanations, oral question samples, practical test and sample projects.

Chapter 10 - Aircraft Instruments
Written questions, answers, explanations, oral question samples, practical test and sample projects.

Chapter 11 - Communications & Navigation
Written questions, answers, explanations, oral question samples, practical test and sample projects.

Chapter 12 - Hydraulic & Pneumatic
Written questions, answers, explanations, oral question samples, practical test and sample projects.

Chapter 13 - Landing Gear
Written questions, answers, explanations, oral question samples, practical test and sample projects.

Chapter 14 - Fuel Systems
Written questions, answers, explanations, oral question samples, practical test and sample projects.

Chapter 15 - Ice & Rain Protection
Written questions, answers, explanations, oral question samples, practical test and sample projects.

Chapter 16 - Cabin Environment
Written questions, answers, explanations, oral question samples, practical test and sample projects.

Chapter 17 - Fire Protection
Written questions, answers, explanations, oral question samples, practical test and sample projects.

HOW TO USE THIS TEST GUIDE

This book is designed to help you pass your FAA knowledge test. But, even more important, it is designed to help reinforce your understanding of the subject which you have been studying in the classroom or with your textbooks and other tools. Rather than this being the first book you pick up, it should be the last. When you take that route, you will find the questions in this book both easy and an excellent reinforcement to your studies.

The process we suggest is: Learn first from the textbooks and your instructors. When you are comfortable with a subject, and can see problems from different sides, then it is time to prepare for the test. This Test Guide, if properly used, will serve as your proof that you know what you need to know or if a subject requires further study. If so, the explanation with each question may refresh your understanding, or the textbook reference given will point you to the right place for review.

WHERE THE QUESTIONS COME FROM:
In 2011, FAA made the decision to stop publishing actual test questions. Previous test guides, where one could memorize questions are no more. Questions in this and other current FAA test guides now contain only examples of the type of question you will see on your actual FAA test.

Questions in this book come from two sources. First are previous FAA written questions which remain relevant to the curricula covered in the FAA 8083 Handbooks. Second are new questions written by Aircraft Technical Book Company and its team of authors to cover topics in the 8083s (the FAA required curricula) for which previous FAA samples did not exist.

Should you "make sure" and buy other test guides as well? In one sense it can't hurt. After all, our question on any particular topic may have different wording or may approach that topic slightly differently than another's. However, all will be different from the actual test questions, and different too from those asked by an examiner, or more important; by an employer.

So your first job is to learn in the classroom, study the textbooks, and understand the subject. With that, all questions, no matter how they are written will be easy and obvious, so making your career in aerospace rich and rewarding. Remember, its not the quick way; its the right way.

PRACTICAL TEST STANDARDS (PTS) AND AIRMAN CERTIFICATION STANDARDS (ACS)

The PTS and ACS are FAA documents which detail the knowledge and skills required to qualify for an A&P license. Your knowledge requirements are tested through your FAA oral and written exams (General, Airframe, Powerplant) via questions similar to those in this book. Your practical skills are assessed by an FAA examiner during that final phase of your testing.

In May 2022 FAA began a transition from the PTS to the ACS format. For the purpose of learning, the ACS will replace the PTS in September of 2022. For the purpose of testing, the ACS standards will replace the PTS in July 2023. This staggered schedule will insure that those presently learning under PTS standards will be tested according to the same.

Each of these documents in their most current editions are available to download and/or print at the following links:

Practical Test Standards (PTS)
   https://www.actechbooks.com/test_standards/amt_pts.pdf

Airman Certification Standards (ACS)
   https://www.actechbooks.com/test_standards/amt_acs.pdf

Learning Statement Codes A&P Mechanic — Airframe

Learning statement codes replace the old subject matter codes and are noted on the test report. They refer to measurable statements of knowledge that a student should be able to demonstrate following a defined element of training. The learning statement corresponding to the learning statement code is on the test report.

AMA001   Aerodynamic Fundamentals
AMA002   Air Conditioning System - Components / Operating Principles / Characteristics
AMA003   Aircraft Component Markings
AMA004   Aircraft Components Material - Flame Resistant
AMA005   Aircraft Cooling System - Charging / Leaking / Oil / Pressure / Water
AMA006   Aircraft Cooling System - Components / Operating Principles / Characteristics
AMA007   Aircraft Corrosion - Principles / Control / Prevention
AMA008   Aircraft Engines - Indicating System
AMA009   Aircraft Exterior Lighting - Systems / Components
AMA010   Aircraft Flight Indicator System
AMA011   Aircraft Hardware - Bolts / Nuts / Fasteners / Fittings /Valves
AMA012   Aircraft Heating System - Exhaust Jacket Inspection
AMA013   Aircraft Instruments - Install / Inspect / Adjust / Repair / Markings
AMA014   Aircraft Instruments - Types / Components / Operating Principles / Characteristics
AMA015   Aircraft Lighting - Install / Inspect / Repair / Service
AMA016   Aircraft Metals - Inspect / Test / Repair / Identify
AMA017   Aircraft Metals - Types / Tools / Fasteners
AMA018   Aircraft Warning Systems - Navigation / Stall / Takeoff
AMA019   Airframe - Inspections
AMA020   Airframe - Repair / Component Installation
AMA021   Airframe Design - Structures / Components
AMA022   Alternators - Components / Operating Principles / Characteristics
AMA023   Antenna System - Install / Inspect / Repair / Service
AMA024   Anti-Icing / Deicing - Methods / Systems
AMA025   Autopilot - Components / Operating Principles / Characteristics
AMA026   Autopilot - Install / Inspect / Repair / Service
AMA027   Avionics - Components / Operating Principles / Characteristics
AMA028   Avionics - Install / Inspect / Repair / Service
AMA029   Basic Hand Tools / Torque Values
AMA030   Batteries - Capacity / Charging / Types / Storage / Rating / Precautions
AMA031   Brake System - Components / Operating Principles / Characteristics
AMA032   Brake System - Install / Inspect / Repair / Service
AMA033   Carburetor - Icing / Anti-Icing
AMA034   Chemical Rain Repellent
AMA035   Combustion Heaters - Components / Operating Principles / Characteristics
AMA036   Compass - Components / Operating Principles / Characteristics
AMA037   Composite Materials - Types / Repairs / Techniques / Processes
AMA038   Control Cables - Install / Inspect / Repair / Service
AMA039   DC Electric Motors - Components / Operating Principles / Characteristics
AMA040   Dope And Fabric - Materials / Techniques / Hazards
AMA041   Electrical System - Components / Operating Principles / Characteristics / Symbols
AMA042   Electrical System - Install / Inspect / Repair / Service
AMA043   Electronic Test Equipment
AMA044   Emergency Locator Transmitter (ELT) - Operation / Battery / Testing
AMA045   Fiberglass - Install / Troubleshoot / Service / Repair
AMA046   Fire Detection System - Types / Components / Operating Principles / Characteristics
AMA047   Fire Detection Systems - Install / Inspect / Repair / Service
AMA048   Fire Extinguishing Systems - Components / Operating Principles / Characteristics
AMA050   Flight Characteristics - Longitudinal Stability / Instability
AMA051   Fluid Lines - Material / Coding
AMA052   Fuel - Types / Characteristics / Contamination / Fueling / Defueling / Dumping
AMA053   Fuel / Oil - Anti-Icing / Deicing
AMA054   Fuel System - Components / Operating Principles / Characteristics
AMA055   Fuel System - Install / Troubleshoot / Service / Repair

AMA056   Fuel System - Types
AMA057   Fuel/Air Mixture - Idle Rich Mixture - Rpm Rise
AMA058   Fundamental Material Properties
AMA059   Fuselage Stations
AMA060   Helicopter Control System
AMA061   Helicopter Control System - Collective
AMA062   Helicopter Drive System - Free Wheeling Unit
AMA063   Hydraulic Systems - Components / Operating Principles / Characteristics
AMA064   Hydraulic Systems - Fluids
AMA065   Hydraulic Systems - Install / Inspect / Repair / Service
AMA066   Instrument Panel Installation - Shock Mounts
AMA067   Instruments - Manifold Pressure Indicating System
AMA068   Landing Gear System - Components / Operating Principles / Characteristics
AMA069   Landing Gear System - Install / Inspect / Repair / Service
AMA070   Maintenance Publications - Service / Parts / Repair
AMA071   Navigation / Communication Systems - Types / Operational Characteristics
AMA072   Oxygen System - Components / Operating Principles / Characteristics
AMA073   Oxygen System - Install / Inspect / Repair / Service / Precautions
AMA074   Oxygen System - Quality / Types / Contamination / Cylinders / Pressure
AMA075   Physics - Work Forces
AMA076   Pitot-Static System - Components / Operating Principles / Characteristics
AMA077   Pitot-Static System - Install / Inspect / Repair / Service
AMA078   Plastic Fundamentals - Installation / Cleaning / Repair / Characteristics
AMA079   Pneumatic System - Components / Operating Principles / Characteristics
AMA080   Pressurization System - Components / Operating Principles / Characteristics
AMA081   Primary Flight Controls - Inspect / Adjust / Repair
AMA082   Primary Flight Controls - Types / Purpose / Functionality
AMA083   Radar Altimeter - Indications
AMA084   Radar Altimeter - Signals
AMA085   Radio System - Components / Operating Principles / Characteristics
AMA086   Radio System - Install / Inspect / Repair / Service
AMA087   Radio System - License Requirements / Frequencies
AMA088   Regulations - Airworthiness Requirements / Responsibilities
AMA089   Regulations - Maintenance Reports / Records / Entries
AMA090   Regulations - Privileges / Limitations Of Maintenance Certificates / Licenses
AMA091   Rotor System - Components / Operating Principles / Characteristics
AMA092   Secondary Flight Control System - Inspect / Adjust / Repair
AMA093   Secondary Flight Control System - Types / Purpose / Functionality
AMA094   Sheet Metal Fabrication - Blueprints / Shaping / Construction
AMA095   Smoke Detection Systems - Types / Components / Operating Principles / Characteristics
AMA096   Static Pressure System - Install / Inspect / Repair / Service
AMA097   Tires - Install / Inspect / Repair / Service / Storage
AMA098   Turbine Engines - Components / Operational Characteristics / Associated Instruments
AMA099   Type Certificate Data Sheet (TCDS) / Supplemental Type Certificate (STC)
AMA100   Weight And Balance - Equipment Installation / Cg / General Principles
AMA101   Welding / Soldering - Types / Techniques / Equipment
AMA102   Wooden Components - Failures / Decay / Patching / Gluing / Substitutions

AIRCRAFT STRUCTURES

Major Structural Stresses, Fixed-Wing Aircraft, Wings, Empennage, Flight Control Surfaces, and Aircraft Structure Maintenance

1-1 AMA021
Which stresses does an operating piston engine apply to its airframe?
  A. Shear and bending.
  B. Tension and torsion.
  C. Compression and shear.

1-2 AMA021
Which type of stress does a stringer in a semi-monocoque fuselage absorb?
  A. Shear
  B. Tension
  C. Torsion

1-3 AMA021
Which type of skin material would most likely be found on a monocoque fuselage?
  A. Fabric
  B. Wood
  C. Metal

1-4 AMA021
Which of the following creates a critical need for frequent inspections on a pressurized fuselage?
  A. Corrosion
  B. Metal fatigue
  C. Humidity and temperature changes

1-5 AMA021
Which of the following wing design features will provide the greatest amount of lateral stability?
  A. Sweepback
  B. Dihedral
  C. Cantilever

1-6 AMA021
Which of the following wing components are positioned chordwise within a wing's structure?
  A. Stringers and formers.
  B. Ribs and stingers.
  C. Ribs and formers.

AIRCRAFT STRUCTURES

ANSWERS

1-1 Answer B.
An operating engine and propeller apply both tension and torsion to the airframe via its engine mounts. Tension, being the pulling force generated by the propeller. Torsion being the twisting force created by the rotating propeller on the non-rotating airframe.
[Ref: Airframe Handbook H-8083-31A-ATB, Chapter 01 Page 7]

1-2 Answer B.
Of the 5 stresses that may act on airframe parts, (tension, compression, torsion, shear, bending) horizontally installed stringers and longerons prevent tension and compression from bending the fuselage.
[Ref: Airframe Handbook H-8083-31A-ATB, Chapter 01 Page 8-9]

1-3 Answer C.
A monocoque fuselage relies on the strength and stiffness of the skin to carry the primary loads in all directions. Thus metal or composites (or in rare cases, wood) would be the likely skin material of choice.
[Ref: Airframe Handbook H-8083-31A-ATB, Chapter 01 Page 8-9]

1-4 Answer B.
Pressurized fuselages are constantly stretching and shrinking as the pressurization inside the fuselage cycles higher and lower with each flight. Thus frequent inspection are required for minute cracks caused by this constant flexing.
[Ref: Airframe Handbook H-8083-31A-ATB, Chapter 01 Page 10]

1-5 Answer B.
Dihedral is the measure of the angle the span of the wing has to the fuselage. The higher this angle, the greater is the lateral stability of the aircraft. Cantilever is a construction method allowing the absence of external bracing. Sweepback provides benefits regarding critical mach numbers in high speed flight.
[Ref: Airframe Handbook H-8083-31A-ATB, Chapter 01 Page 10-11]

1-6 Answer C.
The chordwise direction is from the leading to training edge of the wing; versus spanwise which is from the root to the tip. Ribs and formers are positioned chordwise and are mostly responsible for determining and forming the structure for the aerodynamic shape of the wing.
[Ref: Airframe Handbook H-8083-31A-ATB, Chapter 01 Page 12]

1-7 AMA021
Most manufactured aircraft have wings spars made of
 A. laminated wood.
 B. solid extruded aluminum.
 C. spruce wood.

1-8 AMA021
The purpose of anti-drag wires within the structure of a wing are to add strength to the _____.
 A. Trailing edge fittings
 B. Spar
 C. Ribs

1-9 AMA021
Which term below is also referred to as a pod?
 A. Nacelles
 B. Rib
 C. Spar

1-10 AMA021
Which of the following can be part of an empennage?
 1. Rudder
 2. Elevator
 3. Fuel tank
 A. Only 1
 B. 1 and 2
 C. All of the above

1-11 AMA082
Ailerons control which of an airplane's axes of rotation?
 A. Longitudinal
 B. Lateral
 C. Vertical

1-12 AMA021
To prevent in-flight flutter of a control surface such as an aileron or elevator, the center of gravity of the component is typically set _____.
 A. exactly on the hinge line
 B. slightly forward of its hinge line
 C. slightly aft of its hinge line

AIRCRAFT STRUCTURES

ANSWERS

1-7 Answer B.
Spars may be made of metal, wood, or composite materials depending on the design criteria of a specific aircraft. Wooden spars are usually made from spruce. Lamination of solid wood spars is often used to increase strength. Currently, most manufactured aircraft have wing spars made of solid extruded aluminum or aluminum extrusions riveted together to form the spar.
[Ref: Airframe Handbook H-8083-31A-ATB, Chapter 01 Page 13-14]

1-8 Answer C.
Since ribs are laterally weak, drag and anti-drag wires are mounted between the ribs to reduce fore and aft forces in the chord direction.
[Ref: Airframe Handbook H-8083-31A-ATB, Chapter 01 Page 10-16]

1-9 Answer A.
Nacelles (sometimes called "pods") are streamlined enclosures used primarily to house the engine and its components. They usually present a round or elliptical profile to the wind thus reducing aerodynamic drag.
[Ref: Airframe Handbook H-8083-31A-ATB, Chapter 01 Page 19-20]

1-10 Answer B.
The other components of the typical empennage are of heavier construction than the tail cone. These members include fixed surfaces that help stabilize the aircraft and movable surfaces that help to direct an aircraft during flight. The fixed surfaces are the horizontal stabilizer and vertical stabilizer. The movable surfaces are usually a rudder located at the aft edge of the vertical stabilizer and an elevator located at the aft edge the horizontal stabilizer.
[Ref: Airframe Handbook H-8083-31A-ATB, Chapter 01 Page 22-24]

1-11 Answer A.
An aircraft can rotate in 3 directions: The rudder controls yaw or the vertical axis (nose goes left or right). The elevator controls pitch or the lateral axis (nose goes up or down). The ailerons control roll or the longitudinal axis (the left and right wings go up or down). Page 1-25 of the Airframe textbook shows these directions clearly.
[Ref: Airframe Handbook H-8083-31A-ATB, Chapter 01 Page 25]

1-12 Answer B.
Primary control surfaces must be balanced around their center of gravity so they do not vibrate or flutter in the air stream. Balancing typically consists of assuring that the center of gravity of the movable surface is slightly forward of its hinge line.
[Ref: Airframe Handbook H-8083-31A-ATB, Chapter 01 Page 26]

1-13 AMA093
Which device serves to increase the pilot's sense of feel when operating a primary control surface such as ailerons or rudders?
A. Trim tabs
B. Balance tabs
C. Anti-balance tabs

1-16 AMA001
The primary purpose of stall strips is to
A. provide added lift at high angles of attack.
B. stall the inboard portion of the wings first.
C. provide added lift at slow speeds.

1-14 AMA093
When operating at low speeds, spoilers on transport aircraft are typically interconnected with and operate simultaneously with the
A. flaps.
B. ailerons.
C. elevators.

1-17 AMA021
Which of these wing devices has the purpose of reducing drag created by airflow over the wing tips and so improving the aircraft's overall fuel economy?
A. Vortex generators
B. Winglets
C. Gap seals

1-15 AMA093
Which type of tab can be used in an emergency failure of the hydraulic system to move and control the primary flight control surfaces?
A. Servo tabs
B. Spring tabs
C. Balance tab

1-18 AMA068
An aircraft said to have conventional landing gear, is understood to have
A. fixed landing gear which are not retracted in flight.
B. two main gear under the wing and a nose wheel.
C. two main gear typically forward of the wing and a tail wheel.

AIRCRAFT STRUCTURES

ANSWERS

1-13 Answer C.
Anti-balance or anti-servo tabs move in the same direction as the primary control surface (typically the horizontal stabilizer). These are common when the input to the control surface is too sensitive to the pilot's control. The anti-servo tab increases the force needed to move the control surface thus making the aircraft more stable for the pilot.
[Ref: Airframe Handbook H-8083-31A-ATB, Chapter 01 Page 29-32]

1-14 Answer B.
At low speeds, spoilers are rigged to operate with the ailerons. On the wing where the aileron is moved up, the spoiler also raises to amplify the reduction of lift on that side. On the wing with downward aileron deflection the spoiler remains stowed. As the aircraft speed increases the ailerons become more effective and the spoiler link disconnects.
[Ref: Airframe Handbook H-8083-31A-ATB, Chapter 01 Page 30]

1-15 Answer A.
A servo tab is similar to a balance tab in location and effect, but is designed to fully operate and position the primary control surface in the event of a systems failure, not just reduce the force needed to do so.
[Ref: Airframe Handbook H-8083-31A-ATB, Chapter 01 Page 32]

1-16 Answer B.
A stall strip is a small triangular metal strip installed along the leading edge of an airplane wing near the wing root. Stall strips cause the root section of the wing to stall before the portion of the wing ahead of the ailerons.
[Ref: Airframe Handbook H-8083-31A-ATB, Chapter 01 Page 34]

1-17 Answer B.
A winglet is an aerodynamic addition to the wing tip (an obvious upturn of the wing) which reduces drag which is caused by the circulation of air from the bottom to the top of the wing at the wing tip. Vortex generators help low speed performance by maintaining a stable boundary layer of air flowing over the wing. Gap seals cover the space between the wing and control surfaces smoothing airflow over this area at high angles of attack.
[Ref: Airframe Handbook H-8083-31A-ATB, Chapter 01 Page 34-35]

1-18 Answer C.
As tail wheel type aircraft dominated early aviation, "conventional gear" refers to an aircraft with a tail wheel. Nose wheel aircraft are referred to as "tricycle gear". An aircraft with or without gear retraction is termed either "fixed gear" or "retractable gear".
[Ref: Airframe Handbook H-8083-31A-ATB, Chapter 01 Page 36-37]

1-19 AMA070
If a manufacturer's maintenance manual does not exist for an older aircraft, the correct procedures for maintaining that aircraft can be found by
A. consulting an A&P mechanic with Inspection Authorization.
B. consulting FAA Advisory Circular AC43.13 1B/2B.
C. consulting a current manufacturer's maintenance manual of a similar type airplane.

1-20 AMA059
To locate the position of a hinge on the REAR SPAR OF the vertical stabilizer, you must refer to the hinge's _____.
A. Butt line
B. Waterline
C. Reference datum

1-21 AMA059
Which is the location of FS 137?
A. 137 inches aft of the nose of the aircraft.
B. 137 inches aft of the datum.
C. 137 inches aft of the aircraft center of gravity (CG).

1-22 AMA098
Approximately what percentage of the airflow entering a helicopter's turbine engine is applied to the production of power?
A. 25%
B. 60%
C. 90%

1-23 AMA021
Which type of helicopter rotor system allows movement in the blade positions during speed (RPM) changes to counter variations of centrifugal force?
A. Anti-torque rotor systems
B. Semi rigid rotor systems
C. Articulated rotor systems

1-24 AMA061
Which helicopter flight control causes the rotor to tilt, thus changing the horizontal direction of the aircraft?
A. Cyclic
B. Collective
C. Foot pedals

AIRCRAFT STRUCTURES

ANSWERS

1-19 Answer B.
FAA AC43.13 1B/2B Acceptable Methods of Aircraft Inspection and Repair documents the proper and legal techniques and procedures to maintain non-pressurized aircraft under 10,000 pounds and for which no current manufacturer's manual exists.
[Ref: Airframe Handbook H-8083-31A-ATB, Chapter 01 Page 38]

1-20 Answer B.
The waterline is a vertical reference which identifies points above or below the indicated reference. a point on the vertical spar of the vertical stabilizer is identified from this point. The butt line is a horizontal measurement from the centerline of the aircraft, useful for points along the wing or horizontal stabilizer. The reference datum indicates locations along the length of the fuselage.
[Ref: Airframe Handbook H-8083-31A-ATB, Chapter 01 Page 39-40]

1-21 Answer B
Fuselage stations (Fus. Sta. or FS) are numbered in inches from a reference or zero point known as the reference datum. The reference datum is an imaginary vertical plane at or near the nose of the aircraft from which all fore and aft distances are measured. The distance to a given point is measured in inches parallel to a center line extending through the aircraft from the nose through the center of the tail cone. Some manufacturers may call the fuselage station a body station, abbreviated BS.
[Ref: Airframe Handbook H-8083-31A-ATB, Chapter 01 Page 39]

1-22 Answer A.
Because airflow through the helicopter turboshaft engine is not a straight line pass through as in a jet engine, the cooling efficiency of the airflow is limited. Thus, approximately 75% of the incoming airflow into the engine is re-routed for the purpose of engine cooling.
[Ref: Airframe Handbook H-8083-31A-ATB, Chapter 01 Page 42]

1-23 Answer C.
Fully articulated blade systems provide hinges that allow the rotor blades to move fore and aft. When first starting to spin, the blades lag until centrifugal force is fully developed. Once rotating a reduction in speed causes the blades to lead the main rotor until forces come into balance. In a fully articulated system, they are free to do so due to being mounted on a vertical drag hinge.
[Ref: Airframe Handbook H-8083-31A-ATB, Chapter 01 Page 44]

1-24 Answer A.
The cyclic is the control stick typically located between the pilot's legs. It changes the angle of the swash plate which changes the plane of rotation of the rotor blades moving the aircraft horizontally depending on the position of the cyclic.
[Ref: Airframe Handbook H-8083-31A-ATB, Chapter 01 Page 46-47]

ORAL EXAM

1-1(O).   Name the three major categories of aircraft.

1-2(O).   Name the five principal units that make up a fixed-wing aircraft.

1-3(O).   Name the principal units that make up a helicopter airframe.

1-4(O).   Name the five major stresses to which all aircraft are subjected.

1-5(O).   Define fuselage.

1-6(O).   Explain a monocoque fuselage.

1-7(O).   Explain a semi-monocoque fuselage.

1-8(O).   Explain the purpose of stringers as used the construction of a semi-monocoque fuselage.

1-9(O).   What factors are taken into consideration when designing the wing structure of an aircraft?

1-10(O).   What are nacelles and what purpose do they serve?

1-11(O).   What is the empennage and which components does it house?

1-12(O).   Name the primary flight control surfaces on a fixed-wing aircraft.

1-13(O).   What is a stabilator?

1-14(O).   Explain fuselage stations?

1-15(O).   Define Buttock line or butt line (BL).

1-16(O).   Define Water line (WL).

1-17(O).   Which components make up the rotor section of a helicopter.

1-18(O).   Name the three basic classification of rotor blades.

1-19(O).   Which section of a helicopter help to counteract the effects of torque produced by the main rotors?

AIRCRAFT STRUCTURES

ANSWERS

ORAL EXAM

1-1(O).   Rotorcraft, glider, and lighter-than-air vehicles.
[Ref: Airframe Handbook H-8083-31A-ATB, Chapter 01 Page 5]

1-2(O).   Fuselage, wings, stabilizers, flight control surfaces, and landing gear.
[Ref: Airframe Handbook H-8083-31A-ATB, Chapter 01 Page 6]

1-3(O).   Fuselage, main rotor and related gearbox, tail rotor (on helicopters with a single main rotor), and the landing gear.
[Ref: Airframe Handbook H-8083-31A-ATB, Chapter 01 Page 6]

1-4(O).   Tension, compression, torsion, shear, and bending.
[Ref: Airframe Handbook H-8083-31A-ATB, Chapter 01 Page 7]

1-5(O).   The main structure or body of an aircraft that houses space for cargo, controls, accessories, passengers, and other equipment.
[Ref: Airframe Handbook H-8083-31A-ATB, Chapter 01 Page 8]

1-6(O).   A single-shell type of aircraft structure in which all of the flight loads are carried in the outside skin of the structure..
[Ref: Airframe Handbook H-8083-31A-ATB, Chapter 01 Page 9, G-23]

1-7(O).   A form of aircraft stressed skin structure. Most of the strength of a semi-monocoque structure is in the skin, but the skin is supported on a substructure of formers and stringers that give the skin its shape and increase its rigidity.
[Ref: Airframe Handbook H-8083-31A-ATB, Chapter 01 Page 9, G-31]

1-8(O).   They give the fuselage its shape and, in some types of structure, to provide a small part of fuselage strength.
[Ref: Airframe Handbook H-8083-31A-ATB, Chapter 01 Page 9]

1-9(O).   Wing designs must factor the aircraft's size and weight, the use of the aircraft, the desired speed in flight and at landing, and desired rate of climb.
[Ref: Airframe Handbook H-8083-31A-ATB, Chapter 01 Page 11]

1-10(O). Nacelles are streamlined enclosures used primarily to house the engine and its components, usually with a round or elliptical profile reducing aerodynamic drag.
[Ref: Airframe Handbook H-8083-31A-ATB, Chapter 01 Page 19]

1-11(O). The empennage is the tail section and usually consists the vertical and horizontal stabilizer, rudder, and elevator.
[Ref: Airframe Handbook H-8083-31A-ATB, Chapter 01 Page 22]

1-12(O). Ailerons, elevators, and rudder.
[Ref: Airframe Handbook H-8083-31A-ATB, Chapter 01 Page 24]

1-13(O). It is a flight control on the empennage of an airplane that acts as both a stabilizer and an elevator. The entire horizontal tail surface pivots and is moved as a unit.
[Ref: Airframe Handbook H-8083-31A-ATB, Chapter 01 Page 27, G-34]

1-14(O).   They are used to help locate components on an aircraft. They are numbered in inches from a reference or zero point known as the reference datum.
[Ref: Airframe Handbook H-8083-31A-ATB, Chapter 01 Page 39]

ORAL EXAM

1-15(O). This is a vertical reference plane down the center of the aircraft from which measurements left or right can be made.
[Ref: Airframe Handbook H-8083-31A-ATB, Chapter 01 Page 39]

1-16(O). This is the measurement of height in inches perpendicular from a horizontal plane usually located at the ground, cabin floor, or some other easily referenced location.
[Ref: Airframe Handbook H-8083-31A-ATB, Chapter 01 Page 39]

1-17(O). The mast, hub, and rotor blades.
[Ref: Airframe Handbook H-8083-31A-ATB, Chapter 01 Page 43]

1-18(O). Rigid, semi-rigid, or fully articulated.
[Ref: Airframe Handbook H-8083-31A-ATB, Chapter 01 Page 1-43]

1-19(O). The tail boom and tail rotor, or antitorque rotor, counteract this torque effect.
[Ref: Airframe Handbook H-8083-31A-ATB, Chapter 01 Page 45]

AIRCRAFT STRUCTURES

QUESTIONS

PRACTICAL EXAM

1-1(P). Given an actual aircraft, mock-up, or even a drawing of an aircraft identify the various structures as requested by the examiner.

1-2(P). Given an actual aircraft, mock-up, and a maintenance manual task locate the panels to be removed to complete the required maintenance.

1-3(P). Given an actual aircraft or mock-up complete an operational check of the primarily flight control surfaces and document any discrepancies.

1-4(P). Given an actual aircraft, mock-up complete an operational check of the secondary flight control surfaces and document any discrepancies.

1-5(P). Given a series of pictures, identify the various types of wing designs.

AERODYNAMICS, AIRCRAFT ASSEMBLY, AND RIGGING

Basic Aerodynamics, Aerodynamics and the Laws of Physics, Thrust and Drag, Primary Flight Controls, and High-speed Aerodynamics

CHAPTER 02

QUESTIONS

2-1 AMA001
An aircraft's airspeed is 100 mph. The speed of the airflow under the wing is 105 mph and its speed over the wing is 115 mph. If the angle of attack is then increased by 2 degrees what will be the affect on the speed of airflow above the wing?
  A. It will stay the same.
  B. It will decrease.
  C. It will increase.

2-2 AMA014
A deviation from the measurement 29.92" Hg is best calculated by which device?
  A. An anemometer.
  B. A barometer.
  C. A variometer.

2-3 AMA001
When the atmosphere is considered "saturated", the length of runway required for an aircraft to take off is _____ than/to on an unsaturated day.
  A. shorter
  B. longer
  C. equal

2-4 AMA075
Newton's _____ Law of Motion is the law of action and reaction.
  A. First
  B. Second
  C. Third

2-5 AMA001
According to Bernoulli's Principle, when air flowing through a tube reaches a narrowing of that tube, the speed of that air flowing through that tube is _____ and its pressure is _____.
  A. decreased; decreased
  B. increased; decreased
  C. decreased; increased

2-6 AMA001
Which of the following statements regarding airfoils is True (within limits)?
  A. Lift is increased by decreasing by angle of incidence of an airfoil.
  B. Lift is increased by increased the angle of attack of an airfoil.
  C. Lift is decreased by increasing the angle of attack of an airfoil.

AERODYNAMICS, AIRCRAFT ASSEMBLY, AND RIGGING

ANSWERS

2-1 Answer C.
The airflow over the top and bottom of a wing must reach the trailing edge of the wing at the same time. When angle of attack is increased, the distance the air must flow above the wing increases, and so its speed must then also increase, thus lowering the pressure above the wing and creating additional lift.
[Ref: Airframe Handbook H-8083-31A-ATB, Chapter 02 Page 4-5]

2-2 Answer B.
Inches of Mercury is a measure of atmospheric pressure and so directly provided by a barometer. While a variometer does this as well through an internal barometer, the direct reading it provides is vertical speed changes. An anemometer measures wind speed or the pressure caused by the wind.
[Ref: Airframe Handbook H-8083-31A-ATB, Chapter 02 Page 2]

2-3 Answer B.
The term saturated refers to the amount of humidity in the air. Saturated air contains the most humidity possible at a given temperature. As humid air is less dense than dry air, the performance of an aircraft decreases versus if it were operating in dry air.
[Ref: Airframe Handbook H-8083-31A-ATB, Chapter 02 Page 3]

2-4 Answer C.
Newton's Third Law states that for every action (force) there is an equal and opposite reaction (force). This law can be illustrated by the example of firing a gun. The action is the forward movement of the bullet while the reaction is the backward recoil of the gun.
[Ref: Airframe Handbook H-8083-31A-ATB, Chapter 02 Page 4]

2-5 Answer B.
In Bernoulli's principle states when a fluid (air) flowing through a tube reaches a constriction, or narrowing, of the tube, the speed of the fluid flowing through that constriction is increased and its pressure is decreased.
[Ref: Airframe Handbook H-8083-31A-ATB, Chapter 02 Page 4]

2-6 Answer B.
Within limits, lift can be increased by increasing the Angle Of Attack (AOA), wing area, velocity, density of the air, or by changing the shape of the airfoil. When the force of lift on an aircraft's wing equals the force of gravity, the aircraft maintains level fight.
[Ref: Airframe Handbook H-8083-31A-ATB, Chapter 02 Page 5]

2-7 AMA001

The angle of incidence is that acute angle formed by
  A. a line parallel to the wing from root to tip and a line parallel to the lateral axis of the aircraft.
  B. a line parallel to the wing chord and a line parallel to the longitudinal axis of the aircraft.
  C. the angular difference between the setting of the main airfoil and the auxiliary airfoil (horizontal stabilizer) in reference to the longitudinal axis of the aircraft.

2-8 AMA001

The acute angle formed by the chord line of a wing and the relative wind is known as the
  A. angle of attack.
  B. angle of incidence.
  C. longitudinal dihedral angle.

2-9 AMA001

As the angle of attack of an airfoil increases, the center of pressure will
  A. move toward the leading edge.
  B. remain stationary because both lift and drag components increase proportionally to increased angle of attack.
  C. move toward the trailing edge.

2-10 AMA001

In order to maintain level flight, as thrust increases, the angle of attack must _____.
  A. increase
  B. decrease
  C. remain the same

2-11 AMA001

The angle of incidence of an airplane at rest
  A. does not change when in flight.
  B. affects the dihedral of the wings in flight.
  C. is the same as the angle between the relative wind and the chord of the wing.

2-12 AMA001

As lift increases on an aircraft, parasitic drag _____ and induced drag _____.
  A. increases; increases
  B. increases; decreases
  C. decreases, increases

AERODYNAMICS, AIRCRAFT ASSEMBLY, AND RIGGING

ANSWERS

2-7 Answer B.
The angle of incidence is the acute angle formed between the chord line of an airfoil and the longitudinal axis of the aircraft on which it is mounted.
[Ref: Airframe Handbook H-8083-31A-ATB, Chapter 02 Page 6, G-2]

2-8 Answer A.
The chord of an airfoil or wing section is an imaginary straight line that passes through the section from the leading edge to the trailing edge. The chord line provides one side of an angle that ultimately forms the AOA. The other side of the angle is formed by a line indicating the direction of the relative airstream. Thus, AOA is defined as the angle between the chord line of the wing and the direction of the relative wind.
[Ref: Airframe Handbook H-8083-31A-ATB, Chapter 02 Page 6, G-2]

2-9 Answer A.
The point of intersection of the resultant force line with the chord line of the airfoil is called the Center Of Pressure (CP). The CP moves along the airfoil chord as the AOA changes. Throughout most of the flight range, the CP moves forward with increasing AOA and rearward as the AOA decreases.
[Ref: Airframe Handbook H-8083-31A-ATB, Chapter 02 Page 6]

2-10 Answer B.
As thrust increases additional air flows over the wing and so increases lift. Therefore to prevent the airplane from climbing, the angle of attack must be slightly reduced, thus lowering the lift proportionately. The end result is that by increasing power and lowering lift, the airplane speeds up without gaining altitude.
[Ref: Airframe Handbook H-8083-31A-ATB, Chapter 02 Page 6-7]

2-11 Answer A.
The angle of incidence in most cases is a fixed, built-in angle. The acute angle the wing chord makes with the longitudinal axis of the aircraft is called the angle of incidence, or the angle of wing setting.
[Ref: Airframe Handbook H-8083-31A-ATB, Chapter 02 Page 6]

2-12 Answer A.
Lift is increased by increasing angle of attack and so presenting more of the structure of the aircraft to the airflow. Induced drag is increased because as angle of attack is increased the pressure difference between the top and bottom of the aircraft becomes greater, causing more vortices, more turbulence, and so more drag.
[Ref: Airframe Handbook H-8083-31A-ATB, Chapter 02 Page 2-8]

2-13 AMA050
An airplane is controlled directionally about its vertical axis by the
  A. ailerons.
  B. elevators.
  C. rudder.

2-14 AMA082
The elevators of a conventional airplane are used to provide rotation about the
  A. vertical axis.
  B. longitudinal axis.
  C. lateral axis.

2-15 AMA081
Improper rigging of the elevator trim tab system will affect the balance of the airplane about its
  A. vertical axis.
  B. lateral axis.
  C. longitudinal axis.

2-16 AMA050
An airplane which has good longitudinal stability should have a minimum tendency to
  A. pitch.
  B. roll.
  C. yaw.

2-17 AMA001
An airplane that has a tendency to gradually increase a pitching moment that has been set into motion has
  A. poor lateral stability.
  B. poor longitudinal stability.
  C. good lateral stability.

2-18 AMA001
Stability about the axis which runs parallel to the line of flight is referred to as
  A. longitudinal stability.
  B. lateral stability.
  C. directional stability.

AERODYNAMICS, AIRCRAFT ASSEMBLY, AND RIGGING

ANSWERS

2-13 Answer C.
The axis that passes through the center, from top to bottom, is called the vertical, or yaw, axis. Yaw is controlled by the rudder located at the rear portion of the vertical tail assembly.
[Ref: Airframe Handbook H-8083-31A-ATB, Chapter 02 Page 9]

2-14 Answer C.
The axis that extends crosswise from wing tip to wing tip is the lateral, or pitch, axis. Pitch is affected by the elevators located at the rear portion of the horizontal tail assembly.
[Ref: Airframe Handbook H-8083-31A-ATB, Chapter 02 Page 9]

2-15 Answer B.
When an aircraft has a tendency to keep a constant AOA with reference to the relative wind (i.e., it does not tend to put its nose down and dive or lift its nose and stall); it is said to have longitudinal stability. Longitudinal stability refers to motion in pitch. The horizontal stabilizer is the primary surface that controls longitudinal stability. The action of the stabilizer depends upon the speed and AOA of the aircraft. Trim tabs are small airfoils recessed into the trailing edges of the primary control surfaces. Trim tabs can be used to correct any tendency of the aircraft to move toward an undesirable flight attitude. Their purpose is to enable the pilot to trim out any unbalanced condition which may exist during flight, without exerting any pressure on the primary controls. See Figure 2-10 in the text for a table of flight control surfaces and their relationship to aircraft stability.
[Ref: Airframe Handbook H-8083-31A-ATB, Chapter 02 Page 10]

2-16 Answer A.
When an aircraft has a tendency to keep a constant AOA with reference to the relative wind (i.e., it does not tend to put its nose down and dive or lift its nose and stall); it is said to have longitudinal stability. Longitudinal stability refers to motion in pitch. See Figure 2-10 in the text for a table of flight control surfaces and their relationship to aircraft stability.
[Ref: Airframe Handbook H-8083-31A-ATB, Chapter 02 Page 10]

2-17 Answer B.
When an aircraft has a tendency to keep a constant AOA with reference to the relative wind (i.e., it does not tend to put its nose down and dive or lift its nose and stall); it is said to have longitudinal stability. Longitudinal stability refers to motion in pitch. See Figure 2-10 in the text for a table of flight control surfaces and their relationship to aircraft stability.
[Ref: Airframe Handbook H-8083-31A-ATB, Chapter 02 Page 10]

2-18 Answer B.
Motion about the aircraft's longitudinal (fore and aft) axis is a lateral, or rolling, motion. The tendency to return to the original attitude from such motion is called lateral stability. See Figure 2-10 in the text for a table of flight control surfaces and their relationship to aircraft stability.
[Ref: Airframe Handbook H-8083-31A-ATB, Chapter 02 Page 10]

2-19 AMA001
The purpose of the vertical fin (stabilizer) is to provide
A. lateral stability.
B. directional stability.
C. longitudinal stability.

2-20 AMA082
The purpose of spring tabs or servo tabs is to
A. contribute to the static balance of the control surface.
B. make in flight trim adjustments possible.
C. assist the pilot in moving the control surfaces.

2-21 AMA092
To what is the control rod for the trim tab of an elevator attached?
A. The elevator.
B. An elevator control horn.
C. The horizontal stabilizer.

2-22 AMA091
_____ are often attached on swept-wing aircraft to prevent the spanwise movement of air at high angles or attack.
A. Canard wings
B. Wing fences
C. Winglets

2-23 AMA063
Which type of drag is greater when an aircraft is moving at a slower speed?
A. Induced Drag
B. Profile Drag
C. Parasitic Drag

2-24 AMA091
Which of the following statements is not true in regards to high-speed aerodynamics?
A. High-speed aerodynamics are often called compressible aerodynamics and a special branch of study of aeronautics.
B. The compression effect becomes more important as speed decreases.
C. Mach number is the ratio of the speed of the aircraft to the local speed of sound.

AERODYNAMICS, AIRCRAFT ASSEMBLY, AND RIGGING

ANSWERS

2-19 Answer B.
The vertical stabilizer is the primary surface that controls directional stability.
[Ref: Airframe Handbook H-8083-31A-ATB, Chapter 02 Page 11]

2-20 Answer C.
Spring tabs are similar in appearance to trim tabs, but serve an entirely different purpose. Spring tabs are used for the same purpose as hydraulic actuators to aid the pilot in moving the primary control surface.
[Ref: Airframe Handbook H-8083-31A-ATB, Chapter 02 Page 12]

2-21 Answer C.
The trim tab is connected to the fixed surface of the horizontal stabilizer and operated by a separate control. Servo and balance tabs are attached too, and so move together with the corresponding control surface.
[Ref: Airframe Handbook H-8083-31A-ATB, Chapter 02 Page 12]

2-22 Answer B.
Wing fences are flat metal vertical plates fixed to the upper surface of the wing. They obstruct spanwise airflow along the wing, and prevent the entire wing from stalling at once. They are often attached on swept-wing aircraft to prevent the spanwise movement of air at high angles of attack. Their purpose is to provide better slow speed handling and stall characteristics.
[Ref: Airframe Handbook H-8083-31A-ATB, Chapter 02 Page 14]

2-23 Answer A.
Up through the stall, induced drag is greatest when the airfoil is producing the greatest amount of lift. This occurs when the angle of attack is the greatest such as during the low speed conditions during takeoff, climb and landing. Parasitic and profile drag are greatest at higher speeds when the aircraft is typically in cruise flight.
[Ref: Airframe Handbook H-8083-31A-ATB, Chapter 02 Page 8]

2-24 Answer B.
The compression effect becomes more important as speed increases. Near and beyond the speed of sound, about 760 mph (at sea level), sharp disturbances generate a shockwave that affects both the lift and drag of an aircraft and flow conditions downstream of the shockwave. The shockwave forms a cone of pressurized air molecules, which move outward and rearward in all directions and extend to the ground. The sharp release of the pressure, after the buildup by the shockwave, is heard as the sonic boom.
[Ref: Airframe Handbook H-8083-31A-ATB, Chapter 02 Page 15]

2-25 AMA081
Which of the three major steps are for rigging of the various flight control systems?
1. Placing the control system in a specific position—holding it in position with pins, clamps, or jigs, then adjusting the various linkages to fit the immobilized control component.
2. Placing the control surfaces in a specific reference position—using a rigging jig, a precision bubble protractor, or a spirit level to check the angular difference between the control surface and some fixed surface on the aircraft.
3. Setting the maximum range of travel of the various components—this adjustment limits the physical movement of the control system.
   A. 1 and 3.
   B. 2 and 3.
   C. 1, 2, and 3.

2-26 AMA091
What configuration of a rotary-wing aircraft has two horizontal rotors that provide both lift and directional control?
   A. Autogyro
   B. Single rotor helicopter
   C. Dual rotor helicopter

2-27 AMA091
What do the foot pedals control on a helicopter?
   A. The pitch of the tail rotor blades.
   B. The RPM of the tail rotor blades.
   C. The angle of the disk of the tail rotor.

2-28 AMA060
The auxiliary (tail) rotor of a helicopter permits the pilot to compensate for and/or accomplish which of the following?
   A. Attitude and airspeed.
   B. Lateral and yaw position.
   C. Torque and directional control.

2-29 AMA091
When a helicopter's rotor blade rotates from front to rear, its pitch, as controlled by an articulated rotor head
   A. decreases.
   B. increases.
   C. moves to neutral.

2-30 AMA060
Regarding gyroscopic forces, the movement of the cyclic pitch control changes the AOA of each blade an appropriate amount so that the end result is the same in what type of rotor system?
   A. One-blade rotor system.
   B. Two-blade rotor system.
   C. Three or more blade rotor system.

AERODYNAMICS, AIRCRAFT ASSEMBLY, AND RIGGING

ANSWERS

2-25 Answer C.
All of the statements make up the three major steps for rigging various flight control, the order listed is also correct.
[Ref: Airframe Handbook H-8083-31A-ATB, Chapter 02 Page 16]

2-26 Answer C.
An aircraft with two horizontal rotors that provide both the lift and directional control is a dual rotor helicopter. The rotors are counterrotating to balance the aerodynamic torque and eliminate the need for a separate antitorque system.
[Ref: Airframe Handbook H-8083-31A-ATB, Chapter 02 Page 18]

2-27 Answer A.
Through input from the left and right foot pedals, the tail rotor produces thrust in the opposite direction to the torque produced by the main rotor by increasing or decreasing the angle of attack of the tail rotor blades. This thrust both prevents the helicopter from spinning on its vertical axis and also points the nose in a desired direction when maneuvering.
[Ref: Airframe Handbook H-8083-31A-ATB, Chapter 02 Page 19, 30]

2-28 Answer C.
The force that compensates for torque and provides for directional control can be produced by various means. The defining factor is dictated by the design of the helicopter, some of which do not have a torque issue. Single main rotor designs typically have an auxiliary rotor located on the end of the tail boom. This auxiliary rotor, generally referred to as a tail rotor, produces thrust in the direction opposite the torque reaction developed by the main rotor.
[Ref: Airframe Handbook H-8083-31A-ATB, Chapter 02 Page 19]

2-29 Answer B.
As a helicopter moves forward, the relative wind over the retreating blade decreases. Therefore to maintain a balanced amount of lift produced as the blade advances, an articulated rotor head increases the pitch of that retreating blade.
[Ref: Airframe Handbook H-8083-31A-ATB, Chapter 02 Page 18 and 21]

2-30 Answer C.
In a rotor system using three or more blades, the movement of the cyclic pitch control changes the AOA of each blade an appropriate amount so that the end result is the same.
[Ref: Airframe Handbook H-8083-31A-ATB, Chapter 02 Page 20-23]

2-31 AMA091
What helicopter flight condition is also known as the law of conservation of angular momentum?
  A. Ground Effect
  B. Coriolis Effect
  C. Translating Tendency

2-32 AMA091
_____ is the differential lift between advancing and retreating halves of the rotor disk caused by the different wind flow velocity across each half.
  A. Dissymmetry of lift
  B. Translational lift
  C. Effective translational lift

2-33 AMA062
A freewheeling unit is used in which form of helicopter flight
  A. forward flight.
  B. hovering flight.
  C. autorotation.

2-34 AMA060
The rotorcraft control device that senses rotor and engine RPM and makes the necessary adjustments in order to keep rotor RPM constant is the
  A. throttle control.
  B. swash plate assembly.
  C. governor.

2-35 AMA060
Movement about the longitudinal axis (roll) in a helicopter is effected by movement of the
  A. cyclic pitch control.
  B. collective pitch control.
  C. tail rotor pitch control.

2-36 AMA011
Movement about the lateral axis (pitch) in a helicopter is effected by movement of the
  A. collective.
  B. cyclic.
  C. pedals.

AERODYNAMICS, AIRCRAFT ASSEMBLY, AND RIGGING

ANSWERS

2-31 Answer B.
The Coriolis Effect is also referred to as the law of conservation of angular momentum. It states that the value of angular momentum of a rotating body does not change unless an external force is applied. In other words, a rotating body continues to rotate with the same rotational velocity until some external force is applied to change the speed of rotation.
[Ref: Airframe Handbook H-8083-31A-ATB, Chapter 02 Page 23]

2-32 Answer A.
Dissymmetry of lift is the differential (unequal) lift between advancing and retreating halves of the rotor disk caused by the different wind flow velocity across each half. This difference in lift would cause the helicopter to be uncontrollable in any situation other than hovering in a calm wind. There must be a means of compensating, correcting, or eliminating this unequal lift to attain symmetry of lift.
[Ref: Airframe Handbook H-8083-31A-ATB, Chapter 02 Page 26]

2-33 Answer C.
Autorotation is permitted mechanically by a freewheeling unit, which is a special clutch mechanism that allows the main rotor to continue turning even if the engine is not running. If the engine fails, the freewheeling unit automatically disengages the engine from the main rotor allowing the main rotor to rotate freely. It is the means by which a helicopter can be landed safely in the event of an engine failure; consequently, all helicopters must demonstrate this capability in order to be certificated.
[Ref: Airframe Handbook H-8083-31A-ATB, Chapter 02 Page 28]

2-34 Answer C.
A governor is a sensing device that senses rotor and engine RPM and makes the necessary adjustments in order to keep rotor RPM constant. Once the rotor RPM is set in normal operations, the governor keeps the RPM constant, and there is no need to make any throttle adjustments.
[Ref: Airframe Handbook H-8083-31A-ATB, Chapter 02 Page 29-30]

2-35 Answer A.
This primary flight control allows the pilot to fly the helicopter in any horizontal direction: fore, aft, and sideways.
[Ref: Airframe Handbook H-8083-31A-ATB, Chapter 02 Page 30]

2-36 Answer B.
This primary flight control allows the pilot to fly the helicopter in any horizontal direction: fore, aft, and sideways.
[Ref: Airframe Handbook H-8083-31A-ATB, Chapter 02 Page 30]

2-37 AMA060

Which helicopter stabilizer system reduces the pilot workload by improving basic aircraft control harmony and decreasing disturbances?
- A. Offset flapping hinge.
- B. Bell stabilizer bar system.
- C. Stability augmentation system.

2-38 AMA091

If a helicopter is said to have a vibration of 4/rev to 6/rev, which frequency vibration type would it be?
- A. Low frequency vibration.
- B. Medium frequency vibration.
- C. High frequency vibration.

2-39 AMA091

During helicopter operation; if manifold pressure is high, and RPM is low _____.
- A. raise the collective pitch.
- B. increase the throttle RPM.
- C. lower the collective pitch.

2-40 AMA091

Which type of blade tracking is accomplished with tracking tip cap reflectors and a strobe light?
- A. Electronic Blade
- B. Flag and Pole
- C. Marking Method

2-41 AMA091

Which tail rotor tracking method utilizes a six-inch piece of rubber hose attached to the end of a 1/2 × 1/2 inch pine stick or flexible device?
- A. Electronic Method
- B. Marking Method
- C. Neither

2-42 AMA062

Out of the list below, which component(s) are not part of the helicopter transmission system?
1. Freewheeling Unit
2. Main Rotor Transmission
3. Reciprocating Engine
4. Clutch
5. Tail Rotor Drive System
- A. 1 and 5
- B. 3
- C. 1 and 2

AERODYNAMICS, AIRCRAFT ASSEMBLY, AND RIGGING

ANSWERS

2-37 Answer C.
Stability Augmentation System (SAS) reduces pilot workload by improving basic aircraft control harmony and decreasing disturbances. These systems are very useful when the pilot is required to perform other duties, such as sling loading and search and rescue operations.
[Ref: Airframe Handbook H-8083-31A-ATB, Chapter 02 Page 32]

2-38 Answer B.
Medium frequency vibration (4/rev and 6/rev) is another vibration inherent in most rotors. An increase in the level of these vibrations is caused by a change in the capability of the fuselage to absorb vibration, or a loose airframe component, such as the skids, vibrating at that frequency.
[Ref: Airframe Handbook H-8083-31A-ATB, Chapter 02 Page 32]

2-39 Answer C.
Lowering the collective pitch decreases manifold pressure and increases RPM. Raising it does the opposite. Increasing the throttle increases both manifold pressure and RPM. Reducing the throttle does the opposite.
[Ref: Airframe Handbook H-8083-31A-ATB, Chapter 02 Page 29]

2-40 Answer A.
One of the most common electronic blade tracker is the Strobex blade tracker. It permits blade tracking from inside or outside the helicopter while on the ground or inside the helicopter in flight. Tracking can be accomplished with tracking tip cap reflectors and a strobe light. The tip caps are temporarily attached to the tip of each blade. The high-intensity strobe light flashes in time with the rotating blades. The strobe light operates from the aircraft electrical power supply. By observing the reflected tip cap image, it is possible to view the track of the rotating blades. Tracking is accomplished in a sequence of four separate steps: ground tracking, hover verification, forward flight tracking, and auto rotation RPM adjustment.
[Ref: Airframe Handbook H-8083-31A-ATB, Chapter 02 Page 33]

2-41 Answer B.
Procedures for tail rotor tracking using the marking method: after replacement or installation of tail rotor hub, blades, or pitch change system, check tail rotor rigging and track tail rotor blades. Tail rotor tip clearance shall be set before tracking and checked again after tracking; and the strobe-type tracking device may be used if available. Instructions for use are provided with the device. Attach a piece of soft rubber hose six inches long on the end of a 1/2 × 1/2 inch pine stick or other flexible device. Cover the rubber hose with Prussian blue or similar type of coloring thinned with oil.
[Ref: Airframe Handbook H-8083-31A-ATB, Chapter 02 Page 34]

2-42 Answer B.
The transmission system transfers power from the engine to the main rotor, tail rotor, and other accessories during normal flight conditions. The main components of the transmission system are the main rotor transmission, tail rotor drive system, clutch, and freewheeling unit.
[Ref: Airframe Handbook H-8083-31A-ATB, Chapter 02 Page 36-38]

2-43 AMA062
One purpose of the freewheeling unit required between the engine and the helicopter transmission is to
  A. disconnect the rotor from the engine to relieve the starter load.
  B. automatically disengage the rotor from the engine in case of an engine failure.
  C. permit practice of autorotation landings.

2-44 AMA062
What is the purpose of the freewheeling unit in a helicopter drive system?
  A. It releases the rotor brake for starting.
  B. It relieves bending stress on the rotor blades during starting.
  C. It disconnects the rotor whenever the engine stops or slows below the equivalent rotor RPM.

2-45 AMA100
A tail-heavy condition that causes undesirable flight performance and is not usually allowed is referred to as
  A. static underbalance.
  B. dynamic balance.
  C. static overbalance.

2-46 AMA081
After repairing a control surface the flight control balance condition may be determined by
  A. suspending the control surface from its leading edge in the streamline position and checking weight distribution.
  B. the behavior of the trailing edge when the surface is suspended from its hinge points.
  C. checking for equal distribution of weight throughout the control surface.

2-47 AMA081
After repairing or recovering a rudder, the surface should be rebalanced
  A. in its normal flight position.
  B. to its span wise axis.
  C. to manufacturer's specifications.

2-48 AMA099
Other than the manufacturer maintenance manual what other document could be used to determine the primary flight control surface deflection for an imported aircraft that is reassembled after shipment?
  A. The certificate of airworthiness issued by the importing country.
  B. The import manual for the aircraft.
  C. The aircraft type certificate data sheet.

AERODYNAMICS, AIRCRAFT ASSEMBLY, AND RIGGING

ANSWERS

2-43 Answer B.
Since lift in a helicopter is provided by rotating airfoils, these airfoils must be free to rotate if the engine fails. The freewheeling unit automatically disengages the engine from the main rotor when engine RPM is less than main rotor RPM. This allows the main rotor and tail rotor to continue turning at normal in-flight speeds.
[Ref: Airframe Handbook H-8083-31A-ATB, Chapter 02 Page 38]

2-46 Answer B.
Very often, repairs to a control surface require static rebalancing of the control surface. The control surface must be permitted to rotate freely about the hinge points without binding. Balance condition is determined by the behavior of the trailing edge when the surface is suspended from its hinge points.
[Ref: Airframe Handbook H-8083-31A-ATB, Chapter 02 Page 39]

2-44 Answer C.
Since lift in a helicopter is provided by rotating airfoils, these airfoils must be free to rotate if the engine fails. The freewheeling unit automatically disengages the engine from the main rotor when engine RPM is less than main rotor RPM. This allows the main rotor and tail rotor to continue turning at normal in-flight speeds.
[Ref: Airframe Handbook H-8083-31A-ATB, Chapter 02 Page 38]

2-47 Answer C.
Several methods of balancing (rebalancing) control surfaces are in use by the various manufacturers of aircraft. Several methods of balancing (rebalancing) control surfaces are in use by the various manufacturers of aircraft. The manufacturer's maintenance manual and service instructions must be followed and all precautions observed when handling the weights.
[Ref: Airframe Handbook H-8083-31A-ATB, Chapter 02 Page 40]

2-45 Answer A.
A tail-heavy condition (static underbalance) causes undesirable flight performance and is not usually allowed. Better flight operations are gained by nose-heavy static overbalance. Most manufacturers advocate the existence of nose- heavy control surfaces.
[Ref: Airframe Handbook H-8083-31A-ATB, Chapter 02 Page 38]

2-48 Answer C.
The Type Certificate Data Sheet (TCDS) is a formal description of an aircraft, engine, or propeller. It is issued by the Federal Aviation Administration (FAA) when the FAA determines that the product meets the applicable requirements for certification under 14 CFR. It lists the limitations and information required for type certification, including airspeed limits, weight limits, control surface movements, engine make and model, minimum crew, fuel type, thrust limits, RPM limits, etc., and the various components eligible for installation on the product.
[Ref: Airframe Handbook H-8083-31A-ATB, Chapter 02 Page 41]

2-49 AMA070
Which manual would be used to locate the "life limits" of a product or its components that must be complied with during inspections and maintenance?
A. Structural Repair Manual (SRM)
B. Maintenance Manual
C. Manufacturer's Service Information

2-50 AMA020
Which of these two publications are required for reference if you are reinstalling the flap assembly of an aircraft which weighs more than 12,500 pounds?
A. Manufacturer's Maintenance Manual and Illustrated Parts Catalog.
B. Manufacturer's Maintenance Manual and Type Certificate Data Sheets.
C. Advisory Circular AC43.13 1B/2B and Illustrated Parts Catalog.

2-51 AMA038
The vast majority of aircraft control cables are terminated with swaged terminals that must be
A. corrosion treated to show compliance with the manufacturers requirements after the swaging operation.
B. pull tested to show compliance with the manufactures requirements after the swaging operation.
C. checked with a no-no-go gauge before and after, to show compliance with the manufacturers requirements after the swaging operation.

2-52 AMA038
What is the smallest size cable that may be used in aircraft primary control systems?
A. 1/8 inch
B. 1/4 inch
C. 5/16 inch

2-53 AMA038
Identify the cable that is used in primary control systems and in other place where operation over pulleys is frequent?
A. 2
B. 1
C. 3

  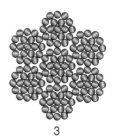

1   2   3

2-54 AMA038
If all instructions issued by the swaging tool manufacturer are followed when swaging a cable terminal, the resultant swaged terminal strength should be
A. the full rated strength of the cable.
B. 70% of the full rated strength of the cable.
C. 80% of the full rated strength of the cable.

AERODYNAMICS, AIRCRAFT ASSEMBLY, AND RIGGING

ANSWERS

2-49 Answer B.
A maintenance manual is developed by the manufacturer of the applicable product and provides the recommended and acceptable procedures to be followed when maintaining or repairing that product. Maintenance personnel are required by regulation to follow the applicable instructions set forth by the manufacturer. The limitations section of the manual lists "life limits" of the product or its components that must be complied with during inspections and maintenance.
[Ref: Airframe Handbook H-8083-31A-ATB, Chapter 02 Page 41]

2-52 Answer A.
Cable designations are based on the number of strands and wires in each strand. The 7 × 19 cable is made up of seven strands of 19 wires each. Six of these strands are laid around the center strand. This cable is very flexible and is used in primary control systems and in other locations where operation over pulleys is frequent. See Figure 2-65, in the Airframe Handbook H-8083-31A-ATB, which specifies that 7 × 19 wire comes in diameters form 1/8-inch to 3/8-inch.
[Ref: Airframe Handbook H-8083-31A-ATB, Chapter 02 Page 40]

2-50 Answer A.
The Illustrated Parts Catalog is required to identify the correct parts and specific hardware required for the installation. Type Certificate Data Sheets do not include maintenance instructions. AC43.13 only specifies procedures for aircraft under 12,500 pounds when current maintenance manuals do not exist.
[Ref: Airframe Handbook H-8083-31A-ATB, Chapter 02 Page 40]

2-53 Answer C.
The 7 × 19 cable is made up of seven strands of 19 wires each. Six of these strands are laid around the center strand. This cable is very flexible and is used in primary control systems and in other locations where operation over pulleys is frequent.
[Ref: Airframe Handbook H-8083-31A-ATB, Chapter 02 Page 42]

2-51 Answer C.
When swaging tools are used, it is imperative that all the manufacturer's instructions, including 'go' and 'no-go' dimensions, be followed exactly to avoid defective and inferior swaging.
[Ref: Airframe Handbook H-8083-31A-ATB, Chapter 02 Page 42]

2-54 Answer A.
Compliance with all of the instructions should result in the terminal developing the full-rated strength of the cable.
[Ref: Airframe Handbook H-8083-31A-ATB, Chapter 02 Page 42-43]

2-55 AMA038
What nondestructive checking method is normally used to ensure that the correct amount of swaging has taken place when installing swaged-type terminals of aircraft control cable?
A. Check the surface of the swaged portion of the terminal for small cracks which indicated incomplete swaging.
B. Measure the finished length of the terminal barrel and compare with the beginning length.
C. Use a terminal gauge to check the diameter of the swaged portion of terminal.

2-56 AMA038
Placing a piece of cloth around a stainless steel control cable and running it back and forth over the length of the cable is generally a satisfactory method of _____.
A. applying anti-corrosion lubricant
B. inspecting for wear or corrosion
C. inspecting for broken wires

2-57 AMA038
Excessive wear on both of the sides of a control cable pulley groove is evidence of
A. excessive cable tension.
B. pulley misalignment.
C. cable misalignment.

2-58 AMA038
A tension regulator in the flight control cable system of a large all metal aircraft is used primarily to
A. provide a means of changing cable tension in flight.
B. maintain a given tension automatically.
C. increase the cable tension in cold weather.

2-59 AMA038
When a control cable is properly rigged, which cable system installation item is the small extra push that is needed for the flight deck control to hit its mechanical stop?
A. Cable Connectors
B. Spring-backs
C. Turnbuckles

2-60 AMA021
If a pilot reports that an airplane flies left wing heavy, this condition may be corrected by
A. increasing the dihedral angle of the left wing, or decreasing the dihedral angle of the right wing, or both.
B. increasing the angle of the incidence of the left wing, or decreasing the angle of incidence of the right wing, or both.
C. adjusting the dihedral angle of the left wing so that differential pressure between the upper and lower wing surfaces is increased.

AERODYNAMICS, AIRCRAFT ASSEMBLY, AND RIGGING

ANSWERS

2-55 Answer C.
Using a go/no-go gauge supplied by the swaging tool manufacturer or a micrometer and swaging chart, check the terminal shank diameter for proper dimension.
[Ref: Airframe Handbook H-8083-31A-ATB, Chapter 02 Page 43]

2-56 Answer C.
Close inspection in these critical fatigue areas can be performed by rubbing a rag along the cable. If there are any broken strands, the rag snags on the cable. A more detailed inspection can be performed in areas that may be corroded or indicate a fatigue failure by loosing or removing the cable and bending it. This technique reveals internal broken strands not readily apparent from the outside.
[Ref: Airframe Handbook H-8083-31A-ATB, Chapter 02 Page 44]

2-57 Answer B.
Excess wear on both sides of a pulley groove indicate that the pulley is misaligned from the direction of travel of the cable. Had the cable been offset to the left or right, only that side of the cable would show wear. Had the cable been excessively tight, wear would show on the inside of the groove.
[Ref: Airframe Handbook H-8083-31A-ATB, Chapter 02 Page 44]

2-58 Answer B.
Cable tension regulators are used in some flight control systems because there is considerable difference in temperature expansion of the aluminum aircraft structure and the steel control cables. Some large aircraft incorporate tension regulators in the control cable systems to maintain a given cable tension automatically.
[Ref: Airframe Handbook H-8083-31A-ATB, Chapter 02 Page 45]

2-59 Answer B.
With a control cable properly rigged, the fight control should hit its stops at both extremes prior to the fight deck control. The spring-back is the small extra push that is needed for the fight deck control to hit its mechanical stop.
[Ref: Airframe Handbook H-8083-31A-ATB, Chapter 02 Page 46]

2-60 Answer B.
A wing heavy condition is an out-of-trim flight condition in which an airplane flies hands off, with one wing low. With a few exceptions, the dihedral and incidence angles of conventional modern aircraft cannot be adjusted. Some manufacturers permit adjusting the wing angle of incidence to correct for a wing-heavy condition. The dihedral and incidence angles should be checked after hard landings or after experiencing abnormal flight loads to ensure that the components are not distorted and that the angles are within the specified limits.
[Ref: Airframe Handbook H-8083-31A-ATB, Chapter 02 Page 49, G-39]

2-61 AMA020
During an airplane rigging process, a grid plate and plumb bob are used when _____.
A. jacking the aircraft
B. checking the aircraft weight and balance
C. measuring symmetry between opposing components

2-62 AMA020
Checking engine alignment on a multi engine aircraft typically involves the use of which tool?
A. A level device.
B. A plumb bob and grid.
C. A measuring line.

2-63 AMA019
Proper wing twist in a sheet metal constructed wing can usually be checked by utilizing a
A. plum bob, string, and straightedge.
B. straightedge, tape measure, and carpenter's square.
C. incidence board described by the manufacturer.

2-64 AMA020
If the vertical stabilizer of a single engine, propeller driven airplane is rigged properly, it should be perpendicular to the
A. longitudinal axis.
B. vertical axis.
C. lateral axis.

2-65 AMA070
Where would you find precise information to perform a symmetry alignment check for a particular aircraft?
A. Aircraft Specification or Type Certificate Data Sheet
B. Manufacturer's Service Bulletins
C. Aircraft Service or Maintenance Manual

2-66 AMA038
Using the chart below, when the outside temperature is 80°F, select the acceptable 3/16 cable tension range.
A. 130 pounds minimum, 140 pounds maximum
B. 120 pounds minimum, 140 pounds maximum
C. 117 pounds minimum, 143 pounds maximum

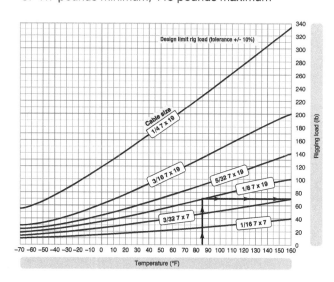

AERODYNAMICS, AIRCRAFT ASSEMBLY, AND RIGGING

ANSWERS

2-61 Answer A.
When a large aircraft is jacked to a level position, a plumb bob is suspended from a predetermined position over a grid plate. Necessary adjustments to the jacks are indicated on the grid scale, and thus jacking heights can be adjusted as needed.
[Ref: Airframe Handbook H-8083-31A-ATB, Chapter 02 Page 48]

2-62 Answer C.
An engine alignment (or symmetry) check on a multi engine aircraft ensures that the thrust line of each engine aligns with the other within factory limits. This is done be measuring the distance from a specified point on each engine to a specified point on the fuselage.
[Ref: Airframe Handbook H-8083-31A-ATB, Chapter 02 Page 50]

2-63 Answer C.
Incidence is usually checked in at least two specified positions on the surface of the wing to ensure that the wing is free from twist. A variety of incidence boards is used to check the incidence angle.
[Ref: Airframe Handbook H-8083-31A-ATB, Chapter 02 Page 50]

2-64 Answer C.
After the rigging of the horizontal stabilizer has been checked, the verticality of the vertical stabilizer relative to the lateral datum can be checked. The measurements are taken from a given point on either side of the top of the fin to a given point on the left and right horizontal stabilizers.
[Ref: Airframe Handbook H-8083-31A-ATB, Chapter 02 Page 51]

2-65 Answer C.
When performing a symmetry alignment check the precise figures, tolerances, and checkpoints for a particular aircraft are found in the applicable service or maintenance manual.
[Ref: Airframe Handbook H-8083-31A-ATB, Chapter 02 Page 52]

2-66 Answer C.
To use the chart, determine the outside air temperature (80°F), follow the 80°F line up until it intersects the curve for 3/16" cable. Extend a horizontal line from the point of intersection to the right edge of the chart. The value at this point indicates the tension, rigging load in pounds, + or – 10%, to establish on the cable. In this example, the tension should be between 117 and 143 pounds.
[Ref: Airframe Handbook H-8083-31A-ATB, Chapter 02 Page 52]

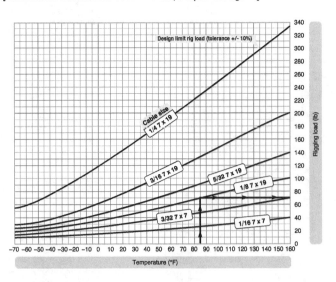

2-67 AMA081

A universal propeller protractor, used to measure the degrees of aileron travel, should be zeroed

    A. with the aileron in the DOWN position.

    B. with the aileron in the NEUTRAL position.

    C. when the aircraft is in a level flight attitude.

2-68 AMA011

When safety wiring 2 standard thread bolts to each other, in which direction should the safety wire be positioned?

    A. Both bolts should be pulled clockwise by the safety wire.

    B. Both bolts should be pulled counterclockwise by the safety wire.

    C. Each bolt should be pulled opposite to the other; one clockwise and the other counter clockwise.

2-69 AMA088

An aircraft self locking nut is identified with a gold coloring. What is this nut designed for?

    A. Location with high temperatures.

    B. Locations subjected to corrosion.

    C. Locations where frequent removal is required.

2-70 AMA088

An aircraft that is required by Section 94.409, to have a 100-hour inspection may be flown beyond the inspection requirement

    A. if necessary to reach a place at which the inspection can be accomplished, but not to exceed 10 flight hours.

    B. if necessary to reach a place at which the inspection can be accomplished, but a special flight permit is necessary.

    C. if necessary to reach a place at which the inspection can be accomplished, but not to exceed 15 flight hours.

2-71 AMA090

Which of the following is true regarding the use of a checklist when performing an annual inspection of a light aircraft?

    A. The use of a checklist provided by the aircraft manufacturer is required.

    B. The use of a checklist created by the inspector is acceptable.

    C. The use of a checklist by a licensed A&P mechanics is recommended but not required.

2-72 AMA088

Where would you find the operating conditions that make a 100-hour inspection mandatory?

    A. 14 CFR part 91

    B. 14 CFR part 43

    C. AC 43.13-2B

AERODYNAMICS, AIRCRAFT ASSEMBLY, AND RIGGING

ANSWERS

2-67 Answer B.

In order for a control system to function properly, it must be correctly adjusted. Correctly rigged control surfaces move through a prescribed arc (surface- throw) and are synchronized with the movement of the flight deck controls. Therefore, the explanations in this chapter are limited to the three general steps listed below:

1. Lock the flight deck control, bellcranks, and the control surfaces in the neutral position.
2. Adjust the cable tension, maintaining the rudder, elevators, or ailerons in the neutral position.
3. Adjust the control stops to limit the control surface travel to the dimensions given for the aircraft being rigged.

[Ref: Airframe Handbook H-8083-31A-ATB, Chapter 02 Page 54]

2-68 Answer A.

A standard thread bolt turns clockwise to tighten, Thus the safety wire should be aligned to pull both bolts in a clockwise direction.

[Ref: Airframe Handbook H-8083-31A-ATB, Chapter 02 Page 54-55]

2-69 Answer B.

Cadmium plated nuts (gold in color) offer exceptionally good corrosion protection but should not be used where temperatures can exceed 450 degree. Non-self locking nuts should be used when frequent removal is expected and secured instead with safety wire, cotter pins or other temporary safety locking devices.

[Ref: Airframe Handbook H-8083-31A-ATB, Chapter 02 Page 55]

2-70 Answer A.

An inspection schedule, specifying the intervals in hours or days when routine and detailed inspections will be performed, and including instructions for exceeding an inspection interval by not more than 10 hours while en route, and for changing an inspection interval because of service experience.

[Ref: Airframe Handbook H-8083-31A-ATB, Chapter 02 Page 62]

2-71 Answer B.

14 CFR Part 43 requires that each person performing a scheduled inspection must use a checklist. While a checklist created by the manufacturer is preferred, one published in another source or even created by the inspector is acceptable.

[Ref: Airframe Handbook H-8083-31A-ATB, Chapter 02 Page 64]

2-72 Answer A.

A 100-hour inspection is required when an aircraft is operated under 14 CFR part 91 and used for hire, such as flight training. It is required to be performed every 100 hours of service in addition to the annual inspection.

[Ref: Airframe Handbook H-8083-31A-ATB, Chapter 02 Page 62]

2-73 AMA088

Large airplanes and turbine-powered multiengine airplanes operated under Federal Aviation Regulation Part 91, General Operating and Flight Rules, must be inspected
- A. in accordance with a continuous airworthiness maintenance program (camp program) authorized under Federal Aviation Regulation Part 91, Subpart E.
- B. in accordance with the progressive inspection requirements of Federal Aviation Regulation Section 91.409(d).
- C. in accordance with an inspection program authorized under Federal Aviation Regulation Part 91, Subpart E.

2-74 AMA088

What determines whether an aircraft must have a 100 hour inspection or an annual inspection?
- A. Whether or not the aircraft is used for hire.
- B. The progressive inspection schedule as approved by FAA.
- C. Manufacturer's requirements and the presence of an approved maintenance manual.

2-75 AMA096

Each static pressure system, altimeter instrument, and automatic pressure altitude reporting system, must be tested and inspected of an airplane or helicopter that was operated in controlled airspace under instrument flight rules (IFR) within the preceding _____ calendar months.
- A. 12
- B. 18
- C. 24

2-76 AMA088

In order to legally operate an on-board air traffic control transponder, the transponder must have been inspected and re-approved for service _____.
- A. within the preceding 12 months
- B. as a part of the aircraft's last 100 hour or annual inspection
- C. within the preceding 24 months

2-77 AMA088

Who is authorized to change the batteries on a portable Emergency Locator Transmitter (ELT)?
- A. A licensed A&P mechanic.
- B. A technician at a certified avionics shop licensed under part 91.413.
- C. Any person, including the pilot.

2-78 AMA089

According to regulation, for long must a record a completed annual inspection be retained?
- A. For 3 years for the date of return to service.
- B. Indefinitely as a part of the aircraft log.
- C. For one year.

AERODYNAMICS, AIRCRAFT ASSEMBLY, AND RIGGING

ANSWERS

2-73 Answer C.
Inspection requirements for large airplanes (over 12,500 lbs) are found under 14 CFR part 91, section 91.409, to include paragraphs (e) and (f). Paragraph (e) applies to large airplanes (to which 14 CFR part 125 is not applicable), turbojet multiengine airplanes, turbo propeller powered multiengine airplanes, and turbine powered rotorcraft. Paragraph (f) lists the inspection programs that can be selected under paragraph (e).
[Ref: Airframe Handbook H-8083-31A-ATB, Chapter 02 Page 62]

2-74 Answer A.
A 100 hour inspection is required when an aircraft is operated under CFR Part 91 for hire. Examples include flight instruction charters, tours, or any other scenario in which compensation is earned. An annual inspection is sufficient when only private use of the aircraft is performed.
[Ref: Airframe Handbook H-8083-31A-ATB, Chapter 02 Page 60]

2-75 Answer C.
To comply with 14 CFR part 43, Appendix E, any person operating an airplane or helicopter in controlled airspace under IFR must have had each static pressure system, each altimeter instrument and each automatic pressure altitude reporting system tested and inspected within the preceding 24 calendar months.
[Ref: Airframe Handbook H-8083-31A-ATB, Chapter 02 Page 63]

2-76 Answer C.
Any person using an air traffic control (ATC) transponder must have had, within the preceding 24 calendar months, that transponder tested and inspected and found to comply with 14 CFR part 43, Appendix F.
[Ref: Airframe Handbook H-8083-31A-ATB, Chapter 02 Page 63]

2-77 Answer C.
Under 14 CFR part 43, section 43.3g; battery removal and reinstallation on a portable ELT is considered simple preventative maintenance and can thus be performed by the pilot, owner, or operator.
[Ref: Airframe Handbook H-8083-31A-ATB, Chapter 02 Page 63]

2-78 Answer C.
FAR part 43.15 requires that the owner/operator of the aircraft retains the records of an inspection until the work/inspection is repeated or for one year after the work is performed.
[Ref: Airframe Handbook H-8083-31A-ATB, Chapter 02 Page 64]

2-79 AMA088

Which regulation applies to airplanes having a seating capacity of 20 or more passengers or a maximum payload capacity of 6,000 pounds or more?
  A. Title 14 CFR part 125, section 125.247
  B. Continuous Airworthiness Maintenance Program (CAMP)
  C. Title 14 CFR part 91

2-80 AMA088

Which of the following additional components for rotorcrafts are required by a person completing an inspection under 14 CFR part 91 in accordance with the maintenance manual?
  1. The drive shaft or similar systems.
  2. The main rotor and center section (or the equivalent are.
  3. The auxiliary rotor.
  4. The main rotor transmission gear box for obvious defects.
  A. 1, 2, and 3
  B. All of the above
  C. 2, 3, and 4

2-81 AMA088

If you are operating under an Experimental certificate for a Light Sport Aircraft, weight-shift control aircraft or a powered parachute, what type of inspection is required?
  A. Annual inspection.
  B. Condition inspection once every 12 months.
  C. 100-Hour inspection.

2-82 AMA057

Before a annual inspection, an initial run up is conducted to check rigging of
  1. full power and idle RPM.
  2. positive switch grounding.
  3. fuel mixture check.
  A. 1 and 3
  B. 2 only
  C. 1, 2, and 3

AERODYNAMICS, AIRCRAFT ASSEMBLY, AND RIGGING

ANSWERS

2-79 Answer A.
Title 14 CFR part 125, section 125.247 applies to airplanes having a seating capacity of 20 or more passengers or a maximum payload capacity of 6,000 pounds or more.
[Ref: Airframe Handbook H-8083-31A-ATB, Chapter 02 Page 68]

2-81 Answer B.
When operating under an Experimental certificated issued for the purpose of operating Light Sport Aircraft, these aircraft must have a condition inspection performed once every 12 months.
[Ref: Airframe Handbook H-8083-31A-ATB, Chapter 02 Page 69]

2-80 Answer B.
A piston-engine helicopter can be inspected in accordance with the scope and detail of 14 CFR part 43, Appendix D for an Annual Inspection. However, there are additional performance rules for inspections under 14 CFR part 43, section 43.15, requiring that each person performing an inspection under 14 CFR part 91 on a rotorcraft, shall inspect these additional components in accordance with the maintenance manual or Instructions for Continued Airworthiness of the manufacturer concerned: the drive shaft or similar systems, the main rotor transmission gear box for obvious defects; the main rotor and center section (or the equivalent area); and the auxiliary rotor.
[Ref: Airframe Handbook H-8083-31A-ATB, Chapter 02 Page 69]

2-82 Answer C.
Initial run-up provides an assessment to the condition of the engine prior to performing the inspection. The run-up should include full power and idle RPM, magneto operation, including positive switch grounding, fuel mixture check, oil and fuel pressure, and cylinder head and oil temperatures.
[Ref: Airframe Handbook H-8083-31A-ATB, Chapter 02 Page 65]

ORAL EXAM

2-1(O).   What material are aircraft control cables made?

2-2(O).   What instrument is used to determine the amount of tension on a cable?

2-3(O).   How can you inspect for broken wires of a control cable?

2-4(O).   What is the purpose of a turnbuckle?

2-5(O).   What are used to guide cables as well as change the direction of cable movement?

2-6(O).   Why are push rods used as links in the flight control system?

2-7(O).   When are torque tubes used in a control system?

2-8(O).   What must be accomplished after repairing a control surface the flight control balance condition?

2-9(O).   Where will you find the procedures and specifications for rigging an aircraft?

2-10(O).   List the three main primary flight controls on an aircraft.

2-11(O).   What is the purpose of trim tabs on a flight control surface?

2-12(O).   What is the main purpose of a Stability Augmentation Systems (SAS)?

2-13(O).   Name the three basic classifications of rotors found on helicopters.

2-14(O).   How is pylon rock reduced in a helicopter?

2-15(O).   What are the most common causes of high frequency vibrations within a helicopter?

2-16(O).   Explain rotor blade tracking.

2-17(O).   Describe the general procedure for leveling a small aircraft after jacking.

2-18(O).   Explain a grid plate as it relates to aircraft leveling.

2-19(O).   If an aircraft must be jacked outside, how should the aircraft be positioned?

2-20(O).   Define a progressive inspection.

2-21(O).   What regulation authorizes the use of a progressive inspection?

2-22(O).   How often must the altimeter instrument and automatic pressure altitude reporting system must be tested and inspected for an aircraft operated in controlled airspace under instrument flight rules (IFR)?

2-23(O).   Can a 100-hour inspection be overflow?

2-24(O).   When must an aircraft owner/operator comply with an airworthiness directive?

AERODYNAMICS, AIRCRAFT ASSEMBLY, AND RIGGING

QUESTIONS

ORAL EXAM

2-25(O). What information needs to be included when recording the approval for return to service of an aircraft after a 100-hour or annual inspection?

2-26(O). What regulation governs the operating conditions that make a 100-hour inspection mandatory?

2-27(O). What operations require a 100-hour inspection when an aircraft is operated under 14 CFR part 91?

AERODYNAMICS, AIRCRAFT ASSEMBLY, AND RIGGING

ORAL EXAM

2-1(O).   Carbon steel or stainless (corrosion resistant) steel.
           [Ref: Airframe Handbook H-8083-31A-ATB, Chapter 02 Page 41]

2-2(O).   A tensiononometer.
           [Ref: Airframe Handbook H-8083-31A-ATB, Chapter 02 Page 52]

2-3(O).   Wrap a piece of cloth around a stainless steel control cable and run it back and forth over the length of the
           cable. A more detailed inspection can be performed by loosening or removing the cable and bending it. This
           technique reveals internal broken strands not readily apparent from the outside.
           [Ref: Airframe Handbook H-8083-31A-ATB, Chapter 02 Page 44]

2-4(O).   It is used for making minor adjustments in cable length and for adjusting cable tension.
           [Ref: Airframe Handbook H-8083-31A-ATB, Chapter 02 Page 46]

2-5(O).   Pulleys.
           [Ref: Airframe Handbook H-8083-31A-ATB, Chapter 02 Page 44]

2-6(O).   The provide give a push-pull motion.
           [Ref: Airframe Handbook H-8083-31A-ATB, Chapter 02 Page 47]

2-7(O).   When an angular or twisting motion is needed in a control system.
           [Ref: Airframe Handbook H-8083-31A-ATB, Chapter 02 Page 48]

2-8(O).   Rapid and uncontrolled oscillation of a flight control surface on an aircraft that is caused by a dynamically
           unbalanced condition.
           [Ref: Airframe Handbook H-8083-31A-ATB, Chapter 02 Page G-16]

2-9(O).   Repairs to a control surface require static rebalancing of the control surface.
           [Ref: Airframe Handbook H-8083-31A-ATB, Chapter 02 Page 39]

2-10(O).   Rigging procedures are detailed in the applicable manufacturer's maintenance or service manuals and
           applicable structural repair manuals. Additionally, aircraft specification or type certificate data sheets (TCDS)
           also provide information regarding control surface movement and weight and balance limits.
           [Ref: Airframe Handbook H-8083-31A-ATB, Chapter 02 Page 48]

2-11(O).   Ailerons, elevator, and the rudder.
           [Ref: Airframe Handbook H-8083-31A-ATB, Chapter 02 Page 12]

2-12(O).   To enable the pilot to trim out any unbalanced condition that may exist during flight, without exerting any
           pressure on the primary controls.
           [Ref: Airframe Handbook H-8083-31A-ATB, Chapter 02 Page 12]

2-13(O).   Reduces pilot workload by improving basic aircraft control harmony and decreasing disturbances.
           [Ref: Airframe Handbook H-8083-31A-ATB, Chapter 02 Page 32]

2-14(O).   Rigid, semirigid, or fully articulated.
           [Ref: Airframe Handbook H-8083-31A-ATB, Chapter 02 Page 18-19]

2-15(O).   To keep the vibration from reaching noticeable levels, transmission mount dampening is incorporated to
           absorb the rocking.
           [Ref: Airframe Handbook H-8083-31A-ATB, Chapter 02 Page 32]

AERODYNAMICS, AIRCRAFT ASSEMBLY, AND RIGGING

ANSWERS

ORAL EXAM

2-16(O).   The most common and obvious causes: loose elevator linkage at swashplate horn, loose elevator, or tail rotor balance and track.
[Ref: Airframe Handbook H-8083-31A-ATB, Chapter 02 Page 32]

2-17(O).   Blade tracking is the process of determining the positions of the tips of the rotor blade relative to each other while the rotor head is turning, and of determining the corrections necessary to hold these positions within certain tolerances.
[Ref: Airframe Handbook H-8083-31A-ATB, Chapter 02 Page 32]

2-18(O).   A spirit level and a straight edge are placed across the fixed pegs or blocks generally attached to the fuselage parallel with the datum lines.
[Ref: Airframe Handbook H-8083-31A-ATB, Chapter 02 Page 49]

2-19(O).   The grid plate is a permanent fixture installed on the aircraft floor or supporting structure. To level the aircraft, a plumb bob is suspended from a predetermined position in the ceiling of the aircraft over the grid plate. The adjustments to the jacks necessary to level the aircraft are indicated on the grid scale. The aircraft is level when the plumb bob is suspended over the center point of the grid.
[Ref: Airframe Handbook H-8083-31A-ATB, Chapter 02 Page 49]

2-20(O).   The aircraft should be positioned with the nose into the wind.
[Ref: Airframe Handbook H-8083-31A-ATB, Chapter 02 Page 49]

2-21(O).   This is an inspection that may be used in place of an annual or 100-hour inspection. It has the same scope as an annual inspection, but it may be performed in increments so the aircraft will not have to be out of service for an extended period.
[Ref: Airframe Handbook H-8083-31A-ATB, Chapter 02 Page G-28]

2-22(O).   14 CFR part 91, section 91.409(d)
[Ref: Airframe Handbook H-8083-31A-ATB, Chapter 02 Page 62]

2-23(O).   24 months
[Ref: Airframe Handbook H-8083-31A-ATB, Chapter 02 Page 63]

2-24(O).   Yes, the maximum time a 100-hour inspection may be extended is 10 hours, if required, to reach a maintenance facility to conduct the inspection.
[Ref: Airframe Handbook H-8083-31A-ATB, Chapter 02 Page 62]

2-25(O).   Always, compliance with an applicable AD is mandatory and must be recorded in the maintenance records.
[Ref: Airframe Handbook H-8083-31A-ATB, Chapter 02 Page 61, G-2]

2-26(O).   Type inspection and a brief description, the date of the inspection and aircraft total time in service, the signature, the certificate number, and kind of certificate held by the person approving or disapproving for return to service, and for the annual and 100-hour inspection, if the aircraft is found to be airworthy and approved for return to service, enter the following statement: "I certify that this aircraft has been inspected in accordance with a (insert type) inspection and was determined to be in airworthy condition."
[Ref: Airframe Handbook H-8083-31A-ATB, Chapter 02 Page 66]

2-27(O).   When used for compensation or hire, or used for flight training when used for flight training provided by a flight instructor.
[Ref: Airframe Handbook H-8083-31A-ATB, Chapter 02 Page 62]

PRACTICAL EXAM

2-1(P).   Given an actual aircraft or mockup, required tools, appropriate publications check or set the tension of a control surface cable and record maintenance.

2-2(P).   Given an actual aircraft or mockup, required tools, appropriate publications install a control surface and record maintenance.

2-3(P).   Given an actual aircraft or mockup, required tools, appropriate publications check the static balance of a control surface and record findings.

2-4(P).   Given a specific helicopter model and the maintenance manuals, locate the procedures for rigging a helicopter.

2-5(P).   Given a specific helicopter model and the maintenance manuals, locate helicopter rotor blade tracking procedures.

2-6(P).   Given an actual aircraft or mockup and the maintenance manuals, identify fixed-wing aircraft rigging adjustment locations.

2-7(P).   Given the appropriate publications for a specific aircraft, locate leveling methods and procedures for a specific aircraft.

2-8(P).   Given an actual aircraft or mockup, inspect a flight control system for travel and security and record findings.

2-9(P).   Given an actual aircraft or mockup, inspect a primary flight control cable and document your findings.

2-10(P).   Given an actual aircraft or mockup, required tools, and appropriate publications install one or more swaged cable terminals, check them with the appropriate gage and record maintenance.

2-11(P).   Given an actual aircraft or mockup, required tools, and appropriate publications install one or more Nicopress sleeves, check with the appropriate gage and record maintenance.

2-12(P).   Given an actual aircraft or mockup, required tools, and appropriate publications check, adjust as necessary a push-pull flight control system and record maintenance.

2-13(P).   Given an actual aircraft or mockup and the appropriate publications for a specific aircraft, locate jacking points and leveling locations.

2-14(P).   Given the appropriate publications for a specific aircraft, determine the jacking requirements for a particular aircraft.

2-15(P).   Given an actual aircraft or mockup, required tools, and appropriate publications jack an aircraft or portion thereof, e.g., as appropriate for tire/wheel change, or gear retraction.

2-16(P).   Given a sample of an aircraft maintenance record, determine if inspection and/or maintenance is due and record findings.

2-17(P).   Given an actual aircraft, mockup, or component, accomplish a 14 CFR part 91 required inspection and record your findings.

2-18(P).   Given an actual aircraft, mockup, or component, accomplish an inspection after maintenance or preventive maintenance and record your findings.

AERODYNAMICS, AIRCRAFT ASSEMBLY, AND RIGGING

QUESTIONS

PRACTICAL EXAM

2-19(P).   Given a specific aircraft and condition, determine the placarding requirements and record results.

2-20(P).   Given a specific aircraft and specific operating conditions, determine if all required instruments and equipment are installed as outlined in 14 CFR part 91 and record findings.

2-21(P).   Given an actual aircraft, mockup, or component, required tools, and appropriate publications accomplish a conformity inspection and record your findings.

2-22(P).   Given the required documentation, generate a checklist for conducting a 100-hour airframe inspection on a specific aircraft.

AIRCRAFT FABRIC COVERING

Fabric Terms, Legal Aspects, Approved Materials, Covering Processes, Determining Fabric Condition, Fabric Strength, Cotton and Polyester

CHAPTER 03

QUESTIONS

3-1 AMA040
What is the purpose of a Selvedge edge woven into the edges of fabric or finishing tape?
A. Prevents the woven fabric from unraveling.
B. Creates a smooth edge negating the need for additional finishing tape.
C. Allows fabric to lay down smoothly around contoured shapes.

3-2 AMA088
An aircraft comes to you with a worn fabric covering. You replace that fabric with a different type of fabric which has previously been approved for that aircraft by an STC. This is considered by FAA as _____.
A. a major alteration
B. a minor repair
C. a major repair

3-3 AMA040
Which type of fabric tape is used on protrusions such as a strut fitting to help prevent the base fabric from tearing?
A. Reinforcing Tape
B. Surface Tape
C. Anti-Chafe Tape

3-4 AMA040
When a fabric seam must be made where there is no structure underneath, what method is typically used to attach the seam?
A. Reinforcing tape
B. A Sewn seam
C. Fabric cement

3-5 AMA040
Fabric rejuvenator is used to
A. restore fabric strength and tautness to at least the minimum acceptable level.
B. restore the condition of dope coatings.
C. penetrate the fabric and restore fungicidal resistance.

3-6 AMA040
Fungus and mildew have no effect on
A. cotton fabric.
B. linen fabric.
C. polyester fabric.

AIRCRAFT FABRIC COVERING

ANSWERS

3-1 Answer A.
A selvedged edge produced during a fabrics manufacture locks the other fabric threads into place to prevent the edges from unraveling. The edge of a piece of fabric which is cut to size, thus eliminating the selvedged edge should be done so only with pinking shears as an alternative method to limit raveling.
[Ref: Airframe Handbook H-8083-31A-ATB, Chapter 03 Page 3]

3-2 Answer A.
According to 14CFR Part 43, changing parts of a wing, tail section or the fuselage when not listed in the original aircraft specifications is considered a major alteration. An FAA form 337 needs to be approved by a certificated A&P mechanic with Inspection Authorization for this alteration to be legal.
[Ref: Airframe Handbook H-8083-31A-ATB, Chapter 03 Page 4]

3-3 Answer C.
Anti-chafe tape provides a smooth surface on protrusions or metal seams underneath the base sections of fabric. It is applied after the aircraft is inspected and primed, but before the primary fabric covering is installed.
[Ref: Airframe Handbook H-8083-31A-ATB, Chapter 03 Page 5]

3-4 Answer B.
When a fabric seam must be made with no structure underneath a sewn seam can be used. Fabric cement is used only to attach fabric to pieces of structure. Reinforcing tape is used after the primary fabric covering is installed to protect or strengthen areas for attaching the fabric to ribs.
[Ref: Airframe Handbook H-8083-31A-ATB, Chapter 03 Page 6]

3-5 Answer B.
Rejuvenator is a finishing material used to restore resilience to an old dope film. It contains strong solvents to open the dried out film and plasticizers to restore resilience to the old dope.
[Ref: Airframe Handbook H-8083-31A-ATB, Chapter 03 Page 8]

3-6 Answer C.
As fungus and mildew do not effect polyester or glass fabric, fungicidal and mildewcidal additives are not required with these materials. On organic fabrics such as cotton and linen, modern topcoats formulas with premixed anti-fungal agents typically provide sufficient insurance from these problems.
[Ref: Airframe Handbook H-8083-31A-ATB, Chapter 03 Page 8]

3-7 AMA040

Which of the following is a factor for the selection of the correct weight of textile fabric to be used in covering any type of aircraft?

A. The aircraft Vne (never exceed speed).
B. The aircraft Vc (design cruising speed).
C. The aircraft's maximum weight.

3-8 AMA088

If an aircraft was originally certified with a Grade A Cotton covering with a breaking strength of 80 pounds, but then the cotton covering was later replaced with a polyester fabric with a breaking strength of 70 pounds, at what tested strength must the new fabric again be replaced

A. 56 pounds.
B. 49 pounds.
C. 80 pounds.

3-9 AMA090

How is it determined whether a test strip of fabric must be cut from the aircraft structure to determine the fabric's strength during an annual or 100-hour inspection?

A. Determined by time in service based on the manufacturer's requirement.
B. Determined by an IA based on his/her knowledge and experience.
C. Determined by passage or failure of a punch test.

3-10 AMA040

Fabric testing using a mechanical punch tester should be done?

A. On a point of fabric on which all coating layers are intact.
B. On a point of fabric where there is a crack or chip in the coatings.
C. On a point of fabric that was purposely left uncoated during the covering process to serve as a test point for this purpose.

3-11 AMA040

Prior to covering, wing ribs are anchored in place to prevent movement during the covering process by

A. gussets placed at all points of attachment.
B. braces placed at 8" intervals connecting one rib to the next.
C. wrapping strips of fabric snugly from one rib to the next.

3-12 AMA040

When a seam is required in an area of critical airflow such as a leading edge, the minimum amount of fabric overlap is

A. 2-4 inches.
B. 4-6 inches.
C. two times the diameter of the leading edge structure to which it is wrapped.

AIRCRAFT FABRIC COVERING

ANSWERS

3-7 Answer A.
Vne is the maximum speed an aircraft is certified to fly in any condition. Therefore, all structural factors must be sufficient to handle these loads. The second factor when selecting fabric is maximum wing loading which represents the maximum pressure per square foot due to the aircraft weight. The actual total weight of the aircraft is not a factor.
[Ref: Airframe Handbook H-8083-31A-ATB, Chapter 03 Page 9-10]

3-8 Answer A.
To maintain airworthiness, the fabric must not deteriorate to a breaking strength of less than 70% of the originally certified material.
80 pounds × 70% = 56 pounds
[Ref: Airframe Handbook H-8083-31A-ATB, Chapter 03 Page 9]

3-9 Answer B.
Although failure of a punch test usually indicates a need to recover an aircraft, the decision of whether a test strip must be cut from the aircraft to determine fabric strength is determined by an IA based on his/her knowledge and experience.
[Ref: Airframe Handbook H-8083-31A-ATB, Chapter 03 Page 10-11]

3-10 Answer B.
Fabric testing should be done on uncovered pieces of fabric so as not to compromise the test by the stiffness of the coatings. If a chipped or cracked point of fabric can not be found in an upper surface area (exposed to UV light) a small piece of coating should be removed to expose a point for testing.
[Ref: Airframe Handbook H-8083-31A-ATB, Chapter 03 Page 11]

3-11 Answer C.
Inter-rib bracing holds ribs in place during the covering process. A single wrap without adhesive is enough to hold each rib in place but still allowing small movements during the final shrinking process.
[Ref: Airframe Handbook H-8083-31A-ATB, Chapter 03 Page 15]

3-12 Answer A.
Typically 2-4 inches of fabric overlap is required where the ends of fabric are joined in areas of critical airflow. In other areas 1-2 inches of overlap is sufficient.
[Ref: Airframe Handbook H-8083-31A-ATB, Chapter 03 Page 16]

3-13 AMA040
When heat shrinking fabric on a wing, in order to get even tightness and a wrinkle free result, it is best to work
  A. from the root end of the wing outwards to the tips.
  B. from the center section first, then work outwards to the ends.
  C. from each end first, then work inwards to the center.

3-16 AMA040
On a tail dragger aircraft drain grommets in the wing are usually placed
  A. in each rib bay at the lowest point when the aircraft is in flight attitude.
  B. in each rib bay at the bottom of the trailing edge.
  C. in each rib bay at the bottom of the leading edge.

3-14 AMA040
Because of the propeller slipstream, rib lace spacing is closer than outside the slipstream area: the size of the slipstream area is considered to be
  A. the propeller diameter plus one additional rib.
  B. twice the propeller diameter.
  C. the propeller diameter added to the distance from the propeller to the leading edge.

3-17 AMA040
When and how is finishing tape applied on a fabric covered aircraft?
  A. Doped on after sealer coats but prior to the finish coat.
  B. Doped on after primary fabric doping but before sealer coats.
  C. Sewn or laced on before dope is applied.

3-15 AMA040
Finishing tape (surface tape) is used for what purpose
  A. to provide additional anti-wear resistance under reinforcement tape.
  B. to help prevent "ripple formation" in covering fabric.
  C. to provide additional wear resistance over the edges of fabric forming structures.

3-18 AMA040
Which layer of coating on a fabric aircraft contains the aluminum pigments used to block ultraviolet rays from damaging the fabric?
  A. Sealer Coat
  B. Fill Coat
  C. Primer Coat

AIRCRAFT FABRIC COVERING

ANSWERS

3-13 Answer C.
Moving the calibrated heating iron from one end to the other and then inwards from each end to the center is more likely to evenly draw the fabric tight with a minimum of wrinkles.
[Ref: Airframe Handbook H-8083-31A-ATB, Chapter 03 Page 17]

3-14 Answer A.
Because of greater turbulence in the area of the prop wash, unless manufacturer's instructions state otherwise, the slipstream area is considered to be the propeller diameter plus one additional rib.
[Ref: Airframe Handbook H-8083-31A-ATB, Chapter 03 Page 18]

3-15 Answer C.
Finishing tape is applied to protect the seams, edges, and above the wing ribs by smoothing aerodynamic resistance and so lessening abrasion and helping to prevent it from coming loose in flight.
[Ref: Airframe Handbook H-8083-31A-ATB, Chapter 03 Page 21]

3-16 Answer B.
As the greatest opportunity for moisture to enter the wing is when the aircraft is parked, the trailing edge becomes the lowest point where most moisture will accumulate. Therefore, drain grommets should be located against the trailing edge.
[Ref: Airframe Handbook H-8083-31A-ATB, Chapter 03 Page 21]

3-17 Answer B.
Finishing tape is applied with dope to cover all seams and edges including those created by the installation of any rings, grommets, and gussets. It is the final pieces of fabric to be installed with the chordwise strips being installed first followed by the spanwise strips.
[Ref: Airframe Handbook H-8083-31A-ATB, Chapter 03 Page 21-22]

3-18 Answer B.
Fill coats contain premixed aluminum solids to block UV rays and are applied as the second coating step following the first sealer coat and before the primer coat. The fourth final topcoat is then applied.
[Ref: Airframe Handbook H-8083-31A-ATB, Chapter 03 Page 22]

ORAL EXAM

3-1(O). What factors are used to determine the proper type of aircraft fabric covering material for an aircraft?

3-2(O). What are some of the approved aircraft fabric coverings and systems?

3-3(O). What kinds of seams are used on fabric coverings?

3-4(O). Explain the terms, 'warp', 'fill', and 'bias' as they refer to aircraft fabric.

3-5(O). Why is structure surface preparation important and when is this performed?

3-6(O). What covering methods are commonly used when recovering fabric-covered aircraft?

3-7(O). How is the fabric covering attached to the airframe?

3-8(O). What areas on aircraft coverings are most susceptible to deterioration?

3-9(O). How is aircraft covering protection and preservation typically accomplished?

3-10(O). How does the technician determine repair procedures for fabric coverings?

3-11(O). What is a major concern when inspecting fabric covering that has been damaged?

AIRCRAFT FABRIC COVERING

ANSWERS

ORAL EXAM

3-1(O).   When a fabric covered aircraft is certified, the aircraft manufacturer uses materials and techniques approved under the type certificate. The same material and techniques must be used to recover the aircraft. However, FAA approved exceptions exist. A Supplemental Type Certificate (STC) for the aircraft in question can be approved by the FAA and materials and techniques there-in may then be used instead of those on the original type certificate. A field approval from the local Flight Standards District Office (FSDO) may also be granted. This provides one-time permission to use materials and techniques other that those found on the original Type Certificate Data Sheet (TCDS). Note that a Form 337 is executed for a field approval. Another method of using materials and techniques not on the original TCDS is when a manufacturer secures approval for a new process. The new process, materials and techniques, is then available for use by operators of that aircraft. Accepting these legal aspects, an owner/ operator may have a choice of more than one recovering process. A personal decision has to be made as to which approved process is preferred.
        [Ref: Airframe Handbook H-8083-31A-ATB, Chapter 03 Page 3-4]

3-2(O).   Ceconite™, Polyfiber™, and Superflight™ are currently approved fabrics for aircraft. The companies that own and sell these fabrics have been awarded Parts Manufacturer's Approvals (PMA's) to legally do so. The holders of the PMA also developed and gained approval for the various tapes, chords, threads, and liquids to be used as well as the procedures and techniques involved. Processes for covering fabric aircraft can also be approved independently of a particular fabric and may enable the use of more than one fabric using the same ancillary products and process approved as an approved process. Approved covering system processes are: Air Tech, Stewart System, Ceconite™/ Randolf System, Stits/Poly-Fiber™, and Superflight™ Systems 1 and VI.
        [Ref: Airframe Handbook H-8083-31A-ATB, Chapter 03 Page 4-9]

3-3(O).   There are two methods of covering an aircraft with fabric. In the envelope method, sewn envelopes for the aircraft surfaces to be covered are used. The sewn seams are executed in accordance with approved data and the technician simply installs the fabric in accordance with the STC or manufacturer's instructions. In the blanket method, a large sheet of approved fabric is draped over the aircraft part, such as a wing, and it is seamed to fit the part using doped or glued seams. In this method, guidelines for seam overlap and placement must be followed by the technician. Some leeway exists as to where to place doped or glued seams so the looks of the finished job can be maximized.
        [Ref: Airframe Handbook H-8083-31A-ATB, Chapter 03 Page 16]

3-4(O).   The warp of a fabric is the direction along the length of a fabric. The fill, or weave, of a fabric is the direction across the width of the fabric. These terms can be used to refer to the fibers that make up the fabric. Fabric bias refers to a cut, fold, or seam made diagonally to the warp and fill.
        [Ref: Airframe Handbook H-8083-31A-ATB, Chapter 03 Page 3]

3-5(O).   Since polyester aircraft fabric covering last so long, before recovering an aircraft, while the old fabric has been removed, a thorough inspection, cleaning, and repairs to the airframe should be performed. It is a rare opportunity to have the structure of the aircraft fully exposed and the technician must take the opportunity to inspect and correct any discrepancies found such as cracks, corrosion, chips, indentations, oil spots, etc. This cleaning, inspection, and repair should involve the IA that is approving the major repair or alteration that is the recovering process. Removal of glue and treatment of leading edges are required to gain maximum performance from the recovering products. Treatment of the structure with primer or a varnish may be prescribed for good adhesion of the fabric but also for protection of the structure. The exposure of the entire structure also allows taping over sharp edges, metal seams, rivet heads and any other feature that might wear through the fabric once installed. Inter-rib bracing, if required, can be done while the structure is fully exposed. This holds the ribs in place during the covering process.
        [Ref: Airframe Handbook H-8083-31A-ATB, Chapter 03 Page 14]

ORAL EXAM

3-6(O). Two basic methods are used when covering an aircraft with fabric. One is the envelope method. In this method, fabric envelopes are pre-sewn to closely fit the components of the aircraft being covered (i.e. wings, fuselage, etc.). The manufacturer then ships these to the technician who installs them on the airframe. The other method is known as the blanket method. Here, the technician uses multiple flat sections of fabric which are trimmed and attached to the airframe.
[Ref: Airframe Handbook H-8083-31A-ATB, Chapter 03 Page 12]

3-7(O). A polyester fabric covering is cemented or glued to the airframe structure at all points where it makes contact. Special formula adhesives have replaced nitrate dope for adhesion in most covering processes. Fabric on wings must be secured to the wing ribs with more than just cement. Screws, rivets, clips, and lacing are used depending on the manufacturer's approved technique.
[Ref: Airframe Handbook H-8083-31A-ATB, Chapter 03 Page 12]

3-8(O). The only significant cause of deterioration of polyester fabric comes from ultra violet (UV) light. Therefore the upper, sun-exposed surfaces of the aircraft covering are the most affected. To protect these areas, sealer coats of product containing UV inhibitors are sprayed on the fabric during the finishing process applied to the covering material.
[Ref: Airframe Handbook H-8083-31A-ATB, Chapter 03 Page 22]

3-9(O). Once all finishing tapes have been installed on the fabric, a sealer coat is applied. This coat saturates and completely surrounds the fibers in the polyester fabric, forming a barrier that keeps water and contaminants from reaching the fabric during its life. It is usually brushed on in a cross coat application for thorough penetration. Two coats are common. Some processes vary on how many coats and whether spray coating is permitted.
[Ref: Airframe Handbook H-8083-31A-ATB, Chapter 03 Page 22]

3-10(O). Repairs to fabric covering are inevitable. Always inspect a damaged area to ensure the damage is confined to the fabric and does not involve the structure below. The source of approved data for the covering job is the same source of approved data for any repair made to that covering. Thus, if the fabric was installed under an STC, the STC holder has included repair procedures and techniques in the STC which the technician is require to follow for a repair of that fabric. If the fabric covering was approved under the aircraft manufacturer's type certificate, then the technician must follow the manufacturer's instruction for any repair.
[Ref: Airframe Handbook H-8083-31A-ATB, Chapter 03 Page 22]

3-11(O). When inspecting a fabric covering that has been damaged it is import to inspect closely to determine the extent of the damage and determine that it is confined to the fabric alone or whether it includes the structure below the fabric. A repair to the fabric only which covers damage to the structure is unacceptable and potentially dangerous.
[Ref: Airframe Handbook H-8083-31A-ATB, Chapter 03 Page 22]

AIRCRAFT FABRIC COVERING

PRACTICAL EXAM

3-1(P).   Given an actual aircraft or mockup, inspect the repair of a damaged covering for airworthiness and record your findings.

3-2(P).   Given an actual aircraft or mockup, test a finished covering sample to determine acceptability of strength and record your findings.

3-3(P).   Given the appropriate publications for a specific aircraft, determine the minimum fabric strength covering requirements.

3-4(P).   Given a covering sample, determine if it has the appropriate identification markings.

3-5(P).   Given an actual aircraft or mockup with a defect, determine the acceptable repairs and summarize your findings.

3-6(P).   Given a sample of a damaged fabric-covered surface, determine the classification, either major or minor of the repair; document your findings and include the reference to the appropriate publications that were consulted.

3-7(P).   Given a specific aircraft and associated publications, locate the requirements for a repair of a specified fabric covering defect.

AIRCRAFT METAL STRUCTURAL REPAIR

CHAPTER 04

Hole Drilling, Forming Tools, Sheet Metal Holding Devices, Aluminum Alloys, Structural Fasteners, Forming Operations, and Repairability

QUESTIONS

4-1 AMA094
Which of the following stresses is a riveted joint primarily designed to resist?
A. Bearing Stresses
B. Tension Stresses
C. Shearing Stresses

4-4 AMA029
When driving out a tight pin or bolt, two punch types are often used in this order. What are they?
A. An awl; and then a drive punch.
B. A drive punch; and then a pin punch.
C. A center punch; and then a chassis punch.

4-2 AMA017
Which is the force that tries to pull two sheets apart?
A. Bearing
B. Torsion
C. Bending

4-5 AMA017
When removing a damaged section on a stringer, the best saw to use is a
A. reciprocating saw.
B. Kett saw.
C. circular cutting saw.

4-3 AMA017
When using a combination square with a center head to determine the exact center of a shaft, how many measurements must be taken?
A. 1
B. 2
C. 4

4-6 AMA017
Which shears have an upper cutting blade that is stationary while the lower blade is movable?
A. Throatless Shears
B. Scroll Shears
C. Squaring Shears

AIRCRAFT METAL STRUCTURAL REPAIR

ANSWERS

4-1 Answer C.
Rivets should not be used in tension applications because the tension strength of a rivet is quite low compared to its shear strength. In addition, a joint held together by multiple rivets resists shear by the combined strength of all the rivets. When the primary stress is bearing or tension, only some of the rivets (typically the end rivets) work to secure the joint.
[Ref: Airframe Handbook H-8083-31A-ATB, Chapter 04 Page 31]

4-2 Answer A.
When a top sheet is bearing against the bottom sheet, the fasteners holding the sheets together are pressing top sheet against bottom sheet. Bearing stress is the force that tries to pull two fastened sheets of material apart. Bearing stress resists the force applied by the rivet or bolt placed to hold the sheets together.
[Ref: Airframe Handbook H-8083-31A-ATB, Chapter 04 Page 3]

4-3 Answer B.
Two measurements (or steps) must be taken. First, place the shaft perpendicular to the square within the center head and draw a line along the square's rule. Next, rotate the shaft approximately 90 degrees and draw a second line. Where the lines intersect is the center.
[Ref: Airframe Handbook H-8083-31A-ATB, Chapter 04 Page 4-5]

4-4 Answer B.
The usual method for driving out a pin or bolt is to start working it out with a drive punch until the shank of the punch is touching the sides of the hole. Then use the correct size pin punch to drive the pin or bolt the rest of the way out of the hole.
[Ref: Airframe Handbook H-8083-31A-ATB, Chapter 04 Page 6-7]

4-5 Answer B.
Since the head of the Kett saw can be turned to any desired angle, it is useful for removing damaged sections on a stringer. The pneumatic circular cutting saw, useful for cutting out damage as well, is similar to the Kett saw. The advantages of a Kett saw include:
  1. Can cut metal up to 3/16-inch in thickness.
  2. No starting hole is required.
  3. A cut can be started anywhere on a sheet of metal.
  4. Can cut an inside or outside radius.
[Ref: Airframe Handbook H-8083-31A-ATB, Chapter 04 Page 8-9]

4-6 Answer B.
Scroll shears are used for cutting irregular lines on the inside of a sheet without cutting through to the edge. The upper cutting blade is stationary while the lower blade is movable. A handle connected to the lower blade operates the machine.
[Ref: Airframe Handbook H-8083-31A-ATB, Chapter 04 Page 10]

4-7 AMA017

When needing to quickly remove corners from sheet metal, the best tool to use is a

A. band saw.

B. rotary punch press.

C. notcher.

4-8 AMA017

To polish surfaces, which is the best tool or tools to use?

1. Disk Sander
2. Belt Sander
3. Wet Or Dry Grinder
4. Grinding Wheels

A. 1 and 4

B. All of the above

C. 2 and 3

4-9 AMA029

Which drill bit size is the largest in diameter?

A. Number 30 drill

B. Number 40 drill

C. Letter A drill

4-10 AMA029

When drilling in tough metals like corrosion-resistant steel and titanium, which drill bit would be used?

A. Step Drill Bits

B. Cobalt Alloy Drill Bits

C. Twist Drill Bits

4-11 AMA029

Which procedure is correct when using a reamer to finish a drilled hole to the correct size?

A. Turn the reamer only in the cutting direction.

B. Apply considerable pressure on the reamer when starting the cut and reduce the pressure when finishing the cut.

C. Turn the reamer in the cutting direction when enlarging the hole and in the opposite direction to remove from the hole.

4-12 AMA029

Which drill accessory or accessories aid in holding the drill perpendicular to the part?

1. Drill Stop
2. Drill Bushing
3. Drill Holder

A. 1

B. 2 and 3

C. 1, 2, and 3

AIRCRAFT METAL STRUCTURAL REPAIR

ANSWERS

4-7 Answer C.
The notcher is used to cut out metal parts, with some machines capable of shearing, squaring, and trimming metal. The notcher consists of a top and bottom die and most often cuts at a 90° angle, although some machines can cut metal into angles up to 180°. Notchers are available in manual and pneumatic models able to cut various thicknesses of mild steel and aluminum. This is an excellent tool for quickly removing corners from sheet metal parts.
[Ref: Airframe Handbook H-8083-31A-ATB, Chapter 04 Page 12]

4-8 Answer A.
Disk sanders have a powered abrasive-covered disk or belt and are used for smoothing or polishing surfaces. Also, grinding wheels are removable. A polishing or buffing wheel can be substituted for the abrasive wheel.
[Ref: Airframe Handbook H-8083-31A-ATB, Chapter 04 Page 11-13]

4-9 Answer C.
Numbered drill sizes are ranked in descending order from the smallest #80 drill at 0.135" to the largest #1 drill at .2280 inches. Lettered drills are ranked in ascending order from an A drill at .2340 to a Z drill at .4130. All larger are ranked in fractional sizes only.
[Ref: Airframe Handbook H-8083-31A-ATB, Chapter 04 Page 18]

4-10 Answer B.
Cobalt alloy drill bits are designed for hard, tough metals like corrosion-resistant steel and titanium. It is important for the aircraft technician to note the difference between HSS and cobalt, because HSS drill bits wear out quickly when drilling titanium or stainless.
[Ref: Airframe Handbook H-8083-31A-ATB, Chapter 04 Page 17]

4-11 Answer A.
Reamer flutes are not designed to remove chips like a drill. Do not attempt to withdraw a reamer by turning it in the reverse direction. Chips can be forced into the material surface scarring the hole.
[Ref: Airframe Handbook H-8083-31A-ATB, Chapter 04 Page 19]

4-12 Answer B.
There are several types of tools available that aid in holding the drill perpendicular to the part. They consist of a hardened bushing anchored in a holder. Some holder types are: standard, egg cup, plate, and arm.
[Ref: Airframe Handbook H-8083-31A-ATB, Chapter 04 Page 20]

4-13 AMA058
Annealing of aluminum
- A. increases the tensile strength.
- B. makes the material brittle.
- C. removes stresses caused by forming.

4-16 AMA029
Which forming technique is usually limited to relatively flat parts with flanges, beads, and lightening holes?
- A. Stretch Forming
- B. Drop Hammer
- C. Hydropress Forming

4-14 AMA094
Any bend formed on a bar folder can also be made on the
1. press brake.
2. cornice brake.
3. box and pan brake.
- A. 2 and 3
- B. 1 and 2
- C. 1, 2, and 3

4-17 AMA094
Which tool is used to stretch and thin a piece of metal before forming it into a desired shape?
- A. A piccolo former.
- B. An english wheel.
- C. A stretch former.

4-15 AMA094
Which of these tools would be used to form a bead down the center of a piece of sheet metal?
- A. Rotary Machine
- B. Slip Roll Former
- C. Stretch Former

4-18 AMA094
All the following are shrinking and stretching tools or devices, except?
1. Dollies and Stakes
2. Hardwood Form Blocks
3. Sandbags
4. C-Clamp
- A. 4
- B. 3
- C. 1

AIRCRAFT METAL STRUCTURAL REPAIR

ANSWERS

4-13 Answer C.
Annealing aluminum makes the metal soft for forming. Forming the metal (stretching, bending, crimping, etc.), work hardens the aluminum. It may need to be re-annealed before the entire job of forming the metal is complete as it may become too brittle to form without damaging it. The annealing removes stresses caused by forming.
[Ref: Airframe Handbook H-8083-31A-ATB, Chapter 04 Page 57-58]

4-14 Answer C.
A brake is similar to a bar folder because it is also used for turning or bending the edges of sheet metal. The cornice brake is more useful than the bar folder because its design allows the sheet metal to be folded or formed to pass through the jaws from front to rear without obstruction. In contrast, the bar folder can form a bend or edge only as wide as the depth of its jaws. Thus, any bend formed on a bar folder can also be made on the cornice brake. The box and pan brake can be used to do everything that the cornice brake can do. Since most cornice brakes and box and pan brakes are limited to a maximum forming capacity of approximately 0.090 inch annealed aluminum, 0.063-inch 7075T6, or 0.063-inch stainless steel, operations that require the forming of thicker and more complex parts use a press brake.
[Ref: Airframe Handbook H-8083-31A-ATB, Chapter 04 Page 22]

4-15 Answer A.
The rotary machine is used on flat stock to form a curved edge or place a bead along a particular length of the material. A slip roller is used to for a straight piece of sheet into an even large radius curved piece. Stretch forming involves shaping a piece of sheet metal over a preformed block.
[Ref: Airframe Handbook H-8083-31A-ATB, Chapter 04 Page 23-24]

4-16 Answer C.
Hydropress forming is usually limited to relatively flat parts with flanges, beads, and lightening holes. However, some types of large radii contoured parts can be formed by a combination of hand forming and pressing operations.
[Ref: Airframe Handbook H-8083-31A-ATB, Chapter 04 Page 24-25]

4-17 Answer B.
The English wheel, a popular type of metal forming tool used to create double curves in metal, has two steel wheels between which metal is formed. The English wheel is primarily a stretching machine, so it stretches and thins the metal before forming it into the desired shape. Thus, the operator must be careful not to over-stretch the metal.
[Ref: Airframe Handbook H-8083-31A-ATB, Chapter 04 Page 25-26]

4-18 Answer A.
Clamps and vises hold materials in place when it is not possible to handle a tool and the work piece at the same time. A clamp is a fastening device with movable jaws that has opposing, often adjustable, sides or parts. The C-clamp is shaped like a large C and has three main parts: threaded screw, jaw, and swivel head.
[Ref: Airframe Handbook H-8083-31A-ATB, Chapter 04 Page 26-29]

4-19 AMA017
What is the benefit of adding magnesium to an aluminum alloy, such as with aluminum alloy 3003?
   A. Improved corrosion resistance.
   B. Increased hardness.
   C. Increased malleability.

4-20 AMA016
When fabricating parts from Alclad™ 2024-T3 aluminum sheet stock
   A. bends should be made with a small radius to develop maximum strength.
   B. all bends must be 90° to the grain.
   C. all scratches, kinks, tool marks, nicks, etc., must be held to a minimum.

4-21 AMA017
Under certain conditions, type A rivets are not used because of their
   A. low strength characteristics.
   B. tendency toward embrittlement when subjected to vibration.
   C. high alloy content.

4-22 AMA017
A rivet with an identifying code of
MS20 426 DD 6 6 _____.
   A. may be used as is from the manufacturer
   B. must be refrigerated upon receipt to maintain their hardness
   C. must be annealed before use

4-23 AMA017
What is the purpose of refrigerating 2017 and 2024 aluminum alloy rivets after heat treatment?
   A. To retard age hardening.
   B. To relieve internal stresses.
   C. To accelerate age hardening.

4-24 AMA016
What is generally the best procedure to use when removing a solid shank rivet?
   A. Drill to the base of the manufactured rivet head with a drill one size smaller than the rivet shank and remove the rivet with a punch.
   B. Drill through the manufactured head and shank with a drill one size smaller than the rivet and remove the rivet with a punch.
   C. Drill through the manufactured head and shank with a shank size drill and remove the rivet with a punch.

AIRCRAFT METAL STRUCTURAL REPAIR

ANSWERS

4-19 Answer B.
Aluminum alloy 3003 is similar to Aluminum 1100 except for containing a small amount of magnesium. Doing so retains most qualities of Aluminum 1100 except for increasing its strength and hardness.
[Ref: Airframe Handbook H-8083-31A-ATB, Chapter 04 Page 30]

4-20 Answer C.
Cladding of any aluminum alloy is performed to prevent corrosion. Therefore, all scratches, kinks, tool marks, nicks, etc., must be held to a minimum to ensure the integrity of the cladding. Fiber-tipped pens are used when marking directly on aluminum because graphite in a No. 2 pencil can cause corrosion. Marking part layout on the protective plastic membrane is preferred, or tape the piece with masking tape and do the layout on the tape if the membrane has been removed.
[Ref: Airframe Handbook H-8083-31A-ATB, Chapter 04 Page 30]

4-21 Answer A.
Alloy code "A" rivets are pure 1100 aluminum or 3003 aluminum alloy. They have the lowest shear strength of all common aluminum rivets and are for nonstructural uses only.
[Ref: Airframe Handbook H-8083-31A-ATB, Chapter 04 Page 33]

4-22 Answer C.
DD rivets will age harden quickly and so must be annealed before use. Storing DD rivets in a freezer will somewhat delay the hardening process and may be used immediately after removal from the freezer. DD rivets are now less common and have been replaced with E type rivets which may be used in its received condition.
[Ref: Airframe Handbook H-8083-31A-ATB, Chapter 04 Page 32]

4-23 Answer A.
Some rivet alloys, such a DD rivets (alloy 2024-T4), are too hard to drive in the condition they are received and must be annealed before they can be installed. Typically, these rivets are annealed and stored in a freezer to retard hardening, which has led to the nickname "ice box rivets". They are removed from the freezer just prior to use.
[Ref: Airframe Handbook H-8083-31A-ATB, Chapter 04 Page 32]

4-24 Answer A.
When removing a rivet, work on the manufactured head. Use a drill bit one size smaller than the rivet shank to drill out the rivet head. Drill the rivet to the depths of its head while holding the drill at a 90 degree angle. The rivet head often breaks away and climbs the drill which is a signal to withdraw the drill. Drive the remaining rivet shank out with a drift punch slightly smaller than the rivet shank diameter.
[Ref: Airframe Handbook H-8083-31A-ATB, Chapter 04 Page 45]

4-25 AMA017
What is the angle of the standard countersunk head rivet?
A. 105°
B. 100°
C. 88°

4-28 AMA017
Which rivet size should be used to join two sheets of
.032 aluminum?
A. MS20455AD5-3
B. MS20425D4-3
C. MS20470AD4-4

4-26 AMA017
MS20426AD-6-5 indicates a countersink rivet which has
A. an overall length of 5/16 inch.
B. a shank length of 5/16 inch (excluding head).
C. a shank length of 5/32 inch (excluding head).

4-29 AMA011
The identifying marks on the heads of aluminum alloy rivets
indicate the
A. degree of dimensional and process control observed
during manufacture.
B. specific alloy used in the manufacture of the rivets.
C. head shape, shank size, material used, and
specifications adhered to during manufacture.

4-27 AMA058
A DD rivet is heat treated before use to
A. soften to facilitate riveting.
B. harden and increase strength.
C. relieve internal stresses.

4-30 AMA017
Which rivet may be used as received without further treatment?
A. 2117-T3
B. 2017-T3
C. 2024-T4

AIRCRAFT METAL STRUCTURAL REPAIR

ANSWERS

4-25 Answer B.
The countersunk head angle can vary from 60° to 120°, but the 100° has been adopted as standard because this head style provides the best possible compromise between tension/shear strength and flushness requirements.
[Ref: Airframe Handbook H-8083-31A-ATB, Chapter 04 Page 31]

4-26 Answer A.
The last number in the identifying code indicates the length of the rivet in sixteenths of an inch. The 426 indicates that this is a countersunk rivet.
Countersunk rivets are measured using the overall length.
[Ref: Airframe Handbook H-8083-31A-ATB, Chapter 04 Page 32]

4-27 Answer A.
Some rivet alloys, such as DD rivets, are too hard to drive in the received condition and must be annealed before they can be installed. Annealing softens the alloy.
[Ref: Airframe Handbook H-8083-31A-ATB, Chapter 04 Page 32]

4-28 Answer C.
As a general rule, the rivet diameter or shank size is equal to 2.5 – 3 times the thickness of the thicker sheet. Or, take the skin thickness (.032) multiply by 3 (.032 × 3 = .096) and use the next larger size of rivet. Diameter of rivets come in 32nd inch intervals and are represented in the rivet identifier by the first dash number. The next largest size of rivet would be 4/32 (.1250). So 4 will be the first dash number in the rivet identifier. To find the length of the rivet to be used, the grip length is added to the length needed to form the shop head. The grip length is the total thickness of the materials (.032 + 032 = .064). The amount needed for the shop head is 1.5 times the shank size being used (1.5 × .1250 = .1875). So, the grip length (.064) plus the length needed for the shop head (.1875) equals (.064 + .1875) = .25. Rivet length is the last dash number in the rivet identifier represented in 16th's of an inch. Since .2515 is closest to 4/16th's of an inch, the last dash number is 4. Therefore, the answer is C because it is a rivet that has a 4/32nd's diameter (dash 4) and a 4/16th's length (dash 4).
[Ref: Airframe Handbook H-8083-31A-ATB, Chapter 04 Page 32-33]

4-29 Answer B.
Standard rivet alloy code marking are manufactured onto the heads of rivets for quick identification. For example, alloy code A rivets have no head markings; alloy code AD have a dimple on the head; alloy code D rivets have a raised dot, etc.
[Ref: Airframe Handbook H-8083-31A-ATB, Chapter 04 Page 33]

4-30 Answer A.
The 2117-T rivet is used for general repair work, since it requires no heat treatment, is fairly soft and strong, and is highly corrosion resistant when used with most types of alloys. Always consult the maintenance manual for correct rivet type and material.
[Ref: Airframe Handbook H-8083-31A-ATB, Chapter 04 Page 33]

4-31 AMA017

Most rivets used in aircraft repair have

A. a raised dot.
B. smooth heads without markings.
C. dimples.

4-32 AMA017

A sheet metal repair is to be made using two pieces of 0.040-inch aluminum riveted together. All rivet holes are drilled for 3/32 inch rivets. The length of the rivets to be used will be

A. 5/16 inch.
B. 1/4 inch.
C. 1/8 inch.

4-33 AMA017

A sheet metal repair is to be made using two pieces of 0.0625-inch aluminum riveted together. All rivet holes are drilled for 1/8 inch rivets. The length of the rivets to be used will be

A. 5/16 inch.
B. 3/16 inch.
C. 5/32 inch.

4-34 AMA017

Clad aluminum alloys are used in aircraft because they _____.

A. can be heat treated faster than the other forms of aluminum
B. are less subject to corrosion than uncoated aluminum alloys
C. are stronger than unclad aluminum alloys

4-35 AMA017

The length of rivet to be chosen when making a structural repair that involves the joining of 0.032 inch and 0.064 inch aluminum sheet, drilled with a No. 30 drill, is

A. 1/4 inch.
B. 7/16 inch.
C. 5/16 inch.

4-36 AMA094

The shop head of a rivet should be

A. one and one-half times the diameter of the rivet shank.
B. one and one-half times the diameter of the manufactured head of the rivet.
C. one-half times the diameter of the rivet shank.

AIRCRAFT METAL STRUCTURAL REPAIR

ANSWERS

4-31 Answer C.
The AD rivet is the most frequently used in aircraft repair. AD rivets are identified by a dimple marked on the head of the rivet.
[Ref: Airframe Handbook H-8083-31A-ATB, Chapter 04 Page 32-33]

4-32 Answer B.
The length of the rivet is calculated by adding the grip or total thickness of the material to be riveted (2 × .040 = .080) plus the amount needed to form the shop head. The amount needed to form the shop head is 1.5 times the rivet diameter (1.5 × 3/32 or 1.5 × .0937 = .141). So, the grip (.080) plus the length needed to form the shop head (.141) equals .221. Therefore, the length of the rivet needed must be the closest to .221 which is a rivet with a length of .250 or 1/4 inch.
[Ref: Airframe Handbook H-8083-31A-ATB, Chapter 04 Page 33]

4-33 Answer A.
The length of the rivet is calculated by adding the grip or total thickness of the material to be riveted (2 × .0625 = .125) plus the amount needed to form the shop head. The amount needed to form the shop head is 1.5 times the rivet diameter (1.5 × 1/8 or 1.5 × .1250 = .1875). So, the grip (.125) plus the length needed to form the shop head (.1875) equals .31. Therefore, the length of the rivet needed must be the closest to .3125 which is a rivet with a length of .3125 or 5/16 inch.
[Ref: Airframe Handbook H-8083-31A-ATB, Chapter 04 Page 33]

4-34 Answer B.
While aluminum alloys are lightweight and strong, they do not possess the corrosion resistance qualities of pure aluminum itself. Therefore with a Alclad process a thin coating of pure aluminum is placed on the alloyed material as a protective coating
[Ref: Airframe Handbook H-8083-31A-ATB, Chapter 04 Page 30]

4-35 Answer C.
A number 30 drill is used to drill a hole for a 1/8 inch diameter rivet (.125 inch). Therefore, the grip of the rivet plus the amount of rivet needed to form the shop head can be calculated to obtain the rivet length required. The grip is .096 (.032 + .064). The amount to form the proper sized shop head is .1875 (1.5 × .125). Added together, the result is the length of the rivet required (.096 + .1875 = .2835).
.2835 is closest in size to a 5/16 rivet.
[Ref: Airframe Handbook H-8083-31A-ATB, Chapter 04 Page 33 & 40]

4-36 Answer A.
The amount of rivet shank needed to form a proper shop head equals one and a half times the diameter of the rivet shank.
[Ref: Airframe Handbook H-8083-31A-ATB, Chapter 04 Page 33]

4-37 AMA016

Alloy 2117 rivets are heat treated

- A. to a temperature of 910 to 930°F and quenched in cold water.
- B. by the manufacturer and do not require heat treatment before being driven.
- C. by the manufacturer and require reheat treatment before being driven.

4-38 AMA016

When repairing a small hole on a piece of metal, the major consideration in the design of the patch should be

- A. that the bond between the patch and the skin is sufficient to prevent dissimilar metal corrosion.
- B. the shear strength of the riveted joint.
- C. to use rivet spacing similar to a seam in the skin.

4-39 AMA094

How many MS20470 AD-4-6 rivets will be required to attach a 10 × 5 inch plate, using a single row of rivets, minimum edge distance, and 4D spacing?

- A. 54
- B. 56
- C. 52

4-40 AMA094

A single lap sheet splice is to be used to repair a section of damaged aluminum skin. If a double row of 1/8 inch rivets is used, the minimum allowable overlap will be

- A. 3/4 inch.
- B. 13/16 inch.
- C. 1/2 inch.

4-41 AMA094

What is the minimum spacing for a single row of aircraft rivets?

- A. Three times the length of the rivet shank.
- B. Three times the diameter of the rivet shank.
- C. Two times the diameter of the river shank.

4-42 AMA094

A factor which determines the minimum space between rivets is the

- A. diameter of the rivets being used.
- B. length of the rivets being used.
- C. thickness of the material being riveted.

AIRCRAFT METAL STRUCTURAL REPAIR

ANSWERS

4-37 Answer B.
The 2117 rivet is used for general repair work, since it requires no heat treatment, is fairly soft and strong, and is highly corrosion resistant when used with most types of alloys.
[Ref: Airframe Handbook H-8083-31A-ATB, Chapter 04 Page 33-34]

4-38 Answer B.
Shear is one of two stresses applied to rivets. The shear strength is the amount of force required to cut a rivet that holds two or more sheets of material together. Tension is the other stress applied to rivets. While rivet spacing is important, consideration for rivet spacing depends more on the size of the rivet since a patch is being discussed. Dissimilar metal corrosion occurs largely irrelevant of bond strength.
[Ref: Airframe Handbook H-8083-31A-ATB, Chapter 04 Page 34]

4-39 Answer B.
The diameter of the rivet used is 1/8 inch because the -4 in the rivet identifier indicates 4/32 inch. Therefore, rivet spacing is 1/2 inch (4D = 4 × 1/8 = 1/2 inch). Minimum edge distance is 1/4 inch (2D = 2 × 1/8 = 2/8 = 1/4 inch). Maximum edge distance is 1/2 inch (4D = 4 × 1/8 = 1/2 inch). The general rule for rivet spacing, as it applies to a straight row layout, is quite simple. In a one-row layout, find the edge distance at each end of the row and then lay off the rivet pitch. The rectangular plate using a single row of rivets has two 10-inch long sides and two 5- inch long sides. Edge distance must be maintained at both ends of each row. Therefore, two times edge distance must be subtracted from each dimension. 10 inches minus 2 × 1/4 inch edge distance (1/2 inch) equals 9 1/2 inches. Spacing the rivets 1/2 inch apart requires 19 rivets for each 10- inch side. 5 inches minus 1/2 inch equals 4 1/2 inch. Spacing of rivets 1/2 inch apart requires 9 rivets for each 5-inch side. Add all of the rivets required:
19 + 19 + 9 + 9 = 56 rivets.
[Ref: Airframe Handbook H-8083-31A-ATB, Chapter 04 Page 35]

4-40 Answer B.
The minimum edge distance for a non-countersunk rivet is 2D (2 × 1/8 = 1/4). The edge distance must be maintained from the edge of the overlapped splice on both ends of the lap sheet. Therefore 2 × 2D or 2 × 1/4 = 1/2. This is the minimum length of overlap for a single row of rivets with the proper edge distance on both ends. However, a second row of rivets is called for. Staggering the rivets allows a closer spacing of rivet rows. The distance from the first row to the second row of staggered rivets is called transverse pitch. It is calculated off of the pitch between the rivets in the first row. The minimum pitch between rivets in the first row is 3D or 3/8 inch (3 × 1/8). Transverse pitch is 75% of the rivet pitch of the first row (.75 × .375 = .28125 or 3/4 × 3/8 = 9/32 = .28125). Thus, the minimum amount allowed for edge distance (1/2) plus the transverse distance between the first and second row (9/32) must be added together to obtain the minimum length of the overlap sheet (1/2 + 9/32 = 25/32 = 781. From the answers given, A (.75) and C (.5) are both shorter than .781. Answer B (13/16 or .8125) is slightly longer than the calculated minimum of .78125 so it is the minimum allowable overlap.
[Ref: Airframe Handbook H-8083-31A-ATB, Chapter 04 Page 35]

4-41 Answer B.
The minimum spacing between rivets in a single row is three times the diameter of the rivet shank.
[Ref: Airframe Handbook H-8083-31A-ATB, Chapter 04 Page 35]

4-42 Answer A.
Rivet pitch is the distance between the centers of neighboring rivets in the same row. The smallest allowable rivet pitch is 3 rivet diameters.
[Ref: Airframe Handbook H-8083-31A-ATB, Chapter 04 Page 35]]

4-43 AMA094
Rivet gauge, or transverse pitch is the distance between the
A. head of the rivets in the same row.
B. centers of the rivets in adjacent rows.
C. centers of adjacent rivets in the same row.

4-44 AMA094
Rivet pitch is the distance between the
A. centers of adjacent rivets in the same row.
B. heads of rivets in the same row.
C. centers of rivets in adjacent rows.

4-45 AMA017
A rivet set used to drive MS20470 rivets should
A. be nearly flat on the end, with a light radius on the edge to prevent damage to the sheet being riveted.
B. have a slightly greater radius than the rivet head and contact the center two thirds of the rivet head.
C. have the same radius as the rivet head.

4-46 AMA017
_____ is/are used if the smoothness of the material, such as skin, requires that all countersunk rivets be driven within a specific tolerance.
A. Rivet Sets/headers
B. Compression riveting
C. Microshavers

4-47 AMA040
As compared to aluminum alloy sheet, when drilling stainless steel sheet, good practice is to drill at a _____.
A. higher speed with less pressure applied to the drill
B. lower speed with less pressure applied to the drill
C. lower speed with more pressure applied to the drill

4-48 AMA016
The form of dimpling that should only be used when the regular male die is broken or not available is
A. hot dimpling.
B. radius dimpling.
C. coin dimpling.

AIRCRAFT METAL STRUCTURAL REPAIR

ANSWERS

4-43 Answer B.
Transverse pitch is the distance between staggered rivet rows. Rows that are not staggered use normal rivet spacing rules.
[Ref: Airframe Handbook H-8083-31A-ATB, Chapter 04 Page 35]

4-44 Answer A.
Rivet spacing is measure between the centerline of rivets in the same row. Rivet pitch is the distance between the centers of neighboring rivets in the same row.
[Ref: Airframe Handbook H-8083-31A-ATB, Chapter 04 Page 34]

4-45 Answer B.
The MS20470 rivet is a universal head rivet. Non- flush rivet headers (sets) should fit to contact the center two-thirds of the rivet head. They must be shallow enough to allow slight upsetting of the head in driving and some misalignment without eyebrowing the riveted surface. A header that is too small marks the rivet; while one too large marks the material.
[Ref: Airframe Handbook H-8083-31A-ATB, Chapter 04 Page 39]

4-46 Answer C.
A microshaver is used if the smoothness of the material (such as skin) requires that all countersunk rivets be driven within a specific tolerance. This tool has a cutter, a stop, and two legs or stabilizers. The cutting portion of the microshaver is inside the stop. When the microshaver is adjusted and held correctly, it can cut the head of a countersunk rivet to within .002 inch without damaging the surrounding material.
[Ref: Airframe Handbook H-8083-31A-ATB, Chapter 04 Page 39]

4-47 Answer C.
When drilling stainless steel, use an HSS drill bit ground to an included angle of 135°. Keep the drill speed about 1/2 that required for drilling mild steel but never exceed 750 RPM. Drilling speed for aluminum is 200 to 300 surface feet per minute (sfm). For mild steel, it is 30 to 50 sfm. Thus, drilling stainless steel would require a speed lower than aluminum. Keep a uniform pressure on the drill so the feed is constant at all times and be sure pressure is on the drill bit when rotation begins.
[Ref: Airframe Handbook H-8083-31A-ATB, Chapter 04 Page 16 & 83]

4-48 Answer C.
The coin dimpling, or coin pressing, method uses a countersink rivet as the male dimpling die. Place the female die in the usual position and back it with a bucking bar. Place the rivet of the required type into the hole and strike the rivet with a pneumatic riveting hammer. Coin dimpling should be used only when the regular male die is broken or not available.
[Ref: Airframe Handbook H-8083-31A-ATB, Chapter 04 Page 43-44]

4-49 AMA016
Joggles in removed rivet shanks would indicate partial
  A. bearing failure.
  B. torsion failure.
  C. shear failure.

4-52 AMA011
CherryMAX and Olympic-Lok rivets
  A. may be installed with ordinary hand tools.
  B. utilize a pulling tool for installation.
  C. utilize a rivet gun, special rivet set, and bucking bar for installation.

4-50 AMA016
What type of loads cause the most rivet failures?
  A. Shear
  B. Head
  C. Bearing

4-53 AMA011
One of the main advantages of Hi-Lok type fasteners over earlier generations is
  A. the squeezed on collar installation provides a more secure, tighter fit.
  B. they can be removed and reused again.
  C. they can be installed with ordinary hand tools.

4-51 AMA011
Which blind rivet was designed to prevent the problem of losing the center stem due to vibration?
  A. Friction-locked blind rivet
  B. Mechanical-lock blind rivet
  C. High-shear fastener

4-54 AMA011
A main difference between Lockbolt/Huckbolt tension and shear fasteners (other than their application) is in the
  A. method of installation.
  B. number of locking collar grooves.
  C. shape of the head.

AIRCRAFT METAL STRUCTURAL REPAIR

ANSWERS

4-49 Answer C.
If, upon examination, the rivet shank appears ogled and the holes in the sheet are misaligned, the rivet has failed in shear. Joggles in removed rivet shanks indicate partial shear failure. In this case, try to determine what is causing the shearing stress and take necessary corrective action. Replacement with the next largest diameter rivet may be possible.
[Ref: Airframe Handbook H-8083-31A-ATB, Chapter 04 Page 45]

4-50 Answer A.
Aircraft structural joint design involves an attempt to find the optimum strength relationship between being critical in shear and critical in bearing (shear and bearing are the two primary loads put on a riveted structure). When critical in shear, the rivets fail if less than the optimal number of fasteners are installed. When bearing is a cause of failure, the material cracks or tears but the rivets remain intact.
[Ref: Airframe Handbook H-8083-31A-ATB, Chapter 04 Page 88]

4-51 Answer B.
The self-plugging, mechanical-lock blind rivet was developed to prevent the problem of losing the center stem due to vibration. This rivet has a device on the puller or rivet head that locks the center stem into place when installed.
[Ref: Airframe Handbook H-8083-31A-ATB, Chapter 04 Page 47-49]

4-52 Answer B.
The CherryMax® mechanical-lock blind rivet is popular with general aviation repair shops because it features the one tool concept for installation.
[Ref: Airframe Handbook H-8083-31A-ATB, Chapter 04 Page 49]

4-53 Answer C.
The advantages of Hi-Lok® two-piece fastener includes its light weight, high fatigue resistance, high strength, and its inability to be over torqued. The hex tip of an Allen wrench engages the recess to prevent rotation of the pin while the collar is being installed. The collar has wrenching flats which are used to install it.
[Ref: Airframe Handbook H-8083-31A-ATB, Chapter 04 Page 51]

4-54 Answer B.
The easiest way to differentiate between tension and shear pins is the number of locking grooves. The tension pins normally have four locking grooves and shear pins have two locking grooves.
[Ref: Airframe Handbook H-8083-31A-ATB, Chapter 04 Page 53]

4-55 AMA011
Threaded rivets (Rivnuts® or rivet nuts) are commonly used to
  A. join two or more pieces of sheet metal where shear strength is desired.
  B. join two or more pieces of sheet metal where bearing strength is desired.
  C. attach parts or components with screws to sheet metal.

4-56 AMA011
Which of the following rivets is not a nonstructural blind fastener?
  A. Pop rivet
  B. Mechanical lock blind rivet
  C. Pull through nut plate blind rivet

4-57 AMA094
Which forming operation involves shaping and forming malleable metal by hammering or tapping with a rubber, plastic or rawhide mallet?
  A. Shrinking
  B. Bumping
  C. Crimping

4-58 AMA094
Unless otherwise specified, the radius of a bend is the
  A. radius of the neutral axis plus one half the thickness of the metal being formed.
  B. inside radius of the metal being formed.
  C. inside radius plus one half the thickness of the metal being formed.

4-59 AMA094
A piece of sheet metal is bent to a certain radius. The curvature of the bend is referred to as the
  A. bend radius.
  B. bend allowance.
  C. neutral line.

4-60 AMA094
The flat layout or blank length of a piece of metal from which a simple L shaped bracket 3 inches by 1 inch is to be bent depends upon the radius of the desired bend. The bracket which will require the greatest amount of material is one which has a bend radius of
  A. 1/2 inch.
  B. 1/4 inch.
  C. 1/8 inch.

AIRCRAFT METAL STRUCTURAL REPAIR

ANSWERS

4-55 Answer C.
Rivnuts® are used for the installation of fairings, trim, and lightly loaded fittings that must be installed after an assembly is completed. Often used for parts that are removed frequently, the rivet nut is available in flat head or countersunk versions. They are installed by crimping from one side. The rivet nut provides a threaded hole into which a machine screw can be installed.
[Ref: Airframe Handbook H-8083-31A-ATB, Chapter 04 Page 56]

4-56 Answer B.
The nonstructural blind fasteners are: pop rivets (a common pull-type rivet produced for non-aircraft related applications) and pull-through nut plate blind rivets (used where the high shear strength of solid rivets is not required or if there is no access to install a solid rivet).
[Ref: Airframe Handbook H-8083-31A-ATB, Chapter 04 Page 57]

4-57 Answer B.
Bumping involves shaping or forming malleable metal by hammering or tapping—usually with a rubber, plastic, or rawhide mallet. During this process, the metal is supported by a dolly, a sandbag, or a die. Each contains a depression into which hammered portions of the metal can sink. Bumping can be done by hand or by machine.
[Ref: Airframe Handbook H-8083-31A-ATB, Chapter 04 Page 58-59]

4-58 Answer B.
Bend radius is the arc that is formed when sheet metal is bent. The bend radius is measured from a radius center to the inside surface of the metal. It is the radius of the bend measured on the inside of the curved material.
[Ref: Airframe Handbook H-8083-31A-ATB, Chapter 04 Page 60 & 62]

4-59 Answer A.
Bend radius is the arc that is formed when sheet metal is bent. The bend radius is measured from a radius center to the inside surface of the metal. It is the radius of the bend measured on the inside of the curved material.
[Ref: Airframe Handbook H-8083-31A-ATB, Chapter 04 Page 60 & 62]

4-60 Answer C.
The radius of the bend is generally proportional to the thickness of the material. Furthermore, the sharper the radius of bend, the less material that is needed for the bend. Since the bend allowance must be subtracted from the total length of the L bracket flat layout, (3 inches + 1 inch = 4 inches), the overall length of the flat layout will be longest with the sharpest radius.
[Ref: Airframe Handbook H-8083-31A-ATB, Chapter 04 Page 63]

4-61 AMA094
The sharpest bend that can be placed in a piece of metal without critically weakening the part is called the
A. minimum radius of bend.
B. bend allowance.
C. maximum radius of bend.

4-62 AMA094
On a sheet metal fitting layout with a single bend, allow for stretching by
A. adding the setback to each leg.
B. subtracting the setback from one leg.
C. subtracting the setback from both legs.

4-63 AMA094
When bending a sheet of metal, if bend allowance is not considered, what will be the result after bending?
A. Cracking at the bend line will result.
B. The resulting sheet will be undersized.
C. The resulting bend will be at an insufficient angle.

4-64 AMA094
Which of the following list of steps for using a sheet metal brake to fold metal are correct?
Step 1: Adjustment of bend radius.
Step 2: Adjusting clamping pressure.
Step 3: Adjusting the nose gap.
A. 1 and 2
B. 2 and 3
C. All of the above

4-65 AMA094
The sight line on a sheet metal flat layout to be bent in a cornice or box brake is measured and marked
A. one radius from either bend tangent line.
B. one-half radius from either bend tangent line.
C. one radius from the bend tangent line that is placed under the brake.

4-66 AMA094
_____ can be curved and not bent sharply by stretching or shrinking either of the flanges.
A. Straight line bends
B. Formed or extruded angles
C. Flanged angles

AIRCRAFT METAL STRUCTURAL REPAIR

ANSWERS

4-61 Answer A.
The bend radius necessary to bend a part can be found on the parts drawings, but if it is not mentioned on the drawing, consult the structural repair manual for a minimum bend radius chart. This chart lists the smallest radius allowable for each thickness and temper of metal that is normally used. To bend tighter than this radius would jeopardize the integrity of the part. Stresses left in the area of the bend may cause it to fail while in service even if it does not crack while bending it.
[Ref: Airframe Handbook H-8083-31A-ATB, Chapter 04 Page 68]

4-62 Answer C.
Setback is the distance the jaws of a brake must be set back from the mold line to form a bend. The setback dimension must be determined prior to making a bend because setback is used in determining the location of the beginning bend line tangent. Thus, when figuring the total length of the flat layout for this fitting with a single bend, subtract the setback from each flat's mold line dimension. By adding in the bend allowance, the length of flat layout is determined.
[Ref: Airframe Handbook H-8083-31A-ATB, Chapter 04 Page 60]

4-63 Answer B.
Because the inside radius of a bend shrinks more than the outside radius stretches, when bending a piece of metal, the location and length of the neutral axis must be determined so that sufficient metal can be provided for the bend. This is called bend allowance.
[Ref: Airframe Handbook H-8083-31A-ATB, Chapter 04 Page 64]

4-64 Answer C.
When using a sheet metal brake to fold metal, the brake set up for box and pan brakes and cornice brakes is identical. A proper set up of the sheet metal brake is necessary because accurate bending of sheet metal depends on the thickness and temper of the material to be formed and the required radius of the part. Any time a different thickness of sheet metal needs to be formed or when a different radius is required to form the part, the operator needs to adjust the sheet metal brake before the brake is used to form the part.
[Ref: Airframe Handbook H-8083-31A-ATB, Chapter 04 Page 68-71]

4-65 Answer C.
A sight line needs to be drawn to help position the bend tangent line directly at the point where the bend should start. Draw a line inside the bend allowance area that is one bend radius away from the bend tangent line that is placed under the brake nose bar. Put the metal in the brake under the clamp and adjust the position of the metal until the sight line is directly below the edge of the radius bar.
[Ref: Airframe Handbook H-8083-31A-ATB, Chapter 04 Page 74]

4-66 Answer B.
Both formed and extruded types of angles can be curved (not bent sharply) by stretching or shrinking either of the flanges. Curving by stretching one flange is usually preferred since the process requires only a V-block and a mallet and is easily accomplished.
[Ref: Airframe Handbook H-8083-31A-ATB, Chapter 04 Page 75-76]

4-67 AMA094

In regards to hand forming curved flanged parts, which of the following is true?

1. The concave flange is formed by stretching.
2. The convex flange is form by shrinking.
3. Bend the flange on the concave first.
4. Convex surfaces are formed by shrinking the material over a form block.

  A. 1, 2, and 4

  B. 1 and 2

  C. All of the above

4-68 AMA094

If a streamline cover plate is to be hand formed using a form block, a piece of dead soft aluminum should first be placed over the hollow portion of the mold and securely fastened in place. The bumping operation should be

  A. started by tapping the aluminum lightly around the edges and gradually working down into the center.

  B. distributed evenly over the face of the aluminum at all times rather than being started at the edges or center.

  C. started by tapping the aluminum in the center until it touches the bottom of the mold and then working out in all directions.

4-69 AMA017

When drilling a hole for a 1/8" rivet, first drill a _____ pilot hole and then drill the final hole with a _____ size bit.

  A. .125"; number 30

  B. number 30; .125"

  C. number 40; .125"

4-70 AMA016

In regards to the basic principles of sheet metal repair, which of the following statements are not true?

1. Ensure that the cross-sectional area of a splice or patch is at least equal to or greater than that of the damaged part.
2. The joint is critical in sheer if more than the optimum number of fasteners of a given sized are installed.
3. The joint is critical in bearing if less than the optimum number of fasteners of a given size are installed.
4. Form all repairs in such a manner to fit the original contour perfectly.
5. Keep the weight of all repairs to a minimum.
6. The importance of retaining the proper balance and rigidity of aircraft control surfaces cannot be overemphasized.

  A. 5

  B. 1 and 6

  C. 2 and 3

4-71 AMA016

What type of damage repair consists of removing the damaged portion from the structure and replacing it with a member identical in material and shape?

  A. Damage repairable by insertion.

  B. Damage necessitating replacement of parts.

  C. Negligible damage.

4-72 AMA016

Which statement is true regarding the inspection of a stressed skin metal wing assembly known to have been critically loaded?

  A. If rivets show no visible distortion, further investigation is unnecessary.

  B. If genuine rivet tipping has occurred, groups of consecutive rivet heads will be tipped in the same direction.

  C. If bearing failure has occurred, the rivet shanks will be joggled.

AIRCRAFT METAL STRUCTURAL REPAIR

ANSWERS

4-67 Answer C.
Curved flanged parts are usually hand formed with a concave flange, the inside edge, and a convex flange, the outside edge. The concave flange is formed by stretching, while the convex flange is formed by shrinking. Such parts are shaped with the aid of hardwood or metal forming blocks. Bend the flange on the concave curve first. This practice may keep the flange from splitting open or cracking when the metal is stretched. Convex surfaces are formed by shrinking the material over a form block. Using a wooden or plastic shrinking mallet and a backup or wedge block, start at the center of the curve and work toward both ends.
[Ref: Airframe Handbook H-8083-31A-ATB, Chapter 04 Page 77-79]

4-68 Answer A.
After clamping the bumping block into a bench vise, use a soft-faced rubber mallet, or a hardwood drive block with suitable mallet, to start the bumping near the edges of the form. Work the material down gradually from the edges with light blows of the mallet. The purpose of bumping is to work the material into shape by stretching rather than forcing it into the form with heavy blows. Always start bumping near the edge of the form. Never start near the center of the blister.
[Ref: Airframe Handbook H-8083-31A-ATB, Chapter 04 Page 80]

4-69 Answer A.
The final rivet hole size should be the smallest size which allows for easy insertion of the rivet, which is typically about .003" larger than the actual rivet diameter. To produce that final hole size, first drill a slightly smaller pilot hole, and then use the correct size bit to ream out the hole to its required dimension. In this example, a #30 drill hole measures .1285"; or approximately .003" larger than the rivet diameter, allowing for that proper insertion force.
[Ref: Airframe Handbook H-8083-31A-ATB, Chapter 04 Page 40]

4-70 Answer C.
Aircraft structural joint design involves an attempt to find the optimum strength relationship between being critical in shear and critical in bearing. These are determined by the failure mode affecting the joint. The joint is critical in shear if less than the optimum number of fasteners of a given size are installed. This means that the rivets will fail, and not the sheet, if the joint fails. The joint is critical in bearing if more than the optimum number of fasteners of a given size are installed; the material may crack and tear between holes, or fastener holes may distort and stretch while the fasteners remain intact.
[Ref: Airframe Handbook H-8083-31A-ATB, Chapter 04 Page 86-89]

4-71 Answer A.
Damage must be repaired by insertion when the area is too large to be patched or the structure is arranged such that repair members would interfere with structural alignment. In this type of repair, the damaged portion is removed from the structure and replaced by a member identical in material and shape. Splice connections at each end of the insertion member provide for load transfer to the original structure.
[Ref: Airframe Handbook H-8083-31A-ATB, Chapter 04 Page 91-92]

4-72 Answer B.
If the heads are tipped or rivets are loose, they show up in groups of several consecutive rivets and are probably tipped in the same direction. If heads that appear to be tipped are not in the same direction, tipping may have occurred during some previous installation.
[Ref: Airframe Handbook H-8083-31A-ATB, Chapter 04 Page 92-93]

4-73 AMA016
What is indicated by the presence of aluminum oxide surrounding the manufactured heads of a rivet installation?
  A. Fretting Corrosion
  B. Loose Rivets
  C. Exfoliation Corrosion

4-74 AMA016
Which patch may be utilized in repairing skin where aerodynamic smoothness is not important?
  A. Flush Patch
  B. Open and Closed Skin Area Repair
  C. Lap or Scab Patch

4-75 AMA094
What is the minimum edge distance for aircraft rivets?
  A. Three times the diameter of the rivet shank.
  B. Two times the diameter of the rivet head.
  C. Two times the diameter of the river shank.

4-76 AMA016
When riveting dissimilar metal together, what precautions must be taken to prevent an electrolytic action?
  A. Avoid the use of dissimilar metals by redesigning the unit according to the recommendations outlined in AC43.13-2A.
  B. Treat the surfaces to be riveted together with a process called anodic treatment.
  C. Place a protective separator between areas of potential electrical difference.

4-77 AMA017
The dimensions of an MS20430AD-4-8 rivet are
  A. 1/8 inch in diameter and 1/2 inch long.
  B. 1/8 inch in diameter and 1/4 inch long.
  C. 4/16 inch in diameter and 8/32 inch long.

4-78 AMA016
Aircraft structural units, such as spars, engine supports, etc., which have been built up from sheet metal, are normally?
  A. Repairable, using approved methods.
  B. not repairable, but must be replaced when damaged or deteriorated.
  C. repairable, except when subjected to compressive loads.

AIRCRAFT METAL STRUCTURAL REPAIR

ANSWERS

4-73 Answer A.
The presence of a black residue around the rivets is not an indication of looseness, but an indication of movement (fretting). The residue, which is aluminum oxide, is formed by a small amount of relative motion between the rivet and the adjacent surface.
[Ref: Airframe Handbook H-8083-31A-ATB, Chapter 04 Page 93]

4-74 Answer C.
The lap or scab type of patch is an external patch where the edges of the patch and the skin overlap each other. The overlapping portion of the patch is riveted to the skin. Lap patches may be used in most areas where aerodynamic smoothness is not important.
[Ref: Airframe Handbook H-8083-31A-ATB, Chapter 04 Page 95-96]

4-75 Answer C.
Edge distance, also called margin by some manufacturers, is the distance from the center of the rivet to the edge of the sheet. It should not be less than 2 or more than 4 rivet diameters and the recommended edge distance is about 2 half diameters of the rivet shank.
[Ref: Airframe Handbook H-8083-31A-ATB, Chapter 04 Page 34]

4-76 Answer C.
Corrosion Resistant Steel (CRES) causes magnesium, aluminum, or cadmium to corrode when it touches these metals. To isolate CRES, from magnesium and aluminum, apply a finish that gives protection between their mating surfaces.
[Ref: Airframe Handbook H-8083-31A-ATB, Chapter 04 Page 83]

4-77 Answer A.
The Alloy Code (AD) is followed by two numbers separated by a dash. The first number is the numerator of a fraction, which specifies the shank diameter in thirty-seconds of an inch. The second number is the numerator of a fraction in sixteenths of an inch and identifies the length of the rivet.
[Ref: Airframe Handbook H-8083-31A-ATB, Chapter 04 Page 32]

4-78 Answer A.
Forming processes used on the flight line and those practiced in the maintenance or repair shop cannot duplicate a manufacturer's resources, but similar techniques of factory metal working can be applied in the handcrafting of repair parts. For exact information about specific repairs, consult the manufacturer's maintenance or Structural Repair Manuals (SRM).
[Ref: Airframe Handbook H-8083-31A-ATB, Chapter 04 Page 2 & 57]

ORAL EXAM

4-1(O).   What are some considerations when inspecting a sheet metal structure?

4-2(O).   Name and describe five types of sheet metal defects.

4-3(O).   What is involved in the selection of repair material?

4-4(O).   When forming a bend in metal, what is K-factor and how is it used?

4-5(O).   How is a rivet selected for a repair?

4-6(O).   What actions are taken to install a rivet?

4-7(O).   What are some precautions and safety practices when working with metals other than aluminum?

AIRCRAFT METAL STRUCTURAL REPAIR

ANSWERS

ORAL EXAM

4-1(O). The extent of the damage is often greater than the area where damage can be seen. An impact, for example, will transfer the shock throughout the structure not just where the external damage is visible. The entire member and surrounding support structure must be inspected for damage. Corrosion often occurs on the inside of structure in pockets and corners where moisture and salt spray may accumulate. Ensure that drain holes are kept clean and open. Surface irregularities may be visible but they may also be covering further damage in the structure that is covered. Clues like smoking from loose rivets, buckled skin, etc. must be interpreted and further inspection of the substructure must be made. Damage to aluminum alloy surface protection should be repaired immediately to prevent corrosion to the core metal. The full extent of cracks and substructure condition often requires eddy current or ultra sound inspection to be performed.
[Ref: Airframe Handbook H-8083-31A-ATB, Chapter 04 Page 90]

4-2(O). 1) Burnishing – a polishing of one surface by sliding contact with a smooth, harder surface. Usually, there is no displacement or removal of metal. 2) Crack – a physical separation of two adjacent portions of metal, evidenced by a fine or thin line across the surface caused by excessive stress at that point. It may extend inward from the surface from a few thousandths of an inch to completely through the section thickness. 3) Dent – indentation in a metal surface produced by an object striking with force. The surface surrounding the indentation is usually slightly upset. 4) Inclusion – presence of foreign or extraneous material wholly within a portion of metal. Such material is introduced during the manufacture of rod, bar, or tubing by rolling or forging. 5) Score - deeper than a scratch, tear, or break in the metal that results from contact under pressure. May show discoloration from temperature produced by friction. Other defects are: Brinelling, Burr, Corrosion, Cut, Erosion, Chattering, Galling, Gouge, Nick, Pitting, Scratch, Stain, and Upsetting.
[Ref: Airframe Handbook H-8083-31A-ATB, Chapter 04 Page 90-91]

4-3(O). The repair material must duplicate the strength of the original structure. The same material as the original is desired. If an alloy weaker than the original material has to be used, a heavier gauge must be used to give equivalent cross-sectional strength. A lighter gauge material should not be used even when using a stronger alloy. Note that extensive repairs that are made too strong can be as undesirable as repairs weaker than the original structure. All aircraft structure must flex slightly to withstand the forces of takeoff, flight, and landing. If a repair is too strong, excessive flexing occurs at the edge of the repair causing accelerated metal fatigue.
[Ref: Airframe Handbook H-8083-31A-ATB, Chapter 04 Page 87, 93]

4-4(O). K-factor is the percentage of material thickness where there is no stretching or compressing of the material, such as the neutral axis. This percentage has been calculated and is one of 179 numbers on a K chart. The number corresponds to the angle to which the metal is bent. The K factor of a 90° bend is 1. All other bend angles must use the K-factor to calculate the setback. The setback is the distance the jaws of a break must be set back from the mold line to form a bend. The K-factor is multiplied by the sum of the radius of the intended bend and the material thickness to arrive at the setback.
[Ref: Airframe Handbook H-8083-31A-ATB, Chapter 04 Page 60]

4-5(O). Normally, the rivet size and material should be the same as the original rivets in the part being repaired. If a rivet hole has been enlarged or deformed, the next size larger rivet can be used after the hole has been reworked. Proper edge distance and rivet spacing must be maintained. Consult the manufacturer's maintenance manual for the correct rivets to be used. The size rivet for any repair can be determined by referring to the rivets used by the manufacturer in the next parallel rivet row inboard on a wing, or forward on the fuselage. Another method is to multiply the thickness of the skin by three and use the next larger size diameter rivet than the resulting product. The number of rivets to be used can be found in the manufacturer's structural repair manual or in Advisory Circular (AC) 43.13-1.
[Ref: Airframe Handbook H-8083-31A-ATB, Chapter 04 Page 87, 94]

ORAL EXAM

4-6(O). The riveting procedure consists of transferring and preparing the hole, drilling, and driving the rivets. First, the holes in which rivets will be inserted must be correctly located. Accomplish transfer of holes from a drilled part to another part by placing one part over the other and using the established holes as a guide. Alternately, scribe the hole locations through from the drilled part onto the part to be drilled. Spot with a center punch and drill. Hole locations may also be laid out following manufacturer instructions or standard acceptable practices. Next, the holes must be drilled. It is critical to use the correct size drill bit for the shank diameter of the rivets to be installed or the rivet may not hold securely. It is necessary to hold the drill at a 90° to the work. Ensure that the drill bit is seated and cutting in the center punched hole. Avoid excess pressure and allow the drill bit to cut completely through the material. After the holes are drilled, they must be prepared for the rivets. All burrs and drill chips must be removed. If countersinking or dimpling is required, use the method that is correct for metal of that thickness. Always keep hammer blows and dimpling pressure to a minimum so that no undue work hardening occurs. Before driving the rivets, make certain that the holes line up perfectly and that they are securely fastened with temporary fasteners. Solo riveting is possible if the riveter can hold the bucking bar and still operate the rivet gun. A team approach is used when this is not possible. A code or a radio set is used by the riveter and the bucking bar person to communicate the status of the riveting process. Always inspect installed rivets for any sign of looseness and proper installation.

[Ref: Airframe Handbook H-8083-31A-ATB, Chapter 04 Page 40-41]

4-7(O). When working with Corrosion Resistant Steel (CRES), a finish must be applied to isolate the steel from aluminum or magnesium parts. Contact with these metals causes corrosion. Also, a larger bend radius prevents cracking of CRES in the bend area. Understand that working with CRES, pressures needed to be applied when sheering, punching, and drilling, etc., will be greater than with mild steel. Working with magnesium, it is important to keep any particles away from sources of ignition. They ignite very easily and, if concentrated, could cause an explosion. Extinguish magnesium fires with dry talc, calcium carbonate, sand, or graphite. Do not use foam, water, carbon tetrachloride, or carbon dioxide on a magnesium fire. Magnesium must also not touch methyl alcohol. Titanium also has working precautions. Small particles of titanium burn very easily and can explode when in sufficient concentration. If water touches molten titanium, a steam explosion could occur. Like magnesium, extinguish titanium fires with dry talc, calcium carbonate, sand, or graphite. Do not use foam, water, carbon tetrachloride, or carbon dioxide.

[Ref: Airframe Handbook H-8083-31A-ATB, Chapter 04 Page 83, 85]

AIRCRAFT METAL STRUCTURAL REPAIR

QUESTIONS

PRACTICAL EXAM

4-1(P).   Given an actual aircraft or mockup and the appropriate tooling, install and remove at least two each of two or more types of rivets.

4-2(P).   Given specific dimensions and appropriate sheet metal tooling, lay out and form a piece of metal, to include at least one bend.

4-3(P).   Given required information, lay out a rivet pattern.

4-4(P).   Given required information, determine the hole size to use in a sheet metal repair.

4-5(P).   Given an actual aircraft or mockup, inspect a sheet metal assembly or repair for airworthiness and record your findings.

4-6(P).   Given appropriate sheet metal tooling, drill and install countersunk rivets.

4-7(P).   Given appropriate sheet metal tooling, drill and install countersunk rivets via dimpling.

AIRCRAFT WELDING

Types of Welding, Gas Welding and Cutting Equipment, Cutting, Brazing and Soldering, and Repair of Steel Tubing

5-1 AMA101
Which statement concerning a welding process is true?
  A. The inert arc welding process uses an inert gas to protect the weld zone from the atmosphere.
  B. In the oxyacetylene welding process, the filler rod used for steel is covered with a thin coating of flux.
  C. In the metallic arc welding process, filler material, if needed, is provided by a separate metal rod of the proper material held in the arc.

5-2 AMA101
The shielding gases generally used in the Gas Tungsten Arc (GTA) welding of aluminum consist of
  A. a mixture of nitrogen and carbon dioxide.
  B. helium or argon.
  C. nitrogen or hydrogen, or a mixture of nitrogen and hydrogen.

5-3 AMA101
Which of the following types of electric arc welding is not well suited for repair work because the weld quality cannot be easily determined?
  A. Shielded Metal Arc Welding
  B. Gas Metal Arc Welding
  C. Gas Tungsten Arc Welding

5-4 AMA101
In Gas Tungsten Arc (GTA) welding, a stream of inert gas is used to?
  A. Concentrate the heat of the arc and prevent its dissipation.
  B. Prevent the formation of oxides in the puddle.
  C. Lower the temperature required to properly fuse the metal.

5-5 AMA101
Which type of welding torch contains a tungsten electrode within a fine bore copper nozzle?
  A. Plasma Arc Torch
  B. Injector Torch
  C. Oxy-Acetylene Torch

5-6 AMA101
What is the benefit of adding acetone to acetylene welding gas?
  A. Increased stability.
  B. A hotter flame.
  C. Decreased combustion rate.

AIRCRAFT WELDING

ANSWERS

5-1 Answer A.
In shielded metal arc welding, the flux on the metal wire rod melts, releasing an inert gas that shields the molten puddle from oxygen in the air to prevent oxidation. The molten flux covers the weld and hardens to an airtight slag that protects the weld bead as it cools.
[Ref: Airframe Handbook H-8083-31A-ATB, Chapter 05 Page 2]

5-2 Answer B.
In Gas Tungsten Arc (GTA) welding, a stream of inert gas, such as argon or helium, flows out around the electrode and envelopes the arc thereby preventing the formation of oxides in the molten puddle.
[Ref: Airframe Handbook H-8083-31A-ATB, Chapter 05 Page 3]

5-3 Answer B.
Gas Metal Arch Welding (GMAW) can be used for large volume manufacturing and production work; it is not well suited to repair work because weld quality cannot be easily determined without destructive testing.
[Ref: Airframe Handbook H-8083-31A-ATB, Chapter 05 Page 3]

5-4 Answer B.
In gas tungsten arc welding, a stream of inert gas, such as argon or helium, flows out around the electrode and envelopes the arc thereby preventing the formation of oxides in the molten puddle.
[Ref: Airframe Handbook H-8083-31A-ATB, Chapter 05 Page 3]

5-5 Answer A.
In the plasma welding the torch is a non- consumable tungsten electrode is located within a fine-bore copper nozzle.
[Ref: Airframe Handbook H-8083-31A-ATB, Chapter 05 Page 6]

5-6 Answer A.
Acetylene is chemically very unstable, and is stored in special cylinders designed to keep the gas dissolved. The cylinders are packed with a porous material and then saturated with acetone. When the acetylene is added to the cylinder, it dissolves; in this solution, it becomes stable. Pure acetylene stored in a free state explodes from a slight shock at 29.4 pounds per square inch (psi). The acetylene pressure gauge should never be set higher than 15 psi for welding or cutting.
[Ref: Airframe Handbook H-8083-31A-ATB, Chapter 05 Page 7]

5-7 AMA101
Which is true regarding the use of hydrogen, rather than acetylene as a welding gas?
- A. Hydrogen must be stored in special cylinders and kept dissolved with acetone.
- B. Hydrogen can be used and stored at a higher pressure than acetylene.
- C. Detecting a Hydrogen leak is easier than with acetylene.

5-8 AMA101
An acetylene welding hose is a two part hose in which the acetylene portion is
- A. red with left hand threads; the oxygen portion is green with right hand threads.
- B. green with left hand threads; the oxygen portion is red with right hand threads.
- C. red with right hand threads; the oxygen portion is green with left hand threads.

5-9 AMA101
In gas welding, the amount of heat applied to the material being welded is controlled by the
- A. amount of gas pressure used.
- B. size of the tip opening.
- C. distance the tip is held from the work.

5-10 AMA101
In selecting a torch tip size to use in welding, the size of the tip opening determines the
- A. melting point of the filler metal.
- B. temperature of the flame.
- C. amount of the heat applied to the work.

5-11 AMA101
The most important consideration(s) when selecting a filler welding rod is
- A. current setting or flame temperature.
- B. material compatibility.
- C. ambient conditions.

5-12 AMA101
To prevent corrosion after successfully brazing two pieces of metal together, the mechanic should _____.
- A. clean with hot water and stainless steel brush
- B. spray immediately with primer
- C. clean with an acid wash

AIRCRAFT WELDING

ANSWERS

5-7 Answer B.
Being more stable than acetylene, hydrogen may be stored at higher pressures in standard cylinders with less risk of explosion and thus is suitable for underwater welding and cutting. However, because it is colorless and odorless it is more difficult to detect leaks.
[Ref: Airframe Handbook H-8083-31A-ATB, Chapter 05 Page 7]

5-10 Answer C.
The torch tip delivers and controls the final flow of gases. It is important that you use the correct tip with the proper gas pressures for the work to be welded satisfactorily. The size of the tip opening—not the temperature—determines the amount of heat applied to the work.
[Ref: Airframe Handbook H-8083-31A-ATB, Chapter 05 Page 11]

5-8 Answer A.
The acetylene hose is red and has left hand threads indicated by a groove cut into the connection nut. The oxygen hose is green and has right hand threads indicated by the absence of a groove on the connection nut.
[Ref: Airframe Handbook H-8083-31A-ATB, Chapter 05 Page 8]

5-11 Answer B.
To insure proper strength and corrosion resistance, the welding rod selected should be compatible with the base metal being welded.
[Ref: Airframe Handbook H-8083-31A-ATB, Chapter 05 Page 15]

5-9 Answer B.
The torch tip delivers and controls the final flow of gases. It is important that you use the correct tip with the proper gas pressures for the work to be welded satisfactorily. The size of the tip opening—not the temperature—determines the amount of heat applied to the work.
[Ref: Airframe Handbook H-8083-31A-ATB, Chapter 05 Page 9]

5-12 Answer A.
As brazing fluxes are water soluble, use a hot water rinse and wire brush to remove the excess flux. If the flux was overheated during welding and has turned green or black, it will need to be removed with an acid solution.
[Ref: Airframe Handbook H-8083-31A-ATB, Chapter 05 Page 20]

5-13 AMA101

Which type of welding flame is most widely used because it has the smallest effect on the composition of the base metal?
- A. Oxidizing Flame
- B. Carburizing Flame
- C. Neutral Flame

5-14 AMA101

A welding torch backfire may be caused by
- A. using too much acetylene.
- B. a loose tip.
- C. a tip temperature that is too cool.

5-15 AMA101

Filing or grinding a weld bead
- A. may be performed to achieve a smoother surface.
- B. reduces the strength of the joint.
- C. may be necessary to avoid adding excess weight or to achieve uniform material thickness.

5-16 AMA101

If too much acetylene is used in the welding of stainless steel
- A. oxide will be formed on the base metal close to the weld.
- B. a porous weld will result.
- C. the metal will absorb carbon and lose its resistance to corrosion.

5-17 AMA101

When welding Chrome Molybdenum steel, the areas sounding the weld site should be preheated to
- A. 300-400 degrees.
- B. 600-700 degrees.
- C. within 100 degrees of the kindling temperature of the filler rod.

5-18 AMA101

How should a welding torch flame be adjusted to weld stainless steel?
- A. Neutral
- B. Slightly Oxidizing
- C. Slightly Carburizing

AIRCRAFT WELDING

ANSWERS

5-13 Answer C.
A neutral flame is produced with a balanced mixture of acetylene and oxygen and is most widely used for most welding as it does not alter the composition of the base metal, and when welding steel allows the metal to flow quietly without burning or sparking.
[Ref: Airframe Handbook H-8083-31A-ATB, Chapter 05 Page 13]

5-14 Answer B.
A backfire may be caused by touching the tip against the work, overheating the tip, by operating the torch at other than recommended pressures, by a loose tip or head, or by dirt or slag in the end of the tip, and may cause molten metal to be splattered when the flame pops.
[Ref: Airframe Handbook H-8083-31A-ATB, Chapter 05 Page 14]

5-15 Answer B.
Welds should never be filed to give them a better appearance, since filing deprives the weld of part of its strength.
[Ref: Airframe Handbook H-8083-31A-ATB, Chapter 05 Page 16]

5-16 Answer C.
Too much acetylene in the flame adds carbon to the metal and causes it to lose its resistance to corrosion.
[Ref: Airframe Handbook H-8083-31A-ATB, Chapter 05 Page 17]

5-17 Answer A.
The welding technique for chrome molybdenum (chromemoly) is practically the same as that for carbon steels, except for sections over 3/16-inch thick. The surrounding area must be preheated to a temperature between 300°F and 400°F before beginning to weld.
[Ref: Airframe Handbook H-8083-31A-ATB, Chapter 05 Page 17]

5-18 Answer C.
A slightly carburizing flame is recommended for welding stainless steel. The flame should be adjusted so that a feather of excess acetylene, about 1/16-inch long, forms around the inner cone.
[Ref: Airframe Handbook H-8083-31A-ATB, Chapter 05 Page 17]

5-19 AMA101

The oxyacetylene flame used for aluminum welding should
  A. be neutral and soft, and slightly carburizing.
  B. contain an excess of acetylene and leave the tip at a relatively low speed.
  C. be slightly oxidizing.

5-22 AMA101

Which statement best describes magnesium welding?
  A. Magnesium can be welded to other metals.
  B. Filler rod should be nickel steel.
  C. Filler rod should be the same composition as base metal.

5-20 AMA101

When brazing; to what temperature should the base metal be preheated?
  A. The filler material boiling point.
  B. The base material flow temperature.
  C. The filler material flow temperature.

5-23 AMA101

Which is true regarding soldering of electrical connections?
  A. Only use solder with a melting point below 293°.
  B. Only use solder which contains rosin.
  C. Always use solder containing at least 50% silver.

5-21 AMA101

What purpose does flux serve in welding aluminum?
  A. Removes dirt, grease, and oil.
  B. Minimizes or prevents oxidation.
  C. Ensures proper distribution of the filler rod.

5-24 AMA101

What is the purpose of using flux during all silver soldering operations?
  A. To remove contaminants from the joint.
  B. To chemically react with the solder to increase adhesion.
  C. To provide even heat conductivity.

AIRCRAFT WELDING

ANSWERS

5-19 Answer A.
To be sure there is no possibility of oxidation, when welding aluminum, the flame should be neutral, soft, and slightly carburizing.
[Ref: Airframe Handbook H-8083-31A-ATB, Chapter 05 Page 18]

5-22 Answer C.
When welding magnesium, for the weld strength to match the base metal strength, the filler material should be of the same composition as the base material in the alloy.
[Ref: Airframe Handbook H-8083-31A-ATB, Chapter 05 Page 19]

5-20 Answer C.
When brazing, the base metal should be preheated slowly until it reaches the flowing temperature of the filler metal, but not as high as the metal's boiling point.
[Ref: Airframe Handbook H-8083-31A-ATB, Chapter 05 Page 20]

5-23 Answer B.
Electrical connections should be soldered only with a soft solder containing rosin, as rosin does not corrode the electrical connections.
[Ref: Airframe Handbook H-8083-31A-ATB, Chapter 05 Page 21]

5-21 Answer B.
Use of the proper flux when welding aluminum is important as aluminum flux is designed to remove aluminum oxide by chemically combining with it during the heating process.
[Ref: Airframe Handbook H-8083-31A-ATB, Chapter 05 Page 18-21]

5-24 Answer A.
Flux must be used in all silver soldering operations to ensure the base metal is chemically clean. The flux removes the film of oxide from the base metal and allows the silver solder to adhere to it.
[Ref: Airframe Handbook H-8083-31A-ATB, Chapter 05 Page 22]

5-25 AMA101
What is the most important factor for successful TIG welding of titanium?
- A. Proper preheat temperatures are achieved.
- B. A clean welding surface.
- C. Proper oxygen/fuel ratios.

5-26 AMA101
Expansion and contraction of metal is of greatest concern when welding
- A. thin material.
- B. thick material.
- C. a thin piece of metal to a thick piece.

5-27 AMA101
What primarily determines the number of beads required when welding a joint?
- A. The type of joint.
- B. The thickness of the metal.
- C. The amperage of your equipment.

5-28 AMA101
Which of the following is not true regarding controlling the expansion of metals during welding?
- A. Chill bars made of nickel are an effective way to control expansion and contraction.
- B. Expansion is a greater problem with thinner sheets of metal.
- C. Expansion can be controlled by tack welding along the joint.

5-29 AMA101
When a butt welded joint is visually inspected for penetration
- A. the penetration should be 25 to 50 percent of the thickness of the base metal.
- B. the penetration should be 100 percent of the thickness of the base metal.
- C. look for evidence of excessive heat in the form of a very high bead.

5-30 AMA101
What method of repair is recommended for a steel tube longeron dented at a cluster?
- A. Welded Patch Plate
- B. Welded Split Sleeve
- C. Welded Outer Sleeve

AIRCRAFT WELDING

ANSWERS

5-25 Answer B.
The techniques for welding titanium are similar to those required for nickel-based alloys and stainless steels. To produce a satisfactory weld, emphasis is placed on the surface cleanliness and the use of inert gas to shield the weld area. A clean environment is one of the requirements to weld titanium.
[Ref: Airframe Handbook H-8083-31A-ATB, Chapter 05 Page 24]

5-28 Answer C.
Expansion and contraction have a tendency to buckle and warp thin sheet metal 1/8-inch or thinner. The most effective method of alleviating this situation is to remove the heat from the metal near the weld, preventing it from spreading across the surface area. This can be done by placing heavy pieces of metal, known as chill bars, on either side of the weld; to absorb the heat and prevent it from spreading. Copper is most often used for chill bars because of its ability to absorb heat readily.
[Ref: Airframe Handbook H-8083-31A-ATB, Chapter 05 Page 30]

5-26 Answer A.
Expansion and contraction have a tendency to buckle and warp pieces of metal 1/8" thick and thinner. This is because of having a low mass large surface area that spreads and dissipates heat quickly. This is often alleviated by placing heavy pieces of metal near the welded point to prevent the heat from spreading along the entire piece of thinner stock.
[Ref: Airframe Handbook H-8083-31A-ATB, Chapter 05 Page 29-30]

5-29 Answer B.
The welded joint should have a penetration that is 100 percent of the thickness of the base metal. When welding butt joints in metal thicker than 1/8th inch it is often necessary to bevel the edges so heat from the torch can completely penetrate the metal.
[Ref: Airframe Handbook H-8083-31A-ATB, Chapter 05 Page 31]

5-27 Answer B.
Grove and fillet welds in heavy metals often require multiple beads to produce the soundest welds with the number of beads determined by the thickness of the metal.
[Ref: Airframe Handbook H-8083-31A-ATB, Chapter 05 Page 26-27]

5-30 Answer A.
Dents at a cluster weld can be repaired by welding a formed steel patch plate over the dented area and surrounding tubes.
[Ref: Airframe Handbook H-8083-31A-ATB, Chapter 05 Page 32-33]

ORAL EXAM

5-1(O).   Name the two most common fuel gases used for gas welding.

5-2(O).   Name the three types of torches used in gas welding.

5-3(O).   Why must acetylene gas be kept at 15 psi or below?

5-4(O).   What do the cylinders containing acetylene contain to help stabilize this gas?

5-5(O).   What determines the amount of heat applied to the material being welded in gas welding?

5-6(O).   What should be considered when selecting a filler welding rod?

5-7(O).   Which type of flame should be used when welding aluminum or nickel?

5-8(O).   What can cause a welding torch to backfire?

5-9(O).   Can a weld bead be filed or grind?

5-10(O). Explain the purpose of tack welding.

5-11(O). What shielding gas is generally used in the Gas Tungsten Arc (GRA) welding of aluminum?

5-12(O). In Gas Tungsten Arc (GTA) welding, what is the purpose of the stream of inert gas?

5-13(O). When inspecting a butt-welded, the weld penetration should be how thick.

5-14(O). What is the recommended repair for engine mounts?

5-15(O). How is the number of beads determined when producing a fillet welds in heavy metals?

5-16(O). What purpose does flux serve in welding aluminum?

5-17(O). Why is it necessary to use flux in all silver soldering operations?

5-18(O). List the protective personal equipment you should use when welding.

5-19(O). What color of glass is used in the protective eye-wear designed especially for aluminum oxy-fuel welding?

AIRCRAFT WELDING

ANSWERS

ORAL EXAM

5-1(O).   Oxygen and acetylene.
[Ref: Airframe Handbook H-8083-31A-ATB, Chapter 05 Page 2]

5-2(O).   Equal pressure, injector, and cutting.
[Ref: Airframe Handbook H-8083-31A-ATB, Chapter 05 Page 9]

5-3(O).   Acetylene is chemically very unstable. The acetylene pressure gauge should never be set higher than 15 psi for welding or cutting.
[Ref: Airframe Handbook H-8083-31A-ATB, Chapter 05 Page 7]

5-4(O).   Acetylene, being very unstable, is stored special cylinders designed to keep the gas dissolved. The cylinders are packed with a porous material and then saturated with acetone.
[Ref: Airframe Handbook H-8083-31A-ATB, Chapter 05 Page 7]

5-5(O).   The size of the tip opening determines the amount of heat applied to the work.
[Ref: Airframe Handbook H-8083-31A-ATB, Chapter 05 Page 9]

5-6(O).   The filler rod selected should be compatible with the base metal being welded.
[Ref: Airframe Handbook H-8083-31A-ATB, Chapter 05 Page 15]

5-7(O).   A carburizing flame is best used for welding such nonferrous alloys as aluminum, nickel, and Monel.
[Ref: Airframe Handbook H-8083-31A-ATB, Chapter 05 Page 13]

5-8(O).   A backfire may be caused by touching the tip against the work, overheating the tip, by operating the torch at other than recommended pressures, by a loose tip or head, or by dirt or slag in the end of the tip, and may cause molten metal to be splattered when the flame pops.
[Ref: Airframe Handbook H-8083-31A-ATB, Chapter 05 Page 14]

5-9(O).   No, welds should never be filed to give them a better appearance, since filing deprives the weld of part of its strength.
[Ref: Airframe Handbook H-8083-31A-ATB, Chapter 05 Page 16]

5-10(O). A method of holding parts together before they are permanently welded. The parts are assembled, and small spots of weld are placed at strategic locations to hold them in position.
[Ref: Airframe Handbook H-8083-31A-ATB, Glossary Page G-35]

5-11(O). Argon or helium is used as the shielding gas for Gas Tungsten Arc when welding aluminum.
[Ref: Airframe Handbook H-8083-31A-ATB, Chapter 05 Page 3]

5-12(O). To prevent the formation of oxides in the puddle.
[Ref: Airframe Handbook H-8083-31A-ATB, Chapter 05 Page 3]

5-13(O). The weld penetration should be 100 percent of the thickness of the base metal.
[Ref: Airframe Handbook H-8083-31A-ATB, Chapter 05 Page 31]

5-14(O). The preferred method to repair an engine mount member is by using a larger diameter replacement tube telescoped over the stub of the original member using fish-mouth and rosette welds.
[Ref: Airframe Handbook H-8083-31A-ATB, Chapter 05 Page 36]

ORAL EXAM

5-15(O).   Fillet welds in heavy metals often require the deposit of a number of beads to complete a weld. It is important that the beads be deposited in a predetermined sequence to produce the soundest welds with the best proportions. The number of beads is determined by the thickness of the metal being welded.
[Ref: Airframe Handbook H-8083-31A-ATB, Chapter 05 Page 28]

5-16(O).   The use of flux in aluminum welding minimizes or prevents oxidation.
[Ref: Airframe Handbook H-8083-31A-ATB, Chapter 05 Page 18, 20, 21]

5-17(O).   Flux must be used in all silver soldering operations to ensure the base metal is chemically clean. The flux removes the film of oxide from the base metal and allows the silver solder to adhere to it.
[Ref: Airframe Handbook H-8083-31A-ATB, Chapter 05 Page 20]

5-18(O).   Welding helmet, welding gloves, protective clothing, and footwear; if not in an adequately ventilated area, appropriate breathing equipment.
[Ref: Airframe Handbook H-8083-31A-ATB, Chapter 05 Page 25]

5-19(O).   Patented green glass by TM Technologies.
[Ref: Airframe Handbook H-8083-31A-ATB, Chapter 05 Page 10]

AIRCRAFT WELDING

PRACTICAL EXAM

5-1(P).   Given appropriate welding equipment and safety equipment, ignite a torch, set one or more specified flame patterns, and properly shutdown torch.

5-2(P).   Given appropriate soldering equipment and safety equipment, solder a joint or connection.

5-3(P).   Given appropriate aircraft quality materials and safety equipment, weld or braze a joint.

5-4(P).   Given a specific welding task, determine the appropriate method and materials that is to be used.

5-5(P).   Given a specific soldering task, determine the appropriate method and materials that is to be used.

5-6(P).   Given a specific brazing task, determine the appropriate method and materials that is to be used.

5-7(P).   Given a specific welding task, determine the appropriate data that is to be used.

5-8(P).   Given a specific soldering task, determine the appropriate data that is to be used.

5-9(P).   Given a specific brazing task, determine the appropriate data that is to be used.

AIRCRAFT WOOD AND STRUCTURAL REPAIR

Wooden Aircraft Construction, Wooden Aircraft Repairs, Materials, Adhesives, Application, Joint Pressures, and Wing Repairs

6-1 AMA070
What is the danger of a wooden aircraft structure in which the wood holds a moisture content of over 20%?
- A. Expansion and contraction of the structure components.
- B. The growth of fungus.
- C. A weakening of the glued joints.

6-2 AMA102
In order to properly inspect wood structure of an aircraft, the wooden components must be
- A. between 60-80°F.
- B. at a moisture content as close as possible to its principle area of operation.
- C. dry.

6-3 AMA102
Glued joints are typically designed to take what type of load?
- A. Shear Loads
- B. Tension Loads
- C. Both Shear and Tension Loads

6-4 AMA102
A faint line running across the grain of a wood spar generally indicates
- A. compression failure.
- B. shear failure.
- C. decay.

6-5 AMA102
Which of the following types of wood has the greatest strength properties?
- A. Spruce
- B. Western Hemlock
- C. Douglas Fir

6-6 AMA102
The slope of the grain of any wood used for aircraft may not be greater than
- A. 1:15.
- B. 1:30.
- C. the width to length ratio of that piece.

AIRCRAFT WOOD AND STRUCTURAL REPAIR

ANSWERS

6-1 Answer B.
The ideal moisture range for wooden aircraft components is 8-12%. Any amount of moisture above 20% promotes the growth of fungus. In addition, a high moisture level can cause the components to swell, making inspection of the glued joints more difficult.
[Ref: Airframe Handbook H-8083-31A-ATB, Chapter 06 Page 3]

6-2 Answer C.
Wet or damp wood causes swelling making it difficult to assess the condition of glue joints. The ideal range is 8-12 percent humidity inside the wood. Meters are available that check internal moisture content without making holes in the structure.
[Ref: Airframe Handbook H-8083-31A-ATB, Chapter 06 Page 3]

6-3 Answer A.
Glued joints are designed to take shear loads. If a tension load is expected, the joint is supplemented with a number of screws or bolts in the areas subjected to tension.
[Ref: Airframe Handbook H-8083-31A-ATB, Chapter 06 Page 6]

6-4 Answer A.
A compression failure is indicated by a rupture across the wood fibers. If suspected, a flashlight beam shown to run parallel to the grain will assist in revealing it. The surface will appear to have minute ridges or lines running across the grain.
[Ref: Airframe Handbook H-8083-31A-ATB, Chapter 06 Page 7]

6-5 Answer C.
Douglas Fir is the strongest of the woods mentioned. Thus, Douglas fir may be used as a substitute for Spruce in most cases. Noble Fir also slightly exceeds Spruce except in shear strength where it is approximately 8% deficient. Hemlock is also slightly stronger than Spruce. A complete chart of wood properties may be found on page 8 of Chapter 06 of the 8083-31-ATB Airframe handbook.
[Ref: Airframe Handbook H-8083-31A-ATB, Chapter 06 Page 8]

6-6 Answer A.
The slope of the grain of any aircraft grade wood species may not be steeper than a 1:15 ratio, meaning it can not angle across the wood length of wood by more than 1" of width to 15" of length.
[Ref: Airframe Handbook H-8083-31A-ATB, Chapter 06 Page 8]

6-7 AMA102

Pin knot clusters are permitted in wood aircraft structure provided

A. no pitch pockets are within 12 inches.
B. they produce a small effect on grain direction.
C. they have no mineral streaks.

6-8 AMA102

Compression failures in wood aircraft structures are characterized by buckling of the fibers that appear as streaks on the surface

A. at right angles to the growth rings.
B. at right angles to the grain.
C. parallel to the grain.

6-9 AMA102

Which of the following is most important for successful gluing of structural wood joints?

A. All moisture is eliminated.
B. The joined surfaces are properly sanded.
C. The ambient temperature.

6-10 AMA102

If the allowable temperature of a wood adhesive is listed as 62-80 degrees, at what temperature will the usable pot life be longest?

A. 62 degrees
B. 71 degrees
C. 80 degrees

6-11 AMA102

When a bevel is being cut to repair a cap strip on a wing rib, the length of the beveled area should be

A. equal to the thickness of the rib cap strip.
B. 16 times the thickness of the rib cap strip.
C. 10 times the thickness of the rib cap strip.

6-12 AMA021

What is the purpose of a gusset plate used in the construction and repair of aircraft structures?

A. To join and reinforce intersecting structural members.
B. To provide access for inspection of structural attachments.
C. To hold structural members in position temporarily until the permanent attachment has been completed.

AIRCRAFT WOOD AND STRUCTURAL REPAIR

ANSWERS

6-7 Answer B.
Pin knot clusters are a group of knots, all having a diameter less than approximately 1/16th inch. They are acceptable provided they produce only a small effect on the grain direction.
[Ref: Airframe Handbook H-8083-31A-ATB, Chapter 06 Page 9]

6-8 Answer B.
Compression failures, often caused by natural forces during the growth of the tree or rough handling of the lumber are characterized by a buckling of the fibers that appear as streaks at right angles to the grain, and vary from pronounced failures to very fine hairlines that are difficult to detect.
[Ref: Airframe Handbook H-8083-31A-ATB, Chapter 06 Page 9]

6-9 Answer C.
Be sure to know what the factory recommended temperature range is for the glue you are using. Otherwise, a moisture content of the wood from 8-12% is recommended, and insure the joining surfaces are planed, not sanded or sawed.
[Ref: Airframe Handbook H-8083-31A-ATB, Chapter 06 Page 11]

6-10 Answer A.
Pot life is a product of time and temperature. The cooler the adhesive mix is kept, within the recommended limits of the manufacturer, the longer it remains usable.
[Ref: Airframe Handbook H-8083-31A-ATB, Chapter 06 Page 6-7]

6-11 Answer C.
The angle and length of a beveled sides to be joined should be 10 times the thickness of the rib cap strip. The "16 times" dimension refers to the length of the reinforcing plywood faceplates on either side of the beveled joint.
[Ref: Airframe Handbook H-8083-31A-ATB, Chapter 06 Page 14]

6-12 Answer A.
Plywood gussets are nailed or glued into place to join and reinforce intersecting structural members on wing and stabilizer ribs, trailing edges, and other locations.
[Ref: Airframe Handbook H-8083-31A-ATB, Chapter 06 Page 14-15]

6-13 AMA102

If elongated bolt holes are discovered while inspecting a wooden wing spar, which is the minimum required repair?

A. It is permissible to ream out the holes and use an oversized bolt.

B. The section of spar or the entire spar must be replaced.

C. The spar may be reinforced using a similar wood as splice plates.

6-14 AMA102

Holes bored for bolts which will hold fittings in place should be cut

A. to match the hole diameter of the fitting.

B. .002" undersized to ensure a tight fit through the wood.

C. exactly to equal the hole diameter of the fitting.

6-15 AMA102

In what circumstances are mineral streaks found in wood to be used for structural aircraft repair acceptable?

A. Never.

B. As long as they are not perpendicular to the natural grain.

C. As long as decay is not found in the streaked area.

6-16 AMA102

When patching a plywood skin, abrupt changes in cross sectional areas which will develop dangerous stress concentration should be avoided by using

A. circular or elliptical patches.

B. square patches.

C. doublers with any desired shaped patches.

AIRCRAFT WOOD AND STRUCTURAL REPAIR

ANSWERS

6-13 Answer B.
Bolts and bushings in all aircraft structures must fit snugly. If one is loose, movement of the structure allows it to further enlarge the hole. In the case of elongated holes in a spar, the repair may require a new section to be spliced into the spar or a replacement of the entire spar.
[Ref: Airframe Handbook H-8083-31A-ATB, Chapter 06 Page 20]

6-15 Answer C.
Mineral streaks are acceptable so long as, with careful inspection, no decay is found in the streaked area. All stains must be carefully examined to determine if they are harmless of in the early stages of decay.
[Ref: Airframe Handbook H-8083-31A-ATB, Chapter 06 Page 9]

6-14 Answer A.
All holes drilled for bolts that are to hold fittings in place should match the hole diameter of the fitting. After drilling the hole through the wood should be sealed with varnish or an acceptable substitute and then allowed to dry prior to installing the bolt or bushing.
[Ref: Airframe Handbook H-8083-31A-ATB, Chapter 06 Page 20]

6-16 Answer A.
Both the damaged area and the patch should be cut out in a circular or oval shape with the radius of corners at least 5 times the thickness of the material to eliminate any sharp corners which could stress the skin.
[Ref: Airframe Handbook H-8083-31A-ATB, Chapter 06 Page 21]

ORAL EXAM

6-1(O).   How can you determine if the wood is dry before you inspect a wood aircraft airframe?

6-2(O).   What effect does moisture/humidity have on wood?

6-3(O).   Name the one characteristic all aircraft approved wood species have in common.

6-4(O).   For wood to be certificated for aircraft usage, what must it have?

6-5(O).   Which wood is the standard for comparisons in aircraft structures?

6-6(O).   Can Northern White pine be substituted for Spruce in an aircraft structure?

6-7(O).   When would mineral streaks cause a piece of aircraft quality wood to be rejected?

6-8(O).   When are pin knot clusters acceptable in a piece of aircraft quality wood?

6-9(O).   Are hard knots acceptable in a piece of aircraft quality wood?

6-10(O).   Name two methods for repairing plywood skin.

AIRCRAFT WOOD AND STRUCTURAL REPAIR

ANSWERS

ORAL EXAM

6-1(O).   A moisture meter should be utilized to verify the percentage of moisture in the structure.
   [Ref: Airframe Handbook H-8083-31A-ATB, Chapter 06 Page 3]

6-2(O).   Moisture and/or humidity causes wood to swell.
   [Ref: Airframe Handbook H-8083-31A-ATB, Chapter 06 Page 3]

6-3(O).   The one item common to all the species is that the slope of the grain cannot be steeper than 1:15.
   [Ref: Airframe Handbook H-8083-31A-ATB, Chapter 06 Page 10]

6-4(O).   For certificated aircraft, the wood should have traceability to a source that can provide certification to a military specification (MIL-SPEC).
   [Ref: Airframe Handbook H-8083-31A-ATB, Chapter 06 Page 10]

6-5(O).   Spruce is the standard by which the other wood is measured.
   [Ref: Airframe Handbook H-8083-31A-ATB, Chapter 06 Page 9]

6-6(O).   Northern White Pine cannot be used as substitute for Spruce without an increase in size to compensate for its lesser strength.
   [Ref: Airframe Handbook H-8083-31A-ATB, Chapter 06 Page 8]

6-7(O).   Mineral streaks—unacceptable, if accompanied by decay.
   [Ref: Airframe Handbook H-8083-31A-ATB, Chapter 06 Page 9]

6-8(O).   Only if they produce a small effect on grain direction.
   [Ref: Airframe Handbook H-8083-31A-ATB, Chapter 06 Page 9]

6-9(O).   Hard knots unacceptable.
   [Ref: Airframe Handbook H-8083-31A-ATB, Chapter 06 Page 9]

6-10(O).   Fabric, splayed, surface, plug, or scarf.
   [Ref: Airframe Handbook H-8083-31A-ATB, Chapter 06 Page 20-24]

PRACTICAL EXAM

6-1(P).   Given a sample of aircraft wood, inspect the sample and record your findings.

6-2(P).   Given an actual wooden aircraft structure or mockup, inspect the structure and record your findings.

6-3(P).   Given an actual wooden aircraft structural repair or mockup, inspect the repair for airworthiness and record your findings.

6-4(P).   Given various samples of wood, identify and select those samples that are acceptable aircraft quality woods.

6-5(P).   Given a specific defect, determine the acceptable repair and reference your documentation.

6-6(P).   Given a specific defect in an actual wooden aircraft structure or mockup, inspect the defect and determine if it within acceptable limits, record your findings.

6-7(P).   Given various actual aircraft woods or a listing of them, locate and list any allowable substitute for the woods.

6-8(P).   Given the appropriate publications, determine the allowable species of wood that can be substituted for spruce, record your findings and include the required dimensional changes, if any that are necessary.

6-9(P).   Given the appropriate publications, locate the repair procedures for a damaged wood spar.

6-10(P).   Given the appropriate publications, locate the repair procedures for a damaged wood rib structure.

PAGE LEFT BLANK INTENTIONALLY

ADVANCED COMPOSITE MATERIALS

Description of Composite Structures, Manufacturing and In-service Damage, Nondestructive Inspection of Surfaces, and Plastics

QUESTIONS

7-1 AMA037
The strength and stiffness of a properly constructed composite buildup depends primarily on
   A. the orientation of the plies.
   B. the curing temperature.
   C. the mix of hardener to resin.

7-2 AMA037
Composite fabric material is considered to be the strongest in what direction?
   A. Fill
   B. Bias
   C. Warp

7-3 AMA037
What reference tool is used to determine how the fiber is to be oriented for a particular ply of fabric?
   A. Fill Clock (or Compass)
   B. Bias Clock (or Compass)
   C. Warp Clock (or Compass)

7-4 AMA045
The classification for high tensile strength fiberglass used in aircraft structures is
   A. S-glass.
   B. G-glass.
   C. E-glass.

7-5 AMA037
Which of the following are generally characteristic of Aramid fiber (Kevlar®) composites?
   1. High tensile strength
   2. Flexibility
   3. Stiffness
   4. High compressive strength
   5. Ability to conduct electricity
   A. 1, 3, and 5
   B. 1 and 2
   C. 2, 3, and 4

7-6 AMA037
Which of the following are generally characteristic of carbon/graphite fiber composites?
   1. Flexibility
   2. Stiffness
   3. High compressive strength
   4. Corrosive effect in contact with aluminum
   5. Ability to conduct electricity
   A. 1, 3, and 5
   B. 2, 3, and 4
   C. 1 and 3

ADVANCED COMPOSITE MATERIALS

ANSWERS

7-1 Answer A.
The strength and stiffness of a composite buildup depends on the orientation sequence of the plies.
[Ref: Airframe Handbook H-8083-31A-ATB, Chapter 07 Page 2]

7-2 Answer C.
Warp indicates the longitudinal fibers of a fabric. The warp is the high strength direction due to the straightness of the fibers.
[Ref: Airframe Handbook H-8083-31A-ATB, Chapter 07 Page 3]

7-3 Answer C.
A warp clock is used to describe direction of fibers on a diagram, spec sheet, or manufacturer's sheets. If the warp clock is not available on the fabric, the orientation is defaulted to zero as the fabric comes off the roll. Therefore, 90° to zero is the width of the fabric across.
[Ref: Airframe Handbook H-8083-31A-ATB, Chapter 07 Page 3]

7-4 Answer A.
There are several types of fiberglass used in the aviation industry. S-glass and S2-glass identify structural fiberglass that have a higher strength than E-glass.
[Ref: Airframe Handbook H-8083-31A-ATB, Chapter 07 Page 4]

7-5 Answer B.
Kevlar® is DuPont's name for Aramid fibers. Aramid fibers are lightweight, strong, and tough as well being flexible.
[Ref: Airframe Handbook H-8083-31A-ATB, Chapter 07 Page 4]

7-6 Answer B.
Carbon fibers are very stiff and strong. Advantages include its high strength and corrosion resistance. Disadvantages include lower conductivity than aluminum; therefore, a lightning protection mesh or coating is necessary for aircraft parts that are prone to lightning strikes. Carbon fibers have a high potential for causing galvanic corrosion when used with metallic fasteners and structures.
[Ref: Airframe Handbook H-8083-31A-ATB, Chapter 07 Page 6]

7-7 AMA037
The maximum tensile strength of fiber reinforced plastic is achieved using _____.
  A. unidirectional fibers
  B. fibers uniformly distributed at 45 degrees to each other
  C. bi-directional fibers

7-8 AMA037
Lightning protective fibers on aircraft provide
  A. less electrically resistive surface to aid in lightning dissipation.
  B. more electrically resistive surface to aid in lightning dissipation.
  C. an electrical pathway to guide static charges to lightning dissipater's on an aircraft.

7-9 AMA037
The principle advantage of polyimide resin is that it offers
  A. high flexibility.
  B. high temperature resistance.
  C. strength for load bearing structural applications.

7-10 AMA037
The curing process of a mixed resin may be temporarily stopped by
  A. thoroughly mixing a resin inhibitor compound
  B. placing it in a freezer
  C. place the uncured resin in a pressure vessel above 125 PSI

7-11 AMA078
On a prepreg composite tape, once the chemical reaction within the resin has begun, _____.
  A. the reaction can be reversed by placing the unused prepreg in a freezer
  B. any unapplied prepreg tape must be discarded
  C. the tape is ready to be applied

7-12 AMA037
Which composite adhesive type must be stored at the coldest temperature of the three?
  A. Paste adhesives
  B. Foaming adhesives
  C. Film adhesives

ADVANCED COMPOSITE MATERIALS

ANSWERS

7-7 Answer A.
Fibers in a unidirectional material have all their strength and stiffness only in that one direction and so are stronger in that direction for a given thickness then multi-directional fibers.
[Ref: Airframe Handbook H-8083-31A-ATB, Chapter 07 Page 2-3]

7-8 Answer A.
The surface of a composite structure often includes a metal laced conductive ply to help dissipate a lightning strike over a larger surface of the aircraft.
[Ref: Airframe Handbook H-8083-31A-ATB, Chapter 07 Page 6]

7-9 Answer B.
Polyimide resins excel in high temperature environments due to temperature resistance and low thermal expansion properties. Typical uses are on electrical circuit boards, near hot engines, and heat effected airframe structural components.
[Ref: Airframe Handbook H-8083-31A-ATB, Chapter 07 Page 7]

7-10 Answer B.
Thermosetting resins use a chemical reaction to cure. When the components of the resin have been mixed and the chemical reaction has started the material will be have thickened and is tacky; the prepreg materials are in the B stage. To prevent further curing the resin is placed in a freezer at 0°F. In the frozen state, the resin of the prepreg material stays in the B stage. The curing starts when the material is removed from the freezer and warmed again.
[Ref: Airframe Handbook H-8083-31A-ATB, Chapter 07 Page 8]

7-11 Answer C.
Prepreg comes from the manufacturer in the B stage of curing, but the curing state is temporarily halted by its storage in a 0°F freezer. Once it is removed from the freezer, its use must occur quickly before the B stage advances to the point of unsuitability. By replacing the unused prepreg back in a freezer, the current cure state can be halted, but not reversed.
[Ref: Airframe Handbook H-8083-31A-ATB, Chapter 07 Page 8]

7-12 Answer C.
Film type adhesives must be stored in refrigerated conditions of under 0°F. Paste and foaming adhesives are stored at room temperature.
[Ref: Airframe Handbook H-8083-31A-ATB, Chapter 07 Page 10]

7-13 AMA037
Which fiber to resin (percent) ratio for advanced composite wet lay-ups is generally considered the best for strength?
- A. 60:40
- B. 40:60
- C. 50:50

7-14 AMA037
The most frequent cause of damage to composite parts are
- A. improper construction techniques.
- B. static electrical buildup.
- C. impacts to the surface by debris.

7-15 AMA037
Corrosion is a factor with composite aircraft components when
- A. assembled with certain aluminum alloys.
- B. lighting protective plies are installed.
- C. in proximity to fuel and other liquid.

7-16 AMA037
1. When performing a ring (coin tap) test on composite structures, a change in sound may be due to damage or to transition to a different internal structure.
2. The extent of separation damage in composite structures is most accurately measured by a ring (coin tap) test.

Regarding the above statements.
- A. Only No. 1 is true.
- B. Only No. 2 is true.
- C. Both No. 1 and No. 2 are true.

7-17 AMA037
When inspecting a composite panel using the ring test/coin test tapping method, a dull thud sound may indicate _____.
- A. insufficient resin in the matrix mix
- B. to much resin in the matrix mix
- C. a delamination in the matrix mix

7-18 AMA037
Composite inspections conducted by means of ultrasonic monitoring
- A. pick up the "noise" of corrosion or other deterioration occurring.
- B. create sonogram pictures of the areas being inspected.
- C. analyze ultrasonic signals transmitted into the parts being inspected.

ADVANCED COMPOSITE MATERIALS

ANSWERS

7-13 Answer A.
A part is resin rich if too much resin is used, for nonstructural applications this is not necessarily bad, but it adds weight. A part is called resin starved if too much resin is bled off during the curing process or if not enough resin is applied during the wet layup process. Resin-starved areas are indicated by fibers that show to the surface. The ratio of 60:40 fiber to resin ratio is considered optimum.
[Ref: Airframe Handbook H-8083-31A-ATB, Chapter 07 Page 13]

7-14 Answer C.
Manufacturing damage includes anomalies, such as porosity, micro-cracking, and delaminations resulting from processing discrepancies. It also includes such items as inadvertent edge cuts, surface gouges and scratches, damaged fastener holes, and impact damage.
[Ref: Airframe Handbook H-8083-31A-ATB, Chapter 07 Page 14]

7-15 Answer B.
Many fiberglass and Kevlar® parts have a fine aluminum mesh for lightning protection. This aluminum mesh often corrodes around the bolt or screw holes. The corrosion affects the electrical bonding of the panel, and the aluminum mesh needs to be removed and new mesh installed to restore the electrical bonding of the panel.
[Ref: Airframe Handbook H-8083-31A-ATB, Chapter 07 Page 15]

7-16 Answer A.
The ring (coin tap) test is accomplished by tapping the inspection area with a solid round disk or lightweight hammer-like device and listening to the response of the structure to the hammer. A clear, sharp, ringing sound is indicative of a well-bonded solid structure, while a dull or thud-like sound indicates a discrepant area.
[Ref: Airframe Handbook H-8083-31A-ATB, Chapter 07 Page 16]

7-17 Answer C.
The coin tap method of inspection is accomplished by tapping the inspection area with a solid round disk or a light hammer. A clear and sharp ringing sound indicates a well bonded structure. A dull thud sound is sign of a discrepancy, typically being a delamination causing gaps in the matrix mix.
[Ref: Airframe Handbook H-8083-31A-ATB, Chapter 07 Page 16]

7-18 Answer A.
A high-frequency (usually several MHz) sound wave is introduced into the part and may be directed to travel normal to the part surface, or along the surface of the part, or at some predefined angle to the part surface ultrasonic sound waves have properties similar to light waves. When an ultrasonic wave strikes an interrupting object, the wave or energy is either absorbed or reflected back to the surface. The disrupted or diminished sonic energy is then picked up by a receiving transducer and converted into a display on an oscilloscope or a chart recorder.
[Ref: Airframe Handbook H-8083-31A-ATB, Chapter 07 Page 18]

7-19 AMA037
Which of the following is an advantage of
prepreg composites?
  A. Does not have a problem of a lean or rich mix.
  B. Does not need to be stored in a freezer.
  C. Is less expensive than a fiber and resin mix.

7-20 AMA037
What is the material layer used within the vacuum bag
pressure system to absorb excess resin during curing called?
  A. Release
  B. Bleeder
  C. Breather

7-21 AMA037
The principle advantage to curing composite parts with an
autoclave versus a standard oven is
  A. eliminates the need for vacuum bagging.
  B. allows curing in higher temperatures and pressures.
  C. allows circulation of the heated air for a more consistent
     temperature over the entire part.

7-22 AMA037
When curing an on-aircraft composite repair, a heat blanket
is used to maintain the proper curing temperature. What
is used to insure a proper contact between the blanket
and the part?
  A. Vacuum Bags
  B. Shrink Wrapping
  C. Shrink Tape

7-23 AMA037
The minimum number of thermocouples used to monitor a
heat cycle is
  A. no fewer than three.
  B. one per two square feet of the structure.
  C. two, one at the heat source and one at the furthest
     point of the heat source.

7-24 AMA037
To prevent premature curing, all prepreg materials must
be stored
  A. in a vacuum sealed environment.
  B. in a refrigerated environment under 32°F.
  C. in a refrigerated environment under 0°F.

ADVANCED COMPOSITE MATERIALS

ANSWERS

7-19 Answer A.
Prepreg material is a factory pre-mixed assembly of resin and fibers. Its benefit is that the optimum mix ratios have already been established. Its concern is that, in order not to begin to cure, it must be stored in freezers at temperatures below 0°F. As soon as it is removed from the cold temperature it will begin to cure and have a limited shelf life.
[Ref: Airframe Handbook H-8083-31A-ATB, Chapter 07 Page 7-8]

7-20 Answer B.
The bleeder ply creates a path for the air and volatiles to escape from the repair. Excess resin is collected In the bleeder. Bleeder material could be made of a layer of fiberglass, non-woven polyester, or it could be a perforated Teflon® coated material.
[Ref: Airframe Handbook H-8083-31A-ATB, Chapter 07 Page 21]

7-21 Answer B.
Unlike a standard oven, autoclaves are specially constructed to allow for high temperatures and regulated pressures.
[Ref: Airframe Handbook H-8083-31A-ATB, Chapter 07 Page 23]

7-22 Answer A.
A heat blanket must conform to and be in 100% contact with the part. This is typically accomplished with vacuum bag pressure. Shrink wrapping and shrink tapes are commonly used for pressure application in curing ovens.
[Ref: Airframe Handbook H-8083-31A-ATB, Chapter 07 Page 22-24]

7-23 Answer A.
Never use fewer than three thermocouples to monitor a heating cycle. Thermocouple placement is the key in obtaining proper cure temperatures throughout the repair. In general, the thermocouples used for temperature control should be placed as close as possible to the repair material without causing it to become embedded in the repair or producing indentations in the repair. They should also be placed in strategic hot or cold locations to ensure the materials are adequately cured but not exposed to excessively high temperatures that could degrade the material structural properties.
[Ref: Airframe Handbook H-8083-31A-ATB, Chapter 07 Page 25]

7-24 Answer C.
Prepreg is a fabric or tape that is impregnated with a resin during the manufacturing process. Store the prepreg material in a freezer below 0°F to prevent further curing of the resin.
[Ref: Airframe Handbook H-8083-31A-ATB, Chapter 07 Page 27]

7-25 AMA037
The principle benefit of vacuum bagging over a wet layup is it
   A. removes excess resin uniformly from the structure.
   B. squeezes resin more deeply into the structure.
   C. prevents expansion of the structure during the curing process.

7-26 AMA045
The maximum design properties of a fiberglass component are achieved at what curing temperature
   A. room temperature.
   B. 150°F.
   C. 250 – 300°F.

7-27 AMA037
A potted compound repair on honeycomb can usually be made on damages less than
   A. 2 inches in diameter.
   B. 1 inch in diameter.
   C. .5 inches in diameter.

7-28 AMA037
The proper sequence of procedures to repair a damaged composite component in which the damage extends to the component's core is
   1. remove the damage.
   2. remove water from damage area.
   3. install the honeycomb core and repair plies.
   4. prepare the damaged area.
   5. inspect the damage.
   6. vacuum bag the repair.
   A. 5, 1, 2, 4, 3, 6
   B. 5, 2, 1, 4, 3, 6
   C. 5, 1, 4, 3, 2, 6

7-29 AMA037
Which is not a step to ensure proper bonding of a composite patch to an aluminum surface
   A. cure the film adhesive material at 250°F.
   B. anodize the aluminum surface.
   C. install anchor tabs on the aluminum surface.

7-30 AMA037
The purpose of a double vacuum debulk process when repairing laminated fiberglass structures is to remove
   A. water from between the laminations.
   B. air from between the laminations.
   C. dirt and foreign substances from between the laminations.

ADVANCED COMPOSITE MATERIALS

ANSWERS

7-25 Answer A.
The pressure applied by the vacuum bag is distributed evenly across the part allowing the resin to be bleed off uniformly while removing excess trapped air.
[Ref: Airframe Handbook H-8083-31A-ATB, Chapter 07 Page 29]

7-26 Answer B.
Room temperature cure repairs can be accelerated by the application of heat. Maximum properties are achieved at 150°F. A vacuum bag can be used to consolidate the plies and to provide a path for air and volatiles to escape.
[Ref: Airframe Handbook H-8083-31A-ATB, Chapter 07 Page 32]

7-27 Answer C.
A potted repair can be used to repair damage to a sandwich honeycomb structure that is smaller than 0.5 inches. The honeycomb material could be left in place or could be removed and is filled up with a potting compound to restore some strength. Potted repairs do not restore the full strength of the part.
[Ref: Airframe Handbook H-8083-31A-ATB, Chapter 07 Page 34]

7-28 Answer B.
The proper procedure sequence for repairing a damaged composite component is: Step 1: Inspect the damage, Step 2: Remove water from damaged area, Step 3: Remove the damage, Step 4: Prepare the damaged area, Step 5: Installation of honeycomb core (wet layup), Step 6: Prepare and install the repair plies, Step 7: Vacuum bag the repair, Step 8: Curing the repair, and Step 9: Post repair inspection.
[Ref: Airframe Handbook H-8083-31A-ATB, Chapter 07 Page 34-36]

7-29 Answer C.
Surface preparation is very important to achieve the adhesive strength. Grit blast silane and phosphoric acid anodizing are used to prepare aluminum skin. Film adhesives using a 250°F (121°C) cure are used routinely to bond the doublers to the metallic structure.
[Ref: Airframe Handbook H-8083-31A-ATB, Chapter 07 Page 40]

7-30 Answer B.
Generally, the properties of a wet layup repair are not as good as a repair with prepreg material; but by using a DVD method, the properties of the wet layup process can be improved. The DVD process is a technique to remove entrapped air that causes porosity in wet layup laminates.
[Ref: Airframe Handbook H-8083-31A-ATB, Chapter 07 Page 42]

7-31 AMA037
Metal fasteners which may be used with repairs of carbon fiber structures are made from?
A. Magnesium
B. Titanium
C. Aluminum

7-32 AMA037
The principle difference between composite structure fasteners and metal structure fasteners is that composite fasteners
A. are made from the same composite material to eliminate corrosion.
B. are more electrically conductive to aid in lightning dissipation.
C. have larger bearing surfaces.

7-33 AMA037
When drilling into composite structures the general rule is to use
A. high speed, low pressure drills.
B. low speed and high pressure drills.
C. low speed and low pressure drills.

7-34 AMA037
The best cutting tool to use on composite honeycomb structures is a
A. water jet cutter.
B. fine tooth saw carbide saw blade.
C. toothless diamond coated saw blade.

7-35 AMA037
Health problems resulting from composite repair processes are best avoided by
A. use of a high quality respirator.
B. consulting Material Data Safety Sheets (MSDS).
C. consulting AC43.13 section 1B.

7-36 AMA078
Which of the following is true regarding thermoplastics versus thermosetting plastics?
A. Thermosetting plastics may be remolded after hardening by reapplying heat.
B. Thermosetting plastics are best suited for forming windshields and canopies.
C. Thermoplastics must be stored in a cool and dry location.

ADVANCED COMPOSITE MATERIALS

ANSWERS

7-31 Answer B.
Titanium or stainless steel fasteners are always used when joining carbon based composites as aluminum and magnesium will corrode quickly when in contact with carbon.
[Ref: Airframe Handbook H-8083-31A-ATB, Chapter 07 Page 44]

7-32 Answer C.
The main differences between fasteners for metal and composite structures are the materials and the footprint diameter of nuts and collars.
[Ref: Airframe Handbook H-8083-31A-ATB, Chapter 07 Page 46]

7-33 Answer A.
A general rule for drilling composites is to use high speed and a low feed rate (pressure). Drilling equipment with a power feed control produces better hole quality than drill motors without power feed control. Drill guides are recommended, especially for thicker laminates.
[Ref: Airframe Handbook H-8083-31A-ATB, Chapter 07 Page 49]

7-34 Answer C.
The band saw is the equipment that is most often used in a repair shop for cutting composite materials. A toothless carbide or diamond-coated saw blade is recommended.
[Ref: Airframe Handbook H-8083-31A-ATB, Chapter 07 Page 52]

7-35 Answer B.
Advanced composite materials including prepreg, resin systems, cleaning solvents, and adhesives could be hazardous, and it is important that you use personal protection equipment. It is important to read and understand the Material Safety Data Sheets (MSDS) and handle all chemicals, resins, and fibers correctly.
[Ref: Airframe Handbook H-8083-31A-ATB, Chapter 07 Page 53]

7-36 Answer C.
Thermoplastics will continuously soften and reform when exposed to heat. Thermosetting plastics may be molded into a form once. Then once hardened, they can not appreciably be reformed again. Because thermoplastics continuously respond to heat, they must be stored in a cool dry location.
[Ref: Airframe Handbook H-8083-31A-ATB, Chapter 07 Page 54]

7-37 AMA078
What is the cause of crazing on an acrylic plastic panel?
A. It was bent beyond its limits in a cold state.
B. It was cooled too quickly after forming.
C. It was heated to an excess temperature when forming.

7-38 AMA078
When drilling through acrylic plastics, a drill bit with an included tip angle of is recommended.
A. 90°
B. 150°
C. 120°

7-39 AMA078
Which is true regarding the use of polymerizable cements with transparent plastics?
A. They expand as the cement hardens.
B. They produce a hazy residue and should be used only around edges or under fairings.
C. Remaining beads of cement are easily machined off.

7-40 AMA078
When installing transparent plastic enclosures that are retained by bolts extending through the plastic material and self-locking nuts, the nuts should be tightened to a
A. firm fit, then backed off one full turn.
B. firm fit, plus on full turn.
C. firm fit.

7-41 AMA078
Which is considered good practice concerning the installation of acrylic plastics?
A. When rivets are used, drill the mounting holes through the plastic oversize by 1/8 inch.
B. When rivets or nuts and bolts are used, slotted holes are not recommended.
C. When nuts and bolts are used, the plastic should be installed hot and tightened to a firm fit before the plastic cools.

7-42 AMA037
Which of the following is an acceptable combination of materials and its fasteners?
A. Kevlar composite materials with cadmium coated fasteners.
B. Carbon fiber composite materials with aluminum fasteners.
C. Carbon fiber composite materials with cadmium coated fasteners.

ADVANCED COMPOSITE MATERIALS

ANSWERS

7-37 Answer C.
The amount that acrylic plastic can be bent or formed in a cold state is very limited. If it is bent beyond these limits, excess stress is imposed to the point that tiny cracks will form throughout; a process known as crazing.
[Ref: Airframe Handbook H-8083-31A-ATB, Chapter 07 Page 54]

7-38 Answer B.
A twist drill with an included angle of 150° is used to drill acrylic plastics.
[Ref: Airframe Handbook H-8083-31A-ATB, Chapter 07 Page 56]

7-39 Answer C.
Polymerizable cements shrink as the cement hardens. Bubbles tend to float to the top of the cement bead in a gap joint after the cement is poured. These cause no problem if the bead is machined off. These cements produce clear, transparent joints and should be used when the color and appearance of the joints are important.
[Ref: Airframe Handbook H-8083-31A-ATB, Chapter 07 Page 56]

7-40 Answer A.
In clamping or bolting plastic panels into their mountings, do not place the plastic under excessive compressive stress. It is easy to develop more than 1,000 psi on the plastic by over-torquing a nut and bolt. Tighten each nut to a firm fit, and then back the nut off one full turn (until they are snug and can still be rotated with the fingers).
[Ref: Airframe Handbook H-8083-31A-ATB, Chapter 07 Page 57]

7-41 Answer A.
In installations involving bolts or rivets make the holes through the plastic oversize by 1/8-inch and center so that the plastic does not bind or crack at the edge of the holes. The use of slotted holes is also recommended.
[Ref: Airframe Handbook H-8083-31A-ATB, Chapter 07 Page 58]

7-42 Answer A.
For corrosion protection purposes, never use a cathodic material fastener such as those made from aluminum or cadmium plating with composites made from carbon or carbon fiber reinforcement materials.
[Ref: Airframe Handbook H-8083-31A-ATB, Chapter 07 Page 46]

ORAL EXAM

7-1(O). What are the advantages of composite materials?

7-2(O). Explain how to perform a ring (corn tap) test and how is a defect detected.

7-3(O). Name several non-destructive testing methods that can be used to inspect a fiberglass/honeycomb structure for entrapped water.

7-4(O). Name several types of damage that can occur to composite parts.

7-5(O). Define a warp clock and how is it used.

7-6(O). How should prepreg materials be stored to prevent premature curing?

7-7(O). Define shelf life.

7-8(O). When can a potted repair be used on a honeycomb structure?

7-9(O). List the steps to repair a damaged composite component when the damage extends to the component's core.

7-10(O). What are the general guidelines for drilling into composite structures?

7-11(O). Define crazing.

7-12(O). Explain how to properly store transparent thermoplastic sheets.

7-13(O). Describe the general rule for clamping or bolting plastic panels into their mountings.

7-14(O). After cleaning transparent plastic what should be done to the surface?

7-15(O). How can you protect yourself against health problems resulting from composite repair materials and processes?

ADVANCED COMPOSITE MATERIALS

ANSWERS

ORAL EXAM

7-1(O).   High strength, relatively low weight, and corrosion resistance.
           [Ref: Airframe Handbook H-8083-31A-ATB, Chapter 07 Page 1]

7-2(O).   The ring (coin tap) test is accomplished by tapping the inspection area with a solid round disk or lightweight hammer-like device and listening to the response of the structure to the hammer. A clear, sharp, ringing sound indicates a well-bonded solid structure, while a dull or thud-like sound indicates a discrepant area.
           [Ref: Airframe Handbook H-8083-31A-ATB, Chapter 07 Page 16]

7-3(O).   Pulse echo (ultrasonic), radiography, and thermography.
           [Ref: Airframe Handbook H-8083-31A-ATB, Chapter 07 Page 18-19]

7-4(O).   Damage from improper cure or processing include porosity, micro-cracking, and delamination. Shop damages include inadvertent edge cuts, surface gouges, and scratches from mishandling, improper machining, improper drilling, tool drops, contamination, improper sanding, inadequate tooling, mislocation of holes or details.
           [Ref: Airframe Handbook H-8083-31A-ATB, Chapter 07 Page 13-14]

7-5(O).   An alignment indicator to show the orientation of the piles of a composite material, the ply direction is shown in relation to a reference direction, usually the warp. It is used to correctly align the fibers for construction or repair of composite parts.
           [Ref: Airframe Handbook H-8083-31A-ATB, Chapter 07 Page 3,29-30 and G-39]

7-6(O).   Store the prepreg material in a freezer below 0°F to prevent further curing of the resin.
           [Ref: Airframe Handbook H-8083-31A-ATB, Chapter 07 Page 27]

7-7(O).   The length of time a product is good when it remains in its original unopened container.
           [Ref: Airframe Handbook H-8083-31A-ATB, Glossary Page 31]

7-8(O).   A potted repair can be used to repair damage to a sandwich honeycomb structure that is smaller than 0.5 inches.
           [Ref: Airframe Handbook H-8083-31A-ATB, Chapter 07 Page 34]

7-9(O).   Step 1: Inspect the Damage, Step 2: Remove Water From Damaged Area, Step 3: Remove the Damage, Step 4: Prepare the Damaged Area, Step 5: Installation of Honeycomb Core (Wet Layup), Step 6: Prepare and Install the Repair Plies, Step 7: Vacuum Bag the Repair, Step 8: Curing the Repair, and Step 9: Post Repair Inspection.
           [Ref: Airframe Handbook H-8083-31A-ATB, Chapter 07 Page 34-36]

7-10(O).   When drilling composites use equipment with power feed control. Drill using high speed and a low feed rate (pressure). Drill guides are recommended, especially for thicker laminates.
           [Ref: Airframe Handbook H-8083-31A-ATB, Chapter 07 Page 49]

7-11(O).   A form of stress-caused damage that occurs in a transparent thermoplastic material. Crazing appears as a series of tiny, hair-like cracks just below the surface of the plastic.
           [Ref: Airframe Handbook H-8083-31A-ATB, Glossary Page 11]

ORAL EXAM

7-12(O).   Store in a cool, dry place away from fumes. Keep paper-masked transparent sheets out of direct sun. Store with masking paper in place in bins tilted at a 10° angle from vertical. If stored horizontally, avoid getting dirt and debris between sheets, never stack over 18 inches high and with smallest sheets stacked on top (do not let sheets overhang). Formed sections should be supported so they do not lose their shape.
[Ref: Airframe Handbook H-8083-31A-ATB, Chapter 07 Page 54]

7-13(O).   Do not place the plastic under excessive compressive stress by over-torquing a nut and bolt. Tighten each nut to a firm fit, and then back the nut off one full turn (until they are snug and can still be rotated with the fingers).
[Ref: Airframe Handbook H-8083-31A-ATB, Chapter 07 Page 57]

7-14(O).   If, after removing dirt and grease, no great amount of scratching is visible, finish the plastic with a good grade of commercial wax. Apply the wax in a thin even coat and bring to a high polish by rubbing lightly with a soft cloth.
[Ref: Airframe Handbook H-8083-31A-ATB, Chapter 07 Page 57]

7-15(O).   Use personal protection equipment and read and understand the Material Safety Data Sheets (MSDS) and handle all chemicals, resins, and fibers correctly.
[Ref: Airframe Handbook H-8083-31A-ATB, Chapter 07 Page 53]

ADVANCED COMPOSITE MATERIALS

ANSWERS

PRACTICAL EXAM

7-1(P).   Given an actual aircraft or mockup, visually inspect an unpainted composite surface and record your findings.

7-2(P).   Given an actual aircraft or mockup, visually inspect a composite structure, perform a tap test, and record your findings.

7-3(P).   Given an actual aircraft or mockup, visually inspect a composite structure, perform an ultrasonic inspection, and record your findings.

7-4(P).   Given an actual aircraft or mockup, visually inspect a composite structure, perform a moisture detection test, and record your findings.

7-5(P).   Given the appropriate documentation, select the correct materials and clean a transparent surface, and record maintenance.

7-6(P).   Given an actual aircraft or mockup, inspect a window or windscreen and record your findings.

7-7(P).   Given the appropriate documentation and supplies, remove one or more minor scratches from a transparent surface and record maintenance.

7-8(P).   Given various laminated composite structure samples, identify the fiber-reinforcing materials of each.

7-9(P).   Given the appropriate documentation, locate the data used for composite structure damage assessment.

AIRCRAFT PAINTING AND FINISHING

Finishing Materials (Polymers, Paint, Ventilation), Methods of Applying Finish, Finishing Equipment, Preparation, and Troubleshooting

CHAPTER
08

QUESTIONS

8-1 AMA007
What is the purpose of adding butanol and alcohol to a wash coat primer prior to spraying?
A. Slows the evaporation rate.
B. Enhances the adhesion qualities of the primer.
C. Quickens the drying time.

8-2 AMA007
Which of the following solvents is often mixed with other solvents for the purpose of reducing its flammability?
A. Naphtha
B. Methylene Chloride
C. Acetone

8-3 AMA007
What is the danger when using Linseed oil as a protective coating on the interior of metal tubing?
A. Linseed oil fumes are toxic.
B. Spontaneous combustion can occur.
C. Spillage on the exterior of the tube can dissolve some primers.

8-4 AMA007
Which type of coating typically contains phosphoric acid as one of its components?
A. Wash Primer
B. Epoxy Primer
C. Zinc Chromate Primer

8-5 AMA007
Which of the following are benefits of epoxy primers?
1. Low toxicity.
2. Good chip resistance.
3. Sandable.
4. Can be sprayed on bare metal.
A. Two of these four are benefits of epoxy primers.
B. Three of these four are benefits of epoxy primers.
C. All four of these are benefits of epoxy primers.

8-6 AMA007
If a brushing is used to touch up an area of paint, what will best eliminate the possibility of remaining brush marks?
A. Slow evaporation time
B. Thinning
C. Very fine brush bristles

AIRCRAFT PAINTING AND FINISHING

ANSWERS

8-1 Answer A.
Butanol and ethanol alcohol are mixed together in ratios ranging from 1:1 to 1:3 to use to dilute wash coat primer for spray applications because the butyl alcohol retards the evaporation rate.
[Ref: Airframe Handbook H-8083-31A-ATB, Chapter 08 Page 2]

8-2 Answer B.
Methylene Chloride can be mixed with other solvents. It is widely used in paint strippers, and as a cleaning agent and degreaser for metal parts. It has no flash point under normal use conditions and can be used to reduce the flammability of other substances.
[Ref: Airframe Handbook H-8083-31A-ATB, Chapter 08 Page 2]

8-3 Answer B.
Linseed oil generates heat as it dries. Oily materials and rags must be properly disposed after use to eliminate the possible cause of spontaneous ignition and fire.
[Ref: Airframe Handbook H-8083-31A-ATB, Chapter 08 Page 3]

8-4 Answer A.
Wash primers are water-thin coatings of phosphoric acid in solutions of vinyl butyral resin, alcohol, and other ingredients. Their functions are to passivate the surface, temporarily provide corrosion resistance, and provide an adhesive base for the next coating, such as a urethane or epoxy primer.
[Ref: Airframe Handbook H-8083-31A-ATB, Chapter 08 Page 3]

8-5 Answer B.
Epoxies are a synthetic, thermosetting resin that produces tough, hard, chemical-resistant coatings and adhesives. They can be used as a non-sanding primer/sealer over bare metal and it is softer than urethane, so it has good chip resistance. They are not classified as hazardous because they contain no isocyanates.
[Ref: Airframe Handbook H-8083-31A-ATB, Chapter 08 Page 4]

8-6 Answer B.
To avoid brush marks or roping, the material to be applied should be thinned to a proper consistency, but not too thin to cause the material to run. Proper thinning and paint temperature allows the finish to flow out and eliminate marks.
[Ref: Airframe Handbook H-8083-31A-ATB, Chapter 08 Page 4]

8-7 AMA007
For use with HVLP spray guns, the critical operating characteristic of the compressed air source is
  A. constant high pressure.
  B. constant air volume.
  C. moisture elimination.

8-8 AMA007
What is not an advantage of airless spraying equipment compared to an air atomized system?
  A. Reduction in overspray.
  B. Quality of the finish.
  C. Increased transfer efficiency.

8-9 AMA007
When making a viscosity measurement of a mixed paint with a Zahn cup or similar, begin the timing when the top edge of the cup breaks the surface of the material, and end the timing _____.
  A. when the cup is empty
  B. when a steady flow from the cup ends
  C. at the amount of time stated by the manufacturer

8-10 AMA007
What is the most important aspect of insuring a successful painting operation?
  A. Temperature and viscosity are at the manufacturer's requirement.
  B. The skill of the painter when handling the spray gun.
  C. The preparation of the surface to be painted.

8-11 AMA040
When spraying topcoat or primer, how far is the spray head held from the painted surface?
  A. 8-10 inches.
  B. 12-16 inches.
  C. Determined by product data sheet based on temperature and viscosity.

8-12 AMA040
What the usual cause of runs and sags in aircraft finishes?
  A. High Atmospheric humidity.
  B. Excess reducer in the paint.
  C. Non-compatible primer.

AIRCRAFT PAINTING AND FINISHING

ANSWERS

8-7 Answer B.
The key to the operation of the newer High-Volume Low-Pressure (HVLP) spray guns is the air volume, not the pressure.
[Ref: Airframe Handbook H-8083-31A-ATB, Chapter 08 Page 6]

8-8 Answer C.
This system increases transfer efficiency and production speed with less overspray than conventional air atomized spray systems. It is used for production work but does not provide the fine finish of air-atomized systems.
[Ref: Airframe Handbook H-8083-31A-ATB, Chapter 08 Page 8]

8-9 Answer B.
With a stopwatch in one hand, lift the cup out of the sample. As the top edge of the cup breaks the surface, start the stopwatch. Stop the timing when the first break in the flow of the liquid is seen at the cup's orifice.
[Ref: Airframe Handbook H-8083-31A-ATB, Chapter 08 Page 8-9]

8-10 Answer C.
The most important and time consuming part of any paint project is the proper cleaning and preparation of the substrate surface, including dirt and grease removal, proper acid wash and alodine coating, and complete drying, thus insuring a long lasting and corrosion free finish.
[Ref: Airframe Handbook H-8083-31A-ATB, Chapter 08 Page 10]

8-11 Answer A.
Hold the spray gun a constant 8-10" from the surface, moving the gun across the surface at approximately 1 foot per second in a straight line across the surface. Do not arc the stroke, as this reduces the distance between the gun and the surface.
[Ref: Airframe Handbook H-8083-31A-ATB, Chapter 08 Page 12]

8-12 Answer B.
Sags and runs are usually caused by applying too much paint to an area, by holding the spray gun too close to the surface, or moving the gun too slowly across the surface.
[Ref: Airframe Handbook H-8083-31A-ATB, Chapter 08 Page 14]

8-13 AMA040
Which defect in aircraft finishes may be caused by adverse humidity, drafts, or sudden changes in temperature?
- A. Orange Peel
- B. Pinholes
- C. Blushing

8-14 AMA007
What is used to prevent blushing when painting in a high humidity environment?
- A. A fast drying reducer can be added to the paint.
- B. A slow drying reducer can be added to the paint.
- C. Increase the air pressure at the spray gun.

8-15 AMA040
What is the common cause of an unwanted Orange Peel finish on a painted surface?
- A. Contaminates in the paint or air lines.
- B. Paint material is too thick (not enough reducer in the mixture).
- C. Paint material is too thin (too much reducer in the mixture).

8-16 AMA040
If a fisheye appearance occurs after painting, the typical cause is
- A. improper cleaning of the surface.
- B. trapped solvents in the paint mixture.
- C. dirt or debris in the paint mixture or airlines.

8-17 AMA040
When removing masking tape following the painting of a trim color, at what point should the masking tape be removed to avoid damage to the underlying surface?
- A. Immediately following the spraying of the new color.
- B. When the new color paint is dry to the touch.
- C. When the new color paint is fully cured.

8-18 AMA088
If registration numbers are to be applied to an aircraft with a letter height of 12 inches, what is the minimum space required for the registration mark N1683C?
- A. 52 inches
- B. 48 inches
- C. 57 inches

AIRCRAFT PAINTING AND FINISHING

ANSWERS

8-13 Answer C.
Blushing is the dull milky haze that appears in a paint finish.
It occurs when moisture is trapped in the paint. Blushing
forms when the solvents quickly evaporate from the sprayed
coating, causing a drop in temperature that is enough
to condense the water in the air. It usually forms when
the humidity is above 80 percent. Other causes include,
incorrect temperature, incorrect reducer (fast drying) being
used, or excessively high air pressure at the spray gun.
[Ref: Airframe Handbook H-8083-31A-ATB, Chapter 08 Page 13]

8-14 Answer B.
Blushing occurs when moisture is trapped in the drying paint
and is common when humidity levels approach 80%. Other
causes are use of an incorrect fast drying reducer and/or too
high air pressure at the gun.
[Ref: Airframe Handbook H-8083-31A-ATB, Chapter 08 Page 13]

8-15 Answer B.
"Orange peel" can be the result of a number of factors with
the first being the improper adjustment of the spray gun.
Other causes include, not enough reducer (too thick) or the
wrong type of reducer for the ambient temperature, material
not uniformly mixed, forced drying method is too quick, too
little flash time between coats, or spray painting when the
ambient or substrate temperature is either too hot or too cold.
[Ref: Airframe Handbook H-8083-31A-ATB, Chapter 08 Page 14]

8-16 Answer A.
Fisheyes appear as small holes in the coating as it is being
applied, which allows the underlying surface to be seen.
Usually, it is due to the surface not being cleaned of all traces
of silicone wax.
[Ref: Airframe Handbook H-8083-31A-ATB, Chapter 08 Page 15]

8-17 Answer B.
With all the trim completed, the masking paper should be
removed as soon as the last trimmed area is dry to the touch.
Carefully remove the Fine Line trim edge tape by slowly
pulling it back onto itself at a sharp angle. Remove all trim
and masking tape from the base coat as soon as possible to
preclude damage to the paint.
[Ref: Airframe Handbook H-8083-31A-ATB, Chapter 08 Page 17]

8-18 Answer A.
The width for the number "1" is $1/6 \times 12" = 2"$. The spacing
between the characters is $1/4 \times (2/3 \times 12") = 2"$. The minimum
space required needed for the registration marking is
$52"$ ($8 + 2 + 2 + 2 + 8 + 2 + 8 + 2 + 8 + 2 + 8 = 52$).
[Ref: Airframe Handbook H-8083-31A-ATB, Chapter 08 Page 18]

8-19 AMA007

Which statement is true regarding paint system compatibility?

A. Acrylic nitrocellulose lacquers may be used over old nitrocellulose finishes.
B. Old type zinc chromate primer may not be used directly for touch up of bare metal surfaces.
C. Old wash primer coats may be overcoated directly with epoxy finishes.

8-20 AMA007

When planning a paint touch-up project following a repair, how can it be determined if the existing topcoat is acrylic or epoxy based?

A. Apply a coating of engine oil; the acrylic finish will soften.
B. Wipe with a wet rag of MEK; the acrylic finish will bleed some color.
C. Remove a small chip of the topcoat and immerse in isopropyl alcohol; within 3-5 minutes an acrylic chip will dissolve.

8-21 AMA007

Which chemical paint stripper type is now considered the safest to use?

A. Methylene Chloride Systems
B. EFS-2500 Systems
C. Benzyl Alcohol Systems

AIRCRAFT PAINTING AND FINISHING

ANSWERS

8-19 Answer C.
Old wash primer coats may be overcoated directly with epoxy finishes. Acrylic nitrocellulose lacquers adhere poorly to bare metal and both nitrocellulose and epoxy finishes. Old type zinc chromate primer may be used directly for touchup of bare metal surfaces and for use on interior finishes.
[Ref: Airframe Handbook H-8083-31A-ATB, Chapter 08 Page 19]

8-20 Answer B.
Wipe a small area of the surface in question with a rag wet with MEK. The MEK picks up the pigment from an acrylic finish, but has no effect on an epoxy coating. Just wipe the surface, and do not rub.
[Ref: Airframe Handbook H-8083-31A-ATB, Chapter 08 Page 19]

8-21 Answer B.
One of the more recent entries into the chemical stripping business is an environmentally friendly product known as EFS-2500, which works by breaking the bond between the substrate and primer. Methylene Chloride has been classified as a toxic air contaminant and carcinogen. Benzyl alcohol is ineffective as a paint stripper and is not considered environmentally friendly.
[Ref: Airframe Handbook H-8083-31A-ATB, Chapter 08 Page 21]

ORAL EXAM

8-1(O).   Why are aircrafts more often painted than not?

8-2(O).   What is the purpose of a primer when preparing an aircraft for painting?

8-3(O).   Name at least three types of primers used in aviation.

8-4(O).   Why is it important that primers and paints be of the same brand when painting an aircraft?

8-5(O).   What are some of the effects of ambient conditions on finishing materials?

8-6(O).   What cases poor adhesion?

8-7(O).   What regulation provides the requirements for registration markings?

8-8(O).   What are the basic requirements for identification and registration marking for aircraft?

8-9(O).   What can cause of runs and sags in aircraft finishes?

8-10(O).   What can cause of "orange peel" on a painted surface?

8-11(O).   What causes a "fisheye" appearance occurs after painting?

8-12(O).   Where can you find safety, hazard, health, and environmental information about finishing products?

8-13(O).   What personal protective equipment should be used when mixing any paint or two-part coatings?

8-14(O).   Where should paint and solvent soaked rags be disposed of?

AIRCRAFT PAINTING AND FINISHING

ANSWERS

ORAL EXAM

8-1(O).   Paint protects the integrity of the airframe by protecting the exposed surfaces from corrosion and deterioration. Also, a properly painted aircraft is easier to clean and maintain because the exposed surfaces are more resistant to corrosion and dirt, and oil does not adhere as readily to the surface.
[Ref: Airframe Handbook H-8083-31A-ATB, Chapter 08 Page 2]

8-2(O).   A primer is the foundation of the finish. Its role is to bond to the surface, inhibit corrosion of metal, and provide an anchor point for the finish coats.
[Ref: Airframe Handbook H-8083-31A-ATB, Chapter 08 Page 3]

8-3(O).   Wash primers, gray enamel undercoat, urethane, epoxy, and zinc chromate.
[Ref: Airframe Handbook H-8083-31A-ATB, Chapter 08 Page 3-4]

8-4(O).   It is highly recommended that a complete system from etching to primers and reducers to the finish topcoat are compatible, are of the same brand, for the entire project because they are formulated to work together. Mixing brands is a risk that may ruin the entire project.
[Ref: Airframe Handbook H-8083-31A-ATB, Chapter 08 Page 10]

8-5(O).   Changes in temperature can cause blushing and orange peel. Also, rapid changes in ambient temperatures while spraying may cause an uneven release of the solvents, causing the surface to dry, shrink, and wrinkle.
[Ref: Airframe Handbook H-8083-31A-ATB, Chapter 08 Page 13-16]

8-6(O).   Improperly cleaned and prepared surfaces.
[Ref: Airframe Handbook H-8083-31A-ATB, Chapter 08 Page 13]

8-7(O).   The complete regulatory requirement for identification and marking of a U.S.-registered aircraft can be found in Title 14 of the Code of Federal Regulations (14 CFR), Part 45, Identification and Registration Marking. *[Ref: Airframe Handbook H-8083-31A-ATB, Chapter 08 Page 17]*

8-8(O).   The regulation states that the marks must be painted on the aircraft or affixed by other means to insure a similar degree of permanence; have no ornamentation; contrast in color with the background; and be legible.
[Ref: Airframe Handbook H-8083-31A-ATB, Chapter 08 Page 17]

8-9(O).   Sags and runs are usually caused by applying too much paint to an area, by holding the spray gun too close to the surface, or moving the gun too slowly across the surface.
[Ref: Airframe Handbook H-8083-31A-ATB, Chapter 08 Page 14]

8-10(O). Improper adjustment of the spray gun is the most common, but other causes include not enough reducer (too thick) or the wrong type of reducer for the ambient temperature, material not uniformly mixed, forced drying method is too quick, too little flash time between coats, or spray painting when the ambient or substrate temperature is either too hot or too cold.
[Ref: Airframe Handbook H-8083-31A-ATB, Chapter 08 Page 14]

8-11(O). Improper cleaning of the surface.
[Ref: Airframe Handbook H-8083-31A-ATB, Chapter 08 Page 15]

8-12(O). The manufacturer's technical or Material and Safety Data Sheets (MSDS).
[Ref: Airframe Handbook H-8083-31A-ATB, Chapter 08 Page 10]

ORAL EXAM

8-13(O).   Eye protection and respirators should be worn at a minimum, protective clothing and gloves are also recommended.
[Ref: Airframe Handbook H-8083-31A-ATB, Chapter 08 Page 21]

8-14(O).   In fireproof containers.
[Ref: Airframe Handbook H-8083-31A-ATB, Chapter 08 Page 21]

AIRCRAFT PAINTING AND FINISHING

PRACTICAL EXAM

8-1(P).   Given a specific aircraft finishing application, select the appropriate finishing materials.

8-2(P).   Given a specified aircraft surface, determine the preparation processes and procedures for applying a specific finishing material.

8-3(P).   Given an actual aircraft surface or mockup, prepare the surface for application of a finishing material.

8-4(P).   Given an actual aircraft or mockup and the appropriate materials and equipment, apply a primer to the surface.

8-5(P).   Given an actual aircraft or mockup and the appropriate materials and equipment, apply a topcoat to the surface.

8-6(P).   Given one or more, various aircraft finished surfaces, inspect and record your findings.

8-7(P).   Given a specific finishing task, locate the appropriate data to use for accomplishing the task.

8-8(P).   Given a specific aircraft registration designation and a specific fixed-wing aircraft make and model, determine where the registration designation should be located on the aircraft and the sizes of the registration numbers.

8-9(P).   Given a specific aircraft registration designation and a specific rotorcraft make and model, determine where the registration designation should be located on the rotorcraft and the sizes of the registration numbers.

AIRCRAFT ELECTRICAL SYSTEM

Aircraft Batteries, Aircraft Electrical Systems,Wiring Installation, Electrical System
Components, Grounding, and Bonding

CHAPTER
09

QUESTIONS

9-1 AMA041
What does the term "free electron" mean in relation to current and conductors?
- A. The inner electrons are tightly bound to the atom and can be easily motivated to move to an atom with more space in their inner rings.
- B. The outer electrons are loosely bound to the atom and can be easily motivated to move.
- C. The inner electrons are loosely bound to the atom and can be easily motivated to move.

9-2 AMA041
Which theory regarding the flow of electricity should be used during the connection or troubleshooting of electrical circuits?
- A. Only the electron current theory can be applied.
- B. The FAA officially defines current flow using the conventional current theory.
- C. The use of either theory may be applied as long as it is used consistently.

9-3 AMA041
What is drift velocity?
- A. The tendency for electrons to "rattle around" through a conductor.
- B. The average velocity of electrons through a conductor when an electric field is introduced.
- C. The force present to "push" the electrons.

9-4 AMA041
Which of the following produces voltage by moving a magnetic field in relationship to a conductor?
- A. EMF
- B. Chemical
- C. Heat

9-5 AMA041
The value of the induced voltage/current depends on which basic factors during the process of electromagnetic induction?
1. Number of turns in the conductor coil.
2. Strength of the electromagnet.
3. Speed of rotation of the conductor or magnet.
- A. 1, 2, and 3
- B. 1 and 2
- C. 2 and 3

9-6 AMA039
Which of the following is an advantage of an AC electrical system over DC?
- A. AC power can be transmitted over long distances more readily and more economically.
- B. AC systems require more space, but are less heavy.
- C. AC systems are larger than DC systems.

AIRCRAFT ELECTRICAL SYSTEM

ANSWERS

9-1 Answer B.
The term "free electron" describes a condition in some atoms where the outer electrons are loosely bound to their parent atom. These loosely bound electrons are easily motivated to move in a given direction when an external source, such as a battery, is applied to the circuit.
[Ref: Airframe Handbook H-8083-31A-ATB, Chapter 09 Page 3]

9-2 Answer C.
There are two competing schools of thought regarding the flow of electricity. The two explanations are the conventional current theory and the electron theory. Both theories describe the movement of electrons through a conductor. They simply explain the direction current moves. Typically during troubleshooting or the connection of electrical circuits, the use of either theory can be applied as long as it is used consistently. The Federal Aviation Administration (FAA) officially defines current flow using electron theory (negative to positive).
[Ref: Airframe Handbook H-8083-31A-ATB, Chapter 09 Page 3]

9-3 Answer B.
When a voltage is applied across the conductor, an electromotive force creates an electric field within the conductor, and a current is established. The electrons do not move in a straight direction, but undergo repeated collisions with other nearby atoms within a conductor. These collisions usually knock other free electrons from their atoms, and these electrons move on toward the positive end of the conductor with an average velocity called the drift velocity, which is relatively low speed.
[Ref: Airframe Handbook H-8083-31A-ATB, Chapter 09 Page 3]

9-4 Answer A.
Voltage is most easily described as electrical pressure force. It is the Electromotive Force (EMF), or the push or pressure from one end of the conductor to the other that ultimately moves the electrons. The symbol for EMF is the capital letter E. EMF is always measured between two points and voltage is considered a value between two points.
[Ref: Airframe Handbook H-8083-31A-ATB, Chapter 09 Page 5]

9-5 Answer A.
During the process of electromagnetic induction, the value of the induced voltage/current depends on three basic factors: 1. Number of turns in the conductor coil (more loops equals greater induced voltage), 2. Strength of the electromagnet (the stronger the magnetic field, the greater the induced voltage), and 3. Speed of rotation of the conductor or magnet (the faster the rotation, the greater the induced voltage).
[Ref: Airframe Handbook H-8083-31A-ATB, Chapter 09 Page 6-7]

9-6 Answer A.
AC can be transmitted over long distances more readily and more economically than DC; space and weight can be saved since AC devices, especially motors, are smaller and simpler than DC devices.
[Ref: Airframe Handbook H-8083-31A-ATB, Chapter 09 Page 9]

9-7 AMA041
In an AC system, at what point of an AC sine wave is instantaneous voltage the greatest?
   A. 90°
   B. 180°
   C. 360°

9-8 AMA041
Which of the following statements in regards to AC current is true?
   1. AC voltages can be increased or decreased by means of transformers.
   2. The polarity and voltage constantly change in DC.
   3. The three values of AC that apply to both voltage and current are instantaneous, peak and effective.
   A. 1 and 3
   B. 1, 2, and 3
   C. 2

9-9 AMA041
A _____ is equal to the number of cycles in on revolution multiplied by the number of revolutions per second.
   A. period
   B. frequency
   C. cycle

9-10 AMA041
The primary effect of a coil is its property to oppose any change in current through it. This property is called
   A. resistance.
   B. inductance.
   C. capacitive reactance.

9-11 AMA041
Doubling the amount of turns in a coil has what affect on the field strength?
   A. Reduces it by half.
   B. Doubles it.
   C. Increases it by a factor of four.

9-12 AMA041
When the length of the coil doubles but the number of turns of the coil remains the same what affect does this have on the field strength?
   A. Reduces it by half.
   B. Doubles it.
   C. Decreases if by a factor of four.

AIRCRAFT ELECTRICAL SYSTEM

ANSWERS

9-7 Answer A.
Instantaneous voltage varies with every instant of time.
Based on its AC wave form, it is at its highest positive value
at 90° and highest negative value at 270°. At the 0°, 180°, and
360° points voltage is zero.
[Ref: Airframe Handbook H-8083-31A-ATB, Chapter 09 Page 9]

9-8 Answer A.
AC systems are more economically than DC, since AC
voltages can be increased or decreased by means of
transformers. AC is constantly changing in value and polarity,
or as the name implies, alternating. There are three values of
AC that apply to both voltage and current. These values help
to define the sine wave and are called instantaneous, peak,
and effective.
[Ref: Airframe Handbook H-8083-31A-ATB, Chapter 09 Page 9]

9-9 Answer B.
The frequency, then, is equal to the number of cycles in
one revolution multiplied by the number of revolutions per
second. The frequency is the number of cycles of AC per
second (CPS).
[Ref: Airframe Handbook H-8083-31A-ATB, Chapter 09 Page 10-11]

9-10 Answer B.
The primary effect of a coil is its property to oppose
any change in current through it. This property is
called inductance.
[Ref: Airframe Handbook H-8083-31A-ATB, Chapter 09 Page 12]

9-11 Answer B.
One of the physical factors that affect inductance is the
number of turns—doubling the number of turns in a coil
produces a field twice as strong if the same current is used.
As a general rule, the inductance varies with the square of
the number of turns.
[Ref: Airframe Handbook H-8083-31A-ATB, Chapter 09 Page 13]

9-12 Answer A.
One of the physical factors that affect inductance is the
length of a coil—doubling the length of a coil, while keeping
the same number of turns, reduces inductance by one-half.
[Ref: Airframe Handbook H-8083-31A-ATB, Chapter 09 Page 13]

9-13 AMA041
The total opposition to current flow in an AC circuit is known as
  A. capacitive reactance.
  B. resistance.
  C. impedance.

9-14 AMA041
What does the electrical equation $X_L = 2\pi \times f \times L$ refer to?
  A. Inductive reactance
  B. Impedance
  C. Power factor

9-15 AMA030
In which Figure are the batteries incorrectly connected?
  A. 1
  B. 2
  C. 3

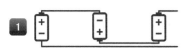
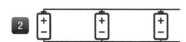
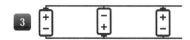

9-16 AMA030
How are the cells in a Ni-Cad battery connected?
  A. In series with nickel copper links
  B. In series with cadmium links
  C. In parallel with nickel copper links

9-17 AMA030
Which of the following is most likely to cause thermal runaway in a nickel-cadmium battery?
  A. Constant current charging of the battery to more than 100% of its capacity.
  B. A high internal resistance condition.
  C. Excessive current draw from the battery.

9-18 AMA030
At what temperature does electrolyte freeze?
  A. -75°F
  B. -90°F
  C. It does not freeze.

AIRCRAFT ELECTRICAL SYSTEM

ANSWERS

9-13 Answer C.
Impedance is the total opposition to current flow in an AC circuit.
[Ref: Airframe Handbook H-8083-31A-ATB, Chapter 09 Page 15]

9-14 Answer A.
The equation regards inductive reactance where XL = inductive reactance in ohms, L = inductance in Henries, f = frequency in cycles per second, and π = 3.14. Inductive reactance is a measure of how much electro-magnetic field (EMF) in a circuit opposes the applied current.
[Ref: Airframe Handbook H-8083-31A-ATB, Chapter 09 Page 13]

9-15 Answer C.
Figure 1, correctly depicts batteries connected in series. Figure 2, correctly depicts batteries connected in parallel. Figure 3, depicts batteries improperly connected in parallel. Because the polarity of the middle battery is reversed it will cause a short circuit condition across the other two batteries.
[Ref: Airframe Handbook H-8083-31A-ATB, Chapter 09 Page 21]

9-16 Answer A.
A NiCad battery consists of a metallic box, usually stainless steel, plastic-coated steel, painted steel, or titanium containing a number of individual cells. These cells are connected in series to obtain 12 volts or 24 volts. The cells are connected by highly conductive nickel copper links.
[Ref: Airframe Handbook H-8083-31A-ATB, Chapter 09 Page 22]

9-17 Answer C.
The combination of high battery temperature (in excess of 160°F) and overcharging can lead to a condition called thermal runaway. The temperature of the battery has to be constantly monitored to ensure safe operation. Thermal runaway can result in a NiCad chemical fire and/or explosion of the NiCad battery under recharge by a constant-voltage source and is due to cyclical, ever- increasing temperature and charging current. One or more shorted cells or an existing high temperature and low charge can produce the following cyclical sequence of events:
1. excessive current,
2. increased temperature,
3. decreased cell(s) resistance,
4. further increased current, and
5. urther increased temperature.

[Ref: Airframe Handbook H-8083-31A-ATB, Chapter 09 Page 22]

9-18 Answer A.
Discharged lead-acid batteries exposed to cold temperatures are subject to plate damage due to freezing of the electrolyte. To prevent freezing damage, maintain each cell's specific gravity at 1.275 or, for sealed lead-acid batteries, check open circuit voltage. NiCd battery electrolyte is not as susceptible to freezing because no appreciable chemical change takes place between the charged and discharged states. However, the electrolyte freezes at approximately –75°F.
[Ref: Airframe Handbook H-8083-31A-ATB, Chapter 09 Page 23]

9-19 AMA030
The specific gravity reading of a fully charged lead acid battery at a temperature of 80°F is 1.300. What is the approximate specific gravity of a battery which is 50% discharged when the temperature drops to 30°F?
A. 1.21
B. 1.41
C. .650

9-20 AMA041
The purpose of a rectifier in an electrical system is to change
A. direct current to alternating current.
B. alternating current to direct current.
C. the frequency of alternating current.

9-21 AMA030
A NiCd battery is observed with an excess spewage of electrolyte. Which action is most likely to correct this problem?
A. Adjust the voltage regulator.
B. Replace the vent cap.
C. Identify and replace the defective cell.

9-22 AMA041
The commutator of a generator
A. changes direct current produced in the armature into alternating current as it is taken from the armature.
B. changes alternating current produced in the armature into direct current as it is taken from the armature.
C. reverses the current in the field coils at the proper time in order to produce direct current.

9-23 AMA039
What enables the output voltage of a generator to approach a steady DC value?
A. Increasing the number of loops
B. Increasing the number of commutators
C. Using a permanent magnet

9-24 AMA041
A commutator, coils, and a shaft are the major components of a(n) _____.
A. armature
B. field frame
C. DC generator

AIRCRAFT ELECTRICAL SYSTEM

ANSWERS

9-19 Answer A.
US manufactured lead-acid batteries are considered fully charged when the specific gravity reading is 1.275 – 1.300 at a standard temperature of 80°F. A 1/3rd discharged battery reads about 1.240 and a 2/3rds discharged battery at about 1.200. In addition, as temperature drops below standard, the fully charged specific gravity drops a small amount as well; in this case for a 50°F drop by .020.
[Ref: Airframe Handbook H-8083-31A-ATB, Chapter 09 Page 23]

9-20 Answer B.
A constant current charging system usually consists of a rectifier to change the normal AC supply to DC.
[Ref: Airframe Handbook H-8083-31A-ATB, Chapter 09 Page 24]

9-21 Answer A.
After cleaning the battery, checking the electrolyte level, and tightening the cap, if the spewage continues, identify and replace the defective cell.
[Ref: Airframe Handbook H-8083-31A-ATB, Chapter 09 Page 27-29]

9-22 Answer B.
Generators use a modified slip ring arrangement, known as a commutator, to change the AC produced in the generator loop into a DC voltage. The action of the commutator allows the generator to produce a DC output.
[Ref: Airframe Handbook H-8083-31A-ATB, Chapter 09 Page 27]

9-23 Answer A.
As the number of loops is increased, the variation between maximum and minimum values of voltage is reduced, and the output voltage of the generator approaches a steady DC value.
[Ref: Airframe Handbook H-8083-31A-ATB, Chapter 09 Page 27]

9-24 Answer A.
A commutator, coils and a shaft are the major components of an armature. Together with the field frame, brush assemblies and a housing, this forms the basic components of a DC generator.
[Ref: Airframe Handbook H-8083-31A-ATB, Chapter 09 Page 29-31]

9-25 AMA041
While charging, a lead acid battery cell fails to reach the required 1.55 volts. Which is the appropriate action?
   A. Replace the cell.
   B. Check and refill the electrolyte.
   C. Clean and retighten its hardware to proper torque values.

9-28 AMA041
A voltage regulator controls generator output by
   A. introducing a resistance in the generator to battery lead in the event of overload.
   B. shorting out the field coil in the event of overload.
   C. varying current flow to the generator field coil.

9-26 AMA041
Which type of DC generator is not used as an airplane generator?
   A. Compound Wound
   B. Externally Grounded
   C. Series Wound

9-29 AMA041
DC generators are classified by the connection of the
   A. armature to the external circuit.
   B. field circuit to the external circuit.
   C. armature and field circuit to the external circuit.

9-27 AMA041
The most common method of regulating the voltage output of a compound DC generator is to vary the
   A. current flowing through the shunt field coils.
   B. resistance of the series field circuit.
   C. total effective field strength by changing the reluctance of the magnetic circuit.

9-30 AMA041
How is a shunt wound DC generator connected?
   A. One field is shunted across the other.
   B. The field and armature are shunted with a capacitor.
   C. Both fields are shunted across the armature.

AIRCRAFT ELECTRICAL SYSTEM

ANSWERS

9-25 Answer A.
If the cell fails to reach 1.55 volts charge, or reaches it and then drops, the cell is defective and must be removed and replaced.
[Ref: Airframe Handbook H-8083-31A-ATB, Chapter 09 Page 28]

9-28 Answer C.
The voltage of the generator is accurately controlled by means of a voltage regulator connected in the field circuit of the generator. The output voltage of the generator is controlled by means of a rheostat inserted in series with the field windings. In the actual aircraft, the field rheostat would be replaced with an automatic control device, such as a voltage regulator.
[Ref: Airframe Handbook H-8083-31A-ATB, Chapter 09 Page 32]

9-26 Answer C.
Since the series wound generator has such poor voltage and current regulation, it is never employed as an airplane generator.
[Ref: Airframe Handbook H-8083-31A-ATB, Chapter 09 Page 32]

9-29 Answer C.
There are three types of DC generator: series wound, parallel (shunt) wound, and series-parallel (or compound wound). The appropriate generator is determined by the connections to the armature and field circuits with respect to the external circuit.
[Ref: Airframe Handbook H-8083-31A-ATB, Chapter 09 Page 32]

9-27 Answer A.
The output voltage of a shunt generator can be controlled by means of a rheostat inserted in series with the field windings. As the resistance of the field circuit is increased, the field current is reduced; consequently, the generated voltage is also reduced. As the field resistance is decreased, the field current increases and the generator output increases. In the actual aircraft, the field rheostat would be replaced with an automatic control device, such as a voltage regulator.
[Ref: Airframe Handbook H-8083-31A-ATB, Chapter 09 Page 32]

9-30 Answer C.
A generator having a field winding connected in parallel with the external circuit is called a shunt generator. It should be noted that, in electrical terms, shunt means parallel. Therefore, this type of generator could be called either a shunt generator or a parallel generator.
[Ref: Airframe Handbook H-8083-31A-ATB, Chapter 09 Page 32]

9-31 AMA041
How is the rheostat in a shunt generator connected?
A. In series with the field winding.
B. In parallel with the field winding.
C. In series with the armature.

9-32 AMA041
The only practical method of maintaining a constant voltage output from an aircraft generator under varying conditions of speed and load is to vary the?
A. Strength of the magnetic field.
B. Number of conductors in the armature.
C. Speed at which the armature rotates.

9-33 AMA041
By what measurement are DC generators rated for power?
A. amperes at rated voltage
B. watts at rated voltage
C. the impedance at rated voltage

9-34 AMA042
What is the cause of generator brush arcing?
A. Low brush block spring tension.
B. Carbon dust particles.
C. Seating brushes with No. 000 sandpaper.

9-35 AMA041
In a generator, what eliminates any possible sparking to the brush guides caused by the movement of the brushes within the holder?
A. Brush spring tension.
B. The brush pigtail.
C. Undercutting the mica on the commutator.

9-36 AMA041
The voltage regulator controls generator voltage by changing the
A. current in the generator output circuit.
B. resistance of the generator field circuit
C. resistance in the generator output circuit.

AIRCRAFT ELECTRICAL SYSTEM

ANSWERS

9-31 Answer A.
The output voltage of a shunt generator can be controlled by means of a rheostat inserted in series with the field windings.
[Ref: Airframe Handbook H-8083-31A-ATB, Chapter 09 Page 32]

9-32 Answer A.
Aircraft generator output can easily be adjusted through control of the generator's magnetic field strength. Remember, the strength of the magnetic field has a direct effect on generator output. More field current means more generator output and vice versa.
[Ref: Airframe Handbook H-8083-31A-ATB, Chapter 09 Page 34]

9-33 Answer A.
A DC generator is typically rated for its voltage and power output. Each generator is designed to operate at a specified voltage, approximately 14 or 28 volts. The power output of any generator is given as the maximum number of amperes the generator can safely supply.
[Ref: Airframe Handbook H-8083-31A-ATB, Chapter 09 Page 33]

9-34 Answer A.
Brushes contain conductive materials that cause arcing between brushes and commutator bars. It is important that the brush spring pressure be correct. Excessive pressure causes rapid wear of brushes. Too little pressure, however, allows bouncing of the brushes, resulting in burned and pitted surfaces.
[Ref: Airframe Handbook H-8083-31A-ATB, Chapter 09 Page 34]

9-35 Answer B.
Flexible low-resistance pigtails are provided on most heavy current carrying brushes, and their connections should be securely made and checked at frequent intervals. The pigtails should never be permitted to alter or restrict the free motion of the brush. The purpose of the pigtail is to conduct the current from the armature, through the brushes, to the external circuit of the generator.
[Ref: Airframe Handbook H-8083-31A-ATB, Chapter 09 Page 34]

9-36 Answer B.
Generator control systems are often referred to as voltage regulators or Generator Control Units (GCU).
[Ref: Airframe Handbook H-8083-31A-ATB, Chapter 09 Page 33]

9-37 AMA041

The over voltage control automatically protects the generator system when excessive voltage is present by
A. opening and resetting the field control relay.
B. breaking a circuit to the trip coil of the field control relay.
C. opening the shunt field circuit.

9-38 AMA041

If a generator is equipped with a vibrator type voltage regulator, the actual time the voltage regulator points remain open
A. is controlled by the reverse current cutout relay point clearance.
B. depends on the load carried by the generator.
C. is increased when the external load is greater than the generator output.

9-39 AMA042

A generator in a 24-V DC system shows low voltage, a likely cause is
A. a defective reverse current cutout relay.
B. shorted or grounded wiring.
C. an out of adjustment voltage regulator.

9-40 AMA041

How do low output generators control generator output power?
A. Modify voltage to the field winding.
B. Modify current flow to the generator field.
C. Modify voltage to the armature.

9-41 AMA041

What controls the resistance of a carbon pile voltage regulator?
A. Field current from the generator.
B. Current output of the generator.
C. Magnetism of the voltage coil.

9-42 AMA041

A circuit protection device called a current limiter is essentially a slow-blow fuse and is designed to be used in
A. starter generator circuit.
B. heavy power circuits.
C. 400 cycle AC circuits.

AIRCRAFT ELECTRICAL SYSTEM

ANSWERS

9-37 Answer C.
The overvoltage protection system compares the sampled voltage to a reference voltage. The overvoltage protection circuit is used to open the relay that controls the field excitation current. It is typically found on more complex generator control systems.
[Ref: Airframe Handbook H-8083-31A-ATB, Chapter 09 Page 35]

9-38 Answer B.
A vibrator-type voltage regulator is a type of voltage regulator used with a generator or alternator that intermittently places a resistance in the field circuit to control the voltage. A set of vibrating contacts puts the resistor in the circuit and takes it out several times a second.
[Ref: Airframe Handbook H-8083-31A-ATB, Chapter 09 Page 36]

9-39 Answer C.
The most basic of the GCU functions is that of voltage regulation. Regulation of any kind requires the regulation unit to take a sample of a generator output and compare that sample to a known reference. If the generator's output voltage falls outside of the set limits, then the regulation unit must provide an adjustment to the generator field current. Adjusting field current controls generator output.
[Ref: Airframe Handbook H-8083-31A-ATB, Chapter 09 Page 36]

9-40 Answer B.
A typical generator control circuit for low-output generators modifies current flow to the generator field to control generator output power. As flight variables and electrical loads change, the GCU must monitor the electrical system and make the appropriate adjustments to ensure proper system voltage and current.
[Ref: Airframe Handbook H-8083-31A-ATB, Chapter 09 Page 36]

9-41 Answer C.
In a carbon pile regulator, the voltage coil acts like an electromagnet. That varying magnetism controls pressure on the carbon stack which alters the resistance of the carbon. The more common voltage regulators operate from the generators field current. Current limiters operate via the current output of the generator.
[Ref: Airframe Handbook H-8083-31A-ATB, Chapter 09 Page 36-37]

9-42 Answer B.
A current limiter is an electrical component used to limit the amount of current a generator can produce. Some current limiters are a type of slow- blow fuse in the generator output. Other current limiters reduce the generator output voltage if the generator tries to put out more than its rated current.
[Ref: Airframe Handbook H-8083-31A-ATB, Chapter 09 Page 37]

9-43 AMA041

If the reverse current cutout relay contact points fail to open after the generator output has dropped below battery potential, current will flow through the generator armature
- A. opposite the normal direction and through the shunt field in the normal direction.
- B. in the normal direction and through the shunt field opposite the normal direction.
- C. and the shunt field opposite the normal direction.

9-44 AMA022

What makes up a rectifier in a DC alternator?
- A. 3 Diodes
- B. 6 Diodes
- C. 6 Transistors

9-45 AMA041

What does a rectifier do?
- A. Changes direct current into alternating current.
- B. Reduces voltage.
- C. Changes alternating current into direct current.

9-46 AMA039

Aircraft which operate only AC generators (alternators) as a primary source of electrical power normally provide current suitable for battery charging through the use of
- A. a stepdown transformer and a rectifier.
- B. a dynamotor with a half wave DC output.
- C. an inverter and a voltage dropping resistor.

9-47 AMA042

A battery generator system provides direct current. On installations requiring alternating current from the battery generator system, it is necessary to have
- A. a variable resistor between the battery and generator.
- B. a transformer.
- C. an inverter.

9-48 AMA022

What is the frequency of an alternator depend upon?
- A. RPM
- B. Voltage
- C. Current

AIRCRAFT ELECTRICAL SYSTEM

ANSWERS

9-43 Answer A.
The third unit of a three-unit regulator is used to prevent current from leaving the battery and feeding the generator. This type of current flow would discharge the battery and is opposite of normal operation. It can be thought of as a reverse current situation and is known as reverse current relay.
[Ref: Airframe Handbook H-8083-31A-ATB, Chapter 09 Page 38]

9-44 Answer B.
The invention of the diode has made the development of the alternator possible. The rectifier assembly is comprised of six diodes. This rectifier assembly replaces the commutator and brushes found on DC generators and helps to make the alternator more efficient.
[Ref: Airframe Handbook H-8083-31A-ATB, Chapter 09 Page 39]

9-45 Answer C.
A rectifier assembly changes the three-phase AC to DC.
[Ref: Airframe Handbook H-8083-31A-ATB, Chapter 09 Page 39]

9-46 Answer A.
The TR unit is used to change AC to DC. The TR contains a transformer to step down the voltage from 115-volt AC to 26-volt AC and a rectifier to change the 26-volt AC to 26-volt DC. The output of the TR is therefore compatible with the aircraft battery at 26-volt DC.
[Ref: Airframe Handbook H-8083-31A-ATB, Chapter 09 Page 62]

9-47 Answer C.
Most airplanes using a 24-volt DC system have special equipment that requires a certain amount of 400 cycle AC current. For these aircraft, a unit called an inverter is used to change DC to AC. Inverters are commonly used when only a small amount of AC is required for certain systems.
Inverters may also be used as a backup AC power source on aircraft that employ an AC alternator.
[Ref: Airframe Handbook H-8083-31A-ATB, Chapter 09 Page 41]

9-48 Answer A.
All AC alternators must rotate at a specific RPM to keep the frequency of the AC voltage within limits. Aircraft AC alternators should produce a frequency of approximately 400Hz.
[Ref: Airframe Handbook H-8083-31A-ATB, Chapter 09 Page 42]

9-49 AM022
How many degrees out of sync is each phase of a
AC alternator to one another?
- A. 90°
- B. 120°
- C. 150°

9-50 AMA022
How does the wave pattern of an AC alternator differ from a
DC alternator?
- A. AC has larger amplitude for each wave.
- B. They have different phase shifts.
- C. They are the same.

9-51 AMA041
A CSD unit drives a generator through the use of
- A. a variable hydraulic pump and a hydraulic motor.
- B. a synchronous electrical motor.
- C. an infinitely variable mechanical gearing system.

9-52 AMA041
How does the speed control unit of a CSD adjust the
hydraulic pressure to control output speed?
- A. Piston Pump
- B. Wobble Plate
- C. Gear Reduction

9-53 AMA022
In an AC alternator control system, the computer that
controls alternator functions on large transport category
aircraft is?
- A. BPCU
- B. GCU
- C. BPCU and GCU

9-54 AMA030
The primary function of which of these devices ensures that
an alternator maintains an AC output of 115-120 volts?
- A. Generator Control Unit (GCU)
- B. Bus Power Control Unit (BPCU)
- C. Constant Speed Drive (CSD)

AIRCRAFT ELECTRICAL SYSTEM

ANSWERS

9-49 Answer B.
AC alternators produce a three-phase AC output. For each revolution of the alternator, the unit produces three separate voltages. The sine waves for these voltages are separated by 120°.
[Ref: Airframe Handbook H-8083-31A-ATB, Chapter 09 Page 42]

9-52 Answer B.
The speed control unit is made up of a wobble plate that adjusts hydraulic pressure to control output speed.
[Ref: Airframe Handbook H-8083-31A-ATB, Chapter 09 Page 43]

9-50 Answer C.
AC alternators produce a three-phase AC output. For each revolution of the alternator, the unit produces three separate voltages. The sine waves for these voltages are separated by 120°. This wave pattern is similar to those produced internally by a DC alternator; however, in this case, the AC alternator does not rectify the voltage and the output of the unit is AC.
[Ref: Airframe Handbook H-8083-31A-ATB, Chapter 09 Page 42]

9-53 Answer B.
The two most common units used to control AC alternators are the bus power control unit (BPCU) and the GCU. In this case, the term "generator" is used, and not alternator, although the meaning is the same. The GCU is the main computer that controls alternator functions.
[Ref: Airframe Handbook H-8083-31A-ATB, Chapter 09 Page 45-46]

9-51 Answer A.
A unit called a Constant-Speed Drive (CSD) is used to ensure the alternator rotates at the correct speed to ensure a 400Hz frequency. The CSD can be an independent unit or mounted within the alternator housing. The CSD is a hydraulic unit.
[Ref: Airframe Handbook H-8083-31A-ATB, Chapter 09 Page 42-43]

9-54 Answer A.
The Generator Control Unit insures that an alternator maintains a constant voltage of 115-120 volts. The Constant Speed Drive insures that voltage is at a continuous frequency of 400 Hz. The Bus Power Control Unit controls the distribution of power to the various electrical busses.
[Ref: Airframe Handbook H-8083-31A-ATB, Chapter 09 Page 46]

9-55 AMA030
An ammeter in a battery charging system is for the purpose of indicating the
A. rate of current used to charge the battery.
B. amperage available for use.
C. total amperes being used in the airplane.

9-56 AMA022
What instrument is used to monitor the output from an aircraft alternator?
A. Volt Meter
B. Dual Polarity Ammeter
C. Single Polarity Ammeter

9-57 AMA041
What kind of protection is in place to prevent an incorrect polarity connection with an external power source?
A. Plug with a ground.
B. Diode
C. Solenoid

9-58 AMA039
Which of the items list below are required for a starter circuit?
1. Solenoid
2. Start Switch
3. Aircraft Battery
4. Starter Motor
5. External Power
A. 1, 2, and 3
B. 1, 2, and 4
C. All can be required.

9-59 AMA068
What is used to monitor the position of each gear during all flight operations?
A. Limit Switch
B. Squat Switch
C. Indicator Switch

9-60 AMA041
In order to provide power for an electroluminescent instrument panel, what must be included with the DC electrical system of a light aircraft?
A. A rectifier.
B. A transformer.
C. An inverter.

AIRCRAFT ELECTRICAL SYSTEM

ANSWERS

9-55 Answer A.
The ammeter shown in the battery circuit is used to monitor the current flow from the battery to the distribution bus. When all systems are operating properly, battery current should flow from the main bus to the battery giving a positive indication on the ammeter. In this case, the battery is being charged. If the aircraft alternator (or generator) experiences a malfunction, the ammeter indicates a negative value.
[Ref: Airframe Handbook H-8083-31A-ATB, Chapter 09 Page 48]

9-56 Answer A.
All alternators must be monitored for correct output. Most light aircraft employ an ammeter to monitor alternator output. A typical ammeter circuit used to monitor alternator output. An ammeter placed in the alternator circuit is a single polarity meter that shows current flow in only one direction.
[Ref: Airframe Handbook H-8083-31A-ATB, Chapter 09 Page 49]

9-57 Answer B.
This diode is used to prevent any accidental connection in the event the external power supply has the incorrect polarity (i.e., a reverse of the positive and negative electrical connections). A reverse polarity connection could be catastrophic to the aircraft's electrical system.
[Ref: Airframe Handbook H-8083-31A-ATB, Chapter 09 Page 50]

9-58 Answer C.
All items listed can be required in a general starter circuit. See Figure 9-91 on p. 9-51 in the text for an example of starter circuit.
[Ref: Airframe Handbook H-8083-31A-ATB, Chapter 09 Page 50-51]

9-59 Answer A.
A series of limit switches are needed to monitor the position of each gear during the operation of the system. (A limit switch is simply a spring-loaded, momentary contact switch that is activated when a gear reaches it limit of travel).
[Ref: Airframe Handbook H-8083-31A-ATB, Chapter 09 Page 52]

9-60 Answer C.
An electroluminescent panel operates only with AC power. Therefore an inverter is needed to change the DC current to AC.
[Ref: Airframe Handbook H-8083-31A-ATB, Chapter 09 Page 55]

9-61 AMA022
What is the process of equalizing alternator outputs in a multiple alternator system?
  A. Paralleling
  B. Strapping
  C. Pairing

9-62 AMA022
On a twin engine aircraft, if one alternator has a higher voltage output than the other, how is the problem corrected by the paralleling circuit?
  A. The paralleling circuit creates a magnetic force to open or close contact points.
  B. The paralleling circuit increases the current to the lower alternator's field winding.
  C. The paralleling circuit disengages the dominant alternator until the voltage of the lesser alternator increases to the proper value.

9-63 AMA041
Generator busses are connected to the isolation bus through which of the following?
  A. Diode and Current Limiter
  B. Reverse Polarity Diode
  C. Circuit Breakers

9-64 AMA041
What prevents the dual fed bus from powering the main generator busses?
  A. Circuit Breaker
  B. Current Limiter
  C. Diode

9-65 AMA022
When two AC generators are operated in parallel, the
  A. amperes and voltage most both be equal.
  B. amperes and frequency must both be equal.
  C. frequency and voltage must both be equal.

9-66 AMA041
Which of the following statements are true regarding split-bus power distributions systems?
  1. The split-bus system does allow both engine- driven generators to power any given bus and at the same time.
  2. On all modern split-bus systems, the auxiliary power unit can be started and operated during flight.
  3. Each engine-driven AC generator powers only on main AC bus during normal conditions.
  A. Only 3
  B. 2 and 3
  C. Only 1

AIRCRAFT ELECTRICAL SYSTEM

ANSWERS

9-61 Answer A.
Since two alternators (or generators) are used on twin engine aircraft, it becomes vital to ensure both alternators share the electrical load equally. This process of equalizing alternator outputs is often called paralleling.
[Ref: Airframe Handbook H-8083-31A-ATB, Chapter 09 Page 57]

9-62 Answer A.
If the two alternators provide equal voltages, the paralleling coil has no effect. If one alternator has a higher voltage output, the paralleling coils create the appropriate magnetic force to open/close the contact points, controlling field current and control alternator output.
[Ref: Airframe Handbook H-8083-31A-ATB, Chapter 09 Page 57]

9-63 Answer A.
An aircraft with two starter generator units used to start the engines and generate DC electrical power has a system that is typically defined as a split-bus power distribution system since there is a left and right generator bus that splits (shares) the electrical loads by connecting to each sub-bus through a diode and current limiter.
[Ref: Airframe Handbook H-8083-31A-ATB, Chapter 09 Page 58]

9-64 Answer C.
The dual-feed busses are connected to the main generator busses through both a current limiter and a diode. Remember, a diode allows current flow in only one direction. The current can flow from the generator bus to the dual-feed bus, but the current cannot flow from the dual fed bus to the main generator bus.
[Ref: Airframe Handbook H-8083-31A-ATB, Chapter 09 Page 60]

9-65 Answer C.
The left and right DC generators are connected to their respective main generator busses. Each generator feeds its respective bus, and since the busses are connected under normal circumstances, the generators operate in parallel. Both generators feed all loads together. If one generator fails or a current limiter opens, the generators can operate independently. This design allows for redundancy in the event of failure and provides battery backup in the event of a dual generator failure.
[Ref: Airframe Handbook H-8083-31A-ATB, Chapter 09 Page 60]

9-66 Answer B.
During normal conditions, each engine-driven AC generator powers only one main AC bus. The busses are kept split from each other, and two generators can never power the same bus simultaneously. The split-bus system does allow both engine-driven generators to power any given bus, but not at the same time. On all modern split bus systems, the APU can be started and operated during flight. This allows the APU generator to provide back-up power in the event of a main generator failure.
[Ref: Airframe Handbook H-8083-31A-ATB, Chapter 09 Page 61]

9-67 AMA042
Which type of wiring diagrams would be used to troubleshoot electronic systems?
   A. Schematic Diagram
   B. Block Diagram
   C. Pictorial Diagram

9-68 AMA088
Wiring approved for use in commercial and military aircraft are specifically designed to meet?
   A. International Civil Aviation Organization (ICAO) standards
   B. Military specifications
   C. Technical Standard Order (TSO) specifications

9-69 AMA042
What is the primary importance in the selection of wire for aircraft use and is the basic factor in wire rating in regards to insulation?
   A. Abrasion Resistance
   B. Heat Resistance
   C. Corrosion Resistance

9-70 AMA042
The primary considerations when selecting electric wire size are
   A. the voltage and amperage load it must carry.
   B. system voltage and cable length.
   C. current carrying capacity and allowable voltage drop.

9-71 AMA042
In the American Wire Gauge (AWG) system of numbers used to designate electrical wire sizes, the number assigned to a size is related to its
   A. cross sectional area.
   B. combined resistance and current carrying capacity.
   C. current carrying capacity.

9-72 AMA042
Which of the following factors must be taken into consideration when determining the wire size to use for an aircraft application?
   1. Mechanical strength
   2. Allowable power loss
   3. Ease of installation
   4. Resistance of current return path through the aircraft structure
   5. Permissible voltage drop
   6. Current carrying capability of the conductor
   7. Type of load (continuous or intermittent)
   A. 1, 2, 4, and 5
   B. 2, 4, 6, and 7
   C. 2, 5, 6, and 7

AIRCRAFT ELECTRICAL SYSTEM

ANSWERS

9-67 Answer B.
A block diagram is used as an aid for troubleshooting complex electrical and electronic systems. A block diagram consists of individual blocks that represent several components, such as a printed circuit board or some other type of replaceable module.
[Ref: Airframe Handbook H-8083-31A-ATB, Chapter 09 Page 65]

9-68 Answer B.
Commercial and military aircraft use wire that is manufactured under MIL-W-22759 specification, which complies with current military and FAA requirements.
[Ref: Airframe Handbook H-8083-31A-ATB, Chapter 09 Page 67]

9-69 Answer B.
Since electrical wire may be installed in areas where inspection is infrequent over extended periods of time, it is necessary to give special consideration to heat-aging characteristics in the selection of wire. Resistance to heat is of primary importance in the selection of wire for aircraft use, as it is the basic factor in wire rating.
[Ref: Airframe Handbook H-8083-31A-ATB, Chapter 09 Page 68]

9-70 Answer C.
Several factors must be considered in selecting the size of wire for transmitting and distributing electric power, these include the wires current carrying capacity and the allowable voltage drop.
[Ref: Airframe Handbook H-8083-31A-ATB, Chapter 09 Page 69]

9-71 Answer A.
Wire is manufactured in sizes according to a standard known as the American Wire Gauge (AWG). The wire diameters (cross sectional area) become smaller as the gauge numbers become larger. Typical wire sizes range from a number 40 to number 0000.
[Ref: Airframe Handbook H-8083-31A-ATB, Chapter 09 Page 69]

9-72 Answer C.
Several factors must be considered in selecting the size of wire for transmitting and distributing electric power, these include the wires current carrying capacity, the allowable voltage drop, allowable power loss, and the type of load.
[Ref: Airframe Handbook H-8083-31A-ATB, Chapter 09 Page 69]

9-73 AMA042
What is the shortest recommended run for aluminum wires?
  A. 2 Feet
  B. 18 Inches
  C. 3 Feet

9-74 AMA042
What is the voltage drop for a No. 18 copper wire 50 feet long to carry 12.5 amperes, continuous operation?
Use the formula:
  VD = RLA;
  VD = Voltage drop;
  R = Resistance per ft = .00644;
  L = length of wire;
  A = amperes
  A. 1/2 V
  B. 1 V
  C. 4 V

9-75 AMA042
The voltage drop of main power wires from the generation or battery source to the bus should not exceed what percentage of the regulated voltage?
  A. 2%
  B. 5%
  C. 10%

9-76 AMA042
What type of identification sleeving should be used for wires exposed to solvent and synthetic hydraulic fluids?
  A. Polyolefin
  B. Polyethylene
  C. Fiberglass

9-77 AMA042
What is the minimum bend radius for an electrical wire bundle?
  A. Ten times the outside diameter of the bundle.
  B. Fifteen times the outside diameter of the bundle.
  C. Five times the outside diameter of the bundle.

9-78 AMA042
Non-printed wires may be identified with printed sleeves which must be placed
  A. no more than 15 inches apart.
  B. no more than 6 feet apart.
  C. centered in between every bracket or clamp.

AIRCRAFT ELECTRICAL SYSTEM

ANSWERS

9-73 Answer C.
When aluminum conductor wire is used, sizes should be selected on the basis of current ratings. Use of aluminum wire is also discouraged for runs of less than 3 feet.
[Ref: Airframe Handbook H-8083-31A-ATB, Chapter 09 Page 71]

9-74 Answer C.
Voltage drop = (.00644) × (50 feet) × (12.5 amps) = 4.25 Volts.
[Ref: Airframe Handbook H-8083-31A-ATB, Chapter 09 Page 72]

9-75 Answer A.
The voltage drop in the main power wires from the generation source or the battery to the bus should not exceed 2 percent of the regulated voltage when the generator is carrying rated current or the battery is being discharged at the 5 minute rate.
[Ref: Airframe Handbook H-8083-31A-ATB, Chapter 09 Page 75]

9-76 Answer A.
In most cases, identification tape can be used in place of sleeving. For sleeving exposed to high temperatures (over 400°F), materials, such as silicone fiberglass, should be used. Polyolefin sleeving should be used in areas where resistance to solvent and synthetic hydraulic fluids is necessary.
[Ref: Airframe Handbook H-8083-31A-ATB, Chapter 09 Page 78]

9-77 Answer A.
The minimum radius of bends in wire groups or bundles must not be less than 10 times the outside diameter of the largest wire or cable, except that at the terminal strips where wires break out at terminations or reverse direction in a bundle.
[Ref: Airframe Handbook H-8083-31A-ATB, Chapter 09 Page 80]

9-78 Answer B.
Indirect marking of cables may be done with heat shrinkable sleeves placed over the wire covering within 3 inches of each end and at intervals not longer than 6 feet.
[Ref: Airframe Handbook H-8083-31A-ATB, Chapter 09 Page 77-78]

9-79 AMA042
When approved, splices may be used to repair manufactured harnesses or installed wiring. The maximum number of splices permitted between any two connectors is?
A. Three
B. Two
C. One

9-80 AMA042
How far away can the nearest splice be from a termination device?
A. 6 Inches
B. 12 Inches
C. 18 Inches

9-81 AMA042
Where electrical cables must pass through holes in bulkheads, formers, ribs, firewalls, etc, the wires should be protected from chafing by
A. wrapping with electrical tape.
B. using a suitable grommet.
C. wrapping with plastic.

9-82 AMA042
If a wire is installed so that it comes in contact with some moving parts, what protection should be given the wire?
A. Wrap with friction tape.
B. Pass through conduit.
C. Wrap with soft wire solder into the shield.

9-83 AMA042
If there is less than 3/8" clearance between the bulkhead and the wire bundle, what must be done?
A. A clamp must be used.
B. A grommet should be installed.
C. An angle bracket must be used.

9-84 AMA042
Clamps should be spaced at intervals not exceeding?
A. 12 Inches
B. 18 Inches
C. 24 Inches

AIRCRAFT ELECTRICAL SYSTEM

ANSWERS

9-79 Answer C.
There should be no more than one splice in any one wire segment between any two connectors or other disconnect points. Exceptions include when attaching to the spare pigtail lead of a potted connector, when splicing multiple wires to a single wire, when adjusting wire size to fit connector contact crimp barrel size, and when required to make an approved repair.
[Ref: Airframe Handbook H-8083-31A-ATB, Chapter 09 Page 80]

9-80 Answer B.
Splices should not be used within 12 inches of a termination device, except when attaching to the pigtail spare lead of a potted termination device, to splice multiple wires to a single wire, or to adjust the wire sizes so that they are compatible with the contact crimp barrel sizes.
[Ref: Airframe Handbook H-8083-31A-ATB, Chapter 09 Page 80]

9-81 Answer B.
Where wires or wire bundles pass through bulkheads or other structural members, a grommet or suitable clamp should be provided to prevent abrasion.
[Ref: Airframe Handbook H-8083-31A-ATB, Chapter 09 Page 80]

9-82 Answer B.
Conduit is manufactured in metallic and nonmetallic materials and in both rigid and flexible forms. Primarily, its purpose is for mechanical protection of cables or wires.
[Ref: Airframe Handbook H-8083-31A-ATB, Chapter 09 Page 83]

9-83 Answer B.
When a wire bundle is clamped into position, if there is less than 3/8-inch of clearance between the bulkhead cutout and the wire bundle, a suitable grommet should be installed.
[Ref: Airframe Handbook H-8083-31A-ATB, Chapter 09 Page 83]

9-84 Answer C.
Wires and cables are supported by suitable clamps, grommets, or other devices at intervals of not more than 24 inches.
[Ref: Airframe Handbook H-8083-31A-ATB, Chapter 09 Page 83]

9-85 AMA042
A piece of rigid electrical conduit should be replaced if the diameter of a bend section in the conduit has been flattened by
A. in excess of 10% of its normal diameter.
B. in excess of 25% of its normal diameter.
C. if any flattening of its diameter is apparent at all.

9-88 AMA042
What is normally used to bond non-continuous stainless steel aircraft components?
A. Aluminum Jumpers
B. Stainless Steel Jumpers
C. Copper Jumpers

9-86 AMA041
Grounding is electrically connecting a conductive object to the primary structure. One purpose of grounding is to
A. prevent development of radio frequency potentials.
B. prevent current return paths.
C. allow static charge accumulation.

9-89 AMA043
Bonding connections should be tested for
A. reactance.
B. amperage value.
C. resistance value.

9-87 AMA041
With regards to grounding, which of the following statements are true?
1. Grounding is the electrical connecting of two or more conducting objects not otherwise adequately connected.
2. To minimize the interaction between various return currents, different types of ground (i.e., AC returns, DC returns and all others) should be identified and used.
3. The design of the ground return circuit should be given as much attention as the other leads of a circuit.
A. 1 and 3
B. 1 and 2
C. 2 and 3

AIRCRAFT ELECTRICAL SYSTEM

ANSWERS

9-85 Answer B.
Kinked or wrinkled bends in rigid conduits are not recommended and should be replaced. Tubing bends that have been flattened into an ellipse and have a minor diameter of less than 75 percent of the nominal tubing diameter should be replaced, because the tube area has been reduced by at least 10 percent.
[Ref: Airframe Handbook H-8083-31A-ATB, Chapter 09 Page 84]

9-86 Answer A.
Electromagnetic Interference (EMI) is caused when electromagnetic fields (radio waves) induce High Frequency (HF) voltages in a wire or component. One of the more important factors in the design and maintenance of aircraft electrical systems is proper bonding and grounding. Inadequate bonding or grounding can lead to unreliable operation of systems, EMI, electrostatic discharge damage to sensitive electronics, personnel shock hazard, or damage from lightning strike.
[Ref: Airframe Handbook H-8083-31A-ATB, Chapter 09 Page 85]

9-87 Answer C.
Grounding is the process of electrically connecting conductive objects to either a conductive structure or some other conductive return path for the purpose of safely completing either a normal or fault circuit.
[Ref: Airframe Handbook H-8083-31A-ATB, Chapter 09 Page 86-87]

9-88 Answer C.
Aluminum alloy jumpers are recommended for most cases; however, copper jumpers should be used to bond together parts made of stainless steel, cadmium plated steel, copper, brass, or bronze.
[Ref: Airframe Handbook H-8083-31A-ATB, Chapter 09 Page 87]

9-89 Answer C.
The resistance of all bond and ground connections should be tested after connections are made before re-finishing.
[Ref: Airframe Handbook H-8083-31A-ATB, Chapter 09 Page 87]

ORAL EXAM

9-1(O).   How are wire sizes determined?

9-2(O).   What factors must be considered in selecting the size of wire for transmitting and distributing electric power?

9-3(O).   Which method of lacing would be used for a bundle of wires 1 inch or less?

9-4(O).   A wire bundle needs several splices, how should they be arranged?

9-5(O).   What is the maximum number of splices permitted between any two connectors?

9-6(O).   How far away can the nearest splice be from a termination device?

9-7(O).   Define the term "derated" at it relates to electrical specifications.

9-8(O).   Why are switches derated for known continuous load current applications?

9-9(O).   Name the two most common types of voltage regulators.

9-10(O).   Explain how a carbon-pile voltage regulator works.

9-11(O).   What is a shunt winding?

9-12(O).   What is a Constant-Speed Drive (CSD).

9-13(O).   What is a switch?

9-14(O).   How are rotary switches activated and where will you commonly find them?

9-15(O).   What is a circuit breaker?

9-16(O).   What is a micro switch and what are they typically used for?

9-17(O).   What is a relay?

9-18(O).   What is the advantage of a circuit breaker when compared to a fuse?

9-19(O).   What should you look for when inspecting wiring?

AIRCRAFT ELECTRICAL SYSTEM

ANSWERS

ORAL EXAM

9-1(O).   Wire sizes are in accordance with the standard known as the American Wire Gauge (AWG) and determined by the wire diameters.
[Ref: Airframe Handbook H-8083-31A-ATB, Chapter 09 Page 69]

9-2(O).   Current carrying ability, allowable voltage drop, mechanical strength, and allowable power loss.
[Ref: Airframe Handbook H-8083-31A-ATB, Chapter 09 Page 69]

9-3(O).   The single cord-lacing method and tying tape may be used for wire groups of bundles 1 inch in diameter or less.
[Ref: Airframe Handbook H-8083-31A-ATB, Chapter 09 Page 88-89]

9-4(O).   Splices in bundles must be staggered to minimize any increase in the size of the bundle, preventing the bundle from fitting into its designated space or causing congestion that adversely affects maintenance.
[Ref: Airframe Handbook H-8083-31A-ATB, Chapter 09 Page 80]

9-5(O).   There should be no more than one splice in any one wire segment between any two connectors or other disconnect points. Exceptions include when attaching to the spare pigtail lead of a potted connector, when splicing multiple wires to a single wire, when adjusting wire size to fit connector contact crimp barrel size, and when required to make an approved repair.
[Ref: Airframe Handbook H-8083-31A-ATB, Chapter 09 Page 80]

9-6(O).   Splices should not be used within 12 inches of a termination device, except when attaching to the pigtail spare lead of a potted termination device, to splice multiple wires to a single wire, or to adjust the wire sizes so that they are compatible with the contact crimp barrel sizes.
[Ref: Airframe Handbook H-8083-31A-ATB, Chapter 09 Page 80]

9-7(O).   It is the reduction in the rated voltage or current of an electrical component.
[Ref: Airframe Handbook H-8083-31A-ATB, Chapter 09 Page 98 & G-12]

9-8(O).   Derating is done to extend the life or reliability of the device.
[Ref: Airframe Handbook H-8083-31A-ATB, Chapter 09 Page 98 & G-12]

9-9(O).   Carbon pile regulators and the three-unit regulators.
[Ref: Airframe Handbook H-8083-31A-ATB, Chapter 09 Page 36]

9-10(O).   It is a type of voltage regulator used with high-output DC generators. Field current is controlled by varying the resistance of a stack of thin carbon disks. This resistance is varied by controlling the amount the stack is compressed by a spring whose force is opposed by the pull of an electromagnet. The electromagnet's strength is proportional to the generator's output voltage.
[Ref: Airframe Handbook H-8083-31A-ATB, Glossary Page 7]

9-11(O).   It is the field coils in an electric motor or generator that are connected in parallel with the armature.
[Ref: Airframe Handbook H-8083-31A-ATB, Glossary Page 32]

9-12(O).   It is a special drive system used to connect an alternating current generator to an aircraft engine. The drive holds the generator speed (and thus its frequency) constant as the engine speed varies.
[Ref: Airframe Handbook H-8083-31A-ATB, Glossary Page 10]

9-13(O).   They are devices that open and close circuits. They consist of one or more pair of contacts.
[Ref: Airframe Handbook H-8083-31A-ATB, Chapter 09 Page 96]

ORAL EXAM

9-14(O).   A rotary switch is activated by twisting a knob or shaft and are commonly found on radio control panels.
[Ref: Airframe Handbook H-8083-31A-ATB, Chapter 09 Page 99]

9-15(O).   An electrical component that automatically opens a circuit any time excessive current flows through it.
[Ref: Airframe Handbook H-8083-31A-ATB, Glossary Page 8]

9-16(O).   A precision switch that uses a short throw of the control plunger to actuate the contacts. Micro switches are used primarily as limit switches to control electrical units automatically.
[Ref: Airframe Handbook H-8083-31A-ATB, Glossary Page 23]

9-17(O).   An electrical component that uses a small amount of current flowing through a coil to produce a magnetic pull to close a set of contacts through which a large amount of current can flow. The core in a relay coil is fixed.
[Ref: Airframe Handbook H-8083-31A-ATB, Glossary Page 29]

9-18(O).   Unlike a fuse that operates once and then has to be replaced, a circuit breaker can be reset, therefore are reusable, to resume normal operation.
[Ref: Airframe Handbook H-8083-31A-ATB, Chapter 09 Page 100 & G-8]

9-19(O).   Check for abrasions, defective insulation, condition of terminations, and potential corrosion. Grounding connections for power, distribution equipment, and electromagnetic shielding must be given particular attention to ensure that electrical bonding resistance has not been significantly increased by the loosening of connections or corrosion.
[Ref: Airframe Handbook H-8083-31A-ATB, Glossary Page 96]

AIRCRAFT ELECTRICAL SYSTEM

PRACTICAL EXAM

9-1(P).   Given an actual aircraft or mockup, appropriate publications, and appropriate tools and/or test equipment, troubleshoot an electrical system or portion thereof, and record your findings.

9-2(P).   Given a specific aircraft electrical system and appropriate publications, select a circuit switch or circuit protection device for a specified application.

9-3(P).   Given an actual aircraft or mockup, appropriate publications, equipment, tools and testing equipment, if applicable, install a circuit switch or circuit protection device.

9-4(P).   Given various materials and tools, select the appropriate materials and tools and complete a wire splice.

9-5(P).   Given an actual aircraft or mockup, appropriate publications, equipment, tools and testing equipment, if applicable adjust a voltage regulator.

9-6(P).   Given an actual aircraft or mockup, appropriate publications, equipment, tools and testing equipment, if applicable, select and install one or more wires and pins and/or sockets in a connector.

9-7(P).   Given various materials, select the appropriate material and fabricate a bonding wire.

9-8(P).   Given a bonding wire, appropriate publications, and the appropriate testing equipment, install and complete a resistance check.

9-9(P).   Given an actual aircraft or mockup, appropriate publications, and the appropriate testing equipment, if necessary, check the operation of an airframe electrical system circuit.

9-10(P).   Given an actual aircraft or mockup, appropriate publications, and the appropriate testing equipment, if necessary, check the operation of an airframe electrical system component.

9-11(P).   Given an actual aircraft or mockup, appropriate publications, and the appropriate testing equipment, if necessary, inspect and check a landing light and record your findings.

9-12(P).   Given an actual aircraft or mockup, appropriate publications, and the appropriate testing equipment, if necessary, inspect and check the anti-collision and position lights and record your findings.

9-13(P).   Given an actual aircraft or mockup, appropriate publications, and the appropriate testing equipment, if necessary, inspect the generator brushes to determine serviceability and record your findings.

AIRCRAFT INSTRUMENT SYSTEMS

Pressure Measuring Instruments, Remote Sensing and Indication, Mechanical Movement Indicators, and Electronic Instruments

10-1 AMA013
Which of the following instruments are located in the "Basic T" on the instrument panel?
A. Altimeter, oil pressure, fuel pressure, attitude indicator.
B. Directional gyro, attitude indicator, altimeter, airspeed indicator.
C. Altimeter, rate of climb, attitude indicator, turn coordinator.

10-2 AMA014
In addition to flight instruments, two major categories of instruments classified by the job they perform are
A. engine instruments and temperature instruments.
B. navigation instruments and airframe instruments.
C. engine instruments and navigation instruments.

10-3 AMA008
The operating mechanism of most hydraulic pressure gauges is
A. a bourdon tube.
B. an evacuated bellows filled with an inert gas to which suitable arms, levers, and gear are attached.
C. an airtight diaphragm.

10-4 AMA014
A Bourbon tube instrument maybe used to indicate
1. pressure.
2. temperature.
3. position.
A. 1
B. 2 and 3
C. 1 and 2

10-5 AMA014
Solid state piezoelectric pressure sensing units can _____.
A. change impedance when under pressure
B. act as diodes when under pressure
C. vary resistance when under pressure

10-6 AMA067
What does a reciprocating engine manifold pressure gauge indicate when the engine is not operating?
A. Zero pressure.
B. Differential between the manifold pressure and the atmospheric pressure.
C. The existing atmospheric pressure.

AIRCRAFT INSTRUMENT SYSTEMS

ANSWERS

10-1 Answer B.
The instruments used in controlling the aircrafts flight attitude are known as flight instruments. Over the years, flight instruments have come to be situated similarly on instrument panels in most aircraft. The basic T arrangement for flight instruments includes the artificial horizon in the center directly in front of the pilot. To the left is the airspeed indicator. To the right is the altimeter. Below the artificial horizon is a heading indicator, often a directional gyro.
[Ref: Airframe Handbook H-8083-31A-ATB, Chapter 10 Page 3]

10-2 Answer C.
While there are many miscellaneous gauges and indicators on the flight deck, the three basic kinds of instruments classified by the job that they perform are the flight instruments, the engine instruments, and the navigation instruments. A fourth category, position/condition instruments, includes gauges and indicators not falling into one of the three basic kinds since they typically report the position of a certain movable component or the condition of various aircraft components or systems.
[Ref: Airframe Handbook H-8083-31A-ATB, Chapter 10 Page 3]

10-3 Answer A.
Bourdon tube gauges are simple and reliable. Some of the instruments that use a Bourdon tube mechanism include the engine oil pressure gauge, hydraulic pressure gauge, oxygen tank pressure gauge, and deice boot pressure gauge.
[Ref: Airframe Handbook H-8083-31A-ATB, Chapter 10 Page 5]

10-4 Answer C.
The Bourdon tube is the internal mechanism for many pressure gauges used on aircraft. Since the pressure of the vapor produced by a heated liquid or gas increases as temperature increases, Bourdon tube mechanisms can also be used to measure temperature.
[Ref: Airframe Handbook H-8083-31A-ATB, Chapter 10 Page 5-6]

10-5 Answer C.
The solid state sensors used in most aviation applications exhibit varying electric output or resistance changes when pressure changes occur.
[Ref: Airframe Handbook H-8083-31A-ATB, Chapter 10 Page 7]

10-6 Answer C.
In reciprocating engine aircraft, the manifold pressure gauge indicates the pressure of the air in the engine's induction manifold. When the engine is not running, the pressure in the induction manifold is the atmospheric pressure and will be indicated on the gauge.
[Ref: Airframe Handbook H-8083-31A-ATB, Chapter 10 Page 9]

10-7 AMA098

Regarding an EPR gauge for a turbine engine?
- A. It is a direct reading gauge.
- B. It is a differential pressure gauge.
- C. It does not require electricity.

10-8 AMA014

Pressure switches
- A. are used to drive a vacuum gauge.
- B. are electro-mechanical devices.
- C. are rarely used on aircraft.

10-9 AMA096

Which instruments are connected to an aircraft's static pressure system only?
1. Vertical Speed Indicator
2. Cabin Altimeter
3. Altimeter
4. Cabin Rate-Of-Change Indicator
5. Airspeed Indicator
- A. 2 and 4
- B. 1 and 3
- C. 2, 4, and 5

10-10 AMA096

In addition to the pressure sensitive flight instruments, which other system requires an accurate static air pressure sensor?
- A. Vacuum System
- B. Autopilot System
- C. Oil and Fuel Pressure Indicators

10-11 AMA076

Air Data Computers (ADC's) and Digital Air Data Computers (DADC's) have many advantages when accepting and processing static system data such as?
- A. One-time processing without the need for compensating devices in each instrument or units.
- B. Eliminating the need for heated static ports.
- C. Standardized input from different sources.

10-12 AMA096

What will be the result if the instrument static pressure line becomes disconnected inside a pressurized cabin during cruising flight?
- A. The altimeter will read low and the airspeed indicator will read high.
- B. The altimeter and airspeed indicator will both read low.
- C. The altimeter and airspeed indicator will both read high.

AIRCRAFT INSTRUMENT SYSTEMS

ANSWERS

10-7 Answer B.
EPR stands for Engine Pressure Ratio. On a turbine engine, an EPR gauge presents an indication of thrust being developed by the engine. Since the EPR gauge compares two pressures (exhaust pressure versus inlet pressure), it is a differential pressure gauge.
[Ref: Airframe Handbook H-8083-31A-ATB, Chapter 10 Page 9]

10-8 Answer B.
A pressure switch is a simple device usually made to open or close an electric circuit when certain pressure is reached in a system. It contains a diaphragm to which the pressure is applied on one side. The opposite side of the diaphragm is connected to a mechanical switching mechanism for an electric circuit. Each switch is rated to close (or open) at a certain pressure and must be installed in the proper location on the aircraft. They are widely used for various components or systems on an aircraft.
[Ref: Airframe Handbook H-8083-31A-ATB, Chapter 10 Page 11-12]

10-9 Answer B.
The vertical speed indicator and the altimeter are connected to the static system. The airspeed indicator is as well but it is also connected to the pitot tube. The static system is designed to collect atmospheric pressure in a static condition. This pressure is irrelevant for a cabin altitude indication or a cabin rate-of-change indication.
[Ref: Airframe Handbook H-8083-31A-ATB, Chapter 10 Page 13-14]

10-10 Answer B.
The autopilot computers require the same sensing data as does the flight crew when performing manual operation. Oil and fuel pressure and the vacuum systems are absolute sensors or indicators requiring only its own source of pressure monitoring.
[Ref: Airframe Handbook H-8083-31A-ATB, Chapter 10 Page 14-15]

10-11 Answer A.
There are numerous benefits of using ADC's (or DADC's). Simplification of pitot static plumbing creates a lighter, simpler system with few connections. One-time compensation calculations can be done in the computer, eliminating the need to build compensating devices into numerous individual instruments or units in the systems using air data. DADC's can run a number of checks to verify the plausibility of data received. Change to an alternate data source can be automatic. Plus solid state technology is more reliable and modern units are small and lightweight.
[Ref: Airframe Handbook H-8083-31A-ATB, Chapter 10 Page 16]

10-12 Answer B.
In a pressurized cabin, the air pressure is greater than the ambient air. In an altimeter, this increase in pressure would fill the case around the aneroid bellows and cause an indication as though the aircraft was at a lower altitude. In the airspeed indicator, the pitot ram air pressure fills an aneroid, which is surrounded by static air pressure in the case. By filling the case with a higher pressure than the static ambient pressure, in this case the cabin air pressure, the aneroid expansion will be suppressed causing a lower airspeed indication.
[Ref: Airframe Handbook H-8083-31A-ATB, Chapter 10 Page 16-24]

10-13 AMA001
Air pressure is inversely proportional to altitude. At what altitude is atmospheric air pressure approximately half of what it is at sea level?
  A. 5,000 Feet
  B. 18,000 Feet
  C. 40,000 Feet

10-14 AMA014
Within an altimeter, when the aneroid capsule expands _____.
  A. the reading of the Kollsman window increases
  B. the altitude reading decreases
  C. the altitude reading increases

10-15 AMA096
Why are most static vents located on the side of the fuselage?
  A. To prevent hysteresis.
  B. To prevent icing.
  C. To reduce position error.

10-16 AMA076
  1. An airspeed indicator measures the differential between pitot and static air pressures surrounding the aircraft at any moment of flight.
  2. An airspeed indicator measures the differential between pitot and cabin air pressures at any moment of flight.

Regarding the above statements,
  A. Both No. 1 and No. 2 are true.
  B. Only No. 2 is true.
  C. Only No. 1 is true.

10-17 AMA014
Machmeter red and white striped pointer is used in high performance aircraft to
  A. simplify monitoring of higher airspeeds.
  B. measure airspeeds above the speed of sound.
  C. prevent operation at or above the speed of sound or maximum allowable speed due to possibility of destructive shock waves.

10-18 AMA010
Which of the following are some uses for a DC Selsyn system?
  1. Indicates position of retractable landing gear.
  2. Indicates the angle of incidence of an aircraft.
  3. Indicates the altitude of an aircraft.
  4. Indicates cowl flaps or coil cooler door position.
  5. Indicates fuel quantity.
  6. Indicates the rate of climb of an aircraft.
  7. Indicates position of wing flaps.
  A. 2, 3, 5, and 6
  B. 2, 3, 4, and 5
  C. 1, 4, 5, and 7

AIRCRAFT INSTRUMENT SYSTEMS

ANSWERS

10-13 Answer B.
At 18,000 feet, atmospheric air pressure (7.34psi) is about 1/2 of atmospheric pressure at sea level on a standard day. This is also the altitude that flight levels begin and all airspace is controlled airspace above this level. Barometric pressure is set at 29.92 in the Kollsman window on all aircraft altimeters operating at 18,000 feet and above.
[Ref: Airframe Handbook H-8083-31A-ATB, Chapter 10 Page 18-20]

10-14 Answer C.
As the pressure within the aneroid capsule always remains the same, it expands or contracts based on the outside pressure pushing on it. When that pressure decreases due to increased altitude, the capsule expands. This expansion then drives the internal mechanisms to move the dials clockwise, thus displaying a higher altitude.
[Ref: Airframe Handbook H-8083-31A-ATB, Chapter 10 Page 19]

10-15 Answer C.
Position error, or installation error, is that inaccuracy caused by the location of the static vent. The amount of air pressure collection error is measured in test flights. Normally, location of static vents is adjusted during these test flight so that position error is minimal.
[Ref: Airframe Handbook H-8083-31A-ATB, Chapter 10 Page 21-22]

10-16 Answer C.
The airspeed indicator is a differential pressure gauge. Ram air pressure is directed from the aircraft's pitot tube into a diaphragm located in an aircraft instrument case. Static air pressure is directed into the case surrounding the diaphragm. As the speed of the aircraft varies, the ram air pressure varies, expanding or contracting the diaphragm. Linkages attached to the diaphragm cause a pointer to move over the instrument face, which is calibrated in knots or miles per hour.
[Ref: Airframe Handbook H-8083-31A-ATB, Chapter 10 Page 24]

10-17 Answer C.
The machmeter is essentially an airspeed instrument that is calibrated in relation to Mach (the speed of sound). It contains an altitude sensing diaphragm that adjusts input to the pointer so changes in the speed of sound with altitude are incorporated. Shock waves can develop when an aircraft travels near the speed of sound that can affect flight controls and, in some cases, literally tear the aircraft apart. A maximum allowable speed is established for the aircraft during certification flight testing. The machmeter is used to ensure this speed is not exceeded.
[Ref: Airframe Handbook H-8083-31A-ATB, Chapter 10 Page 25]

10-18 Answer C.
A synchro system is an electric system used for transmitting information from one point to another. Most position indicating instruments are designed around a synchro system, such as the flap position indicator or indicators to display the position of landing gear, autopilot systems, or radar. Fluid pressure indicators also commonly used the synchro system. Fluid pressure can be directed into a remote transmitter. The motion of a pressure bellows can be geared to the transmitter rotor in such a way as to make the rotor turn. The position of an aircraft, such as the altitude above sea level or the rate of climb of the aircraft are displayed via direct reading, pressure instruments. The angle of incidence of an aircraft is fixed on most aircraft.
[Ref: Airframe Handbook H-8083-31A-ATB, Chapter 10 Page 26-28]

10-19 AMA010

1. A DC Selsyn system is a widely used electrical method of indicating a remote mechanical movement or position.
2. A synchro type indicating system is an electrical system used for transmitting information from one point to another.

Regarding the above statements,
  A. Both No. 1 and No. 2 are true.
  B. Only No. 2 is true.
  C. Only No. 1 is true.

10-20 AMA014

Which best describes the basic operation of a DC Selsyn system when transmitting information between of a remote position indicator such as wing flaps and the cockpit indicator?
  A. A transmitter sends varying voltages to an indicator motor which moves a pointer.
  B. Resistances based on the flap position are compared and sent to an indicator motor to position a pointer.
  C. A magnetic field in the transmitter is mirrored to a magnetic field in the indicator to align a pointer.

10-21 AMA010

The basic difference between an Autosyn and a Magnesyn indicating system is the
  A. rotor.
  B. transmitter.
  C. receiver.

10-22 AMA010

The rotor in a Magnasyn remote indicating system uses
  A. an electromagnet.
  B. an electromagnet and a permanent magnet.
  C. a permanent magnet.

10-23 AMA014

A mechanical accelerometer operates on the principle of
  A. gravity.
  B. rigidity in space.
  C. inertia.

10-24 AMA018

The pneumatic (reed) type stall warning system installed in some light aircraft is activated by
  A. positive air pressure.
  B. static air pressure.
  C. negative air pressure.

AIRCRAFT INSTRUMENT SYSTEMS

ANSWERS

10-19 Answer A.
A synchro system is an electric system used for transmitting information from one point to another. Most position-indicating instruments are designed around a synchro system. The common synchro system that uses direct current is called a DC Selsyn system. AC systems are known as either a Magnasyn system or an Autosyn system.
[Ref: Airframe Handbook H-8083-31A-ATB, Chapter 10 Page 26-28]

10-20 Answer C.
A circular resistance windings with three tap-offs is fed voltage by a center transmitter rotor. As the rotor changes position, the voltage at the tap-off points changes as does the magnetic field created by the voltage flowing through the resistance coil. The magnetic field change is directional. Wires transfer the resistance coil tap-off voltage to a resistance coil in the indicator. The direction of the magnetic field established in the indicator is the same as that in the transmitter. A permanent magnet is attached to the center rotor shaft in the indicator, as is the indicator pointer. The magnet and pointer align with the magnetic field for the correct indication.
[Ref: Airframe Handbook H-8083-31A-ATB, Chapter 10 Page 27]

10-21 Answer A.
Aircraft with Alternating Current (AC) electrical power systems make use of Autosyn or Magnasyn synchro remote indicating systems. Magnasyn systems use permanent magnet rotors. Autosyn systems are distinguished by the fact that the transmitter and indicator rotors are electro-magnets rather than permanent magnets.
[Ref: Airframe Handbook H-8083-31A-ATB, Chapter 10 Page 28]

10-22 Answer C.
Aircraft with alternating current (AC) electrical power systems make use of Autosyn or Magnasyn synchro remote indicating systems. Magnasyn systems use permanent magnet rotors.
[Ref: Airframe Handbook H-8083-31A-ATB, Chapter 10 Page 28]

10-23 Answer C.
Simple accelerometers are mechanical, direct reading instruments calibrated to indicate force in G's. The accelerometer operates on the principle of inertia. A mass inside is free to slide along a shaft in response to the slightest acceleration force. When a maneuver creates an acceleration force, the aircraft and instrument move but inertia causes the mass to stay at rest in space. As the shaft slides through the mass, the relative position of the mass on the shaft changes. This position corresponds to the force experienced. Through a series of pulley's, springs, and shafts, the pointers are moved on the dial to indicate the relative strength of the acceleration force.
[Ref: Airframe Handbook H-8083-31A-ATB, Chapter 10 Page 33]

10-24 Answer C.
A reed-type stall warning device is located behind an opening precisely located in the leading edge of the wing. When the angle of attack increases to near the point of stall, low pressure air flows over the opening. This causes a suction and the air leaving the wing through the opening flows past the reed which vibrates audibly to warn the pilot.
[Ref: Airframe Handbook H-8083-31A-ATB, Chapter 10 Page 34]

10-25 AMA018
Stall warning systems are generally designed to begin warning the pilot when a stall
A. is starting to occur.
B. first affects the outboard portions of the wings.
C. is imminent.

10-26 AMA010
The operation of an Angle Of Attack (AOA) indicating system is based on
A. airflow parallel to the longitudinal axis of the aircraft.
B. airflow parallel to the angle of attack of the aircraft.
C. detecting the angular difference between the relative wind and the fuselage, which is used as a reference plane.

10-27 AMA014
Which of these readings would be measured with electrical resistance type temperature indicators?
A. Cylinder Head Temperature
B. Exhaust Gas Temperature
C. Carburetor Air Temperature

10-28 AMA014
An electrical resistance thermometer
A. is used for measuring extremely high temperatures.
B. uses a bridge circuit and a variable resistor sensor.
C. compares the resistance of two dissimilar metals.

10-29 AMA098
Turbine engine exhaust gas temperatures are measured by using
A. iron/constantan thermocouples.
B. chromel/alumel thermocouples.
C. ratiometer electrical resistance thermometers.

10-30 AMA098
Which of the following is true of Exhaust Gas Temperature (EGT) and turbine inlet temperature (TIT) systems?
A. Several thermocouples are used.
B. They are high amperage devices.
C. The total voltage produced drives the indicator motor.

AIRCRAFT INSTRUMENT SYSTEMS

ANSWERS

10-25 Answer C.
A stall warning device uses an aural tone to warn of an impending stall due to an increase in angle of attack.
[Ref: Airframe Handbook H-8083-31A-ATB, Chapter 10 Page 34]

10-26 Answer C.
There are two main types of AOA sensors in common use. Both detect the angular difference between the relative wind and the fuselage, which is used as a reference plane. The slotted probe airstream direction detector measures angle of attack using two slots. The probe extends out of the side of the fuselage into the airflow. The slots lead to different sides of movable paddles in a chamber of the unit just inside the fuselage skin. As the angle of attack varies, the pressure ported by each of the slots changes and the paddles rotate to neutralize this pressure difference. The shaft upon which the paddles rotate connects to a potentiometer wiper contact. The changing resistance is used to balance a bridge circuit that signals a motor in the indicator to move the pointer proportional to the angle of attack.
[Ref: Airframe Handbook H-8083-31A-ATB, Chapter 10 Page 35]

10-27 Answer C.
Electrical resistance thermometers are used widely in many types of aircraft to measure carburetor air temperature, oil temperature, free air temperature, and more. They are used to measure low and medium temperatures in the -70°C to 150°C range. Ratiometer temperature measuring systems are used to measure engine oil, outside air, carburetor air and other temperatures in many types of aircraft. Thermocouples are used to measure high temperatures. Two common applications are the measurement of Cylinder Head Temperature (CHT) and Exhaust Gas Temperature (EGT).
[Ref: Airframe Handbook H-8083-31A-ATB, Chapter 10 Page 36-39]

10-28 Answer B.
Typically, the resistance of a metal increases as the temperature rises. An electrical resistance thermometer has a sensor that is manufactured so that it has a definite resistance for each temperature value in its working range. A bridge circuit in the indicator balances this variable resistance against the other known resistances of the circuit. A galvanometer attached across the bridge circuit, which is also the indicator pointer, indicates proportionally to the changing resistance of the sensor.
[Ref: Airframe Handbook H-8083-31A-ATB, Chapter 10 Page 37]

10-29 Answer B.
Thermocouple leads are made from a variety of metals depending on the maximum temperature to which they are exposed. Iron and constantan, or copper and constantan are common for cylinder head temperature measurement. Chromel and alumel are used for turbine engine exhaust gas temperature.
[Ref: Airframe Handbook H-8083-31A-ATB, Chapter 10 Page 39]

10-30 Answer A.
Several thermocouples are used to measure EGT or TIT. They are spaced at intervals around the perimeter of the engine exhaust duct or turbine casing. An average of the voltage produced by the thermocouples is used. The tiny thermocouple voltage is typically amplified to drive the indicator servo motor.
[Ref: Airframe Handbook H-8083-31A-ATB, Chapter 10 Page 40]

10-31 AMA014
How many of the following are controlled by gyroscopes?
1. Attitude indicator.
2. Heading indicator.
3. Turn needle of the turn and slip indicator.
 A. Three
 B. One
 C. Two

10-32 AMA036
Magnetic compass bowls are filled with a liquid to
 A. dampen the oscillation of the float.
 B. reduce deviation errors.
 C. retard precession of the float.

10-33 AMA036
Which of the following causes of aircraft magnetic compass inaccuracies may be compensated for by mechanics?
 A. Variation
 B. Magnetic Compass Current
 C. Deviation

10-34 AMA036
When swinging a magnetic compass, the compensator's are adjusted to correct for
 A. magnetic variations.
 B. compass card oscillations.
 C. magnetic influence deviation.

10-35 AMA036
A direction indicating instrument that combines the use of a gyro and a magnetic compass is called
 A. a ring gyro heading indicator.
 B. a flux gate compass.
 C. a directional gyro.

10-36 AMA036
Solid state devices containing layered structure that react to magnetism on a molecular level are called
 A. magnetrons.
 B. flux chambers.
 C. magnetometers.

AIRCRAFT INSTRUMENT SYSTEMS

ANSWERS

10-31 Answer A.
Gyroscopic instruments are essential instruments used on all aircraft. They provide the pilot with critical attitude and directional information.
[Ref: Airframe Handbook H-8083-31A-ATB, Chapter 10 Page 42-59]

10-32 Answer A.
The entire magnetic assembly of the compass is enclosed in a sealed case that is filled with a liquid similar to kerosene. This dampens vibration and oscillation of the moving float assembly and decreases friction.
[Ref: Airframe Handbook H-8083-31A-ATB, Chapter 10 Page 43]

10-33 Answer C.
Magnetic deviation is caused by influences around a compass that cause the earth magnetic field to be altered. The compass magnet aligns with the altered field. The result is a compass indication called deviation. The technician can compensate for deviation by "swinging" the compass.
[Ref: Airframe Handbook H-8083-31A-ATB, Chapter 10 Page 44]

10-34 Answer C.
The main magnets of a compass align not only with the earth's magnetic field. They align with the composite field made up of all magnetic influences around the unit such as the local electromagnetic influence from metallic structures near the compass and operation of the aircraft engine and electrical system. This is called magnetic deviation. Compensating screws move small magnets within the compass to correct for this deviation. The process for adjusting for deviation is know as swinging the compass.
[Ref: Airframe Handbook H-8083-31A-ATB, Chapter 10 Page 44]

10-35 Answer B.
An elaborate and very accurate method of direction indication has been developed that combines the use of a gyro, a magnetic compass, and a remote indicating system. It is called the slaved gyro compass or flux gate compass system. It is a gyroscopic indicator augmented by magnetic direction information from a remotely located compass.
[Ref: Airframe Handbook H-8083-31A-ATB, Chapter 10 Page 45]

10-36 Answer C.
Solid state magnetometers are used on many modern aircraft. They have no moving parts and are extremely accurate. Tiny layered structures react to magnetism on a molecular level resulting in variations in electron activity. These low-power consuming devices can sense not only direction to the earth's magnetic poles, but also the angle of the flux field. They are free from oscillation that plagues a standard magnetic compass. They feature integrated processing algorithms and easy integration with digital systems.
[Ref: Airframe Handbook H-8083-31A-ATB, Chapter 10 Page 46]

10-37 AMA014
The most common type of pump in an aircraft vacuum system is
  A. piston.
  B. centrifugal.
  C. vane.

10-38 AMA013
Which condition would be most likely to cause excessive vacuum in a vacuum system?
  A. Vacuum relief valve improperly adjusted.
  B. Vacuum pump overspeed.
  C. Vacuum relief valve spring weak.

10-39 AMA071
When flags such as NAV, HDG, or GS are displayed on an HSI, the indication is
  A. that function is operating.
  B. that function is inoperative.
  C. to call attention to deviation from the desired setting, or flight path, or heading, etc.

10-40 AMA014
A gyro spinning at high speed has a unique property called rigidity in space. This means
  A. it will spin indefinitely if all friction is removed.
  B. it cannot be moved if a force less than its mass acts upon it.
  C. the rotor of a free gyro always points in the same direction regardless of the positioning of the base.

10-41 AMA014
When a force is applied to a spinning gyroscope, the gyroscope acts as though the force came from 90 degrees further around the rotor in the direction it is spinning. This property is known as
  A. rigidity in space.
  B. displaced inertia.
  C. precession.

10-42 AMA014
Which of the following describes the principle upon which a ring laser gyro operates?
  A. A laser beam will speed up when traveling a longer distance.
  B. The wavelength of a laser beam will compress or expand when traveling in a plane of rotation.
  C. The frequency of a laser beam remains constant once generated.

AIRCRAFT INSTRUMENT SYSTEMS

ANSWERS

10-37 Answer C.
The vane-type engine-driven pump is the most common source of vacuum for gyros installed in general aviation, light aircraft. One type of engine- driven pump is geared to the engine and is connected to the lubricating system to seal, cool, and lubricate the pump. Another commonly used pump is a dry vacuum pump. It operates without external lubrication.
[Ref: Airframe Handbook H-8083-31A-ATB, Chapter 10 Page 48-49]

10-40 Answer C.
A gyroscope with two rings plus a mounting bracket is said to be a free gyro because it is free to rotate about two axis that are both perpendicular to the rotor's spin axis. Rigidity in space means that the rotor of a free gyro always points in the same direction no matter which way the base of the gyro is positioned.
[Ref: Airframe Handbook H-8083-31A-ATB, Chapter 10 Page 53]

10-38 Answer A.
Vacuum system capacity is more than is needed for operation of the instruments. An adjustable vacuum regulator is set for the vacuum desired for the instruments. Excess suction in the instrument lines is reduced when the spring-loaded valve opens to atmosphere pressure. Therefore, if the relief valve is improperly adjusted, it could cause excess vacuum in the system.
[Ref: Airframe Handbook H-8083-31A-ATB, Chapter 10 Page 50-86]

10-41 Answer C.
Precession is a second important characteristic of a spinning gyroscope. By applying force to the horizontal axis of the gyro, the applied force is resisted and motion occurs around its vertical axis.
[Ref: Airframe Handbook H-8083-31A-ATB, Chapter 10 Page 54]

10-39 Answer B.
When an electric instrument is not getting sufficient power such as an electric attitude indicator, an OFF flag will be displayed. Similarly, when power is lost or the VOR signal is weak or interrupted to a CDI, a NAV warning flag is displayed. The display of a flag indicating that a function in an instrument is not operative or, perhaps, should not be trusted, is a convention in aviation.
[Ref: Airframe Handbook H-8083-31A-ATB, Chapter 10 Page 52-58]

10-42 Answer B.
A ring laser gyro produces laser beams that travel in opposite directions around a closed triangular cavity (the ring). It is mounted aligned with one of the aircraft's axis of rotation. The wavelength of the light traveling around the ring is fixed. As the loop rotated due to the aircraft rotating around the axis with which the ring is aligned, the path that the light must travel lengthens or shortens. The light wavelengths compress or expand to complete travel around the ring as the ring changes its effective length. As the wavelengths change, the frequencies also change. By examining the difference in the frequencies of the two counter- rotating beams of light, the rate at which the path is rotating can be measured with great accuracy.
[Ref: Airframe Handbook H-8083-31A-ATB, Chapter 10 Page 54]

10-43 AMA014
In a Microelectromechanical Systems (MEMS) gyroscopes, what devise replaces the spinning gyro of the mechanical gyroscope?
A. A vibrating or oscillating piezoelectric device.
B. An electro magnet.
C. A rotating semi conductor.

10-44 AMA013
The lubber line on a directional gyro is used to
A. represent the wings of the aircraft.
B. represent the nose of the aircraft.
C. align the instrument glass in the case.

10-45 AMA014
A turn coordinator instrument indicates
A. both roll and yaw.
B. the need for corrections in pitch and bank.
C. the longitudinal attitude of the aircraft during climb and descent.

10-46 AMA025
The typical analog autopilot system flies the aircraft by using electrical signals developed
A. at the control surface mounted sensors.
B. a quadrant position sensors.
C. in gyro-sensing units.

10-47 AMA025
What are the four basic elements of an auto pilot system?
A. Sensing, feedback, control, reset.
B. Command, adjustment, control, feedback.
C. Sensing, computing, output, command.

10-48 AMA025
A flight director system
A. is integrated with the turn coordinator instrument.
B. moves the control surfaces in accordance with computer commands.
C. moves a command bar in the attitude indicator.

AIRCRAFT INSTRUMENT SYSTEMS

ANSWERS

10-43 Answer A.
The basis of operation of tiny MEMS gyroscopes is the same rigidity concept used in mechanical gyroscopes. The difference is that a vibrating or oscillating piezoelectric device replaces the spinning, weighted ring of the mechanical gyro. Once set in motion, any out-of-plane motion is detectable by the varying microvoltages or capacitances detected through geometrically arranged pickups.
[Ref: Airframe Handbook H-8083-31A-ATB, Chapter 10 Page 55]

10-44 Answer B.
On a Directional Gyro (DG), the nose of a small, fixed airplane on the instrument glass indicates the aircraft's heading.
[Ref: Airframe Handbook H-8083-31A-ATB, Chapter 10 Page 58]

10-45 Answer A.
The gyroscopic turn coordinator works on the principle of precession. The rotor of a turn coordinator is canted upwards 30°. As such, it responds not only to movement about the vertical axis, but also to roll movements about the longitudinal axis.
[Ref: Airframe Handbook H-8083-31A-ATB, Chapter 10 Page 58-59]

10-46 Answer C.
The attitude and directional gyros, the turn coordinator, and altitude control are the autopilot sensing elements. These units sense the movement of the aircraft. They generate electric signals that are used by the autopilot to automatically take the required corrective action needed to keep the aircraft flying as intended.
[Ref: Airframe Handbook H-8083-31A-ATB, Chapter 10 Page 61-64]

10-47 Answer C.
Most autopilots consist of four basic components, plus various switches and auxiliary units. The four basic components are: sensing elements, computing elements, output elements, and command elements. Many advanced autopilots contain a fifth element: feedback or follow-up.
[Ref: Airframe Handbook H-8083-31A-ATB, Chapter 10 Page 61]

10-48 Answer C.
Essentially, a flight director system is an autopilot system without the servos. All of the same sensing and computations are made, but the pilot controls the aircraft and makes maneuvers by following the command bar positioned by the flight director in the attitude indicator instrument.
[Ref: Airframe Handbook H-8083-31A-ATB, Chapter 10 Page 65]

10-49 AMA014

In addition to the information given by an attitude indicator, an Electronic Attitude Director Indicator (EADI) typically displays
- A. ILS approach information and flight director command bars.
- B. horizontal situation indicator (his) data.
- C. weather radar information and estimated time of arrival.

10-50 AMA014

The function of an EHSI is primarily to display information concerning
- A. aircraft attitude.
- B. navigation.
- C. aircraft systems.

10-51 AMA014

Data transmitted between components in an EFIS are converted into
- A. digital signals.
- B. analog signals.
- C. carrier wave signals.

10-52 AMA014

The function of a CRT in an EFIS is to
- A. allow the pilot to select the appropriate system configuration for the current flight situation.
- B. display alphanumeric data and representations of aircraft instruments.
- C. receive and process input signals from aircraft and engine sensors and send the data to the appropriate display.

10-53 AMA014

The function of a Symbol Generator (SG) in and EFIS is to
- A. receive and process input signals from aircraft and engine sensors and send the data to the appropriate display.
- B. allow the pilot to select the appropriate system configuration for the current flight situation.
- C. display alphanumeric data and representations of aircraft instruments.

10-54 AMA014

The function of a display controller in an EFIS is to
- A. display alphanumeric data and representations of aircraft instruments.
- B. receive and process input signals from aircraft and engine sensors and send the data to the appropriate display.
- C. allow the pilot to select the appropriate system configuration for the current flight situation.

AIRCRAFT INSTRUMENT SYSTEMS

ANSWERS

10-49 Answer A.
The EADI is an advanced version of attitude and electric attitude indicators. Numerous additional situational flight parameters are displayed. Most notable are those that relate to instrument approaches such as the Instrument Landing System (ILS) and the flight director command bars. Annunciation of active systems, such as the automatic flight control system and navigation systems, is typical.
[Ref: Airframe Handbook H-8083-31A-ATB, Chapter 10 Page 67]

10-50 Answer B.
The EHSI is an evolved version of the Horizontal Situation Indicator (HIS), which was born from the gyroscopic direction indicator or Directional Gyro (DG). The HIS incorporates directional information to two different navigational aids, as well as the heading of the aircraft. The EHSI does this and more. Its primary purpose is to display as much useful navigational information as possible.
[Ref: Airframe Handbook H-8083-31A-ATB, Chapter 10 Page 68]

10-51 Answer A.
Early EFIS systems have analog technology while newer models are digital systems.
[Ref: Airframe Handbook H-8083-31A-ATB, Chapter 10 Page 70]

10-52 Answer B.
In an EFIS system, digital processors or symbol generators are used to drive the CRT which displays the information selected by the pilot with the display controller.
[Ref: Airframe Handbook H-8083-31A-ATB, Chapter 10 Page 70]

10-53 Answer A.
In an EFIS system, digital processors or symbol generators are used to drive the CRT which displays the information selected by the pilot with the display controller.
[Ref: Airframe Handbook H-8083-31A-ATB, Chapter 10 Page 70]

10-54 Answer C.
Through a display controller, the pilot can select the various mode or screen features available to be displayed.
[Ref: Airframe Handbook H-8083-31A-ATB, Chapter 10 Page 70]

10-55 AMA027

The primary function of an ECAM system is to
- A. combine autopilot input with engine power settings to position the throttles.
- B. monitor engine controls to ensure programmed navigation targets are met.
- C. monitor airframe and engine parameters for the pilot.

10-56 AMA027

An Engine Indicating and Crew Alerting System (EICAS) displays full-time engine parameters on the upper screen of the two-screen, two-computer system. The bottom screen displays
- A. flight control position.
- B. navigational messages related to the programmed flight plan.
- C. secondary engine parameters and non-engine system status.

10-57 AMA027

How are ECAM and EICAS system displays controlled?
- A. Automatically depending on the position of the throttle.
- B. With touch screen prompts.
- C. Via a separate control panel.

10-58 AMA043

What is BITE?
- A. Built-In Test Equipment
- B. Built-In Test For Engines
- C. Built-In Test Envelope

10-59 AMA027

What is a Flight Management System (FMS)?
- A. A hand-off auto pilot from throttle up to after touchdown.
- B. A programmable navigation control system that guides the pilot from the starting airport to the destination airport.
- C. A master computer system that has control over all other systems.

10-60 AMA014

Cases for electrically operated instruments are made of
- A. iron or steel cases.
- B. plastic or composite cases.
- C. aluminum or Bakelite cases.

AIRCRAFT INSTRUMENT SYSTEMS

ANSWERS

10-55 Answer C.
The basic concept behind Electronic Centralized Aircraft Monitor (ECAM) is automatic performance of monitoring duties for the pilot. When a problem is detected or a failure occurs, the primary display, along with an aural and visual cue, alert the pilot. Corrective action that needs to be taken is displayed as well as suggested action due to the failure. Early ECAM systems only monitored airframe systems, however, later model ECAM systems incorporate engine monitoring as well.
[Ref: Airframe Handbook H-8083-31A-ATB, Chapter 10 Page 71]

10-56 Answer C.
EICAS provides full time primary engine parameters (EPR, N1, EGT, etc.) on the top, primary monitor. Advisory and warnings are also shown there. Secondary engine parameters and non- engine system status are displayed on the bottom monitor. The lower screen is also used for maintenance diagnosis when the aircraft is on the ground.
[Ref: Airframe Handbook H-8083-31A-ATB, Chapter 10 Page 72]

10-57 Answer C.
Display modes are selected via a separate ECAM control panel. The manual mode of an ECAM is set by pressing one of the display buttons on the control panel. The display select panel for an EICAS allows the pilot to choose which computer is actively supplying information. It also controls the display of secondary engine information and system status displays on the lower monitor.
[Ref: Airframe Handbook H-8083-31A-ATB, Chapter 10 Page 72]

10-58 Answer A.
BITE stands for Built-In Test Equipment. It is standard for monitoring systems to monitor themselves as well as the aircraft systems. ECAM flight warning computers, for example, self test upon startup. The signal generators are also tested. Further tests can be initiated manually. EICAS uses BITE for systems and components.
[Ref: Airframe Handbook H-8083-31A-ATB, Chapter 10 Page 72-73]

10-59 Answer C.
An FMS cab be thought of as a master computer system that has control over all other systems, computerized and otherwise. As such, it coordinates adjustment of flight, engine, and airframe parameters either automatically or by instructing the pilot how to do so. Literally, all aspects of the flight are considered, from preflight planning to pulling up to the Jet-way upon landing, including in-flight amendments to planned courses of action.
[Ref: Airframe Handbook H-8083-31A-ATB, Chapter 10 Page 73]

10-60 Answer A.
Electric instruments usually have a steel or iron alloy case to contain electromagnetic flux caused by current flow inside.
[Ref: Airframe Handbook H-8083-31A-ATB, Chapter 10 Page 77]

10-61 AMA088

Which simple device is required on the flight deck of all IFR certified aircraft?

A. A flashlight.
B. An AM radio.
C. A clock.

10-62 AMA013

Which of the following instrument discrepancies would require replacement of the instrument?

1. Red line missing
2. Case leaking
3. Glass cracked
4. Mounting screws loose
5. Case paint chipped
6. Leaking at line B nut
7. Will not zero out
8. Fogged

A. 1, 3, 5, and 8
B. 1, 4, 6, and 7
C. 2, 3, 7, and 8

10-63 AMA066

Instrument panel shock mounts absorb

A. low frequency, high-amplitude shocks.
B. high g-shock loads imposed by turbulent air.
C. high energy impact shocks caused by hard landings.

10-64 AMA066

An aircraft instrument panel is electrically bonded to the aircraft structure to

A. act as a restraint strap.
B. provide current return paths.
C. aid in the panel installation.

10-65 AMA066

What must be done to an instrument panel that is supported by shock mounts?

A. Bonding straps must be installed across the instrument mounts as a current path from the instrument panel to the aircraft structure.
B. The instrument mounts must be grounded to the aircraft structure as a current path.
C. The instrument mounts must be tightened to the specified torque required by the maintenance manual.

10-66 AMA018

A typical takeoff warning indication system, in addition to throttle setting, monitors the position of which of the following?

A. Ailerons, elevators, speed brake, and steerable nose wheel.
B. Fuselage landing gear.
C. Elevators, speed brake, flaps, and stabilizer trim.

AIRCRAFT INSTRUMENT SYSTEMS

ANSWERS

10-61 Answer C.
Whether called a clock or chronometer, an FAA approved time indicator is required in the cockpit of IFR certified aircraft. Pilots use a clock during flight to time maneuvers and for navigational purposes. The clock is usually mounted near the turn coordinator. It indicates hours, minutes and seconds.
[Ref: Airframe Handbook H-8083-31A-ATB, Chapter 10 Page 76]

10-62 Answer C.
A crack in an airtight instrument case renders it unairworthy. It follows that a cracked glass would as well since the integrity of the airtight unit has been breached. An instrument that will not zero is not indicating correctly and must be replaced. A fogged instrument may be difficult read and clearly contains moisture and should be replaced.
[Ref: Airframe Handbook H-8083-31A-ATB, Chapter 10 Page 77]

10-63 Answer A.
Instrument panels are usually shock-mounted to absorb low frequency, high amplitude shocks. The mounts absorb most of the vertical and horizontal vibration, but permit the instruments to operate under conditions of minor vibration.
[Ref: Airframe Handbook H-8083-31A-ATB, Chapter 10 Page 78]

10-64 Answer B.
Instrument panels are usually made of sheet aluminum alloy and are painted a dark, nonglare color. Bonding straps are used to ensure electrical continuity from the panel to the airframe.
[Ref: Airframe Handbook H-8083-31A-ATB, Chapter 10 Page 78]

10-65 Answer A.
Instrument panels are usually made of sheet aluminum alloy and are painted a dark, nonglare color. Bonding straps are used to ensure electrical continuity from the panel to the airframe.
[Ref: Airframe Handbook H-8083-31A-ATB, Chapter 10 Page 78]

10-66 Answer C.
During takeoff, the cause of a warning signal activation can occur when the throttles are advanced and any of the following exist: speed brakes are not down, flaps are not in takeoff range, auxiliary power exhaust door is open, stabilizer is not in the takeoff setting.
[Ref: Airframe Handbook H-8083-31A-ATB, Chapter 10 Page 79]

10-67 AMA013

How is a flangeless instrument case mounted in an instrument panel?
- A. By four machine screws which extend through the instrument panel.
- B. By an expanding type clamp secured to the back of the panel and tightened by a screw from the front of the instrument panel.
- C. By a metal shelf separate from and located behind the instrument panel.

10-68 AMA013

The method of mounting aircraft instruments in their respective panel depends on the
- A. instrument manufacturer.
- B. design of the instrument panel.
- C. design of the instrument case.

10-69 AMA013

Aircraft instruments should be marked and graduated in accordance with
- A. both the aircraft and engine manufacturers' specifications.
- B. the instrument manufacturer's specifications.
- C. the specific aircraft maintenance or flight manual.

10-70 AMA013
1. Aircraft instruments are color-coded to direct attention to operational ranges and limitations.
2. Aircraft instruments range markings are not specified by Title 14 of the code of Federal Regulations but are standardized by aircraft manufacturers.

Regarding the above statements,
- A. Only No. 1 is true.
- B. Both No. 1 and No. 2 are true.
- C. Only No. 2 is true.

10-71 AMA090

Which of the following instrument discrepancies could be corrected by an aviation mechanic?
1. Red Line Missing
2. Case Leaking
3. Glass Cracked
4. Mounting Screws Loose
5. Case Paint Chipped
6. Leaking At Line B Nut
7. Will Not Adjust
8. Fogged
- A. 1, 4, and 6
- B. 1, 4, 5, and 6
- C. 3, 4, 5, and 6

10-72 AMA090

A certificated mechanic may perform
- A. minor repairs to instruments.
- B. instrument overhaul.
- C. 100-hour inspections of instruments.

AIRCRAFT INSTRUMENT SYSTEMS

ANSWERS

10-67 Answer B.
To mount a flangeless instrument, a special clamp, shaped and dimensioned to fit the instrument case, is permanently secured to the rear face of the instrument panel. The instrument is slid into the panel from the front and into the clamp. The clamp's tightening screw is accessible from the front side of the panel.
[Ref: Airframe Handbook H-8083-31A-ATB, Chapter 10 Page 80]

10-68 Answer C.
The method of mounting instruments in their respective panels depends on the design of the instrument case. Flanged and flangeless instrument cases are employed and mounting systems for each type of instrument case are used.
[Ref: Airframe Handbook H-8083-31A-ATB, Chapter 10 Page 80]

10-69 Answer C.
Instrument range markings are put on the instrument by the original equipment manufacturer in accordance with the aircraft specifications on the type certificate data sheet. Data describing these limitations can also sometimes be found in the aircraft manufacturer's operating and maintenance manuals.
[Ref: Airframe Handbook H-8083-31A-ATB, Chapter 10 Page 81]

10-70 Answer A.
Many instruments contain markings on the dial face to indicate, at a glance, whether a particular system or component is within a range of operation that is safe and desirable or if an undesirable condition exists. These markings are put on the instrument by the original equipment manufacturer in accordance with the Aircraft Specifications on the FAA Type Certificate Data Sheet.
[Ref: Airframe Handbook H-8083-31A-ATB, Chapter 10 Page 81]

10-71 Answer B.
Occasionally, the aircraft technician may find it necessary to apply range marking to an instrument. Correcting a "B" nut leak and tightening mounting screws are not maintenance on an instrument. Touching up the paint on the outside of an instrument case is permitted. FAA airframe and powerplant technicians are not qualified to do internal maintenance on an instrument.
[Ref: Airframe Handbook H-8083-31A-ATB, Chapter 10 Page 81]

10-72 Answer C.
An FAA airframe and powerplant technician is not qualified to do internal maintenance on instruments and related line replaceable units. However, licensed airframe technicians and A&P technicians are charged with a wide variety of maintenance functions related to instrument systems. Installation, removal, inspection, troubleshooting, and functional checks are all performed in the field by licensed personnel.
[Ref: Airframe Handbook H-8083-31A-ATB, Chapter 10 Page 81]

10-73 AMA013
The red radial lines on the face of an engine oil pressure gauge indicates
A. minimum engine safe RPM operating range.
B. minimum precautionary safe operating range.
C. minimum and/or maximum safe operating limits.

10-76 AMA090
When installing an instrument in an aircraft, who is responsible for making sure it is properly marked?
A. The instrument manufacturer
B. The aircraft owner
C. The instrument installer

10-74 AMA013
Which procedure should you use if you find a vacuum operated instrument glass loose?
A. Mark the case and glass with a slippage mark.
B. Replace the glass.
C. Install another instrument.

10-77 AMA013
How would an airspeed indicator be marked to show the best rate of climb speed (one engine inoperative)?
A. A green arc.
B. A blue radial line.
C. A red radial line.

10-75 AMA070
The requirements for testing and inspection of instrument static systems required by Section 91.411 are contained in
A. AC 43.13-1B.
B. Type Certificate Data Sheets.
C. Part 43, Appendix E.

10-78 AMA013
How many of the following instruments will normally have range markings?
1. Airspeed indicator
2. Altimeter
3. Cylinder head temperature gauge
A. Two
B. One
C. Three

AIRCRAFT INSTRUMENT SYSTEMS

ANSWERS

10-73 Answer C.
The colors used in range markings are red, yellow, green, blue, or white. The markings can be in the form of an arc or a radial line. Red is used to indicate maximum and minimum ranges; operations beyond these markings are dangerous and should be avoided.
[Ref: Airframe Handbook H-8083-31A-ATB, Chapter 10 Page 81-82]

10-74 Answer C.
A loose glass on a vacuum operated instrument compromises the integrity of the vacuum system. The aircraft technician is responsible for the prevention or correction of vacuum system malfunctions. Since an FAA airframe and powerplant technician is not qualified to do internal maintenance on instruments, another instrument must be installed.
[Ref: Airframe Handbook H-8083-31A-ATB, Chapter 10 Page 81-85]

10-75 Answer C.
When an aircraft is to be operated under Instrument Flight Rules (IFR), an altimeter test must have been performed within the previous 24 months. Title 14 of the Code of Federal Regulations (14CFR) part 91, section 91.411, requires this test, as well as tests on the pitot-static system and on the automatic pressure altitude reporting system. The licensed airframe or A&P mechanic is not qualified to perform the altimeter inspection. They must be conducted by either the manufacturer or a certified repair station. 14CFR part 43, Appendix E and F detail the requirements for these tests.
[Ref: Airframe Handbook H-8083-31A-ATB, Chapter 10 Page 82]

10-76 Answer C.
An FAA airframe and powerplant technician is not qualified to do internal maintenance on instruments and related line replaceable units.
However, licensed airframe technicians and A&P technicians are charged with a wide variety of maintenance functions related to instrument systems. Installation, removal, inspection, troubleshooting, and functional checks are all performed in the field by licensed personnel. It is also a responsibility of the licensed technician holding an airframe rating to know what maintenance is required and to access the approved procedures for meeting those requirements.
[Ref: Airframe Handbook H-8083-31A-ATB, Chapter 10 Page 82]

10-77 Answer B.
On an airspeed indicator, a blue radial line is used to indicate the best single-engine rate-of-climb airspeed.
[Ref: Airframe Handbook H-8083-31A-ATB, Chapter 10 Page 82]

10-78 Answer A.
Altimeters do not have instrument range makings.
[Ref: Airframe Handbook H-8083-31A-ATB, Chapter 10 Page 82]

10-79 AMA077

Instrument static system leakage can be detected by observing the rate of change in indication of the

A. airspeed indicator after suction has been applied to the static system to cause a prescribed equivalent airspeed to be indicated.

B. altimeter after suction has been applied to the static system to cause a prescribed equivalent altitude to be indicated.

C. altimeter after pressure has been applied to the static system to cause a prescribed equivalent altitude to be indicated.

10-80 AMA096

The maximum altitude loss permitted during an unpressurized aircraft instrument static pressure system integrity check is

A. 200 feet in 1 minute.

B. 100 feet in 1 minute.

C. 50 feet in 1 minute.

10-81 AMA096

When an unpressurized aircraft's static pressure system is leak checked to comply with the requirements of Section 91.411, what aircraft instrument may be used in lieu of a pitot-static system tester?

1. Vertical Speed Indicator
2. Cabin Altimeter
3. Altimeter
4. Cabin Rate-Of-Change Indicator

A. 2 or 4

B. 1 or 5

C. 3

10-82 AMA096

If a static pressure system check reveals excessive leakage the leak(s) may be located by

A. pressurizing the system and adding leak detection dye.

B. isolating portions of the line and testing each portion systematically, starting at the instrument connections.

C. removing and visually inspecting the line segments.

10-83 AMA036

An aircraft magnetic compass is swung to up-date the compass correction card when?

A. The compass is serviced.

B. Equipment is added that could effect compass deviation.

C. An annual inspection is accomplished on the aircraft.

10-84 AMA036

The maximum deviation (during level flight) permitted in a compensated magnetic direction indicator installed on an aircraft certificated under Federal Aviation Regulation Part 23 is

A. 10°.

B. 6°.

C. 8°.

AIRCRAFT INSTRUMENT SYSTEMS

ANSWERS

10-79 Answer B.
A testing device is connected into the static system at the static vent end, and pressure is reduced in the system by the amount required to indicate 1000 feet on the altimeter. Then the system is sealed and observed for one minute. A loss of altitude of more than 100 feet is not permissible.
[Ref: Airframe Handbook H-8083-31A-ATB, Chapter 10 Page 83]

10-82 Answer B.
When leak checking a static system, pressure is reduced in the system by the amount to indicate 1000 feet on the altimeter. Then, the system is sealed and observed for one minute. A loss of altitude of more than 100 feet is not permissible. If a leak exists, a systematic check of portions of the system is conducted until the leak is isolated. Most leaks occur at fittings.
[Ref: Airframe Handbook H-8083-31A-ATB, Chapter 10 Page 83]

10-80 Answer B.
A testing device is connected into the static system at the static vent end, and pressure is reduced in the system by the amount required to indicate 1000 feet on the altimeter. Then the system is sealed and observed for one minute. A loss of altitude of more than 100 feet is not permissible.
[Ref: Airframe Handbook H-8083-31A-ATB, Chapter 10 Page 83]

10-83 Answer B.
Follow the aircraft manufacturer's for method and frequency of swinging the magnetic compass. This is usually accomplished at flight hour or calendar intervals. Compass calibration is also performed when a new electric component is installed on the flight deck, such as a new radio. A complete list of conditions requiring a compass swing and procedure can be found in FAA Advisory Circular (AC) 43.13-1 (as revised), Chapter 12-37.
[Ref: Airframe Handbook H-8083-31A-ATB, Chapter 10 Page 84]

10-81 Answer C.
The method of leak testing depends on the type of aircraft, its pitot static system, and the testing equipment available. Essentially, pressure is reduced in the static system by the amount to indicate 1000 feet on the altimeter. Then, the system is sealed and observed for one minute.
[Ref: Airframe Handbook H-8083-31A-ATB, Chapter 10 Page 83]

10-84 Answer A.
Once a compensated magnetic direction indicator (compass) has been swung, the aircraft is returned to alignment with the North-South radial of the airport compass rose and the indication is recorded. Up to 10° deviation is allowed. The aircraft is aligned with radials every 30 degrees around the compass rose and the compass indications are recorded on the compass compensation card.
[Ref: Airframe Handbook H-8083-31A-ATB, Chapter 10 Page 85]

ORAL EXAM

10-1(O). What are the basic components of an auto pilot system?

10-2(O). Explain the operation of a magnetic compass.

10-3(O). Explain the basic procedure for swinging a compass.

10-4(O). Explain the purpose and operation of a gyroscopic instrument.

10-5(O). How does a pitot and static system operate?

10-6(O). What are the 14 CFR 43 and/or 91 requirements for static system checks?

10-7(O). Describe instrument range markings and their various meanings.

AIRCRAFT INSTRUMENT SYSTEMS

ANSWERS

ORAL EXAM

10-1(O).   The four basic components of an autopilot system are: the sensing elements, the computing element, the output elements, and the command elements. Many advanced autopilots contain a fifth element known as the feedback, or follow-up element. The sensing elements include the attitude and directional gyro, the turn coordinator, and an altitude sensing device. These can be instrument mounted or remotely mounted. The most modern autopilots use solid-state devices rather than gyros. The sensing elements provide input signals to the autopilot computer. The computing element of an autopilot system may be analog or digital. Its function is to interpret sensing element data, integrate commands and navigational input, and send signals to the output element to move the flight controls as required. The output elements are the servos that cause actuation of the flight control surfaces. Systems are usually electric, electro-pneumatic, or electro-hydraulic in operation. The command element, often known as the flight controller, is the human interface of the autopilot. It is the means for the pilot to tell the autopilot system what to do. The feedback or follow-up element provides signals that slow the adjustment of control surfaces as they reach the position required so that the aircraft does not continually over correct its position. Transducers on the surface actuators or the autopilot servo units accomplish the reduction in control surface deflection. In a rate autopilot, control surface pickups cancel error messages when the surface has been moved to the correct position.
           [Ref: Airframe Handbook H-8083-31A-ATB, Chapter 10 Page 61-64]

10-2(O).   A magnetic compass is comprised of permanent magnets that are free to move. They naturally align themselves with the earth's magnetic field. An indicating "lubber line" attached to the magnets displays direction on a graduated dial which allows 360° of movement and indication. The magnetic compass magnets are influenced by other magnetic fields in addition to the earth's. Therefore, precautions must be made during flight deck installations to guard the compass from these influences that cause deviation. Users must also note magnetic variation caused by the earth's magnetic field not being exactly aligned with the geographic landmarks such as the north and south poles. Dip error also occurs when operating near the poles.
           [Ref: Airframe Handbook H-8083-31A-ATB, Chapter 10 Page 43-44]

10-3(O).   Swinging a compass is performed to reduce magnetic deviation caused by electromagnetic interference from onboard aircraft equipment. A compass rose, usually painted somewhere on the surface of the airport, is required or one must be made. Either should be located away from any possible electromagnetic influences on the compass. Follow the manufacturer's instructions. The aircraft should be placed in normal flight attitude with normal equipment operating and the engine(s) running. Use a non-ferrous screwdriver to make adjustments to the compass. Begin by aligning the aircraft with the compass rose facing north (0° or 360°). Rotate the adjusting screws on the compass so that the indication is 0° or 360°. Then, position the aircraft so that it is aligned with east on the compass rose. Rotate the adjusting screws on the compass so that the compass indicates 90°. Reposition the aircraft to be facing south aligned with the compass rose. If the compass indicates 180°, no adjustment is made. If it does not, rotate the adjusting screws on the compass so that 2 of the deviation from 180° is removed. Finally, align the aircraft of the compass rose facing west (270°). Rotate the adjusting crews to removed 2 of any deviation from an indication of 270°. Align the aircraft with the compass rose radials every 30°. Record the indications on the compass correction card which should be displayed near the compass on the flight deck. Date and sign the card and ensure it is in full view to the pilot.
           [Ref: Airframe Handbook H-8083-31A-ATB, Chapter 10 Page 85]

ORAL EXAM

10-4(O). Most gyroscopic instruments are used for direction or attitude indication. They can be driven by air pressure, vacuum, or electricity since the spinning armature of a motor can act as a gyroscope. When rotating, a gyroscope possesses unique characteristics. One is rigidity in space. That is, it will continue to rotate in the same plane of rotation no matter which way its mounting gimbals are moved. This is the basis of the directional gyro. The directional gyro, or DG, is commonly relied upon more than a magnetic compass to indicate direction in an aircraft. The gyro spins in the vertical plane and stays aligned with the direction to which it is set. The instrument case and aircraft move around the rigid gyro. This causes a vertical compass card geared to the rotor gimbal to rotate. Typically, a small fixed airplane in front of the moving card indicates the direction in degrees.
[Ref: Airframe Handbook H-8083-31A-ATB, Chapter 10 Page 58]

10-5(O). A pitot system is designed to capture the impact air pressure caused by the aircraft moving forward through the atmosphere. Typically, air enters the system through an opening in the end of a pitot tube that is directed into the relative wind. Airtight tubing conveys this sensed pressure to the airspeed indicator and to the digital air data computer (if in use). The pressure is used to calculate and display airspeed. The static system is designed to sense ambient atmospheric pressure. Input air is either from static ports in the pitot tube, or from dedicated flush-mounted, heated, static ports located on the sides of the fuselage. The pressure is conveyed through a series of airtight tubes to the instruments that require the use of atmospheric pressure. This includes the airspeed indicator, the variometer and the altimeter. On a modern more complex aircraft, the static system conveys ambient air pressure to a digital air data computer. In addition to the instruments mentioned, the computer processes ambient air pressure outputs for the auto-pilot system, the transponder, the flight management computers, IRS navigation units and more.
[Ref: Airframe Handbook H-8083-31A-ATB, Chapter 10 Page 12-17]

10-6(O). Aircraft static systems must be tested for leaks after the installation of any component parts or when system malfunction is suspected. It must also be tested every 24 months if on an IFR certified aircraft intended to be flown as such. This is specified in 14 CFR 91.411. Licensed airframe and A&P technicians may perform this check. A test unit is used to check the system. It is attached to the static port end of the static system. Air pressure is then reduced by the test unit until it causes 1000 feet to be indicated on the altimeter. This pressure is held for 1 minute. A reduction of altitude indication of more than 100 feet is not allowed. Systematic leak checking must be performed until the leak is located, repaired, and the static system passes the check.
[Ref: Airframe Handbook H-8083-31A-ATB, Chapter 10 Page 38]

10-7(O). Many instruments contain colored markings on the dial face to indicate, at a glance, whether a particular system or component is within a range of operation that is safe and desirable or if an undesirable condition exists. These markings are put on the instrument by the original equipment manufacturer in accordance with the aircraft specifications in the Type Certificate Data Sheet. Data describing these limitations may also sometimes be found in the aircraft manufacturer's operating and maintenance manuals. Occasionally, the airframe technician may find it necessary to apply these markings. Application must only be in accordance with approved data. The marks can be in the form of a colored arc, or, as a radial line. Red is used to indicate maximum and minimum range values. Green indicates normal operating range. Yellow is used to indicate caution. Blue and white are used on airspeed indicators to define specific conditions.
[Ref: Airframe Handbook H-8083-31A-ATB, Chapter 10 Page 81]

AIRCRAFT INSTRUMENT SYSTEMS

QUESTIONS

PRACTICAL EXAM

10-1(P).   Given an actual aircraft or mockup, appropriate publications, and the appropriate testing equipment, if necessary, remove and install an aircraft instrument.

10-2(P).   Given an actual aircraft or mockup, appropriate publications, and the appropriate testing equipment, if necessary, accomplish a magnetic compass swing.

10-3(P).   Given an actual aircraft or mockup of an aircraft instrument, determine the range or limit markings.

10-4(P).   Given an actual aircraft or mockup, appropriate publications, and the appropriate testing equipment, if necessary, remove, inspect, and install a vacuum system filter and record your findings.

10-5(P).   Given an actual aircraft or mockup, appropriate publications, and the appropriate testing equipment, if necessary, remove, inspect, and install a pressure system filter and record your findings.

10-6(P).   Given an actual aircraft or mockup, appropriate publications, and the appropriate testing equipment, if necessary, determine the proper setting of a vacuum system.

10-7(P).   Given an actual aircraft or mockup, appropriate publications, and the appropriate testing equipment, if necessary, determine the proper setting of a pressure system.

10-8(P).   Given an actual aircraft or mockup, appropriate publications, and the appropriate testing equipment, if necessary, inspect a vacuum operated instrument power system and record your findings.

10-9(P).   Given an actual aircraft or mockup, appropriate publications, and the appropriate testing equipment, if necessary, inspect a pressure operated instrument power system and record your findings.

10-10(P).   Given an actual aircraft or mockup, appropriate publications, and the appropriate testing equipment, if necessary, inspect an electrically operated instrument power system and record your findings.

10-11(P).   Given an actual aircraft or mockup, appropriate publications, and the appropriate testing equipment, if necessary, troubleshoot a vacuum operated instrument power system and record your findings.

10-12(P).   Given an actual aircraft or mockup, appropriate publications, and the appropriate testing equipment, if necessary, troubleshoot a pressure operated instrument power system and record your findings.

10-13(P).   Given an actual aircraft or mockup, appropriate publications, and the appropriate testing equipment, if necessary, troubleshoot an electrically operated instrument power system and record your findings.

10-14(P).   Given an actual aircraft or mockup, appropriate publications, and the appropriate testing equipment, if necessary, inspect the pitot-static system or a portion thereof and record your findings.

10-15(P).   Given an altimeter, find the barometric pressure.

10-16(P).   Given an actual aircraft or mockup, appropriate publications, and the appropriate testing equipment, if necessary, inspect an electrically operated engine temperature instrument and record your findings.

10-17(P).   Given an actual aircraft or mockup, appropriate publications, and the appropriate testing equipment, if necessary, inspect an electrically operated pressure instrument and record your findings.

10-18(P).   Given an actual aircraft or mockup, appropriate publications, and the appropriate testing equipment, if necessary, inspect an electrically operated RPM instrument and record your findings.

PRACTICAL EXAM

10-19(P). Given an actual aircraft or mockup, appropriate publications, and the appropriate testing equipment, if necessary, inspect an electrically operated rate of flow instrument and record your findings.

10-20(P). Given an actual aircraft or mockup, appropriate publications, and the appropriate testing equipment, if necessary, inspect a mechanically operated rate of flow instrument and record your findings.

10-21(P). Given an actual aircraft or mockup, appropriate publications, and the appropriate testing equipment, if necessary, inspect a mechanically operated RPM instrument and record your findings.

10-22(P). Given an actual aircraft or mockup, appropriate publications, and the appropriate testing equipment, if necessary, inspect a mechanically operated pressure instrument and record your findings.

10-23(P). Given an actual aircraft or mockup, appropriate publications, and the appropriate testing equipment, if necessary, inspect a mechanically operated temperature instrument and record your findings.

10-24(P). Given an actual aircraft or mockup, verify the proper operation and markings of an indicating system and record your findings.

10-25(P). Given an actual aircraft or mockup, replace a temperature-sensing unit and record the maintenance.

10-26(P). Given an actual aircraft or mockup, and the appropriate publications, remove, inspect, and install fuel flow transmitter and record your findings.

10-27(P). Given an actual aircraft or mockup, appropriate publications, and the appropriate testing equipment, if necessary, troubleshoot an oil pressure indicating system and record your findings.

10-28(P). Given an actual aircraft or mockup, appropriate publications, and the appropriate testing equipment, if necessary, locate and inspect a fuel flow component on an engine and record your findings.

10-29(P). Given an actual aircraft or mockup, appropriate publications, and the appropriate testing equipment, if necessary, replace an Exhaust Gas Temperature (EGT) indication probe and record the maintenance.

10-30(P). Given an actual aircraft or mockup, appropriate publications, and the appropriate testing equipment, if necessary, troubleshoot a manifold pressure gage that is slow to indicate the correct reading and record your findings.

10-31(P). Given an actual aircraft or mockup, appropriate publications, and the appropriate testing equipment, if necessary, inspect a flap position indication system and record your findings.

10-32(P). Given an actual aircraft or mockup, appropriate publications, and the appropriate testing equipment, if necessary, adjust a flap position indicating system and record maintenance.

10-33(P). Given an actual aircraft or mockup, appropriate publications, accomplish an operational check of a flap indicating and/or warning system and record maintenance and findings, if any.

PAGE LEFT BLANK INTENTIONALLY

COMMUNICATION AND NAVIGATION

Aircraft Communication Systems, Aircraft Navigational Systems, Amplifiers, Electronic Oscillation, and Types of Navigational Equipment

CHAPTER
11

QUESTIONS

11-1 AMA027
Analog electrical representations of real world phenomenon are
- A. continuous.
- B. discontinuous.
- C. incremental.

11-4 AMA041
Diodes, triodes, tetrodes, and pentodes are useful in
- A. electron control valves.
- B. electronic relays.
- C. low-power solid-state circuits.

11-2 AMA027
Is noise more or less of an issue with digitized data compared to analog representation of the same information?
- A. More because if the signal contains noise, it cannot be removed.
- B. More because of amplification in the final stage.
- C. Less because the real world phenomenon is represented by a series of ones and zeros.

11-5 AMA041
An atomic characteristic shared by conductors is
- A. a full electron valence shell.
- B. an electron valence shell with two electrons.
- C. an electron valence shell with one or three electrons.

11-3 AMA041
A diode allows
- A. a current to flow during both halves of the AC (alternating current) cycle.
- B. a current to flow during half of the AC (alternating current) cycle.
- C. a DC current to flow but blocks AC current.

11-6 AMA058
Pure silicon is
- A. a conductor.
- B. an insulator.
- C. a semiconductor.

COMMUNICATION AND NAVIGATION

ANSWERS

11-1 Answer A.
Analog representations of real world phenomenon are continuous. Some aspect of an electric signal is modified proportionally to the real world item that is being represented. Analog signals are continuous voltage modified by all external events, including those that are not desired called noise.
[Ref: Airframe Handbook H-8083-31A-ATB, Chapter 11 Page 3-4]

11-2 Answer C.
Noise is any alteration of the represented real world phenomenon that is not intended or desired. During the processing of digitized data, there is little or no signal degradation. The real world phenomenon is represented in a string of binary code. A series of ones and zeros are electronically created as a sequence of voltage or no voltage and carried through the processing stages. Once established, it is relatively immune to outside alteration. If a signal is close to the set value of the voltage, it is considered to be that voltage. If the signal is close to zero, it is considered to be no voltage. Small variations or modifications from undesired phenomenon are ignored.
[Ref: Airframe Handbook H-8083-31A-ATB, Chapter 11 Page 4]

11-3 Answer B.
A diode acts as a check valve in an Alternating Current (AC) circuit. It allows current to flow during half of the AC cycle but not the other half. In this manner it creates a pulsating Direct Current (DC) with current that drops to zero in between pulses.
[Ref: Airframe Handbook H-8083-31A-ATB, Chapter 11 Page 4]

11-4 Answer A.
Electron control valves are an essential part of an electronic circuit. Control of electron flow enables the circuit to produce the desired outcome. A diode acts as an electron check valve. A triode is often used to control a large amount of current with a smaller amount of current. A tetrode is used at higher frequencies than a triode. A pentode is especially useful in high power circuits. All are considered electron control valves.
[Ref: Airframe Handbook H-8083-31A-ATB, Chapter 11 Page 4-6]

11-5 Answer C.
In atoms with an incomplete valence shell, the electrons are bound less strongly to the nucleus. Electrons in incomplete shells may move freely from valence shell to valence shell of different atoms or compound. These are known as free electrons. The movement of electrons is known as electric current or current flow. When electrons move freely from atom to atom or compound to compound, the substance is known as a conductor. The valence shells of elements that are common conductors have one or three electrons (i.e. Copper-1, Silver – 1, Gold – 1, Aluminum – 3).
[Ref: Airframe Handbook H-8083-31A-ATB, Chapter 11 Page 7]

11-6 Answer B.
Pure silicon has 4 electrons in the valence shell of each atom. As such it combines readily with itself and forms a lattice of silicon atoms in which adjacent atoms share electrons to fill out the valence shell of each to the maximum of eight electrons. Once bound together, the valence shells of each silicon atom are complete. In this state, movement of electrons does not occur easily. There are no free electrons. Therefore, silicon in this form is a good insulator.
[Ref: Airframe Handbook H-8083-31A-ATB, Chapter 11 Page 7-8]

11-7 AMA058

Silicon is doped to create

    A. N-type and P-type semiconductors.

    B. N-type semiconductors.

    C. P-type semiconductors.

11-8 AMA058

A semiconductor diode has a junction area between N-type semiconductor material and P- type semiconductor material. When the electrons of the N-type material fill in the valence shells of the P-type material, this junction area is said to be

    A. neutralized.

    B. depleted.

    C. doped.

11-9 AMA041

In a semiconductor diode, what determines whether electricity can flow

    A. the type of semiconductor used.

    B. the width of the depletion area.

    C. the total resistance of the circuit.

11-10 AMA041

Avalanche current flows when a

    A. diode is forward biased and excessive voltage is applied.

    B. transistor base electrode receives current flow and triggers collector – emitter current flow.

    C. diode is reversed biased and excessive voltage is applied.

11-11 AMA041

A transistor is

    A. a reversed biased diode.

    B. a sandwich of dissimilar semiconductor material.

    C. a control valve with two terminals.

11-12 AMA015

Which device can be used instead of a resister as a dimmer for lighting?

    A. UJT

    B. SCR

    C. FET

ANSWERS

11-7 Answer A.
When silicon is doped with an element or compound containing five electrons in its valence shell, the result is a negatively charged material due to the excess free electrons and the fact that electrons are negatively charged. This is known as an N-type semiconductor. Doping silicon can also be performed with an element that has only three valence electrons such as boron, gallium, or indium. This results in many valence shells where there are only seven electrons. This greatly changes the properties of the material and encourages electron flow. This type of doped silicon is known as P-type semiconductor material.
[Ref: Airframe Handbook H-8083-31A-ATB, Chapter 11 Page 8]

11-8 Answer B.
When joined, the junction of N-type semiconductor material and P-type semiconductor material exhibits unique properties. Since there are holes in the P-type material, free electrons from the N-type material are attracted to fill these holes. Once combined, the area at the junction of the two materials where this happens is said to be depleted. There are no longer free electrons or holes.
[Ref: Airframe Handbook H-8083-31A-ATB, Chapter 11 Page 9]

11-9 Answer B.
The depletion area at the junction of two semiconductors materials constitutes a barrier or potential hill. The intensity of the potential hill is proportional to the width of the depletion area. A voltage source attached to the diode with the negative terminal attached to the N-type material forces electrons towards the junction area. The depletion area narrows and current can flow. A reverse bias (with the negative voltage source attached to the P-type material) widens the depletion area, thus blocking the flow of electricity.
[Ref: Airframe Handbook H-8083-31A-ATB, Chapter 11 Page 9-10]

11-10 Answer C.
A small amount of current does flow through a semiconductor diode when it is reversed biased. This is known as leakage current and it is in the micro amperage range. However, at a certain voltage, the blockage of current flow in a reversed bias diode breaks down completely. The voltage is known as avalanche voltage because the diode can no longer hold back the current and the diode fails.
[Ref: Airframe Handbook H-8083-31A-ATB, Chapter 11 Page 11]

11-11 Answer B.
A transistor is little more than a sandwich of N-type semiconductor material between two pieces of P-type semiconductor material or visa versa. The emitter and the collector are on the outside of the sandwiched semiconductor material. The center material is known as the base. A change in a relatively small amount of voltage applied to the base of the transistor allows a relatively large amount of current to flow from the collector to the emitter. Therefore, the transistor is a control valve but it has three terminals; one for the emitter, one for the base, and one for the collector.
[Ref: Airframe Handbook H-8083-31A-ATB, Chapter 11 Page 11]

11-12 Answer B.
A slight modification to the four-layer Shockley diode creates a Silicon Controlled Rectifier (SCR). An additional terminal gate is added. SCR's can be used to produce variable DC voltages for motors and are found in welding power supplies. Often, lighting dimmer switches use SCR's to reduce the average voltage applied to the lights by only allowing current flow during part of the AC cycle, this is controlled by controlling the pulses to the SCR gate and eliminating the massive heat dissipation caused when using resistors to reduce voltage.
[Ref: Airframe Handbook H-8083-31A-ATB, Chapter 11 Page 13-14]

11-13 AMA041

Which device uses and controls both polarities of an AC power source?

A. SCR
B. Triac
C. Diode

11-14 AMA041

When enough reversed bias voltage is applied to the gate of a FET?

A. The channel widens and current flows.
B. The gate will burn out.
C. The channel narrows and current flow is cut off.

11-15 AMA041

Which of the following statements are true concerning MOSFET's?

1. They are analogous to normally open and normally closed switches.
2. They are used in pairs when constructing integrated circuits.
3. They are used in the construction of digital logic gates.
4. They come in N-channel only.
5. Millions are used to construct integrated circuits.

A. 1, 2, and 5
B. 4 only
C. 1, 2, 3, and 5

11-16 AMA041

The color of a light emitting diode depends on

A. the amount of current applied.
B. the size of the PN junction.
C. the type of material used.

11-17 AMA041

A rectifier

A. changes AC voltage to pulsating DC voltage.
B. changes DC voltage into full wave AC voltage.
C. eliminates the peaks and valleys in AC voltage.

11-18 AMA027

What is the function of an amplifier?

A. To change DC voltage to AC voltage
B. To change the amplitude of an electric signal
C. To change the frequency of an electric signal

ANSWERS

11-13 Answer B.
SCR's are limited to allowing current flow in one direction only. To access the voltage in the reverse cycle of an AC power source, a triac can be used. A triac is also a 4-layer semiconductor device. It differs from an SCR in that it allows current flow in both directions. A triac has a gate that works the same way as in an SCR; however, a positive or negative pulse to the gate triggers current flow in a triac. The pulse polarity determines the direction of the current flow through the device.
[Ref: Airframe Handbook H-8083-31A-ATB, Chapter 11 Page 16]

11-14 Answer C.
In an FET, the channel is the substrate through which the controlled current flows. The polarity and amount of voltage applied to the gate can widen or narrow the channel due to the expansion or shrinking of the depletion area at the junction of the semiconductors. This increases or decreases the amount of current that can flow through the channel. Enough reversed biased voltage can be applied to the gate to prevent the flow of current through the channel. This allows the FET to be used as a switch.
[Ref: Airframe Handbook H-8083-31A-ATB, Chapter 11 Page 17]

11-15 Answer C.
MOSFETS come with N-channels or P-channels. They can be constructed as depletion mode or enhancement mode devices. This is analogous to a switch being normally opened or normally closed. Depletion mode MOSFET's have an open channel that is restricted or closed when voltage is applied to the gate (i.e. normally open). Enhancement mode MOSFET's allow no current to flow at zero bias but create a channel for current to flow when voltage is applied to the gate (normally closed). Millions of enhancement mode MOSFET's are used in the construction of integrated circuits. They are installed in complementary pairs such that when one pair is open, the other is closed. Through the use of these transistors, digital logic gates can be formed and digital circuitry is constructed.
[Ref: Airframe Handbook H-8083-31A-ATB, Chapter 11 Page 17]

11-16 Answer C.
When a free electron from a semiconductor drops into a semiconductor hole, energy is given off. This is true in all semiconductor materials. The energy released in certain materials is in the frequency range of visible light. From these various materials, LED's are constructed. Different materials at different voltages produce different colors when the energy is given off.
[Ref: Airframe Handbook H-8083-31A-ATB, Chapter 11 Page 18-19, Figure 11-41]

11-17 Answer A.
Rectifier circuits change AC voltage into DC voltage and are one of the most commonly used type of circuits in aircraft electronics. When the AC voltage cycles below zero, the diode shuts off and does not allow current to flow until the AC cycles through zero voltage again. The result is pronounced pulsing DC.
[Ref: Airframe Handbook H-8083-31A-ATB, Chapter 11 Page 20]

11-18 Answer B.
An amplifier is a circuit that changes the amplitude of an electric signal. This is done through the use of transistors.
[Ref: Airframe Handbook H-8083-31A-ATB, Chapter 11 Page 21]

11-19 AMA041

In a transistor amplifier, Beta (β) refers to

A. the amount of output current produced.
B. the amount of input current capacity.
C. the ratio of collector current to base current.

11-20 AMA041

When creating AC voltage from DC voltage, a _____ circuit is used.

A. transformer
B. amplifier
C. oscillator

11-21 AMA090

Maintenance of the interior electronics of most avionics devices is performed

A. only by certified repair stations and trained avionics technicians.
B. by holders of an airframe certification.
C. only by the avionics manufacturer.

11-22 AMA041

A digital logic gate is

A. a diode that returns current to the source.
B. used to apply power to an avionics device.
C. constructed with transistors.

11-23 AMA041

The three basic logic gates are

A. AND, OR, NOR.
B. AND, OR, NOT.
C. AND, NAND, OR.

11-24 AMA071

Digital tuners and audio panels

A. are integral to the multi-functional display.
B. create a centralized location for switching from one device to another or for changing frequencies.
C. are found primarily on glass cockpit aircraft.

ANSWERS

11-19 Answer C.
Transistors are rated by the ratio of the collector current to the base current, or Beta (β). For example, a 100 β transistor can handle 100 times more current through a collector emitter circuit than the base input signal. So the amplitude of amplification is a factor of the Beta of the transistor and any in-line resistors used in the circuit.
[Ref: Airframe Handbook H-8083-31A-ATB, Chapter 11 Page 22]

11-20 Answer C.
Oscillators function to make AC from DC. They can produce various waveforms as required by electronic circuits.
[Ref: Airframe Handbook H-8083-31A-ATB, Chapter 11 Page 24]

11-21 Answer A.
The discussion of semiconductors and semiconductor devices, and circuitry is only an introduction to electronics found in communication and navigation avionics. In-depth maintenance of the interior electronics of most avionics devices is performed only by certified repair stations and trained avionics technicians. The airframe technician is responsible for installation, maintenance, inspection, and proper performance of avionics in the aircraft.
[Ref: Airframe Handbook H-8083-31A-ATB, Chapter 11 Page 26]

11-22 Answer C.
Transistors are used in digital electronics to construct circuits that act as digital logic gates. The purpose and task of an avionics device is achieved by manipulating electric signals through logic gates.
[Ref: Airframe Handbook H-8083-31A-ATB, Chapter 11 Page 26]

11-23 Answer B.
The AND, OR, and NOT gates are the basic logic gates. A few other logic gates are also useful. They can be derived from combining the AND, OR, and NOT gates.
[Ref: Airframe Handbook H-8083-31A-ATB, Chapter 11 Page 28]

11-24 Answer B.
Numerous communication and navigation devices must be tuned to the desired frequency and retuned during flight. Switching from one piece of equipment to another and retuning can occur frequently. An audio panel or digital tuner consolidates various communication and navigation radio selection controls into a single unit. The pilot can select and use, or select and tune most of the aircraft's avionics from this single control interface.
[Ref: Airframe Handbook H-8083-31A-ATB, Chapter 11 Page 30]

11-25 AMA085
The relationship between radio wave frequency and wavelength is
  A. directly proportional.
  B. indirectly proportional.
  C. relationship.

11-26 AMA085
What determines the length of an antenna used to transmit and receive a radio signal?
  A. The frequency of the signal.
  B. The wavelength of the signal.
  C. The power of the signal.

11-27 AMA071
VHF radio signals are commonly used in
  A. both VOR navigation and ATC communications.
  B. ATC Communications.
  C. VOR navigation.

11-28 AMA085
A carrier wave _____.
  A. is the term used for the information being transmitted
  B. is combined with a secondary wave which carries useful information
  C. must be modified to contain useful information

11-29 AMA085
Demodulation occurs in the radio receiver. It
  A. is the process of amplifying the radio signal so it can be heard.
  B. reduces noise so the information signal can be heard.
  C. removes the original information signal from the carrier wave.

11-30 AMA085
Single Side Band (SSB) transmissions
  A. contain all of the information signal but use less bandwidth.
  B. use less bandwidth but require more power to transmit.
  C. cannot be used because they do not contain the entire information signal.

COMMUNICATION AND NAVIGATION

ANSWERS

11-25 Answer B.
The atmosphere is filled with radio waves as well as other types of waves. Each wave occurs at a specific frequency and has a corresponding wavelength. The relationship between frequency and wavelength is inversely proportional. A high frequency wave has a short wave length and a low frequency has a long wavelength.
[Ref: Airframe Handbook H-8083-31A-ATB, Chapter 11 Page 31]

11-26 Answer B.
Ideally, the size of the antenna should match the size of the wavelength of the signal with which the antenna will most resonate. However, for practical purposes fractional antenna lengths are also possible such as 1/2 or 1/4 wavelength. This is especially so at 1/2 wavelengths in which case it is the same as half the AC Sine wave or cycle.
[Ref: Airframe Handbook H-8083-31A-ATB, Chapter 11 Page 32-33]

11-27 Answer A.
VHF communication radios are the primary communication radios used in aviation. They are used for communication between aircraft and Air Traffic Control (ATC), as well as air-to-air communication between aircraft. VOR navigation also uses VHF radio waves (108 – 117.95MHz).
[Ref: Airframe Handbook H-8083-31A-ATB, Chapter 11 Page 32-43]

11-28 Answer C.
The production and broadcast of radio waves does not convey any significant information. The basic radio wave is known as a carrier wave. To transmit and receive useful information, the carrier wave is altered or modulated by an information signal. The information signal contains the unique voice or data information desired to be conveyed. The modulated carrier wave then carries the information from the transmitting radio to the receiving radio via their respective antennas. Two common methods of modulating carrier waves are Amplitude Modulation (AM) and Frequency Modulation (FM).
[Ref: Airframe Handbook H-8083-31A-ATB, Chapter 11 Page 32]

11-29 Answer C.
When the modulated carrier wave strikes the receiving antenna, voltage is generated that is the same as that which was applied to the transmitter antenna. However, the signal is weaker. It is amplified so that it can be demodulated. Demodulation is the process of removing the original information signal from the carrier wave. Electronic circuits containing capacitors, inductors, diodes, filters, etc., remove all but the desired information signal identical to the original input signal. Then, the information signal is typically amplified again to drive speakers or other output devices.
[Ref: Airframe Handbook H-8083-31A-ATB, Chapter 11 Page 34]

11-30 Answer A.
SSB transmissions are a narrow bandwidth solution. Each sideband represents the initial information signal in its entirety. Therefore, in a SSB broadcast, the carrier wave and either the upper or lower sidebands are filtered out. Only one sideband with its frequencies is broadcast since it contains all of the needed information. This cuts the bandwidth required in half and allows more efficient use of the radio spectrum. SSB transmissions also use less power to transmit the same amount of information over an equal distance.
[Ref: Airframe Handbook H-8083-31A-ATB, Chapter 11 Page 36]

11-31 AMA085
Radio transmitters contain which of the following basic elements
- A. oscillator, amplifier, modulator.
- B. generator, oscillator, modulator.
- C. amplifier, transformer, oscillator.

11-32 AMA085
Radio receivers contain which of the following basic elements
- A. amplifiers, mixer, local oscillator, demodulator.
- B. transceiver, oscillator, bridge circuit, demodulator.
- C. demodulator, amplifier, rectifier, speaker.

11-33 AMA085
A transceiver
- A. sends communication and navigation radio signals.
- B. uses antennas to lengthen radio coverage area.
- C. receives and transmits radio signals.

11-34 AMA085
The ideal radio antenna is
- A. an insulator, an equal length of the wavelength of the transmitted frequency.
- B. a conductor, 1/2 the length of the wavelength of the transmitted frequency.
- C. an insulator, 1/2 the length of the wavelength of the transmitted frequency.

11-35 AMA085
An antenna that is 1/4 wavelength
- A. is resonant but is not as effective as a 1/2 wavelength.
- B. cannot be used in aviation.
- C. uses the metal of the fuselage to create a 1/2 wavelength antenna.

11-36 AMA023
For the best reception of a radio signal, a receiving antenna should be polarized
- A. the same as the transmitting antenna.
- B. 90 degrees to the transmitting antenna.
- C. parallel to the electromagnetic component of the radio wave.

COMMUNICATION AND NAVIGATION

ANSWERS

11-31 Answer A.
A transmitter consists of a precise oscillating circuit or oscillator that creates an AC carrier wave frequency. This is combined with amplification circuits or amplifiers. Other circuits are used in a transmitter to accept the input information signal and process it for loading on to the carrier wave. Modulator circuits modify the carrier wave with the processed information signal.
[Ref: Airframe Handbook H-8083-31A-ATB, Chapter 11 Page 37]

11-32 Answer A.
A common receiver is the superheterodyne receiver. It must amplify the desired radio frequency captured by the antenna. An oscillator is used to compare and select the desired frequency from all of the frequencies picked up by the antenna. The local oscillator frequency and the carrier wave frequency are mixed in the mixer. The sum and difference frequencies contain the information signal. The detector, or demodulator, is where the information signal is separated from the carrier wave. Finally, amplification occurs for the output device.
[Ref: Airframe Handbook H-8083-31A-ATB, Chapter 11 Page 37-38]

11-33 Answer C.
A transceiver is a communication radio that transmits and receives. The same frequency is used for both. When transmitting the receiver does not function.
[Ref: Airframe Handbook H-8083-31A-ATB, Chapter 11 Page 38]

11-34 Answer B.
Antennas are conductors that are used to transmit and receive radio frequency waves. When an AC signal is applied to an antenna, it has a certain frequency. There is a corresponding wavelength for that frequency. Antenna that is half the length of this wavelength is resonant. It is able to allow full voltage and full current flow for the positive phase of the AC signal in one direction. The negative phase of the full AC signal is accommodated by the voltage and current changing direction in the conductor.
[Ref: Airframe Handbook H-8083-31A-ATB, Chapter 11 Page 38]

11-35 Answer C.
VHF antennas are relatively long. Antennas ¼ wavelength of the transmitted frequency are often used. This is possible when mounted on a metal fuselage. A ground plane is formed and the fuselage acts as the missing one-quarter length of a half wavelength antenna.
[Ref: Airframe Handbook H-8083-31A-ATB, Chapter 11 Page 39]

11-36 Answer A
Receiving antennas with the same polarization as the transmitting antenna generate the strongest signal. For example, a vertically polarized antenna is mounted up and down. It radiates waves out from it in all directions. To receive the strongest signal from the waves, the receiving antenna should also be positioned vertically so the electromagnetic component of the radio wave can cross it at as close to a 90 degree angle as possible for most of the possible proximities.
[Ref: Airframe Handbook H-8083-31A-ATB, Chapter 11 Page 39]

11-37 AMA085

A dipole antenna commonly used for VOR radio signal is shaped
- A. like a "U".
- B. in a loop.
- C. like a "V".

11-38 AMA085

A loop antenna receiving a radio signal produces the strongest signal
- A. when the radio signal strikes the loop broadside.
- B. when the radio signal strikes the loop in line with the plane of the loop.
- C. when equal current is caused to flow in both sides of the loop.

11-39 AMA071

The navigational aid that broadcasts a reference signal and a rotating variable signal which are compared in the receiver for phase relationship is called a
- A. VOR.
- B. ADF.
- C. ILS.

11-40 AMA071

If an aircraft is so equipped, which of the following may display VOR navigational information?
1. ADF
2. CDI
3. OBS
4. EADI
5. HIS
6. EFIS
7. RMI
- A. 1, 5, 6
- B. 2, 3, 4, 5, 6, 7
- C. 1, 2, 3, 5, 7

11-41 AMA071

An Automatic Direction Finder (ADF) system uses which type of antenna(s)?
- A. Sense and loop antennas.
- B. V shaped bi-pole antenna.
- C. Marconi antenna.

11-42 AMA071

A Radio Magnetic Indicator (RMI) combines
- A. ILS, marker beacon and heading indications all in one gauge.
- B. horizontal and vertical situational indications all in one gauge.
- C. a magnetic compass, VOR and ADF all in one gauge.

COMMUNICATION AND NAVIGATION

ANSWERS

11-37 Answer C.
A common dipole antenna is the V-shaped VHF navigation antenna, known as a VOR antenna, found on numerous aircraft. Each arm of the V is one-fourth wavelength creating a half wave antenna which is fed in the center. The antenna is horizontally polarized. For a dipole receiving antenna, this means it is most sensitive to signal approaching the antenna from the sides rather than head-on in the direction of flight.
[Ref: Airframe Handbook H-8083-31A-ATB, Chapter 11 Page 40]

11-38 Answer B.
Used as a receiving antenna, the loop antenna's properties are highly direction sensitive. A radio wave intercepting the loop directly broadside causes equal current to flow in both sides of the loop. However, the polarity of the current flow is opposite each other. This causes them to cancel out and produce no signal. When a radio wave strikes the loop antenna in line with the plane of the loop, current is generated first in one side , and then in the other side. This causes the current flows to have different phases and the strongest signal can be generated from this angle.
[Ref: Airframe Handbook H-8083-31A-ATB, Chapter 11 Page 41]

11-39 Answer A.
A VOR terminal produces two signals that a receiver on board the aircraft uses to locate itself in relation to the ground station. One signal is a reference signal. The second is produced by electronically rotating a variable signal. The variable signal is in phase with the reference signal when at magnetic north, but becomes increasingly out of phase as it is rotated 180 degrees. As it continues to rotate to 360 degrees, the signal become increasingly in phase until the two signals are in phase again at magnetic north. The receiver in the aircraft deciphers the phase difference and determines the aircraft's position in degrees from the VOR ground based unit.
[Ref: Airframe Handbook H-8083-31A-ATB, Chapter 11 Page 43]

11-40 Answer B.
Older aircraft are often equipped with a VOR gauge dedicated to display only VOR information. This is also called an Omni-Bearing Selector (OBS) or a Course Deviation Indicator (CDI). A separate gauge for the VOR information is not always used. As flight instruments and displays have evolved, VOR navigational information has been integrated into other instrument displays, such as the Radio Magnetic Indicator (RMI), the Horizontal Situation Indicator (HSI), an EFIS display or an Electronic Attitude Director Indicator (EADI).
[Ref: Airframe Handbook H-8083-31A-ATB, Chapter 11 Page 44-45]

11-41 Answer A.
An Automatic Direction Finder (ADF) operates off of a ground signal transmitted from a non-directional beacon (NDB). Using a loop antenna, the direction to or from the broadcast antenna can be determined by monitoring the strength of the signal received. In modern ADF systems, an additional sense antenna is used to remove the ambiguity concerning whether the aircraft is heading to or from the transmitter. The reception field of the sense antenna is omnidirectional. When combined with the fields of the loop antenna, it forms a field with a single significant null reception area on one side. This is used for tuning and produces an indication in the direction towards the ADF station at all times.
[Ref: Airframe Handbook H-8083-31A-ATB, Chapter 11 Page 46]

11-42 Answer C.
The RMI combines indications from a magnetic compass, VOR, and ADF into one instrument. The azimuth card of the RMI is rotated by a remotely located flux gate compass. Thus, the magnetic heading of the aircraft is always indicated. The VOR receiver drives a solid pointer to indicate the magnetic position to a tuned VOR station. When the ADF is tuned to an NDB, the double or hollow pointer indicates the magnetic bearing to the NDB.
[Ref: Airframe Handbook H-8083-31A-ATB, Chapter 11 Page 48-49]

11-43 AMA071

An Instrument Landing System (ILS) includes which of the following?
1. Marker beacon
2. Localizer
3. RNAV
4. Glideslope
5. GPS
  A. 1. 2, 3, 4
  B. 1, 2, 4
  C. 1, 2, 4, 5

11-44 AMA071

The purpose of a localizer is to
  A. set the airplane on the proper approach angle to the runway.
  B. indicate the distance the airplane is from the end of the runway.
  C. align the airplane with the center of the runway.

11-45 AMA071

The purpose of a glideslope system is to
  A. indicate the distance the airplane is from the end of the runway.
  B. assist the pilot in making a correct angle of descent to the runway.
  C. provide for automatic altitude reporting to air traffic control.

11-46 AMA023

A DME antenna should be located in a position on the aircraft that will?
  A. Permit interruptions in DME operation.
  B. Not be blocked by the wing when the aircraft is banked.
  C. Eliminate the possibility of the DME locking on a station.

11-47 AMA071

In general, the purpose of an aircraft transponder is to
  A. continually transmit heading, speed, and rate of climb/descent, etc., information to Aircraft Tower.
  B. monitor aircraft speed, heading, altitude, and attitude whenever the autopilot system is engaged.
  C. receive an interrogation signal from a ground station and automatically send a reply back.

11-48 AMA071

RNAV allows a pilot to navigate from point to point
  A. by creating intermediate waypoints to which the CDI guides the pilot.
  B. by flying over VOR and VORTAC stations using CDI guidance.
  C. without the CDI.

COMMUNICATION AND NAVIGATION

ANSWERS

11-43 Answer B.
Multiple radio transmissions are used that enable an exact approach to landing with an ILS. A localizer is one of the transmissions. It is used to provide horizontal guidance to the center line of the runway. A separate glideslope broadcast provides vertical guidance of the aircraft down the proper slope to the touch down point. Compass locator transmissions for outer and middle approach marker beacons aid the pilot in intercepting the approach navigational aid system.
[Ref: Airframe Handbook H-8083-31A-ATB, Chapter 11 Page 49]

11-44 Answer C.
Multiple radio transmissions are used that enable an exact approach to landing with an ILS. A localizer is one of the radio transmissions. It is used to provide horizontal guidance to the centerline of the runway.
[Ref: Airframe Handbook H-8083-31A-ATB, Chapter 11 Page 49]

11-45 Answer B.
Multiple radio transmissions are used that enable an exact approach to landing with an ILS. A separate glideslope broadcast provides vertical guidance of the aircraft down the proper slope to the touch down point.
[Ref: Airframe Handbook H-8083-31A-ATB, Chapter 11 Page 49]

11-46 Answer B.
A DME system calculates the distance from the aircraft to the DME unit at the VORTAC ground station and displays it on the flight deck. In most cases, the UHF of the DME is transmitted and received via a small blade-type antenna mounted to the underside of the aircraft fuselage centerline.
[Ref: Airframe Handbook H-8083-31A-ATB, Chapter 11 Page 52-54]

11-47 Answer C.
A transponder provides positive identification and location of an aircraft on the radar screen of air traffic control (ATC). The ground station transmits a pulse of energy at 1030 MHz and the transponder transmits a reply with the assigned code attached at 1090MHz. This confirms the aircraft's location typically by altering its target symbol on the radar screen. In the ALT or Mode C mode, the transponder reply is transmitted with pressure altitude information, which is then displayed next to the aircraft target symbol on the radar screen.
[Ref: Airframe Handbook H-8083-31A-ATB, Chapter 11 Page 54-55]

11-48 Answer A.
Area navigation, or RNAV, is a general term used to describe the navigation from point to point without direct over flight of navigational aids such as VOR stations. VOR/DME and VORTAC stations are used to create phantom waypoints that are over flown rather than the actual stations. The RNAV computer causes the aircraft's CDI to operate as though they are actual VOR stations. The computer also uses basic geometry and trigonometry calculations to produces heading, speed, and time readouts for each waypoint.
[Ref: Airframe Handbook H-8083-31A-ATB, Chapter 11 Page 54]

11-49 AMA088
All transponders flown into controlled airspace are require to be inspected and tested in accordance with 14CFR part 43, Appendix F every
- A. 12 months.
- B. 24 months.
- C. occurrence of a recorded hard landing.

11-50 AMA018
Traffic Collision Avoidance Systems (TCAS)
- A. are transponder based systems.
- B. are air to ground units.
- C. use ultra high frequencies for interrogation.

11-51 AMA018
Automatic Dependent Surveillance Broadcast (ADS-B)
- A. uses ground radar and broadcast technology to alert aircraft of a potential collision.
- B. is more reliable than ground radar but is more expensive.
- C. combines air-to-air broadcast and air-to- ground broadcast with GPS positioning to avoid accidents.

11-52 AMA084
A radar altimeter determines altitude by
- A. means of transponder interrogation.
- B. receiving signals transmitted from ground radar stations.
- C. transmitting a signal and receiving back a reflected signal.

11-53 AMA083
A radar altimeter indicates
- A. altitude above ground level.
- B. altitude above sea level.
- C. altitude level (pressure) altitude.

11-54 AMA018
The Ground Proximity Warning System (GPWS) uses input from which of the following?
- A. Airspeed Indicator
- B. Pressure Altimeter
- C. Radar Altimeter

COMMUNICATION AND NAVIGATION

ANSWERS

11-49 Answer B.
Title 14 of the Code of Federal Regulations (CFR) part 91, section 91.413 states that all transponders on aircraft flown into controlled airspace are required to be inspected and tested in accordance with 14CFR part 43, Appendix F every 24 calendar months. Installation or maintenance that may introduce a transponder error is also cause for inspection and test in accordance with Appendix F.
[Ref: Airframe Handbook H-8083-31A-ATB, Chapter 11 Page 58]

11-50 Answer A.
TCAS are transponder based air-to-air traffic monitoring and alerting systems. The transponder of an aircraft with TCAS is able to interrogate the transponder of other aircraft nearby using SSR technology. This is done with a 1030 MHz signal.
[Ref: Airframe Handbook H-8083-31A-ATB, Chapter 11 Page 59-60]

11-51 Answer C.
ADS-B OUT combines the positioning information available from a GPS receiver with on-board flight status information, i.e. location, altitude, velocity, time. It then broadcasts this information to other ADS-B equipped aircraft and ground stations. Data is transferred without the need for human acknowledgement. ADS-B IN AND TIS-B supplement the ADS-B OUT information giving the pilot greatly enhanced situational awareness.
[Ref: Airframe Handbook H-8083-31A-ATB, Chapter 11 Page 61]

11-52 Answer C.
Using a transceiver and a directional antenna, a radio altimeter broadcasts a carrier wave at 4.3 GHz from the aircraft directly towards the ground. It strikes the surface features and bounces back toward the aircraft where a second antenna receives the return signal. The transceiver processes the signal by measuring the elapsed time the signal traveled and the frequency modulation that occurred.
[Ref: Airframe Handbook H-8083-31A-ATB, Chapter 11 Page 62]

11-53 Answer A.
A radar altimeter is used to measure the distance from the aircraft to the terrain directly beneath it.
[Ref: Airframe Handbook H-8083-31A-ATB, Chapter 11 Page 62]

11-54 Answer C.
Large aircraft may incorporate radio altimeter information into a ground proximity warning system (GPWS) which aurally alerts the crew of potentially dangerous proximity to the terrain below the aircraft.
[Ref: Airframe Handbook H-8083-31A-ATB, Chapter 11 Page 62]

11-55 AMA027

What precaution must be utilized when maintaining and operating on-board weather radar?
- A. The aircraft airframe must be grounded.
- B. Approved paint must be used on the radome.
- C. The radar must be pointed at a building or other solid object.

11-56 AMA027

Lightning detectors typically use which type of antenna?
- A. Loop
- B. Marconi
- C. Dipole

11-57 AMA044

The preferred location of an ELT is
- A. where it is readily accessible to the pilot or a member of the flight crew while the aircraft is in flight.
- B. as far aft as possible, but forward of the vertical fin.
- C. as far aft as possible.

11-58 AMA044

How may the battery replacement date be verified for an emergency locator transmitter (ELT)?
- A. By activating the transmitter and measuring the signal strength.
- B. By removing the batteries and testing them under a measured load to determine if 50 percent of the useful life remains.
- C. By observing the battery replacement date marked on the outside of the transmitter.

11-59 AMA071

Long Range Navigation (LORAN) systems determine aircraft location by
- A. measuring the inertial forces acting on the aircraft.
- B. means of pulsed signals transmitted from ground stations.
- C. means of signals transmitted to and from navigation satellites.

11-60 AMA071

The user segment of the Global Positioning System (GPS) consists of
- A. 24 satellites, the aircraft receiver, and the antenna.
- B. the aircraft receiver, antenna, and display unit.
- C. the control center, the satellites, and the aircraft receiver.

COMMUNICATION AND NAVIGATION

ANSWERS

11-55 Answer B.
Special precautions must be followed by the technician during maintenance and operation of weather radar systems. The radome covering the antenna must only be painted with approved paint to allow radio signals to pass unobstructed. Operation of radar should not take place while the radar is pointed toward a building or when refueling takes place. Note that physical harm is possible from the high-energy radiation emitted, especially to the eyes and testes.
[Ref: Airframe Handbook H-8083-31A-ATB, Chapter 11 Page 64-65]

11-56 Answer A.
Lightning gives off its own electromagnetic signal. The azimuth of a lightening strike can be calculated by a receiver using a loop antenna such as that used in ADF. Some lightning detectors make use of the ADF antenna. The range of the lightning strike is closely associated with its intensity. Intense strikes are plotted as being closer to the aircraft.
[Ref: Airframe Handbook H-8083-31A-ATB, Chapter 11 Page 65]

11-57 Answer B.
Emergency Locator Transmitters (ELT's) are typically installed as far aft in the fuselage of an aircraft as practicable just forward of the empennage. Helicopter ELT's may be located elsewhere on the airframe.
[Ref: Airframe Handbook H-8083-31A-ATB, Chapter 11 Page 68]

11-58 Answer C.
ELT inspection must occur within 12 months of the previous inspection. Inspection must be recorded in the maintenance records including the new expiration date of the battery. This must also be recorded on the outside of the ELT unit.
[Ref: Airframe Handbook H-8083-31A-ATB, Chapter 11 Page 68]

11-59 Answer B.
Precisely timed, synchronized pulse signals are transmitted from towers in a LORAN tower chain. The LORAN receiver measures the time to receive the pulses from the master tower and two other towers. It calculates the aircraft's position based on the intersection of parabolic curves representing elapsed signal times from each of these known points. The accuracy and proliferation of GPS navigation has caused the U.S. Government to cease support for LORAN. Signals are no longer generated from the tower network.
[Ref: Airframe Handbook H-8083-31A-ATB, Chapter 11 Page 69]

11-60 Answer B.
There are three segments of GPS: the space segment, the control segment, and the user segment. Aircraft technicians are only involved with user segment equipment such as GPS receivers, displays, and antennas.
[Ref: Airframe Handbook H-8083-31A-ATB, Chapter 11 Page 69]

11-61 AMA071
To determine an aircraft's position and altitude, a GPS receiver must receive signals from a minimum of _____ GPS satellites.
  A. 3
  B. 4
  C. 5

11-62 AMA071
What is used to augment satellite GPS to increase its accuracy in fixing the location of an aircraft?
  A. ADS-B IN uploads
  B. VOR augmentation
  C. WAAS

11-63 AMA071
An Inertial Reference System (IRS) navigation unit incorporates which of the following for extreme navigational accuracy?
  A. GPS, solid state accelerometers, and laser gyros.
  B. GPS, WAAS, and VOR.
  C. GPS, ADS-B, and WAAS.

11-64 AMA028
Installation of a modern Technical Standard Order (TSO'd) avionics device in an aircraft previously approved for the installation by the airframe manufacturer is a
  A. minor alteration.
  B. major alteration.
  C. MEL item.

11-65 AMA028
Installation of new avionics equipment not on the airframe manufacturer's approved equipment list is a
  A. major repair.
  B. major alteration.
  C. minor alteration.

11-66 AMA028
What is the purpose of a cable installed between a shock mounted radio tray to a structural member of the airframe?
  A. Radio noise suppression.
  B. Protect the radio in the event of lightning strikes.
  C. Provide an electrical grounding.

COMMUNICATION AND NAVIGATION

ANSWERS

11-61 Answer B.
The GPS receiver measures the time it takes for signals to arrive from three transmitting satellites. Since radio waves travel at 186,000 miles per second, the distance to each satellite can be calculated. The intersection of these ranges provides a two dimensional position of the aircraft. It is expressed in latitude and longitude coordinates. By incorporating the distance to a fourth satellite, the altitude above the surface of the earth can be calculated as well. This results in a three dimensional fix. Additional satellite inputs refine the accuracy of the position.
[Ref: Airframe Handbook H-8083-31A-ATB, Chapter 11 Page 70]

11-62 Answer C.
To increase the accuracy of GPS for aircraft navigation, the Wide Area Augmentation System (WAAS) was developed. It consists of approximately 25 precisely surveyed ground stations that receive GPS signals and ultimately transmit correction information to the aircraft. A WAAS enabled GPS receiver is required to use the wide area augmentation system. WAAS is known to reduce position errors to 1-3 meters laterally and vertically.
[Ref: Airframe Handbook H-8083-31A-ATB, Chapter 11 Page 71]

11-63 Answer A.
Modern Inertial Navigation Systems (INS) are known as Inertial Reference Systems (IRS). They are completely solid state units with no moving parts. Three-ring laser gyros replace mechanical gyros used in the old INS platform systems. The use of three solid-state mechanical accelerometers also increases accuracy. The accelerometer and gyro output are input to the IRS computer for continuous calculation of the aircraft's position. The most modern IRS integrate satellite GPS. The GPS is extremely accurate in itself. When combined with IRS, it creates one of the most accurate navigation systems available.
[Ref: Airframe Handbook H-8083-31A-ATB, Chapter 11 Page 72]

11-64 Answer A.
Avionics equipment to be installed must be a Technical Standard Order (TSO'd) device that is approved for installation in the aircraft in question. The addition of a new piece of avionics equipment and/or antenna is a minor alteration if previously approved by the airframe manufacturer. A licensed airframe technician is qualified to perform the installation and return the aircraft to service.
[Ref: Airframe Handbook H-8083-31A-ATB, Chapter 11 Page 72]

11-65 Answer B.
The addition of new avionics not on the aircraft's approved equipment list is considered a major alteration and requires an FAA Form 337 to be enacted. A technician with an inspection authorization is required to complete a Form 337.
[Ref: Airframe Handbook H-8083-31A-ATB, Chapter 11 Page 72]

11-66 Answer C.
As most shock mounting material are electrical insulator, a bonding wire must be installed so that the avionics gear can maintain a ground path.
[Ref: Airframe Handbook H-8083-31A-ATB, Chapter 11 Page 74]

11-67 AMA086

Radio equipment is bonded to the aircraft
   A. in order to provide a low impedance ground and to minimize radio interference from static electrical charges.
   B. ensure minimum movement should the attaching hardware become loose.
   C. to increase impedance of the antenna(s) to the proper value for maximum signal reception.

11-68 AMA085

Static dischargers help eliminate radio interference by
   A. acting like capacitor for static electricity.
   B. grounding static electric build-up to the airframe structure.
   C. dissipating static electricity into the atmosphere.

11-69 AMA028

When installing coaxial cable, it should be secured firmly along its entire length
   A. where ever the cable sags.
   B. at 1 foot intervals.
   C. at 2 foot intervals.

11-70 AMA023

When an antenna is installed, it should be fastened
   A. to the primary structure at the approximate intersection of the three aircraft axes.
   B. with a reinforcing doubler on each side of the aircraft skin.
   C. so that loads imposed are transmitted to the aircraft structure.

11-71 AMA023

Doublers are used when antennas are installed to?
   A. Prevent oil canning of the skin.
   B. Eliminate antenna vibration.
   C. Reinforce the aircraft skin.

11-72 AMA087

What is the radio transponder code reserved for Visual Flight Rules (VFR) flight not under ATC control?
   A. 7600
   B. 7700.
   C. 1200.

COMMUNICATION AND NAVIGATION

ANSWERS

11-67 Answer A.
One of the most important measures taken to eliminate unwanted electrical charges which may damage or interfere with avionics equipment is bonding. Bonding provides the necessary electrical connection between metallic parts of an aircraft to prevent variable resistance in the airframe. It provides a low-impedance ground return that minimizes interference from static electricity charges.
[Ref: Airframe Handbook H-8083-31A-ATB, Chapter 11 Page 74]

11-68 Answer C.
Static dischargers, or wicks, are installed on aircraft to reduce radio receiver interference. This interference is caused by corona discharge emitted from the aircraft as a result of precipitation static. They discharge precipitation static at points a critical distance away from avionics antennas where there is little or no coupling of the static to cause interference or noise.
[Ref: Airframe Handbook H-8083-31A-ATB, Chapter 11 Page 75]

11-69 Answer C.
When installing coaxial cable, secure the cables firmly along their entire length at intervals of approximately 2 feet.
[Ref: Airframe Handbook H-8083-31A-ATB, Chapter 11 Page 76]

11-70 Answer C.
Airborne antennas must be mechanically secure. The air loads on an antenna are significant and must be considered. Antennas must be mounted in interference free locations and in areas where signal can be optimally transmitted and received. They must also have the same polarization as the ground station. Reinforcing the antenna mounting area on each side of the aircraft skin would not be considered a doubler by definition.
[Ref: Airframe Handbook H-8083-31A-ATB, Chapter 11 Page 76]

11-71 Answer C.
After the antenna mounting template has been located and the holes drilled for the transmission cable and the mounting holes, a doubler is installed to reinforce to aircraft skin in the area of the antenna mounting.
[Ref: Airframe Handbook H-8083-31A-ATB, Chapter 11 Page 76]

11-72 Answer C.
Code 7500 is used in a hijack situation and 7600 and 7700 are also reserved for emergency use. Even the inadvertent transmission of code 1200 reserved for Visual Flight Rules (VFR) flight not under ATC direction could result in evasion action.
[Ref: Airframe Handbook H-8083-31A-ATB, Chapter 11 Page 58]

ORAL EXAM

11-1(O). What are the (part 91) maintenance requirements for an Emergency Locator Transmitter (ELT)?

11-2(O). What are the record keeping requirements for a (part 91) Emergency Locator Transmitter (ELT)?

11-3(O). Name some concerns when inspecting coaxial cable installations on aircraft.

11-4(O). What are the requirements for routing coaxial cable?

11-5(O). Name some communication and navigation systems commonly used in aviation.

11-6(O). What is involved when properly installing a NAV/COM radio in an existing radio rack?

11-7(O). What is the means of identification of commonly used communication and/or navigation antennas?

11-8(O). Describe the function and operation of a static discharger.

11-9(O). What are the maintenance procedures for static dischargers?

COMMUNICATION AND NAVIGATION

ANSWERS

ORAL EXAM

11-1(O). An ELT must be inspected within 12 months of the previous inspection. The inspection includes: proper installation, battery corrosion, battery life, operation of the controls and the crash sensor, and the presence of a sufficient signal at the antenna.
[Ref: Airframe Handbook H-8083-31A-ATB, Chapter 11 Page 68]

11-2(O). A record of the inspection of an ELT must be recorded in the aircraft maintenance logbook including the expiration date of the battery. This must also be recorded on the outside of the ELT.
[Ref: Airframe Handbook H-8083-31A-ATB, Chapter 11 Page 68]

11-3(O). Some coax cable used on pulse-type transceivers must be a specified length. Attachment of cable ends must be secure. Coaxial cable should be secured along its entire run at intervals of approximately two feet. Proper impedance must exist.
[Ref: Airframe Handbook H-8083-31A-ATB, Chapter 11 Page 76-77]

11-4(O). Coax cable should be secured to the aircraft structure approximately every two feet. It should not be tied to or routed with other wire bundle. When bending coaxial cable, be sure the bend is at least 10 times the size of the cable diameter. Always follow manufacturer's instructions.
[Ref: Airframe Handbook H-8083-31A-ATB, Chapter 11 Page 76]

11-5(O). Communication: VHF, HF, Transponder
Navigation: VOR, ADF, Loran, NDB's, Marker Beacons, Glideslope, DME, GPS Radar Altimeter, Doppler NAV (weather radar), ILS, RNAV, TCAS, ADS-B, LORAN, INS, IRS, WAAS
[Ref: Airframe Handbook H-8083-31A-ATB, Chapter 11 Page 32-71]

11-6(O). Any installation of radio navigation or communication equipment must only be accomplished with equipment approved for installation on the aircraft. When this is the case, the installation is considered a minor alteration and can be accomplished by a technician holding an airframe certificate. Installation of equipment not on the aircraft manufacturer's approved equipment list, constitutes a major alteration. It required that a form 337 be executed. It could be installed under an STC (supplemental type certificate) in which case the hold of the STC supplies the list of aircraft upon which the installation is approved. Considerations such as space, the size and weight of the equipment, and previously accomplished alterations are important. Electrical requirements and power consumption are as well. Maximum continuous electrical load for the aircraft must be maintained. Provision for easy access for inspection, maintenance, and exchange must also be considered.
[Ref: Airframe Handbook H-8083-31A-ATB, Chapter 11 Page 72-73]

11-7(O). The shape and length of an antenna can sometimes be used to reason what type of antenna is under consideration. The orientation or polarization and location on the aircraft also can give clues. The three basic types of antenna are: the dipole, the Marconi, and the loop. Dipole antennas, often used for VOR frequencies, may have a "V" shape. They are commonly located at the empennage or mounted on the underside of the fuselage. The "V" shape indicates its horizontal polarization that makes the antenna good at receiving signals that are not coming from head on. The Marconi antenna is simply a straight conductor. It uses the aircraft skin or, on fabric aircraft, conductive material under the skin, to form a conductor of 2 wavelength of the signals it is designed to receive or transmit. The Marconi antenna is vertically polarized and creates a field that is omnidirectional. VHF communication radios can use this type of antenna. The conductor in a loop antenna forms a loop. Having a loop shape to receive radio signals significantly affects the field characteristics of the antenna. It is highly sensitive to the direction from which the signal is received. Loop antennas are used extensively in navigation such as for an ADF radio. Often the loop is enclosed in a housing broad enough to conceal the entire antenna which is frequently mounted on the underside of the fuselage.
[Ref: Airframe Handbook H-8083-31A-ATB, Chapter 11 Page 40-41]

ORAL EXAM

11-8(O).   Static dischargers, or wicks, are installed on aircraft to reduce radio receiver interference. The interference is caused by corona discharge emitted from the aircraft as a result of precipitation static. Corona occurs in short pulses that produce noise at the radio frequency spectrum. Static dischargers are normally mounted on the trailing edge of control surfaces, wing tips, and the vertical stabilizer. They discharge precipitation static at points a critical distance away from avionics antennas where there is little or no coupling of the static to cause interference or noise.

[Ref: Airframe Handbook H-8083-31A-ATB, Chapter 11 Page 75]

11-9(O).   Dischargers can be flexible or rigid. They are attached to the aircraft structure with screws, rivets, or epoxy. These connections should be checked periodically for security. A resistance measurement from the mount to the airframe should not exceed 0.1 ohm. The condition of the static dischargers should be inspected in accordance with manufacturer's instructions.

[Ref: Airframe Handbook H-8083-31A-ATB, Chapter 11 Page 75]

COMMUNICATION AND NAVIGATION

QUESTIONS

PRACTICAL EXAM

11-1(P). Given various communication/navigation cables and connectors identify them and record your findings.

11-2(P). Given various communication/navigation cables and connectors in varying conditions, inspect and record your findings.

11-3(P). Given an actual aircraft or mockup, appropriate publications, and the appropriate testing equipment, if necessary, inspect an ELT and record your findings.

11-4(P). Given an actual aircraft or mockup, appropriate publications, and the appropriate testing equipment, if necessary, inspect an ELT installation and record your findings.

11-5(P). Given an actual aircraft or mockup, appropriate publications, and the appropriate testing equipment, if necessary, determine ELT battery serviceability or status and record your findings.

11-6(P). Given an actual aircraft or mockup, appropriate publications, and the appropriate testing equipment, if necessary, inspect an antenna installation and record your findings.

11-7(P). Given an actual aircraft or mockup, appropriate publications, and the appropriate testing equipment, if necessary, inspect a coaxial cable installation and record your findings.

11-8(P). Given an actual aircraft or mockup, appropriate publications, and the appropriate testing equipment, if necessary, inspect a communication/navigation radio installation and record your findings.

11-9(P). Given an actual aircraft or mockup, appropriate publications, and the appropriate testing equipment, if necessary, inspect a shock mount base and record your findings.

11-10(P). Given an actual aircraft or mockup, locate and identify the various antennas installed.

11-11(P). Given an actual aircraft or mockup, appropriate publications, and the appropriate testing equipment, if necessary, inspect a static discharger for security and resistance and record your findings.

HYDRAULIC & PNEUMATIC POWER SYSTEMS

Aircraft Hydraulic Systems, Hydraulic Fluid, Basic Hydraulic Systems,
Hydraulic Power Systems, and Large Aircraft Hydraulic Systems

CHAPTER
12

QUESTIONS

12-1 AMA063
Which characteristics apply to aircraft hydraulic systems?
1. Minimum maintenance requirements.
2. Lightweight.
3. About 80% operating efficiency (20% loss due to fluid friction).
4. Simple to inspect.
  A. 1, 2, 3, and 4
  B. 1, 2, and 4
  C. 1, 3, and 4

12-2 AMA064
Which statement about fluids is correct?
  A. All fluids are considered to be highly compressible.
  B. Any fluid will completely fill its container.
  C. All fluids readily transmit pressure.

12-3 AMA064
Which of the following is a unique characteristic of Polyalphaolefin hydraulic fluid?
  A. It is the most fire resistant type.
  B. It has high viscosity at low temperatures.
  C. It is the most resistant to oxidation.

12-4 AMA064
1. When servicing aircraft hydraulic systems, use the type fluid specified in the aircraft manufacturer's maintenance manual or on the instruction plate affixed to the reservoir or unit.
2. Hydraulic fluids for aircraft are dyed a specific color for each type of fluid.

Regarding the above statements,
  A. Only No. 1 is true
  B. Only No. 2 is true
  C. Both No. 1 and No. 2 are true.

12-5 AMA065
If a hydraulic brake system uses neoprene rubber packing materials, the correct hydraulic fluid to service the system is
  A. mineral based oil.
  B. phosphate ester based oil.
  C. vegetable based oil.

12-6 AMA065
If an aircraft hydraulic system requires mineral base hydraulic fluid, but phosphate ester based hydraulic fluid is used, what will be the effect on the system?
  A. System will be contaminated, fluids will not blend, and the seals will fail.
  B. No effect.
  C. System will be contaminated, fluids will not blend, but there will be no seal problem.

HYDRAULIC & PNEUMATIC POWER SYSTEMS

ANSWERS

12-1 Answer B.
Hydraulic systems combine the advantages of light weight, ease of installation, simplification of inspection, and minimum maintenance requirements. Hydraulic operations are almost 100% efficient with only negligible loss due to fluid friction.
[Ref: Airframe Handbook H-8083-31A-ATB, Chapter 12 Page 2]

12-2 Answer C.
Hydraulic system liquids are used primarily to transmit and distribute forces to various units to be actuated. Liquids are able to do this because they are almost incompressible.
[Ref: Airframe Handbook H-8083-31A-ATB, Chapter 12 Page 2]

12-3 Answer B.
Polyalphaolefin hydraulic fluids have some flammability improvements from older fluid types, but their main concern is their unacceptable high viscosity at temperatures below -40, and so its use is limited to small aircraft which do not reach very high altitudes.
[Ref: Airframe Handbook H-8083-31A-ATB, Chapter 12 Page 3]

12-4 Answer C.
When adding fluid to a hydraulic system, use the type specified in the manufacturer's maintenance manual or on the instruction plate affixed to the reservoir being serviced. Mineral-based hydraulic fluid (5606) is dyed red. Phosphate ester-based fluid is purple.
[Ref: Airframe Handbook H-8083-31A-ATB, Chapter 12 Page 3]

12-5 Answer A.
Appropriate seals, gaskets, and hoses must be specifically designed for the type of fluid in use. Skydrol® type V fluid is compatible with natural fibers and a number of synthetics. Petroleum based (mineral) hydraulic fluid system seals of neoprene or Buna-N® are not compatible with Skydrol®.
[Ref: Airframe Handbook H-8083-31A-ATB, Chapter 12 Page 4]

12-6 Answer A.
Due to the differences in composition, petroleum-based (mineral) hydraulic fluid and phosphate ester-based fluids will not mix; neither are the seals for any one fluid usable with or tolerant of any of the other fluids. Should an aircraft hydraulic system be serviced with the wrong type of fluid, immediately drain and flush the system and maintain the seals in accordance with the manufacturer's specifications.
[Ref: Airframe Handbook H-8083-31A-ATB, Chapter 12 Page 3]

12-7 AMA064
1. Paints that are Skydrol® compatible include polyurethane and epoxy paints.
2. Skydrol® hydraulic fluid is compatible with neoprene and Buna-N® seals.

Regarding the above statements,
A. Both No. 1 and No. 2 are true.
B. Only No. 1 is true.
C. Neither No. 1 nor No. 2 is true.

12-8 AMA063
One of the distinguishing characteristics of an open center selector valve used in a hydraulic system is that
A. fluid flows through the valve in the off position.
B. a limited amount of fluid flows in one direction and no fluid flows in the opposite direction.
C. fluid flows in three directions in the ON position.

12-9 AMA063
Unless specifically stated by the manufacturer, which of these hydraulic system filter types typically has the longest service life?
A. Pressure Filters
B. Return Filters
C. Case Drain Filters

12-10 AMA063
A hydraulic system referred to as a "power pack" system will
A. have an engine driven pump for greater pressure.
B. have all hydraulic power components located in one unit.
C. have a pressurized reservoir.

12-11 AMA063
Hydraulic fluid reservoirs are sometimes designed with a standpipe in one of the outlet ports in order to assure emergency supply of fluid. The outlet post with the standpipe in it furnishes fluid to the
A. emergency pump when the fluid supply to the normal system has been depleted.
B. emergency pump at any time it is required.
C. normal system power pump.

12-12 AMA063
What is the main purpose of a pressurized reservoir in a hydraulic system?
A. Prevent hydraulic pump cavitation.
B. Prevent hydraulic fluid from foaming.
C. Prevent tank collapse at altitude.

HYDRAULIC & PNEUMATIC POWER SYSTEMS

ANSWERS

12-7 Answer B.
Paints that are Skydrol® resistant include epoxies and polyurethanes, however, seals of neoprene or Buna-N® are not compatible with Skydrol® and must be replaced with seals of butyl rubber or ethylene-propylene.
[Ref: Airframe Handbook H-8083-31A-ATB, Chapter 12 Page 4]

12-8 Answer A.
An open center system is one having fluid flow, but no pressure, in the system when the actuating mechanisms are idle. The pump circulates the fluid from the reservoir through the selector valves and back to the reservoir. The system pressure line goes through each selector valve and back to the reservoir until one of the selector valves is positioned to operate a mechanism.
[Ref: Airframe Handbook H-8083-31A-ATB, Chapter 12 Page 6]

12-9 Answer A.
Unless otherwise stated, pressure filters should be replaced after 3,000 hours of service. Return filters at 1,500 hours, and Case drain filters every 600 hours.
[Ref: Airframe Handbook H-8083-31A-ATB, Chapter 12 Page 5]

12-10 Answer B.
A hydraulic power pack is a small unit that consists of an electric pump, filters, reservoir and pressure relief valve.
[Ref: Airframe Handbook H-8083-31A-ATB, Chapter 12 Page 7]

12-11 Answer C.
Most aircraft have emergency hydraulic systems that take over if main systems fail. In many such systems, the pumps of both systems obtain fluid from a single reservoir. Under such circumstances, a supply of fluid for the emergency pump is ensured by drawing the hydraulic fluid from the bottom of the reservoir. The main system draws its fluid through a standpipe located at a higher level. With this arrangement, should the main system's fluid supply becomes depleted, adequate fluid is left at the bottom of the reservoir below the standpipe for operation of the emergency system.
[Ref: Airframe Handbook H-8083-31A-ATB, Chapter 12 Page 9]

12-12 Answer A.
Pressurizing a reservoir assures a positive flow of fluid to the pump at high altitude when low atmospheric pressures are encountered. At high altitude there is not enough pressure to move fluid to the pump inlet. Cavitation will occur unless a pressurized reservoir is used to force fluid to the pump inlet.
[Ref: Airframe Handbook H-8083-31A-ATB, Chapter 12 Page 10]

12-13 AMA065
Hydraulic fluid filtering elements constructed of porous paper are normally
- A. discarded at regular intervals and replaced with new filtering elements.
- B. not approved for use in certificated aircraft.
- C. cleaned and reused.

12-14 AMA065
Before removing the filter cap of a pressurized hydraulic reservoir
- A. relieve the hydraulic system pressure.
- B. relieve the air pressure.
- C. actuate several components in the system.

12-15 AMA063
What happens to the output of a constant displacement hydraulic pump when the hydraulic system pressure regulator diverts the fluid from the system to the reservoir?
- A. The output pressure and volume remain the same.
- B. The output pressure reduces, but the volume remains the same.
- C. The output pressure remains the same, but the volume reduces.

12-16 AMA063
A hydraulic pump is a constant-displacement type if it
- A. produces an unregulated constant pressure.
- B. produces a continuous positive pressure.
- C. delivers a uniform rate of fluid flow.

12-17 AMA063
What safety device is usually located between the driving unit and hydraulic pump drive shaft?
- A. Thermal Relief Valve
- B. Pump Motor Safety Switch
- C. Pump Drive Coupling Shear Section

12-18 AMA063
Most variable displacement hydraulic pumps of current design
- A. contain a built in means of system pressure regulation.
- B. must be driven at a nearly constant speed in order to practical for use.
- C. are not practical for use with a closed center hydraulic system.

HYDRAULIC & PNEUMATIC POWER SYSTEMS

ANSWERS

12-13 Answer A.
Hydraulic system filters are cleaned or changed at regular intervals since a small amount of debris can damage components in the system that have close tolerances. The micron hydraulic filter element is made of a specially treated paper and is normally thrown away when removed.
[Ref: Airframe Handbook H-8083-31A-ATB, Chapter 12 Page 13]

12-14 Answer B.
During hydraulic system maintenance, it is necessary to relieve reservoir pressure. A manual bleeder is installed on most reservoirs with a push button. When the bleeder valve push button is pushed, pressurized air from the reservoir flows through the valve to an overboard vent until the air pressure is depleted.
[Ref: Airframe Handbook H-8083-31A-ATB, Chapter 12 Page 11]

12-15 Answer B.
A constant displacement pump, regardless of pump rotations per minute, forces a fixed volume of fluid through the outlet port for each revolution. If a pressure regulator is required, the output volume does not change but the pressure is reduced.
[Ref: Airframe Handbook H-8083-31A-ATB, Chapter 12 Page 17]

12-16 Answer C.
Constant-displacement pumps are sometimes called constant volume or constant delivery pumps. They deliver a fixed quantity of fluid during each revolution, regardless of the pressure demands.
[Ref: Airframe Handbook H-8083-31A-ATB, Chapter 12 Page 17]

12-17 Answer C.
Pump drive couplings are designed to serve as safety devices. The shear section of the drive coupling, located midway between the engine drive spines and the pump drive spines is smaller in diameter than the splines. If the pump becomes unusually hard to turn or becomes jammed, this section shears, preventing damage to the pump or the drive unit.
[Ref: Airframe Handbook H-8083-31A-ATB, Chapter 12 Page 18]

12-18 Answer A.
A variable displacement pump has a fluid output that is varied to meet the pressure demands of the system. The pump output is changed automatically by a pump compensator within the pump.
[Ref: Airframe Handbook H-8083-31A-ATB, Chapter 12 Page 20]

12-19 AMA063
Select the valve used in a hydraulic system that directs pressurized fluid to one end of an actuating cylinder and simultaneously directs return fluid to the reservoir from the other end.
- A. Sequence
- B. Shuttle
- C. Selector

12-20 AMA063
A sequence valve which is designed to activate a secondary function after a set pressure has been reached in a primary function may be found in some aircraft
- A. flap overload systems.
- B. landing gear systems.
- C. engine cowl flap systems.

12-21 AMA063
The purpose of an orifice check valve is to
- A. restrict flow in one direction and allow free flow in the other.
- B. relieve pressure to a sensitive component.
- C. relieve pressure in one direction and prevent flow in the other direction.

12-22 AMA063
The unit which causes one hydraulic operation to follow another in a definite order is called a
- A. selector valve.
- B. shuttle valve.
- C. sequence valve.

12-23 AMA065
Quick disconnect couplings in hydraulic systems provide a means of
- A. easily replacing hydraulic lines in areas where leaks are common.
- B. quickly connecting and disconnecting hydraulic lines and eliminate the possibility of contaminates entering the system.
- C. quickly connecting and disconnecting hydraulic lines without loss of fluid or entrance of air into the system.

12-24 AMA063
Some hydraulic systems incorporate a device which is designed to remain open to allow a normal fluid flow in the line, but closed if the fluid flow increases above an established rate. This device is generally referred to as a
- A. hydraulic fuse.
- B. metering check valve.
- C. flow regulator.

HYDRAULIC & PNEUMATIC POWER SYSTEMS

ANSWERS

12-19 Answer C.
A selector valve is used to control the direction of movement of a hydraulic actuating cylinder or similar device. It provides for the simultaneous flow of hydraulic fluid both into and out of the unit. When the selector valve is positioned to connect pressure to one port on the actuator, the other actuator port is simultaneously connected to the reservoir return line through the selector valve.
[Ref: Airframe Handbook H-8083-31A-ATB, Chapter 12 Page 23-24]

12-20 Answer B.
Sequence valves control the sequence of operation between two branches in a circuit. After a set pressure has been reached in a primary component actuator, the sequence valve diverts fluid to a second actuator to do work in another part of the system. An example is a landing gear actuating system where the gear doors must open before the landing gear starts to extend.
[Ref: Airframe Handbook H-8083-31A-ATB, Chapter 12 Page 25]

12-21 Answer A.
An orifice check valve allows full fluid flow in one direction and restricts flow in the opposite direction. Also called a damping valve, it may be included on a hydraulic landing gear actuation system. When the gear is raised, the orifice check valve allows full fluid flow to lift the heavy gear at maximum speed. When lowering the gear, the orifice in the check valve prevents the gear from violently dropping by restricting the fluid flow out of the actuating cylinder.
[Ref: Airframe Handbook H-8083-31A-ATB, Chapter 12 Page 25]

12-22 Answer C.
A sequence valve controls the sequence of operation between two branches in a circuit. It enables one unit to automatically set another unit into motion. There are various types of sequence valves. Some are controlled by pressure, some are controlled mechanically, and some are controlled by electric switches.
[Ref: Airframe Handbook H-8083-31A-ATB, Chapter 12 Page 25]

12-23 Answer C.
Quick disconnect valves are installed in hydraulic lines to prevent loss of fluid when units are removed. Such valves are installed in the pressure and suction lines of the system. Each valve section has a piston and poppet assembly that is spring loaded in the closed position when the unit is disconnected.
[Ref: Airframe Handbook H-8083-31A-ATB, Chapter 12 Page 26-27]

12-24 Answer A.
A hydraulic fuse is a safety device. It detects a sudden increase in flow, such as from a burst line downstream, and shuts off the fluid flow. By closing, the fuse preserves hydraulic fluid for use by the rest of the system.
[Ref: Airframe Handbook H-8083-31A-ATB, Chapter 12 Page 27]

12-25 AMA063
What device in a hydraulic system with a constant delivery pump allows circulation of the fluid when no demands are on the system?
A. Pressure Regulator
B. Pressure Relief Valve
C. Shuttle Valve

12-26 AMA063
The purpose of the pressure regulator in a hydraulic system is to
A. prevent failure of components or rupture of hydraulic lines under pressure.
B. regulate the amount of fluid flow to the actuating cylinders within the system.
C. maintain system operating pressure within a predetermined range and to unload the pump.

12-27 AMA063
Unloading valves are used with many engine driven hydraulic pumps to
A. dampen out pressure surges.
B. relieve system pressure.
C. relieve the pump pressure.

12-28 AMA063
The hydraulic component that automatically directs fluid from either the normal source or an emergency source to an actuating cylinder is called a
A. bypass valve.
B. crossflow valve.
C. shuttle valve.

12-29 AMA063
A fully charged hydraulic accumulator provides
A. positive fluid flow to the pump inlet.
B. a source for additional hydraulic power when heavy demands are placed on the system.
C. air pressure to the various hydraulic components.

12-30 AMA063
In a hydraulic system of a typical large aircraft such as a Boeing 777 the nose wheel steering system's isolation valve _____ when it senses that airspeed is below a preset point.
A. closes
B. opens
C. bypasses

HYDRAULIC & PNEUMATIC POWER SYSTEMS

ANSWERS

12-25 Answer A.

A pressure regulator is used in a system that is pressurized by a constant delivery-type pump. Its purpose is to manage the output of the pump to maintain system operating pressure within a predetermined range. It permits the pump to turn without resistance (unloading the pump) when pressure in the system is within normal operating range and no demands are on the system.

[Ref: Airframe Handbook H-8083-31A-ATB, Chapter 12 Page 28]

12-28 Answer C.

The main purpose of a shuttle valve is to isolate the normal system from the alternate or emergency system. In the normal position, fluid from the normal source flows through the valve and out to the actuating unit. When the emergency source is selected, fluid pressure allows the emergency source fluid into the valve and out to the actuator. In the process, the emergency fluid pressure moves the shuttle to block off flow from the normal system.

[Ref: Airframe Handbook H-8083-31A-ATB, Chapter 12 Page 29-30]

12-26 Answer C.

A pressure regulator is used in a system that is pressurized by a constant delivery-type pump. Its purpose is to manage the output of the pump to maintain system operating pressure within a predetermined range. It permits the pump to turn without resistance (unloading the pump) when pressure in the system is within normal operating range and no demands are on the system.

[Ref: Airframe Handbook H-8083-31A-ATB, Chapter 12 Page 28]

12-29 Answer B.

One of the function of an accumulator is to aid or supplement the power pump when several units are operating at once by supplying extra power from its accumulated, or stored, power.

[Ref: Airframe Handbook H-8083-31A-ATB, Chapter 12 Page 30]

12-27 Answer C.

A pressure regulator valve is also known as an unloading valve because it permits the pump to run without resistance at times when pressure in the system is within normal operating range but there are no demands on the system.

[Ref: Airframe Handbook H-8083-31A-ATB, Chapter 12 Page 28]

12-30 Answer B.

A nose gear isolation valve automatically opens when it senses that the airspeed on the ground is at a point in which nose wheel steering is required to control the aircraft. In a Boeing 777, that point is 60 knots.

[Ref: Airframe Handbook H-8083-31A-ATB, Chapter 12 Page 47]

12-31 AMA063
Hydraulic system accumulators serve which of the following functions?
1. Dampen pressure surges.
2. Supplement the system pump when demand is beyond the pump's capacity.
3. Store power for limited operation of components if the pump is not operating.
4. Ensure a continuous supply of fluid to the pump.
A. 1, 2, and 3
B. 2 and 3
C. 1, 2, 3, and 4

12-32 AMA065
If hydraulic fluid is released when the air valve core of the accumulator is depressed, it is evidence of
A. leaking check valve.
B. a ruptured diaphragm or leaking seals.
C. excessive accumulator air pressure.

12-33 AMA065
After a hydraulic accumulator has been installed and air chamber charged, the main system hydraulic pressure gauge will not show a hydraulic pressure reading until
A. the fluid side of the accumulator has been charged.
B. at least one selector valve has been actuated to allow fluid to flow into the fluid side of the accumulator.
C. the air pressure has become equal to the fluid pressure.

12-34 AMA063
A hydraulic accumulator is charged with an air preload of 1,000 PSI. When a hydraulic system pressure of 3,000 PSI is developed, the pressure on the air side of the accumulator will be
A. 4,000 PSI.
B. 3,000 PSI.
C. 1,000 PSI.

12-35 AMA063
A unit which transforms hydraulic pressure into linear motion is called
A. an accumulator.
B. an actuating cylinder.
C. a hydraulic pump.

12-36 AMA063
Heat exchanger cooling units are required in some aircraft hydraulic systems to
A. combat fluid flammability.
B. cool the fluid for braking.
C. extend service life of the fluid and components.

HYDRAULIC & PNEUMATIC POWER SYSTEMS

ANSWERS

12-31 Answer A.
Hydraulic accumulators are located on the pressure side of the hydraulic system and pump. They function to dampen pressure surges caused by actuation of a unit. They aid or supplement the power pump when several units are operating at once. Accumulators also store power for limited operation of a hydraulic unit when the pump is not operating and they may also supply fluid pressure to compensate for small internal or external leaks that would cause the system to cycle continuously.
[Ref: Airframe Handbook H-8083-31A-ATB, Chapter 12 Page 30]

12-32 Answer B.
A hydraulic accumulator contains two separate chambers, one for hydraulic fluid and one for a nitrogen or air charge. The chambers are separated by a diaphragm, bladder or piston seals (cylindrical type). There is no mixing of the hydraulic fluid and the gas charge. If fluid is present in the air/nitrogen chamber, the diaphragm is ruptured or the piston seals are leaking.
[Ref: Airframe Handbook H-8083-31A-ATB, Chapter 12 Page 30-31]

12-33 Answer A.
The accumulator preload through the gas-servicing valve moves the piston (or diaphragm in a spherical accumulator) towards to opposite end of the accumulator until it bottoms out. The pressure indicator on the accumulator will show the preload pressure. The hydraulic fluid pressure indicator will show zero fluid pressure. When the hydraulic pump is activated, it will develop normal hydraulic system fluid pressure. As it does so, the piston (or diaphragm) will be pushed back toward the servicing valve end of the accumulator by the pump pressure. The space for the gas charge becomes smaller and pressure in the gas chamber rises to that equal to the fluid pressure developed by the pump. At this point the piston (or diaphragm) stops moving.
[Ref: Airframe Handbook H-8083-31A-ATB, Chapter 12 Page 31]

12-34 Answer B.
Because of the movable separator between the fluid chamber and the air chamber, system pressure will enter the fluid side of the accumulator and push against the diaphragm, bladder, or piston and move it. As the system pressure moves the separator, it reduces the volume of the air chamber and raises the pressure in the air chamber. When the force on both sides of the diaphragm, bladder, or piston equalize, movement stops. This occurs at fluid system pressure (3000psi)
[Ref: Airframe Handbook H-8083-31A-ATB, Chapter 12 Page 31-32]

12-35 Answer B.
An actuating cylinder transforms energy in the form of fluid pressure into mechanical force, or action, to perform work. It is used to impart powered linear motion to some movable object or mechanism.
[Ref: Airframe Handbook H-8083-31A-ATB, Chapter 12 Page 32]

12-36 Answer C.
Transport category aircraft use heat exchangers in their hydraulic power supply system to cool the hydraulic fluid from the hydraulic pumps. This extends the life of the fluid and the hydraulic pumps.
[Ref: Airframe Handbook H-8083-31A-ATB, Chapter 12 Page 32]

12-37 AMA063
The primary purpose of a hydraulic actuating unit is to transform
   A. fluid pressure into useful work.
   B. fluid motion into mechanical pressure and back again.
   C. energy from one form to another.

12-38 AMA063
A hydraulic motor converts fluid pressure to
   A. linear motion.
   B. rotary motion.
   C. angular motion.

12-39 AMA065
A flexible sealing element subject to motion is a
   A. gasket.
   B. compound.
   C. packing.

12-40 AMA065
An O-ring intended for use in a hydraulic system using MIL-H-5606 (mineral base) fluid will be marked with
   A. one or more white dots.
   B. a blue stripe or dot.
   C. a white and yellow stripe.

12-41 AMA065
What type of packings should be used in hydraulic components to be installed in a system containing Skydrol®?
   A. AN packings made of neoprene.
   B. Packing materials made for ester base fluids.
   C. AN packings made of natural rubber.

12-42 AMA063
What is the purpose of using backup rings with O- rings in high-pressure hydraulic systems?
   A. To prevent high pressure from extruding the seal between the moving and stationary part.
   B. To provide a seal between two parts of a unit which move in relation to each other.
   C. To prevent internal and external leakage of all moving parts within a hydraulic system.

HYDRAULIC & PNEUMATIC POWER SYSTEMS

ANSWERS

12-37 Answer A.
An actuating cylinder transforms energy in the form of fluid pressure into mechanical force, or action, to perform work. It is used to impart powered linear motion to some movable object or mechanism.
[Ref: Airframe Handbook H-8083-31A-ATB, Chapter 12 Page 32]

12-40 Answer B.
Color codes that are compatible with MIL-H-5606 fluid always contain blue.
[Ref: Airframe Handbook H-8083-31A-ATB, Chapter 12 Page 36-37]

12-38 Answer B.
Piston-type motors are the most commonly used in hydraulic systems. They are basically the same as hydraulic pumps except they are used to convert hydraulic energy into mechanical (rotary) energy.
[Ref: Airframe Handbook H-8083-31A-ATB, Chapter 12 Page 34]

12-41 Answer B.
Hydraulic system seals of neoprene are not compatible with Skydrol®. Skydrol® is a phosphate ester-based fluid. Thus, seals used with it must be compatible and made for ester based fluids. O-rings are available in individually hermetically sealed envelopes labeled with all pertinent data. When selecting an O-ring for installation, the basic part number on the sealed envelope provides the most reliable compound identification.
[Ref: Airframe Handbook H-8083-31A-ATB, Chapter 12 Page 35]

12-39 Answer C.
Seals are divided into three main classes: packings, gaskets and wipers. Hydraulic seals used internally on a sliding or moving assembly are normally called packings. Hydraulic seals used between non-moving fittings and bosses are normally called gaskets.
[Ref: Airframe Handbook H-8083-31A-ATB, Chapter 12 Page 35]

12-42 Answer A.
Backup rings made of Teflon™ do not deteriorate with age and can tolerate temperature extremes in excess of those encountered in high pressure hydraulic systems. An O-ring without a backup ring may extrude into the gap which it is sealing. Backup rings are installed downstream of some O-rings to prevent extrusion.
[Ref: Airframe Handbook H-8083-31A-ATB, Chapter 12 Page 39]

12-43 AMA063

Which unit houses multiple filters, bypasses, and bypass indicators in a single location

   A. filter panel
   B. filter module
   C. filter exchange unit (FEU)

12-44 AMA065

To protect packing rings or seals from damage when it is necessary to install them over or inside threaded sections, the

   A. packings should be stretched during installation to avoid contact with the threads.
   B. threaded section should be covered with a suitable sleeve.
   C. threaded section should be coated with a heavy grease.

12-45 AMA079

A pneumatic braking system on an aircraft derives its air from which source?

   A. An onboard compressor such as the APU.
   B. Ground-filled pressure bottles.
   C. Engine compressor bleed air.

12-46 AMA079

  1. Relief valves are used in pneumatic systems as damage preventing units.
  2. Check valves are used in both hydraulic and pneumatic systems.

Regarding the above statements,

   A. Only No. 1 is true.
   B. Neither No. 1 nor No. 2 is true.
   C. Both No. 1 and No. 2 are true.

12-47 AMA079

Relief valves are used in pneumatic systems

   A. as damage preventing units.
   B. for one direction flow control.
   C. to reduce the rate of airflow.

12-48 AMA079

What function does a restrictor perform in the pneumatic power system?

   A. Regulates the compressor outlet air pressure to stabilize the system pressure.
   B. Regulates the inlet air to provide a stabilized source of airflow and pressure.
   C. Regulates the pneumatic system pressure to protect the moisture separator from internal explosion.

HYDRAULIC & PNEUMATIC POWER SYSTEMS

ANSWERS

12-43 Answer B.
Modern design often uses a filter module that contains multiple filters and other components such as temperature and pressure transducers. For example, a return filter module may have more than one filter to clean the return flow of hydraulic fluid from the user systems. It also contains the filter bypasses and the bypass indicators that pop out to indicate a clogged filter.
[Ref: Airframe Handbook H-8083-31A-ATB, Chapter 12 Page 45]

12-46 Answer C.
Relief valves are used in pneumatic systems to prevent damage. They act as pressure limiting units and prevent excessive pressures from bursting lines and blowing out seals. Check valves are used in both pneumatic and hydraulic systems. A pneumatic check valve is a one-direction flow control valve.
[Ref: Airframe Handbook H-8083-31A-ATB, Chapter 12 Page 49-50]

12-44 Answer B.
When the O-ring installation requires spanning or inserting through sharply threaded areas, ridges, slots, and edges, use protective measures such as O-ring entering sleeves. Some of these measures are shown in FAA-H-8083-31-ATB, Page 40, Figure 12-61.
[Ref: Airframe Handbook H-8083-31A-ATB, Chapter 12 Page 38-40]

12-47 Answer A.
Relief valves are used in pneumatic systems to prevent damage. They act as pressure limiting units and prevent excessive pressures from bursting lines and blowing out seals.
[Ref: Airframe Handbook H-8083-31A-ATB, Chapter 12 Page 49]

12-45 Answer B.
Pneumatic braking systems are typically used as an emergency backup in case hydraulic systems failed. To operate pressures of up to 3,000 psi are required. This type of pressure is only available from ground filled high pressure bottles.
[Ref: Airframe Handbook H-8083-31A-ATB, Chapter 12 Page 48]

12-48 Answer B.
Restrictors are a type of control valve used in pneumatic systems. A small outlet port reduces the rate of airflow and the speed of operation of an actuating unit.
[Ref: Airframe Handbook H-8083-31A-ATB, Chapter 12 Page 50]

12-49 AMA079

An aircraft pneumatic system, which incorporates an engine-driven, multistage reciprocating compressor, also requires
- A. a surge chamber.
- B. an oil separator.
- C. a moisture separator.

12-50 AMA079

What aspect of an aircraft pneumatic system must be considered on a daily basis?
- A. Removal of moisture.
- B. Compressor oil.
- C. Leaking air bottles.

12-51 AMA079

What is done with expended air when an actuating unit is operated in a pneumatic system?
- A. It is returned to the compressor.
- B. It is exhausted overboard.
- C. It is returned to a holding tank.

12-52 AMA063

A hydraulic system operational check during ground run-up of an aircraft indicates that the wing flaps cannot be lowered using the main hydraulic system, but can be lowered by using the emergency hand pump. Which is the most likely cause?
- A. The pressure accumulator is not supplying pressure to the system.
- B. The fluid level in the reservoir is low.
- C. The flap selector valve has a severe internal leak.

12-53 AMA065

A pilot reports that when the hydraulic pump is running, the pressure is normal. However, when the pump is stopped, no hydraulic pressure is available. This is an indication of a
- A. leaking selector valve.
- B. low accumulator fluid preload.
- C. leaking accumulator air valve.

12-54 AMA065

When flushing a hydraulic system thought to be contaminated, _____ should be used.
- A. varsol
- B. mineral spirits
- C. clean hydraulic fluid that is the same as specified for the system

HYDRAULIC & PNEUMATIC POWER SYSTEMS

ANSWERS

12-49 Answer C.
The moisture separator in a pneumatic system is always located down stream of the compressor. Its purpose is to remove any moisture caused by the compressor.
[Ref: Airframe Handbook H-8083-31A-ATB, Chapter 12 Page 50]

12-50 Answer B.
The air compressor's oil level should be checked daily according to the manufacturer's instructions. The components and lines should be drained periodically to eliminate moisture and other containments. When reconnecting; all lines, valves, and air bottles must be checked for leaks.
[Ref: Airframe Handbook H-8083-31A-ATB, Chapter 12 Page 53]

12-51 Answer B.
An advantage of a pneumatic system for component actuation is that there need not be any return line(s). For example, when used for emergency gear actuation, pulling the handle fully upward releases compressed nitrogen into the landing gear extension system. Pushing the handle fully downward closes the outlet valve and allows any nitrogen present in the emergency landing gear extension system to be vented overboard.
[Ref: Airframe Handbook H-8083-31A-ATB, Chapter 12 Page 51]

12-52 Answer B.
Many aircraft have emergency hydraulic systems that obtain fluid from the same reservoir as the normal system. This is possible because the normal system draws fluid through a standpipe. All fluid remaining below the top of the standpipe is available for the emergency system pump. In this case, since the emergency pump functions to deploy the flaps, the problem is that the normal system pump is not receiving any fluid (i.e. the fluid level is below the top of the stand pipe but still high enough for the emergency pump to utilize).
[Ref: Airframe Handbook H-8083-31A-ATB, Chapter 12 Page 9]

12-53 Answer C.
The accumulator air charge exerts pressure on the hydraulic fluid through movement of the internal accumulator diaphragm, bladder, or piston. When the hydraulic pump is running, full pump pressure is developed in the system. When it is shut off, the accumulator pressure remains against the system fluid. If this is not the case, the accumulator air pressure has leaked out – most likely through the air valve.
[Ref: Airframe Handbook H-8083-31A-ATB, Chapter 12 Page 31-32]

12-54 Answer C.
When inspection of the hydraulic filters or hydraulic fluid evaluation indicates that the fluid is contaminated, flushing the system may be necessary. This must be done in accordance with manufacturer's instructions. In a typical procedure, connect a ground hydraulic test stand to the inlet and outlet test ports of the system. Verify that the ground test unit fluid is clean and contains the same fluid as specified for the aircraft. Clean the filters and pump clean filtered fluid through the system and subsystems.
[Ref: Airframe Handbook H-8083-31A-ATB, Chapter 12 Page 5]

12-55 AMA063
Which of the following systems would be powered by a medium pressure pneumatic system?
A. Wing Deicing Boots
B. Engine Starts
C. Vacuum Powered Instruments

12-56 AMA063
Which type of pump is most commonly use in aircraft hydraulic systems?
A. Positive Displacement
B. Nonpositive Displacement
C. Centrifugal

12-57 AMA063
Hydraulic fluid enters a bent axis piston pump
A. through a single intake port at the baseplate.
B. through a check valve in the pistons.
C. through the suction action of the pistons while over the inlet port.

12-58 AMA063
To reduce the output of a variable displacement piston hydraulic pump, make sure
A. the relief valve is opened.
B. the yoke angle is reduced.
C. the shaft rotation is slowed.

12-59 AMA063
A common type of rotary actuator often used on nose wheel steering is
A. grooved vane type.
B. wheel and sprocket.
C. rack and pinion.

12-60 AMA063
Power transfer units on transport category aircraft
A. allow any pump to operate any hydraulic component.
B. work at reduced capacity.
C. use an operating EDP to drive components in a system with an inoperative EDP.

HYDRAULIC & PNEUMATIC POWER SYSTEMS

ANSWERS

12-55 Answer B.
Medium pressure pneumatic systems source air from engine bleed air or APU driven pumps. While most deicing equipment operates in this way, deicing boots operate off lower pressures of under 10 lbs. Instrument vacuum pumps operate with still less pressure.
[Ref: Airframe Handbook H-8083-31A-ATB, Chapter 12 Page 52]

12-56 Answer A.
Most pumps used in hydraulic systems are positive displacement pumps. The output of a non-positive displace pump varies as output pressure varies. Centrifugal and propeller pumps are examples of non-positive displacement pumps. In a positive displacement pump, slippage is negligible compared to the pump's volumetric output. If the output port is plugged on a positive displacement pump, pressure would increase instantaneously to the point that the pump pressure relief valve opens.
[Ref: Airframe Handbook H-8083-31A-ATB, Chapter 12 Page 16-17]

12-57 Answer C.
At any given moment of operation, three of the pistons are moving away from the top face of the cylinder block, producing a partial vacuum in the bores in which these pistons operate. This occurs over the inlet port so fluid is drawn into these bores at this time.
[Ref: Airframe Handbook H-8083-31A-ATB, Chapter 12 Page 19]

12-58 Answer B.
When system pressure exceeds the preset setting, the pressure-compensating spool moves to admit outlet pressure against the yoke. The yoke is supported inside the housing by two bearings. At outlet pressure below maximum, the yoke is at its maximum angle. As maximum outlet pressure is reached the compensator allows outlet pressure to act on the yoke actuating piston which reduces the angle of the yoke. This results in a shorter stroke of the pistons and reduced displacement.
[Ref: Airframe Handbook H-8083-31A-ATB, Chapter 12 Page 21-22]

12-59 Answer C.
Rotary actuators can mount right at the part needing to be moved without taking up the long stroke lengths require by linear actuators. An often used type of rotary actuator is the rack and pinion actuator used for many nose steering wheel mechanisms. In a rack and pinion actuator, a long piston with one side machined into a rack engages a pinion to rotate the output shaft. One side of the piston receives fluid pressure while the other side is connected to the return. When the piston moves, it rotates the pinion.
[Ref: Airframe Handbook H-8083-31A-ATB, Chapter 12 Page 33-34]

12-60 Answer C.
The purpose of a Power Transfer Unit (PTU) is to supply the additional volume of hydraulic fluid needed to operate components at a normal rate when the Engine Drive Pump (EDP) that normally operates those components malfunctions. The PTU consists of a hydraulic motor and a hydraulic pump connected by a shaft. The hydraulic motor and connected pump are driven by an operative EDP. The PTU pump uses the fluid of the system with the inoperative EDP to drive the components in that system. There is no transfer of fluid from one system to another.
[Ref: Airframe Handbook H-8083-31A-ATB, Chapter 12 Page 40-41]

ORAL EXAM

12-1(O).   What are the components of a basic hydraulic system?

12-2(O).   What are the functions of a hydraulic accumulator?

12-3(O).   What is the difference between a packing and a gasket and how are hydraulic seals identified?

12-4(O).   What are some general maintenance procedures for removing and replacing hydraulic seals?

12-5(O).   What type of hydraulic filter is used on aircraft and how does a hydraulic filter operate?

12-6(O).   Describe some maintenance procedures used for hydraulic filters?

12-7(O).   Describe the purpose of relief valves and pressure regulators in a hydraulic system.

12-8(O).   What are some hydraulic system maintenance precautions used to prevent contamination?

12-9(O).   What are some common types and characteristics of hydraulic fluids, where are they used, and how can they be identified?

12-10(O). What are some health and handling factors when using phosphate ester-based hydraulic fluid?

HYDRAULIC & PNEUMATIC POWER SYSTEMS

ANSWERS

ORAL EXAM

12-1(O).   A basic hydraulic system consists of a pump, reservoir, directional valve, check valve, pressure relieve valve, and a filter.
[Ref: Airframe Handbook H-8083-31A-ATB, Chapter 12 Page 6]

12-2(O).   Dampen hydraulic system pressure surges; Supplement the hydraulic pump when several units are operated simultaneously; Store power for limited operation of a hydraulic unit without using the pump; Supply fluid under pressure to compensate for small internal or external hydraulic fluid leaks.
[Ref: Airframe Handbook H-8083-31A-ATB, Chapter 12 Page 30]

12-3(O).   Hydraulic seals used internally on a sliding or moving assembly are normally called packings. Seals used between non moving parts are called gaskets. Hydraulic seals are made of different materials to be compatible various types of hydraulic fluid. They are often color coded by the manufacturer as a means of identifying with which fluid they are compatible. However, seals come individually packaged in hermetically sealed envelopes labeled with all pertinent data. The basic part number on the sealed envelope provides the most reliable compound identification.
[Ref: Airframe Handbook H-8083-31A-ATB, Chapter 12 Page 37]

12-4(O).   When removing and replacing o-rings, special tools may be required. It is important to not scratch or mar the metallic surface of the hydraulic component or to damage the o-ring itself during installation. Replace hydraulic seals with new seals from a sealed envelope with the correct part number on the outside. Clean and inspect the area where the seal is to be installed. Inspect the seal itself for imperfections that may cause it to not seal properly. An o-ring can be rolled to inspect the internal diameter surface. Use of a magnifying glass may be helpful. Prior to installation, immerse the new seal in clean hydraulic fluid. Care must be used to not damage the o-ring on sharp edges, threads, ridges and slots when installing it. A protective sleeve may be used. Once in place, the o-ring should be gently rolled with a finger to ensure it is not twisted.
[Ref: Airframe Handbook H-8083-31A-ATB, Chapter 12 Page 38-40]

12-5(O).   Most hydraulic filters used on aircraft are inline micronic filters. They can be located anywhere in the system the designer feels filtering is needed. The filter assembly contains a head which is bolted to the aircraft structure. A bowl attaches to the head and contains a filter element inside. Elements may be micronic, porous metal, or magnetic type. Micron filters are usually paper that trap particles much smaller than the diameter of a human hair. Fluid enters the filter through a port in the head and must pass through the element to exit the filter. Should the element be clogged, a bypass in the head will permit unfiltered fluid to flow to the hydraulic system. Differential pressure indicators are used to alert the technician or crew that the filter is being bypassed.
[Ref: Airframe Handbook H-8083-31A-ATB, Chapter 12 Page 12-15]

12-6(O).   Hydraulic filters are cleaned or replaced periodically in accordance with the manufacturer's maintenance instructions. They are also typically inspected or replaced in the event of a major hydraulic system component failure. Typically, paper micronic filter elements are discarded and replaced with new elements when performing maintenance. Porous metal and magnetic filters are cleaned and reinstalled per manufacturer's instructions. Replaceable elements should be inspected closely to insure that they are completely undamaged before reinstallation. When replacing filter elements, it is critical to ensure there is no pressure on the filter bowl before removing it. Protective gear, especially eye protection, should be used. After the element installation is complete, the hydraulic system must be pressurized and the filter inspected for leaks before returning the aircraft to service.
[Ref: Airframe Handbook H-8083-31A-ATB, Chapter 12 Page 14]

ORAL EXAM

12-7(O). A relief valve is used to limit the pressure being exerted on a confined liquid. In a hydraulic system, this protects components from failure due to excessive pressure. The pressure relief valve can be thought of as the system safety valve. When pressure increased to the value for which the relief valve is set, the valve opens to relieve the pressure. Relief valves can be installed as protection against failure of the normal pressure regulating device in a system or as protection against excess pressure due to thermal expansion of the hydraulic fluid. A pressure regulator is a device used in hydraulic systems that are pressurized by constant-delivery pumps. One purpose of the pressure regulator is to manage the output of the pump to maintain system operating pressure within a predetermined range. The other purpose is to permit the pump to turn without resistance at times when pressure within the system is within normal operating range. This is known as unloading the pump.
[Ref: Airframe Handbook H-8083-31A-ATB, Chapter 12 Page 27-28]

12-8(O). Contamination of the hydraulic system fluid can lead to premature failure of components and the system. Only the correct, specified fluid must be used to service an aircraft hydraulic system. When performing maintenance, keep all tools and the work area clean. Use a suitable container for capturing hydraulic fluid. Before disconnecting hydraulic lines and fittings, clean the fittings and the area around them. Cap or plug all hydraulic lines and fittings immediately after disconnecting. Before assembly, wash all parts in approved solvent. Lubricate parts before assembly in accordance with manufacturer's instructions. Replace all seals and gaskets with new. Use only seals and gaskets with the correct manufacturer's part number. Connect threaded components and fittings with care to prevent stripping metal slivers from threaded areas. Install and torque all lines and fittings in accordance with manufacturer's instructions. Ensure all hydraulic system servicing equipment is clean and in good operating condition.
[Ref: Airframe Handbook H-8083-31A-ATB, Chapter 12 Page 5]

12-9(O). There are three basic types of hydraulic fluids: mineral-based, polyalaphaolefins, and phosphate esters. Mineral-based fluid is processed from petroleum. It is dyed red and has an odor similar to penetrating oil. The most common is MIL-H-5606. It is predominantly used in small aircraft hydraulic systems where the fire hazard is low. Polyalaphaolefin oil is a more fire resistant type of hydraulic oil sometimes used in aircraft that normally use MIL-H-5606. It is compatible with the same seals used in mineral-based hydraulic systems. Phosphate ester-based hydraulic fluid is used in most commercial transport category aircraft. It is fire-resistant but not fire proof. The most common brand name of phosphate ester-based hydraulic fluid is Skydrol®. It is purple in color. Due to the differences in composition, mineral-based hydraulic oils and phosphate ester-based fluids will not mix; neither are the seals for MIL-H-5606 and Skydrol® interchangeable. Always check the manufacturer's maintenance information for the correct type of hydraulic fluid to be used in the aircraft system and ensure the container from which fluid is obtained is clearly labeled as the proper fluid.
[Ref: Airframe Handbook H-8083-31A-ATB, Chapter 12 Page 3-4]

12-10(O). Phosphate esters are good solvents and dissolve away some of the fatty materials of human skin. Repeated and prolonged exposure may cause drying of the skin which, if left unattended, could result in dermatitis or secondary infection from bacteria. Skydrol® on one's skin could cause a burning or itching sensation. Always wear proper gloves and eye protection when handling phosphate ester-based hydraulic fluid or any type of hydraulic fluid. When vapor exposure is possible, a respirator should be worn. Avoid ingesting any type of hydraulic fluid. Although small amounts ingested do not seem highly hazardous, any significant amount of hydraulic fluid ingestion should be followed by medically supervised testing and surveillance in accordance with the manufacturer's instructions.
[Ref: Airframe Handbook H-8083-31A-ATB, Chapter 12 Page 5-6]

HYDRAULIC & PNEUMATIC POWER SYSTEMS

PRACTICAL EXAM

12-1(P).   Given an actual aircraft or mockup and appropriate publications, select and install a hydraulic seal.

12-2(P).   Given an actual aircraft or mockup and appropriate publications, service a pneumatic system filter.

12-3(P).   Given an actual aircraft or mockup and appropriate publications, service a hydraulic system filter.

12-4(P).   Given an actual aircraft or mockup and appropriate publications, inspect the components or portion of a hydraulic system and record your findings.

12-5(P).   Given an actual aircraft or mockup and appropriate publications, inspect the components or portion of a pneumatic system and record your findings.

12-6(P).   Given an actual aircraft or mockup and appropriate publications, locate the fluid servicing instructions and identify or select a fluid for a particular aircraft.

12-7(P).   Given an actual aircraft or mockup, appropriate publications, and appropriate equipment and tooling, service a hydraulic reservoir.

12-8(P).   Given an actual aircraft or mockup, appropriate publications, and appropriate equipment and tooling, troubleshoot a hydraulic system and record your findings.

12-9(P).   Given an actual aircraft or mockup, appropriate publications, and appropriate equipment and tooling, troubleshoot a pneumatic system and record your findings.

12-10(P).   Given an actual aircraft or mockup, appropriate publications, and appropriate equipment and tooling, repair a hydraulic system defect.

12-11(P).   Given an actual aircraft or mockup, appropriate publications, and appropriate equipment and tooling, repair a pneumatic system defect.

12-12(P).   Given an actual aircraft or mockup, appropriate publications, and the appropriate testing equipment, if necessary, remove and install a hydraulic system component, complete an operational check, and record your findings.

12-13(P).   Given an actual aircraft or mockup, appropriate publications, and the appropriate testing equipment, if necessary, remove and install a pneumatic system component, complete an operational check, and record your findings.

12-14(P).   Given an actual aircraft or mockup, appropriate publications, and equipment, service a hydraulic system accumulator.

13-1 AMA068
The purpose of the torque links attached to the cylinder and piston of a landing gear oleo strut is to
   A. limit compression stroke.
   B. maintain correct wheel alignment.
   C. hold the strut in place.

13-2 AMA068
When an air/oil type of landing gear shock strut is used, the initial shock of landing is cushioned by the
   A. compression of the fluid.
   B. fluid being forced through a metered opening.
   C. compression of the air charge.

13-3 AMA069
The purpose of a locking/disconnect pin on a nose gear strut is to
   A. manually retract the nose gear when the aircraft is on jacks for maintenance.
   B. remove the wheel assembly from the axle.
   C. disconnect steering when the aircraft is being towed.

13-4 AMA068
What is the purpose of a hydraulic restrictor on the piston end of a landing gear shock strut?
   A. Restricts the speed of the extension stroke.
   B. Limits compression in case of a hard landing.
   C. Dampens oscillation when on rough surfaces.

13-5 AMA068
The metering pins in hydraulic shock struts serve to
   A. retard the flow of oil as the struts are compressed.
   B. meter the proper amount of air in the struts.
   C. lock the struts in the DOWN position.

13-6 AMA068
A sleeve, spacer, or bumper ring is incorporated in a landing gear hydraulic shock strut to
   A. limit the extension stroke.
   B. limit the extension of the torque arm.
   C. reduce the rebound effect.

AIRCRAFT LANDING GEAR SYSTEMS

ANSWERS

13-1 Answer B.
Most shock struts are equipped with torque links or torque arms to keep the piston and wheels aligned. One end of the links is attached to the fixed upper cylinder, other end is attached to the lower cylinder (piston) so it cannot rotate. This keeps the wheels aligned. The links also retain the piston in the end of the upper cylinder when the strut is extended, such as after takeoff.
[Ref: Airframe Handbook H-8083-31A-ATB, Chapter 13 Page 8]

13-2 Answer B.
In an oleo-shock strut absorber, the initial landing impact is absorbed by oil transferring from one compartment in the shock strut into another compartment through a metering orifice. A cushion of compressed air takes up the shocks of taxiing.
[Ref: Airframe Handbook H-8083-31A-ATB, Chapter 13 Page 8, G-24]

13-3 Answer C.
Nose gear struts are often equipped with a locking or disconnect pin to enable quick turning of the aircraft while towing or positioning the aircraft when on the ramp or in a hangar. Disengagement of this pin allows the wheel fork spindle on some aircraft to rotate 360°, thus enabling the aircraft to be turned in a tight radius. At no time should the nose wheel of any aircraft be rotated beyond limit lines marked on the airframe.
[Ref: Airframe Handbook H-8083-31A-ATB, Chapter 13 Page 9]

13-4 Answer A.
Upon rebound from compression, the shock strut tends to extend rapidly which could result in a sharp impact at the end of the stroke and damage the strut. A recoil device restricts the flow of fluid during this extension which slows the extension.
[Ref: Airframe Handbook H-8083-31A-ATB, Chapter 13 Page 8]

13-5 Answer A.
The compression stroke of the shock strut begins as the aircraft wheels touch the ground. As the center of mass of the aircraft moves downward, the strut compresses, and the lower cylinder or piston is forced upward into the upper cylinder. The metering pin is moved up through the orifice. The taper of the pin controls the rate of fluid flow from the bottom cylinder to the top cylinder at all points during the compression stroke.
[Ref: Airframe Handbook H-8083-31A-ATB, Chapter 13 Page 23]

13-6 Answer A.
The snubbing of fluid flow during the extension stroke dampens the strut rebound and reduces oscillation caused by the spring action of the compressed air. A sleeve, spacer, or bumper ring incorporated into the strut limits the extension stroke.
[Ref: Airframe Handbook H-8083-31A-ATB, Chapter 13 Page 12]

13-7 AMA069
When servicing an air/oil shock strut with fluid, the strut should be
  A. collapsed and fluid added at the filler opening.
  B. partially extended and fluid added at the filler opening.
  C. fully extended and fluid added at the filler opening.

13-8 AMA069
Extension of a shock strut is measured to determine the
  A. physical condition of the strut itself.
  B. amount of oil in the strut.
  C. proper operating position of the strut.

13-9 AMA069
When filling a shock strut with hydraulic fluid, fluid is added when the strut is in its _____ position?
  A. fully extended
  B. fully compressed
  C. normal service

13-10 AMA068
Within an hydraulic landing gear retraction system on a small aircraft at what point in the circuit is an emergency freefall valve located?
  A. Between the shuttle valve and each actuator.
  B. Between the high and low pressure control valves.
  C. Between the fluid reservoir and pump.

13-11 AMA068
The purpose of hydraulic restrictors when used in a small aircraft nose gear retraction system actuator is to
  A. keep the wheel aligned in flight with the direction of the aircraft.
  B. slow the downward motion of the gear leg.
  C. dampen the shock of impact with the ground.

13-12 AMA068
The purpose of a sequence valve in a hydraulic retractable landing gear system is to
  A. prevent heavy landing gear from falling.
  B. provide a means of disconnecting the normal source of hydraulic power and connecting the emergency source of power.
  C. ensure operation of the landing gear and gear doors in the proper order.

AIRCRAFT LANDING GEAR SYSTEMS

ANSWERS

13-7 Answer A.
Efficient operation of the shock struts requires that proper fluid and air pressure be maintained. To check the fluid level, most struts need to be deflated and compressed into the fully compressed position.
[Ref: Airframe Handbook H-8083-31A-ATB, Chapter 13 Page 12]

13-8 Answer C.
The correct amount of inflation is measured in psi on some struts. Other manufacturers specify struts to be inflated until extension of the lower strut is a certain measurement. Always follow manufacturer's instructions.
[Ref: Airframe Handbook H-8083-31A-ATB, Chapter 13 Page 13]

13-9 Answer A.
When filling a shock strut; fully extend the strut; release any air pressure in the strut; remove the service valve; fill the strut to the service valve port; then attach a bleed hose to the service port and continue the bleeding operation to remove any unwanted air.
[Ref: Airframe Handbook H-8083-31A-ATB, Chapter 13 Page 14]

13-10 Answer A.
A freefall emergency extension system disconnects each actuator from the hydraulic system and allows each gear to freefall into a down and locked position prior to landing.
[Ref: Airframe Handbook H-8083-31A-ATB, Chapter 13 Page 19]

13-11 Answer B.
Restrictors are used in the nose wheel actuator inlet and outlet ports to slow down the motion of this lighter gear. While hydraulic fluid is pumped to extend the gear, fluid from the upside of the actuators returns to the reservoir through the gear- up check valve. When the gear reach the down and locked position, pressure builds in the gear-down line from the pump and the low-pressure control valve unseats to return the fluid to the reservoir.
[Ref: Airframe Handbook H-8083-31A-ATB, Chapter 13 Page 18]

13-12 Answer C.
Devices used in a hydraulically-operated retraction system include actuating cylinders, selector valves, uplocks, downlocks, sequence valves, priority valves, tubing, and other conventional hydraulic system components. These units are interconnected so that they permit properly sequenced retraction and extension of the landing gear and the landing gear doors.
[Ref: Airframe Handbook H-8083-31A-ATB, Chapter 13 Page 20]

13-13 AMA068
On all aircraft equipped with retractable landing gear, some means must be provided to
  A. extend the landing gear if the normal operating mechanism fails.
  B. retract and extend the landing gear if the normal operating mechanism fails.
  C. prevent the throttle from being reduced below a safe power setting while the landing gear is retracted.

13-14 AMA069
On a large aircraft which uses proximity sensors to indicate the position of the landing gear, which is the primary task of a mechanic during inspection of this components?
  A. To ensure sufficient voltage from the inductor.
  B. To ensure that the target is clean.
  C. To check the spacing between the target and inductor.

13-15 AMA068
On an aircraft which is equipped with a squat switch to prevent inadvertent gear retraction, when the aircraft is on the ground, the squat switch circuit is _____.
  A. open; inserting a lock pin
  B. closed; inserting a lock pin
  C. open; retracting a lock pin

13-16 AMA068
What typically controls the engagement of the centering cam on a light aircraft nosewheel?
  A. Hydraulic pressure during retraction.
  B. Weight on wheels.
  C. An electric solenoid switch.

13-17 AMA068
Nose gear centering cams are used in many retractable landing gear systems. The primary purpose of the centering device is to
  A. engage the nosewheel steering.
  B. center the nosewheel before it enters the wheel well.
  C. align the nosewheel prior to touchdown.

13-18 AMA069
When inspecting retractable landing gear rigging, always check the cylinder piston for over travel. Over travel is
  A. caused by low fluid levels in the cylinder.
  B. a design feature to accommodate rough surface operation.
  C. a design feature to accommodate the landing gear latching mechanism.

AIRCRAFT LANDING GEAR SYSTEMS

ANSWERS

13-13 Answer A.
The emergency extension system lowers the landing gear if the main power system fails. There are numerous ways in which this is done depending on the size and complexity of the aircraft.
[Ref: Airframe Handbook H-8083-31A-ATB, Chapter 13 Page 22]

13-14 Answer C.
The technician is required to ensure that sensor targets are installed the correct distance from the sensor; typically with the use of go-no go gauges. As the sensor works via electrical inductance, extreme cleanliness is not required.
[Ref: Airframe Handbook H-8083-31A-ATB, Chapter 13 Page 23]

13-15 Answer A.
A landing gear squat switch, or safety switch, is found on most aircrafts. This is a switch positioned to open and close depending on the extension or compression of the main landing gear strut. The squat switch is wired into any number of system operating circuits. One circuit prevents the gear from being retracted while the aircraft is on the ground.
[Ref: Airframe Handbook H-8083-31A-ATB, Chapter 13 Page 22]

13-16 Answer B.
A centering cam which is built into the shock strut remains engaged due to the lack of compression of the strut when airborne. Once weight is on the wheels and the strut compressed, the locking cam disengages and allows control of the wheel.
[Ref: Airframe Handbook H-8083-31A-ATB, Chapter 13 Page 24]

13-17 Answer B.
Since most aircrafts have steerable nose wheel gear assemblies for taxiing, a means for aligning the nose gear before retraction is needed. Centering cams built into the shock strut structure accomplish this. An upper cam is free to mate into a lower cam recess when the gear is fully extended. This aligns the gear for retraction.
[Ref: Airframe Handbook H-8083-31A-ATB, Chapter 13 Page 24]

13-18 Answer C.
When landing gear actuating cylinders are replaced and when length adjustments are made, over- travel must be checked. Over-travel is the action of the cylinder piston beyond the movement necessary for landing gear extension and retraction. The additional action operates the landing gear latch mechanisms.
[Ref: Airframe Handbook H-8083-31A-ATB, Chapter 13 Page 26]

13-19 AMA069
After performing maintenance on an aircraft's landing gear system that may have affected the system's operation, it is usually necessary to
 A. conduct a flight test.
 B. re-inspect the area after the first flight.
 C. make an operational check with the aircraft on jacks.

13-20 AMA069
Which repair would require a landing gear retraction test?
 A. Red warning light bulb.
 B. Landing gear safety switch.
 C. Gear lockdown microswitch.

13-21 AMA069
When inspecting wheel bearings, which condition is caused by friction heat from the movement between the bearing and its mating surface
 A. spalling.
 B. brinelling.
 C. galling.

13-22 AMA069
Why is dye penetrant inspection typically ineffective when checking wheel halves for cracks?
 A. Wheel cracks tend to close up tightly after being formed.
 B. Dye penetrant inspection is typically ineffective on non-ferrous metals.
 C. Wheel heat incurred on a hard landing can refuse the damaged area.

13-23 AMA068
When a properly operating fusible plug has allowed a tire to deflate
 A. it and all additional fusible plugs in that assembly should be replaced.
 B. the affected fusible plug and tire should be replaced.
 C. the affected fusible plug can be repacked and returned to service.

13-24 AMA068
The fusible plugs installed in some aircraft wheels will
 A. melt at a specified elevated temperature.
 B. prevent over inflation.
 C. indicate tire tread separation.

AIRCRAFT LANDING GEAR SYSTEMS

ANSWERS

13-19 Answer C.
Retraction tests are performed at various times, such as during annual inspection. Any time a landing gear component is replaced that could affect the correct functioning of the landing gear system, a retraction test should follow when adjustments to landing gear linkages or components that affect gear system performance are made. It may be necessary to swing the gear after a hard or overweight landing. It is also common to swing the gear while attempting to locate a malfunction within the system. For all required retraction tests and the specific inspection points to check, consult the manufacturer's maintenance manual for the aircraft in question as each landing gear system is unique.
[Ref: Airframe Handbook H-8083-31A-ATB, Chapter 13 Page 29]

13-20 Answer C.
Retraction tests are performed at various times, such as during annual inspection. Any time a landing gear component is replaced that could affect the correct functioning of the landing gear system, a retraction test should follow when adjustments to landing gear linkages or components that affect gear system performance are made. It may be necessary to swing the gear after a hard or overweight landing. It is also common to swing the gear while attempting to locate a malfunction within the system. For all required retraction tests and the specific inspection points to check, consult the manufacturer's maintenance manual for the aircraft in question, as each landing gear system is unique.
[Ref: Airframe Handbook H-8083-31A-ATB, Chapter 13 Page 29]

13-21 Answer C.
Galling is caused by rubbing of mating surfaces. The metal gets so hot it welds, and the surface metal is destroyed as the motion continues and pulls the metal apart in the direction of motion.
[Ref: Airframe Handbook H-8083-31A-ATB, Chapter 13 Page 39, Figure 13-64]

13-22 Answer A.
Dye penetrant inspection is generally ineffective when checking for cracks in the bead area. There is a tendency for cracks to close up tightly once the tire is dismounted, and the stress is removed from the metal. Eddy current inspection of the bead seat area is required.
[Ref: Airframe Handbook H-8083-31A-ATB, Chapter 13 Page 41]

13-23 Answer A.
Fusible plugs or thermal plugs must be inspected visually. These threaded plugs have a core that melts at a lower temperature than the outer part of the plug. This is to release air from the tire should the temperature rise to a dangerous level. A close inspection should reveal whether any core has experienced deformation that might be due to high temperature. If detected, all thermal plugs in the wheel should be replaced with new plugs.
[Ref: Airframe Handbook H-8083-31A-ATB, Chapter 13 Page 42]

13-24 Answer A.
Fusible plugs in the wheels of high-performance airplanes that use tubeless tires. The centers of the plugs are filled with a metal that melts at a relatively low temperature. If a takeoff is aborted and the pilot uses the brakes excessively, the heat transferred into the wheel will melt the center of the fusible plugs and allow the air to escape from the tire before it builds up enough pressure to cause an explosion.
[Ref: Airframe Handbook H-8083-31A-ATB, Chapter 13 Page 42, G-17]

13-25 AMA068

The greatest risk to an aircraft wheel assembly is due to

A. shock of hard landings or runway FOD.
B. drag pressure caused by an over-torqued axle nut.
C. heat from excessive braking.

13-26 AMA031

The braking action of a Cleveland disk brake is accomplished by compressing a rotating brake disk between two opposite brake linings. Equal pressure on both sides of the rotating disk is assured by allowing the

A. brake rotor to float to automatically equalize as pressure is applied to the rotor.
B. brake linings to automatically equalize as pressure is applied to the rotor.
C. caliper to float to automatically equalize as pressure is applied to the rotor.

13-27 AMA031

Why are segmented disc brakes typically used on large high performance aircraft?

A. If one disc segment fails, others can still stop the aircraft.
B. For better heat dissipation.
C. A single disc could not withstand the high pressure hydraulics.

13-28 AMA031

What mostly limits the amount of heat, which can be dissipated by carbon brakes?

A. The alloying metal in which the carbon is infused.
B. The melting point of adjacent system components.
C. The amount of cooling space between adjacent carbon rotors.

13-29 AMA031

What brake component builds up all the pressure required for braking?

A. Master Cylinder
B. Individual Wheel Cylinders
C. Expander Tube

13-30 AMA031

What is the purpose of a compensating port or valve in a brake master cylinder of an independent brake system?

A. Permits the fluid to flow toward or away from the reservoir as temperature changes.
B. Prevents fluid from flowing back to the reservoir.
C. Assists in the master cylinder piston return.

AIRCRAFT LANDING GEAR SYSTEMS

ANSWERS

13-25 Answer C.
The basic operation of brakes involves converting the kinetic energy of motion into heat energy through the creation of friction. A great amount of heat is developed and forces on the brake system components are demanding.
[Ref: Airframe Handbook H-8083-31A-ATB, Chapter 13 Page 43]

13-26 Answer C.
Cleveland brakes are a fixed-disc brake, allowing the brake caliper to move laterally on anchor bolts to deliver even pressure to each side of the brake disc.
[Ref: Airframe Handbook H-8083-31A-ATB, Chapter 13 Page 45, Figure 13-81]

13-27 Answer B.
The large amount of heat generated while slowing the rotation of the wheels on large and high performance aircraft is problematic. To better dissipate this heat, segmented rotor disc brakes have been developed.
[Ref: Airframe Handbook H-8083-31A-ATB, Chapter 13 Page 47]

13-28 Answer B.
Carbon brakes are able to withstand temperatures fifty percent higher than steel component brakes. The maximum designed operating temperature is limited by the ability of adjacent components to withstand the high temperature.
[Ref: Airframe Handbook H-8083-31A-ATB, Chapter 13 Page 50]

13-29 Answer A.
The master cylinders are used to develop the necessary hydraulic pressure to operate the brakes. This is similar to the brake system of an automobile.
[Ref: Airframe Handbook H-8083-31A-ATB, Chapter 13 Page 52]

13-30 Answer A.
Hydraulic fluid expands as temperature increases. Trapped fluid can cause a brake to drag against the rotor(s). Leaks may also result. When the brakes are not applied, fluid must be allowed to expand safely without causing these issues. A compensating port is included in most master cylinders to facilitate this. In the master cylinder, this port is opened when the piston is fully retracted. Fluid in the brake system is allowed to expand into the reservoir, which has the capacity to accept the extra fluid volume. The typical reservoir is also vented to the atmosphere to provide positive pressure on the fluid.
[Ref: Airframe Handbook H-8083-31A-ATB, Chapter 13 Page 54]

13-31 AMA032
A pilot reports that the right brake on an aircraft is spongy when the brake pedal is depressed in a normal manner. The probable cause is
  A. the hydraulic master cylinder piston return spring is weak.
  B. air in the brake hydraulic system.
  C. the hydraulic master cylinder piston is sticking.

13-32 AMA031
What type of valve is used in the brake actuating line to isolate the emergency brake system from the normal power brake control valve system?
  A. Shuttle Valve
  B. Bypass Valve
  C. Orifice Check Valve

13-33 AMA031
In large aircraft, what area of redundancy provides emergency braking in case of a partial system failure
  A. both pilot and copilot operate independent systems.
  B. secondary cylinders and actuators are installed on each wheel assembly.
  C. inboard and outboard wheels on each assembly are served separately.

13-34 AMA031
If a brake debooster is used in a hydraulic brake system, its position in the system will be
  A. in the brake pressure line between the brake pedal and the brake accumulator.
  B. between the brake control valve and the brake actuating cylinder.
  C. between the pressure manifold of the main hydraulic system and the power brake control valve.

13-35 AMA031
Lockout deboosters are primarily pressure reducing valves that
  A. cannot allow full debooster piston travel without fluid from the high pressure side entering the low pressure chamber.
  B. allow full debooster piston travel without fluid from the high pressure side entering the low pressure chamber.
  C. must be bled separately after brake bleeding has been completed.

13-36 AMA031
Debooster cylinders are used in brake systems primarily to
  A. reduce the pressure to the brake and increase the volume of fluid flow.
  B. relieve excessive fluid and ensure a positive release.
  C. reduce brake pressure and maintain static pressure.

AIRCRAFT LANDING GEAR SYSTEMS

ANSWERS

13-31 Answer B.
A common requirement of all braking systems is for there to be no air mixed in with the hydraulic fluid. Since air is compressible and hydraulic fluid essentially is not, any air under pressure when the brakes are applied causes spongy brakes. The pedals do not feel firm when pushed down due to the air compressing.
[Ref: Airframe Handbook H-8083-31A-ATB, Chapter 13 Page 55]

13-32 Answer A.
Shuttle valves are used to direct flow from optional sources of fluid, such as in redundant systems or during the use of an emergency brake power source. Some simpler power brake systems may use an emergency source of brake power that is delivered directly to the brake assemblies and bypasses the remainder of the brake system completely. A shuttle valve immediately upstream of the brake units shifts to accept this source when pressure is lost from the primary supply sources. Compressed air or nitrogen is sometimes used. A pre-charged fluid source can also be used as an alternate hydraulic source.
[Ref: Airframe Handbook H-8083-31A-ATB, Chapter 13 Page 56-60]

13-33 Answer C.
Typically, brake metering valves not only receive hydraulic pressure from two separate hydraulic systems, they also feed two separate brake assemblies. The inboard wheel brake and the outboard wheel brake, located in their respective wheel rims, are independent from each other. In case of hydraulic system failure or brake failure, each is independently supplied to adequately slow and stop the aircraft without the other. More complicated aircraft may involve another hydraulic system for back-up or use a similar alternation of sources and brake assemblies to maintain braking in case of hydraulic system or brake failure.
[Ref: Airframe Handbook H-8083-31A-ATB, Chapter 13 Page 59]

13-34 Answer B.
To supply the lower pressure, a brake debooster cylinder is installed downstream of the control valve and antiskid valve.
[Ref: Airframe Handbook H-8083-31A-ATB, Chapter 13 Page 61]

13-35 Answer B.
A lockout debooster functions as a debooster and a hydraulic fuse. If fluid is not encountered as the piston moves down in the cylinder, the flow of fluid to the brakes is stopped. This prevents the loss of all system hydraulic fluid should a rupture downstream of the debooster occur. Lockout deboosters have a handle to reset the device after it closes as a fuse. If not reset, no braking action is possible.
[Ref: Airframe Handbook H-8083-31A-ATB, Chapter 13 Page 61]

13-36 Answer A.
Debooster valve lowers the pressure of the fluid going to the brake and increases its volume. A debooster valve increases the smoothness of brake application and aids in rapid release of the brakes.
[Ref: Airframe Handbook H-8083-31A-ATB, Chapter 13 Page 61, G-11]

13-37 AMA031
In a brake antiskid system, when an approaching skid is sensed, an electrical signal is sent to the skid control valve which?
  A. Relieves the hydraulic pressure on the brake.
  B. Acts as a bypass for the debooster cylinders.
  C. Equalizes the hydraulic pressure in adjacent brakes.

13-38 AMA031
At what point in the landing operation does normal skid control perform its function
  A. when wheel rotation deceleration indicates an impending skid.
  B. anytime the wheel is rotating.
  C. when wheel rotation indicates hydroplaning.

13-39 AMA031
  1. An antiskid system is designed to apply enough force to operate just below the skid point.
  2. To operate the anti-skid system, flight deck switches must be placed in the ON position.

Regarding the above statements,
  A. Only No. 1 is true.
  B. Both No. 1 and No. 2 are true.
  C. Only No. 2 is true.

13-40 AMA031
In an antiskid system, wheel skid is detected by
  A. a sudden rise in brake pressure.
  B. a discriminator.
  C. an electrical sensor.

13-41 AMA031
Antiskid braking systems are generally armed by
  A. the rotation of the wheels above a certain speed.
  B. a centrifugal switch.
  C. a switch in the cockpit.

13-42 AMA031
An antiskid system is
  A. a hydraulic system.
  B. an electrical system.
  C. an electrohydraulic system.

AIRCRAFT LANDING GEAR SYSTEMS

ANSWERS

13-37 Answer A.
The anti-skid system not only detects wheel skid, it also detects when wheel skid is imminent. It automatically relieves pressure to the brake pistons of the wheel in question by momentarily connecting the pressurized brake fluid area to the hydraulic system return line. This allows the wheel to rotate and avoid a skid. Lower pressure is then maintained to the brake at a level that slows the wheel without causing it to skid.
[Ref: Airframe Handbook H-8083-31A-ATB, Chapter 13 Page 61]

13-38 Answer A.
The anti-skid system detects when wheel skid is imminent. It automatically relieves pressure to the brake pistons of the wheel in question by momentarily connecting the pressurized brake fluid area to the hydraulic system return line. This allows the wheel to rotate and avoid a skid. Lower pressure is then maintained to the brake at a level that slows the wheel without causing it to skid.
[Ref: Airframe Handbook H-8083-31A-ATB, Chapter 13 Page 61]

13-39 Answer B.
The anti-skid system automatically relieves pressure to the brake pistons of the wheel in question by momentarily connecting the pressurized brake fluid area to the hydraulic system return line. This allows the wheel to rotate and avoid a skid. An anti-skid system must be turned ON to operate; this is usually a step within the pilot's checklists.
[Ref: Airframe Handbook H-8083-31A-ATB, Chapter 13 Page 61-62]

13-40 Answer C.
There are various designs of anti-skid systems. Most contain three main types of components: wheel speed sensors, antiskid control valves, and a control unit. Wheel speed sensors are located on each wheel equipped with a brake assembly. Wheel speed sensors are transducers. They may be Alternating Current (AC) or Direct Current (DC).
[Ref: Airframe Handbook H-8083-31A-ATB, Chapter 13 Page 62]

13-41 Answer C.
To operate the anti-skid system, flight deck switches must be placed in the ON position.
[Ref: Airframe Handbook H-8083-31A-ATB, Chapter 13 Page 62]

13-42 Answer C.
An antiskid brake system is an electrohydraulic system in an airplane's power brake system that senses the deceleration rate of every main landing gear wheel. If any wheel decelerates too rapidly, indicating an impending skid, pressure to that bake is released and the wheel stops decelerating. Pressure is then reapplied at a slightly lower value.
[Ref: Airframe Handbook H-8083-31A-ATB, Chapter 13 Page 64, G-3]

13-43 AMA031
In the air with the antiskid armed, current cannot flow to the antiskid control box because
  A. landing gear squat switch is open.
  B. landing gear down and lock switch is open.
  C. landing gear antiskid valves are open.

13-44 AMA031
When a landing gear safety switch on a main gear strut closes at liftoff, which system is deactivated?
  A. Antiskid System
  B. Aural Warning System
  C. Landing Gear Position System

13-45 AMA032
Brake linings may remain in service until
  A. the measured wear exceeds 75% of their original thickness.
  B. less than .25" of material thickness remains and no damage or a glazed sheen is evident.
  C. it exceeds the individual manufacturer's wear specifications.

13-46 AMA032
In brake service work, the term "bleeding brakes" is the process of
  A. replacing small amounts of fluid in reservoir.
  B. withdrawing air only from the system.
  C. withdrawing fluid from the system for the purpose of removing air that has entered the system.

13-47 AMA032
How can it be determined that all air has been purged from a master cylinder brake system?
  A. By operating a hydraulic unit and watching the system pressure gauge for smooth, full scale deflection.
  B. By noting whether the brake is firm or spongy.
  C. By noting the amount of fluid return to the master cylinder upon brake release.

13-48 AMA031
The pressure source for power brakes is
  A. the main hydraulic system.
  B. a master cylinder.
  C. the power brake reservoir.

AIRCRAFT LANDING GEAR SYSTEMS

ANSWERS

13-43 Answer A.
The landing gear squat switch, or safety switch, is found on most aircraft. This is a switch positioned to open and close depending on the extension or compression of the main landing gear strut. On takeoff, the anti-skid system receives input through a switch located on the gear selector that shuts off the anti-skid system. This allows the brakes to be applied as retraction occurs so that no wheel rotation exists while the gear is stowed.
[Ref: Airframe Handbook H-8083-31A-ATB, Chapter 13 Page 22 & 66]

13-44 Answer A.
On takeoff, the anti-skid system receives input through a switch located on the gear selector that shuts off the anti-skid system. This allows the brakes to be applied as retraction occurs so that no wheel rotation exists while the gear is stowed.
[Ref: Airframe Handbook H-8083-31A-ATB, Chapter 13 Page 66]

13-45 Answer C.
Brake lining material is made to wear as it causes friction during application of the brakes. This wear must be monitored to ensure it is not worn beyond limits and sufficient lining is available for effective braking. The aircraft manufacturer gives specifications for lining wear in its maintenance information.
[Ref: Airframe Handbook H-8083-31A-ATB, Chapter 13 Page 68]

13-46 Answer C.
Bleeding of brakes is the maintenance procedure of removing air entrapped in hydraulic fluid in the brakes. Fluid is bled from the brake system until fluid with no bubbles flows out. The brake caliper has the necessary passages machined into it to facilitate hydraulic fluid movement and the application of pressure when the brakes are utilized. The caliper housing also contains a bleed port used by the technician to remove unwanted air from the system. Brake bleeding should be done in accordance with the manufacturer's maintenance instructions.
[Ref: Airframe Handbook H-8083-31A-ATB, Chapter 13 Page 44, G-5]

13-47 Answer B.
The presence of air in the brake system fluid causes the brake pedal to feel spongy. The air can be removed by bleeding to restore firm brake pedal feel. Brake systems must be bled according to manufacturers' instructions. Brakes are bled when the pedals feel spongy or whenever the brake system has been opened.
[Ref: Airframe Handbook H-8083-31A-ATB, Chapter 13 Page 69]

13-48 Answer A.
Power brakes on aircraft use the main hydraulic system to supply fluid for the brake actuation. Aircraft that require a large amount of fluid for their brake actuation normally use power brakes, and the volume of fluid sent to the brakes is increased by the use of deboosters.
[Ref: Airframe Handbook H-8083-31A-ATB, Chapter 13 Page 56, G-27]

13-49 AMA032

If it is determined that poor brake action is not caused by air in the brake system, what is the next most likely cause when hydraulic fluid is found on the floor away from the landing gear?

A. Loose or leaky brake system fittings.
B. Internal leakage in the master cylinder.
C. Worn brake lining.

13-50 AMA032

The left brake is dragging excessively on an airplane on which no recent brake service work has been performed. The most probable cause is

A. excessively worn brake linings.
B. low fluid supply in the brake system reservoir.
C. a weak return mechanism.

13-51 AMA032

A pilot reports that the brakes squeal when applied. What is the likely cause?

A. Foreign matter has gotten in between the linings and disk.
B. A brake disk is misaligned or warped.
C. The brake fluid level is low or contains air.

13-52 AMA097

What is the purpose of chines on an aircraft tire?

A. To deflect water away the fuselage.
B. To reduce the possibility of hydroplaning.
C. To improve lateral traction for operations in snow.

13-53 AMA097

How long should you wait after a flight before checking tire pressure?

A. 2 hours after a typical landing.
B. 3 hours after a typical landing.
C. When the wheel and tire are cool to the touch.

13-54 AMA097

The best safeguards against heat buildup in aircraft tires are

A. proper tire inflation, minimum braking, and ground rolls into the wind.
B. minimum braking, proper tire inflation, and long ground rolls.
C. short ground rolls, slow taxi speeds, minimum braking, and proper tire inflation.

AIRCRAFT LANDING GEAR SYSTEMS

ANSWERS

13-49 Answer A.
Many leaks are found at brake system fittings. While this type of leak may be fixed by tightening an obviously loose connection, the technician is cautioned against over-tightening fittings. Removal of hydraulic pressure from the brake system followed by disconnection and inspection of the connectors is recommended.
[Ref: Airframe Handbook H-8083-31A-ATB, Chapter 13 Page 72]

13-50 Answer C.
A brake may drag when the return mechanism is not functioning properly. This could be due to a weak return spring, the return pin slipping in the auto adjuster pin grip, or similar malfunction.
[Ref: Airframe Handbook H-8083-31A-ATB, Chapter 13 Page 75]

13-51 Answer B.
Brakes may chatter or squeal when the linings do not ride smoothly and evenly along the disc. A warped disc(s) in a multiple brake disc stack produces a condition wherein the brake is actually applied and removed many times per minute. This causes chattering and, at high frequency, it causes squealing. Any misalignment of the disc stack out of parallel causes the same phenomenon.
[Ref: Airframe Handbook H-8083-31A-ATB, Chapter 13 Page 76]

13-52 Answer A.
A chine is a special built-in deflector used on nose wheels of certain aircraft, usually those with fuselage-mounted engines. The chine diverts runway water to the side and away from the intake of the engines.
[Ref: Airframe Handbook H-8083-31A-ATB, Chapter 13 Page 79]

13-53 Answer B.
When checking tire pressure, allow 3 hours to elapse after a typical landing to ensure the tire has cooled to ambient temperature. The correct tire pressure for each ambient temperature is typically provided by the manufacturer on a table or graph.
[Ref: Airframe Handbook H-8083-31A-ATB, Chapter 13 Page 81]

13-54 Answer C.
The most important factor impinging on tire performance and wear, as well as resistance to damage is proper inflation. Taxiing for long distances or at high speeds increase the temperature of aircraft tires. This makes them more susceptible to wear and damage. Short taxi distances at moderate speeds are recommended. Caution should also be used to prevent riding the brakes while taxiing, which adds unnecessary heat to the tires. Heavy use of aircraft brakes introduces heat into the tires. Sharp radius turns do the same and increase tread abrasion and side loads on the tire. Plan ahead to allow the aircraft to slow without heavy braking and make large radius turns to avoid these conditions.
[Ref: Airframe Handbook H-8083-31A-ATB, Chapter 13 Page 81 & 94]

13-55 AMA097
Excessive wear in the center of the tread of an aircraft tire is an indication of
A. incorrect camber.
B. excessive toe out.
C. over inflation.

13-56 AMA097
Excessive wear in the shoulder area of an aircraft tire is an indication of
A. excessive toe-in.
B. under inflation.
C. over inflation.

13-57 AMA097
When inspecting an aircraft tire you notice multiple small chevron shaped cuts throughout its tread area. You should
A. remove the tire and inspect for further damage.
B. replace the tire before further flight.
C. do nothing; this is an acceptable condition.

13-58 AMA097
A high speed aircraft tire with a sound cord body and bead may be retread
A. a maximum of three times.
B. only by the tire manufacturer.
C. an indefinite number of times.

13-59 AMA097
A stripe or mark applied to a wheel rim and extending onto the sidewall of a tube type tire is a
A. wheel weight reference mark.
B. wheel-to-tire balance mark.
C. slippage mark.

13-60 AMA097
The primary purpose for balancing aircraft wheel assemblies is to
A. prevent heavy spots and reduce vibration.
B. reduce excessive wear and turbulence.
C. distribute the aircraft weight properly.

AIRCRAFT LANDING GEAR SYSTEMS

ANSWERS

13-55 Answer C.
The most important factor impinging on tire performance and wear, as well as resistance to damage is proper inflation. Over inflation of aircraft tires is another undesirable condition. While carcass damage due to overheating does not result, adherence to the landing surface is reduced. Over a long period of time, over inflation leads to premature tread wear. Therefore, over inflation reduces the number of cycles in service before the tire must be replaced. It makes the tire more susceptible to bruises, cutting, shock damage, and blowout.
[Ref: Airframe Handbook H-8083-31A-ATB, Chapter 13 Page 82]

13-56 Answer B.
Under inflated aircraft tires wear unevenly, which leads to premature tire replacement. They may also creep or slip on the wheel rim when under stress or when the brakes are applied. Severely under inflated tires can pinch the sidewall between the rim and the runway causing sidewall and rim damage. Damage to the bead and lower sidewall area are also likely. This type of abuse like any over flexing damages the integrity of the tire and it must be replaced. In dual-wheel setups, a severely under inflated tire affects both tires and both should be replaced.
[Ref: Airframe Handbook H-8083-31A-ATB, Chapter 13 Page 82]

13-57 Answer C.
Operation on a grooved runway can cause an aircraft tire tread to develop shallow chevron shaped cuts. These cuts are allowed for continued service, unless chunks or cuts into the fabric of the tire result. Deep chevrons that cause a chunk of the tread to be removed should not expose more than 1 square inch of the reinforcing or protector ply. Consult the applicable inspection parameters to determine the allowable extent of chevron cutting.
[Ref: Airframe Handbook H-8083-31A-ATB, Chapter 13 Page 85]

13-58 Answer C.
Tires that are retreaded are marked as such. They are not compromised in strength and give the performance of a new tire. No limits are established for the number of times a tire can be retreaded. This is based on the structural integrity of the tire carcass.
[Ref: Airframe Handbook H-8083-31A-ATB, Chapter 13 Page 88-89]

13-59 Answer C.
A slippage mark is a paint mark extending across the edge of an aircraft wheel onto a tube-type tire. When this mark is broken, it indicates the tire has slipped on the wheel, and there is a good reason to believe the tube has been damaged.
[Ref: Airframe Handbook H-8083-31A-ATB, Glossary Page G-32]

13-60 Answer A.
Once an aircraft tire is mounted, inflated, and accepted for service, it can be balanced to improve performance. Vibration is the main result of an imbalanced tire and wheel assembly.
[Ref: Airframe Handbook H-8083-31A-ATB, Chapter 13 Page 93]

ORAL EXAM

13-1(O).   How are shock struts measured for proper inflation?

13-2(O).   What is the purpose of a locking/disconnect pin on a nose gear strut.

13-3(O).   What is used to power large aircraft nose wheel steering.

13-4(O).   How does the pilot or mechanic control (steer) the aircraft while on the ground?

13-5(O).   What device is designed to prevent accidental gear retraction when an aircraft is on the ground?

13-6(O).   What should be done if a properly operating fusible plug has allowed a tire to deflate?

13-7(O).   Prior to performing an inspection how should the mechanic prepare the area?

13-8(O).   How can you detect the wear on a brake assembly?

13-9(O).   If a pilot reports that the brakes feel spongy, what might the cause be?

13-10(O).   What is the usually repair for a pilot discrepancy that the brakes feel spongy?

13-11(O).   How are the typical modern two-piece aircraft wheel constructed.

13-12(O).   Name the various classifications of tires.

13-13(O).   Why should the tires on split rim wheels be deflated before removing the wheel from the axle?

13-14(O).   How long can brake linings remain in service?

13-15(O).   Explain the phrase "bleeding the brakes".

13-16(O).   How can it be determined that all air has been purged from a master cylinder brake system?

13-17(O).   What should you look for when inspecting wheel bearings?

13-18(O).   How should tires be stored?

13-19(O).   What does excessive wear in the center of the tread of an aircraft tire indicate?

13-20(O).   How does over inflation affect tire life?

13-21(O).   How is a wheel skid detected by an antiskid system?

13-22(O).   How is the antiskid braking system generally armed by the pilot?

13-23(O).   What is the purpose of the skid control valve in a brake antiskid system?

13-24(O).   What is the purpose of landing gear position indicators and where are they located?

13-25(O).   How is the pilot warned that the landing gear is not down and locked?

13-26(O).   Explain the general operation of a landing gear warning system.

AIRCRAFT LANDING GEAR SYSTEMS

ANSWERS

ORAL EXAM

13-1(O). The correct amount of inflation is measured in psi on some struts. Other manufacturers specify struts to be inflated until extension of the lower strut is a certain measurement. Always follow manufacturer's instructions.
[Ref: Airframe Handbook H-8083-31A-ATB, Chapter 13 Page 13]

13-2(O). To disconnect steering when the aircraft is being towed or positioned in place.
[Ref: Airframe Handbook H-8083-31A-ATB, Chapter 13 Page 9]

13-3(O). Hydraulic power predominates.
[Ref: Airframe Handbook H-8083-31A-ATB, Chapter 13 Page 30]

13-4(O). Control of the steering is from the flight deck through the use of a small wheel, tiller, or joystick.
[Ref: Airframe Handbook H-8083-31A-ATB, Chapter 13 Page 30]

13-5(O). A landing gear squat switch, or safety switch, is found on most aircraft.
[Ref: Airframe Handbook H-8083-31A-ATB, Chapter 13 Page 23]

13-6(O). Fusible plugs or thermal plugs must be inspected visually. A close inspection should reveal whether any core has experienced deformation that might be due to high temperature. If detected, all thermal plugs in the wheel should be replaced with new plugs.
[Ref: Airframe Handbook H-8083-31A-ATB, Chapter 13 Page 42]

13-7(O). All surfaces should be cleaned to ensure that no trouble spots are undetected.
[Ref: Airframe Handbook H-8083-31A-ATB, Chapter 13 Page 25]

13-8(O). Many brake assemblies contain a built-in wear indicator pin. Typically, the exposed pin length decreases as the linings wear, and a minimum length is used to indicate the linings must be replaced.
[Ref: Airframe Handbook H-8083-31A-ATB, Chapter 13 Page 68]

13-9(O). The presence of air in the brake system fluid causes the brake pedal to feel spongy.
[Ref: Airframe Handbook H-8083-31A-ATB, Chapter 13 Page 69]

13-10(O). Trapped air in the lines can be removed by bleeding the breaks to restore firm brake pedal feel.
[Ref: Airframe Handbook H-8083-31A-ATB, Chapter 13 Page 69]

13-11(O). They are either cast or forged from aluminum or magnesium alloy.
[Ref: Airframe Handbook H-8083-31A-ATB, Chapter 13 Page 34]

13-12(O). Aircraft tires are classified in various ways including by: type, ply rating, whether they are tube-type or tubeless, and whether they are bias ply tires or radials. Identifying a tire by its dimensions is also used.
[Ref: Airframe Handbook H-8083-31A-ATB, Chapter 13 Page 76]

13-13(O). As a safety precaution, in case the bolts that hold the wheel halves together have been damaged or weakened.
[Ref: Airframe Handbook H-8083-31A-ATB, Chapter 13 Page 37]

13-14(O). Brake linings can remain in service until they exceed the individual manufacturer's wear specifications.
[Ref: Airframe Handbook H-8083-31A-ATB, Chapter 13 Page 68]

ORAL EXAM

13-15(O). Bleeding the brakes is a maintenance procedure that removes trapped air in hydraulic fluid in the brakes. Fluid is bled from the brake system until fluid with no bubbles flows out.
[Ref: Airframe Handbook H-8083-31A-ATB, Chapter 13 Page 44, G-5]

13-16(O). After bleeding the brakes, operate the brakes and note their feel; firm brakes have had the air properly removed, if they feel spongy air is still in the system.
[Ref: Airframe Handbook H-8083-31A-ATB, Chapter 13 Page 69]

13-17(O). Defects that would render it unserviceable, such as cracks, flaking, broken bearing surfaces, roughness due to impact pressure or surface wear, corrosion or pitting, discoloration from excessive heat, cracked or broken bearing cages, and scored or loose bearing cups or cones that would affect proper seating on the axle or wheel.
[Ref: Airframe Handbook H-8083-31A-ATB, Chapter 13 Page 25]

13-18(O). They should always be stored vertically so that it is resting on its treaded surface. Storage of tires on a tire rack with a minimum 3–4-inch flat resting surface for the tread is ideal and avoids tire distortion.
[Ref: Airframe Handbook H-8083-31A-ATB, Chapter 13 Page 89]

13-19(O). That the tire has been over inflated.
[Ref: Airframe Handbook H-8083-31A-ATB, Chapter 13 Page 82]

13-20(O). Over a long period of time, over inflation leads to premature tread wear, reducing the number of cycles in service before the tire must be replaced. It makes the tire more susceptible to bruises, cutting, shock damage, and blowout.
[Ref: Airframe Handbook H-8083-31A-ATB, Chapter 13 Page 82]

13-21(O). Wheel speed sensors are located on each wheel equipped with a brake assembly.
[Ref: Airframe Handbook H-8083-31A-ATB, Chapter 13 Page 62]

13-22(O). To arm the anti-skid system, flight deck switches must be placed in the ON position.
[Ref: Airframe Handbook H-8083-31A-ATB, Chapter 13 Page 62]

13-23(O). It relieves the hydraulic pressure on the brake.
[Ref: Airframe Handbook H-8083-31A-ATB, Chapter 13 Page 61]

13-24(O). They are used to inform the pilot of gear position status, and located on the instrument panel adjacent to the gear selector handle.
[Ref: Airframe Handbook H-8083-31A-ATB, Chapter 13 Page 24]

13-25(O). The most common display for the landing gear being down and locked is an illuminated green light. Some manufacturer's use a gear disagree annunciation when the landing gear is not in the same position as the selector system.
[Ref: Airframe Handbook H-8083-31A-ATB, Chapter 13 Page 24]

13-26(O). A system of lights used to indicate the condition of the landing gear. A red light illuminates when any of the gears are in an unsafe condition; a green light shows when all of the gears are down and locked, and no light is lit when the gears are all up and locked. An aural warning system is installed that sounds a horn if any of the landing gears are not down and locked when the throttles are retarded for landing.
[Ref: Airframe Handbook H-8083-31A-ATB, Glossary Page G-21]

AIRCRAFT LANDING GEAR SYSTEMS

QUESTIONS

PRACTICAL EXAM

13-1(P). Given an actual aircraft or mockup, perform an inspection of an install brake for serviceability and record your findings.

13-2(P). Given the appropriate documentation, determine the proper lubricant(s) for a specified landing gear.

13-3(P). Given an actual aircraft or mockup, perform an inspection of a landing gear and record your findings.

13-4(P). Given an actual aircraft or mockup, perform an inspection of a landing gear component(s) and record your findings.

13-5(P). Given an actual aircraft or mockup and the appropriate documentation, service an oleo strut.

13-6(P). Given an actual aircraft or mockup and the appropriate documentation, install a brake lining.

13-7(P). Given an actual aircraft or mockup and the appropriate documentation, install a brake assembly.

13-8(P). Given an actual aircraft or mockup and the appropriate documentation, clean and inspect wheel bearings.

13-9(P). Given an actual aircraft or mockup and the appropriate documentation, disassemble, clean as necessary, and inspect a wheel, record your findings.

13-10(P). Given an actual aircraft or mockup and the appropriate documentation, select lubricant, and lubricate wheel bearings.

13-11(P). Given an actual aircraft or mockup and the appropriate documentation, remove and replace a wheel and tire assembly on a landing gear.

13-12(P). Given an actual aircraft or mockup and the appropriate documentation, inspect a wheel and tire assembly, check tire pressure, and service as necessary, record maintenance and any findings.

13-13(P). Given an actual aircraft or mockup and the appropriate documentation, service a nose wheel shimmy damper, record maintenance.

13-14(P). Given an actual aircraft or mockup and the appropriate documentation, accomplish a landing gear retraction/ extension check and record maintenance.

13-15(P). Given an actual aircraft or mockup and the appropriate documentation, replace a tire, check for leaks, and record maintenance.

13-16(P). Given an actual aircraft or mockup and the appropriate documentation, replace a tube valve core, check for leaks and record maintenance.

13-17(P). Given an actual aircraft or mockup and the appropriate documentation, complete an operational check of an anti-skid warning system.

13-18(P). Given an actual aircraft or mockup and the appropriate documentation, inspect a landing gear position switch and record your findings.

PRACTICAL EXAM

13-19(P). Given an actual aircraft or mockup and the appropriate documentation, adjust a landing gear position switch and record maintenance.

13-20(P). Given an actual aircraft or mockup and the appropriate documentation, accomplish an operational check of a landing gear position indicating and/or warning system and record maintenance.

13-21(P). Given an actual aircraft or mockup, the appropriate documentation, and an unknown discrepancy troubleshoot a landing gear warning system.

13-22(P). Given an actual aircraft or mockup identify landing gear position/warning system components.

13-23(P). Given an actual aircraft or mockup and the appropriate documentation, locate the troubleshooting procedures for an anti-skid system.

13-24(P). Given an actual aircraft or mockup and the appropriate documentation, locate the troubleshooting procedures for a landing gear warning system.

PAGE LEFT BLANK INTENTIONALLY

Basic Fuel System Requirements, Types of Aviation Fuel, Aircraft Fuel Systems, Fuel System Repair, and Fuel System Servicing

14-1 AMA052
If a piston engine aircraft is fueled with Avgas of an insufficient octane rating, there will be an increased danger of
  A. insufficient combustion.
  B. vapor lock.
  C. detonation.

14-2 AMA052
The primary purpose of a fuel tank sump is to provide a
  A. place where water and dirt accumulations in the tank can collect and be drained.
  B. positive system of maintaining the design minimum fuel supply for safe operation.
  C. reserve supply of fuel to enable the aircraft to land safely in the event of fuel exhaustion.

14-3 AMA054
What precautions must be observed if a gravity feed fuel system is permitted to supply fuel to an engine from more than one tank at a time?
  A. Each tank must have a valve in its outlet that automatically shuts off the line when the tank is empty.
  B. The fuel outlet ports of each tank must have the same cross sectional area.
  C. The tank airspaces must be interconnected.

14-4 AMA052
Before fueling an aircraft by using the pressure fueling method, what important precaution should be observed?
  A. The truck pump pressure must be adjusted for minimum filter pressure.
  B. The aircraft's electrical system must be on to indicate quantity gauge readings.
  C. The truck pump pressure must be correct for that refueling system.

14-5 AMA052
  1. The fuel jettison valve must be designed to allow flight personnel to close the valve during any part of the jettisoning operation.
  2. During the fuel jettisoning operation, the fuel must discharge clear of any part of the airplane.

Regarding the above statements,
  A. Neither No. 1 nor No. 2 is true.
  B. Both No. 1 and No. 2 are true.
  C. Only No. 2 is true.

14-6 AMA052
Entrained water in aviation turbine fuel is a hazard because of its susceptibility to freezing as it passes through the filters. What are common methods of preventing this hazard?
  A. Micromesh fuel strainers and fuel heater.
  B. Anti-icing fuel additives and fuel heater.
  C. High-velocity fuel pumps and fuel heater.

AIRCRAFT FUEL SYSTEM

ANSWERS

14-1 Answer C.
An octane rating describes a fuel's resistance to detonation, meaning a tendency to pre-ignite due to heat and pressure too early in the 4 stroke cycle, possibly even before the piston reaches top dead center, and so risking structural damage to the engine. To raise the octane level in a fuel, certain chemicals such as Tetraethyl lead are added to increase the critical pressure and temperature of the fuel.
[Ref: Airframe Handbook H-8083-31A-ATB, Chapter 14 Page 5-6]

14-2 Answer A.
Each fuel tank must have a drainable sump that must allow drainage of any hazardous quantity of water from any part of the tank to its sump with the aircraft in the normal ground attitude. Reciprocating engine fuel systems must have a sediment bowl or chamber that is accessible for drainage.
[Ref: Airframe Handbook H-8083-31A-ATB, Chapter 14 Page 4]

14-3 Answer C.
High-wing aircraft with a fuel tank in each wing are common. With the tanks above the engine, gravity is used to deliver the fuel. The space above the liquid fuel is vented to maintain atmospheric pressure on the fuel as the tank empties. The two tanks are also vented to each other to ensure equal pressure when both tanks feed the engine.
[Ref: Airframe Handbook H-8083-31A-ATB, Chapter 14 Page 13]

14-4 Answer C.
Valves in the aircraft fuel system are controlled at the fueling station to direct fuel into the proper tank. Ensure that pressure developed by the refueling pump is correct for the aircraft before pumping fuel.
[Ref: Airframe Handbook H-8083-31A-ATB, Chapter 14 Page 6]

14-5 Answer B.
Fuel jettisoning systems must meet several standards. The fuel must discharge clear of any part of the aircraft and the jettisoning operation must not adversely affect the controllability of the airplane. The fuel jettisoning valve must be design to allow flight crew members to close the valve during any part of the jettisoning operation.
[Ref: Airframe Handbook H-8083-31A-ATB, Chapter 14 Page 6]

14-6 Answer B.
The formation of ice on the filter element blocks the flow of fuel through the filter. A valve in the filter unit bypasses fuel when this occurs. Use of an anti-icing solution in turbine fuel tanks helps prevent filter blockage from water that condenses out of the fuel as ice during flight.
[Ref: Airframe Handbook H-8083-31A-ATB, Chapter 14 Page 39 & 54]

14-7 AMA052
The primary purpose of an aircraft's fuel jettison system is to quickly achieve a
  A. lower landing weight.
  B. reduced fire hazard.
  C. balanced fuel load.

14-8 AMA052
Fuel jettisoning is usually accomplished
  A. by gravity flow into the outboard wing tanks and overboard through a common outlet in each wing.
  B. through individual outlets for each tank.
  C. through a common manifold and outlet in each wing.

14-9 AMA033
Carburetor icing may be eliminated by which of the following methods
  A. ethylene glycol spray and heated induction air.
  B. electrically heating air intake, ethylene glycol spray, or alcohol spray.
  C. heated induction air.

14-10 AMA052
What is one disadvantage of using aromatic aviation fuels?
  A. Results in low fuel volatility.
  B. A fuel inter-cooler is required.
  C. Deteriorates rubber parts.

14-11 AMA003
What markings are placed on or near each appropriate fuel filler cover on aircraft?
  A. The tank capacity.
  B. The correct type of fuel to be used.
  C. The words "Aviation Fuel".

14-12 AMA052
Which of the following precautions is most important during refueling operations?
  A. Fuel to be used must be appropriately identified.
  B. All electrical switches must be in the OFF position.
  C. All outside electrical sources must be disconnected from the aircraft.

AIRCRAFT FUEL SYSTEM

ANSWERS

14-7 Answer A.
If an aircraft's design landing weight is less than that of the maximum takeoff weight, a situation could occur in which a landing is desired before sufficient fuel has burned off to lighten the aircraft. Fuel jettisoning systems are required on these aircraft so that fuel can be jettisoned in flight to avoid structural damage caused by landing the aircraft when it is too heavy.
[Ref: Airframe Handbook H-8083-31A-ATB, Chapter 14 Page 6]

14-8 Answer C
The fuel transfer system (a common manifold) is used to feed the fuel dump valves that send fuel overboard. Boost pumps are used to move the fuel in the transfer system. While the exact location of the dump outlets is not given, it is clear that they are not in each tank since there are only two dump valve outlets and three tanks.
[Ref: Airframe Handbook H-8083-31A-ATB, Chapter 14 Page 21]

14-9 Answer C.
To combat carburetor icing, air preheated by the exhaust manifold is directed into the carburetor via a push/pull control on the flight deck. The control changes the position of the air diverter butterfly valve in the carburetor heat valve box.
[Ref: Airframe Handbook H-8083-31A-ATB, Chapter 14 Page 8]

14-10 Answer C.
In years past, considerable quantities of aromatic hydrocarbons were sometimes added to increase the rich mixture performance of AVGAS. Special hoses and seals were required for use of aromatic fuels. These additives are no longer available.
[Ref: Airframe Handbook H-8083-31A-ATB, Chapter 14 Page 8]

14-11 Answer B.
Each fuel tank receptacle or fuel cap is clearly marked to indicate which fuel is required.
[Ref: Airframe Handbook H-8083-31A-ATB, Chapter 14 Page 57]

14-12 Answer A.
The existence of more than one fuel makes it imperative that fuel be positively identified and never introduced into a fuel system that is not designed for it.
[Ref: Airframe Handbook H-8083-31A-ATB, Chapter 14 Page 10]

14-13 AMA052

Why are jet fuels more susceptible to water contamination than aviation gasoline?

- A. Jet fuel is lighter than gasoline; therefore, water is more easily suspended.
- B. Condensation is greater because of the higher volatility of jet fuels.
- C. Jet fuel has a higher viscosity than gasoline.

14-14 AMA052

The vapor pressure of aviation gasoline is

- A. lower than the vapor pressure of automotive gasoline.
- B. approximately 20 PSI at 100°F.
- C. higher than the vapor pressure of automotive gasoline.

14-15 AMA052

What is the maximum vapor pressure allowable for an aircraft fuel?

- A. 7 PSI
- B. 3 PSI
- C. 5 PSI

14-16 AMA054

On an aircraft with an integral fuel take, the out most bay of the tank, located near the tip of the wing is used primarily _____.

- A. as an overflow tank
- B. for extended range
- C. to fill in flight as needed for the purpose of lateral weight and balance

14-17 AMA054

Why are integral fuel tanks used in many large aircraft?

- A. To facilitate servicing.
- B. To reduce weight.
- C. To reduce fire hazards.

14-18 AMA056

Normal fuel cross-feed system operation in multiengine aircraft

- A. reduces contamination and/or fire hazards during fueling or defueling operations.
- B. provides a means to maintain a balanced fuel load condition.
- C. calls for jettisoning of fuel overboard to correct lateral instability.

AIRCRAFT FUEL SYSTEM

ANSWERS

14-13 Answer C.
The presence of water and fuel-consuming microbes is more prominent in jet fuel, which has different molecular structure than AVGAS and retains water in two principle ways. Some water is dissolved in the fuel. Other water is entrained in the fuel, which is more viscous than AVGAS.
[Ref: Airframe Handbook H-8083-31A-ATB, Chapter 14 Page 13]

14-14 Answer A.
AVGAS has a relatively low maximum vapor pressure compared to automotive gasoline – only 7 psi.
[Ref: Airframe Handbook H-8083-31A-ATB, Chapter 14 Page 13]

14-15 Answer A.
AVGAS has a relatively low maximum vapor pressure compared to automotive gasoline – only 7 psi.
[Ref: Airframe Handbook H-8083-31A-ATB, Chapter 14 Page 13]

14-16 Answer A.
For fuel management purposes, a wing may include a surge tank (or overflow tank) which is normally empty but may hold fuel when needed due to overflow from fuel expansion or over filling of the tanks.
[Ref: Airframe Handbook H-8083-31A-ATB, Chapter 14 Page 22]

14-17 Answer B.
The sealed skin and structure members of an integral fuel provide the highest volume of space available with the lowest weight.
[Ref: Airframe Handbook H-8083-31A-ATB, Chapter 14 Page 25]

14-18 Answer B.
In-tank fuel boost pumps move fuel into a manifold and, by opening the fuel valve for the desired tank, the fuel is transferred to that tank. Through the use of a fuel feed manifold and cross-feed valves, some aircraft allow engines to be run off fuel from any tank as a means of managing fuel location.
[Ref: Airframe Handbook H-8083-31A-ATB, Chapter 14 Page 20]

14-19 AMA054
The purpose of the baffle plate in a fuel tank is to
 A. resist fuel surging within the fuel tank.
 B. provide internal structural integrity.
 C. provide an expansion space for the fuel.

14-20 AMA055
If a bladder type fuel tank is to be left empty for an extended period of time, the inside of the tank should be coated with a film of
 A. ethylene glycol.
 B. engine oil.
 C. linseed oil.

14-21 AMA055
Which type of fuel valve will likely contain a 2nd thermal relief valve?
 A. Cone Valve
 B. Gate Valve.
 C. Poppet Valve

14-22 AMA055
Fuel system components must be bonded and grounded in order to
 A. retard galvanic corrosion.
 B. drain off static charges.
 C. prevent stray currents.

14-23 AMA055
When routing rigid fuel lines in the proximity of electrical wiring, it is considered best practice to _____.
 A. route the fuel line and wiring in a common harness
 B. route the fuel line below the height of the wiring
 C. route the fuel line above the height of the wiring

14-24 AMA054
Fuel boost pumps are operated
 A. automatically from fuel pressure.
 B. primarily for fuel transfer.
 C. to provide a positive flow of fuel to the engine.

AIRCRAFT FUEL SYSTEM

ANSWERS

14-19 Answer A.
When an aircraft maneuvers, the long, horizontal nature of an integral wing tank requires baffling to keep the fuel from sloshing. The wing ribs and box beam structural members serve as baffles and other may be added specifically for that purpose. Baffle check valves are commonly used. These valves allow fuel to move to the low, inboard sections of the tank but prevent it from moving outboard.
[Ref: Airframe Handbook H-8083-31A-ATB, Chapter 14 Page 25]

14-20 Answer B.
The soft flexible nature of bladder fuel tanks requires that they remain wet. Should it become necessary to store a bladder tank without fuel in it for an extended period of time, it is common to wipe the inside of the tank with a coating of clean engine oil.
[Ref: Airframe Handbook H-8083-31A-ATB, Chapter 14 Page 25]

14-21 Answer B.
Simple gate valves are common on large aircraft with large capacity fuel systems and tanks. The thermal relief valve will provide a pressure release should excess pressure build up against the gate due to fuel temperature increases.
[Ref: Airframe Handbook H-8083-31A-ATB, Chapter 14 Page 26]

14-22 Answer B.
Metal fuel lines and all aircraft fuel system components need to be electrically bonded and grounded to the aircraft structure. This is important because fuel flowing through the fuel system generates static electricity that must have a place to flow to ground rather than build up.
[Ref: Airframe Handbook H-8083-31A-ATB, Chapter 14 Page 26]

14-23 Answer B.
When routing both rigid or flexible fuel line and electrical wiring in close proximity, always route the wiring above the level of the fuel line. This ensures if the fuel line leaks, fuel will not drip on the wires.
[Ref: Airframe Handbook H-8083-31A-ATB, Chapter 14 Page 26 & 29]

14-24 Answer C.
Boost pumps are used to provide fuel under pressure to the engine driven pump and during starting when the engine driven pump is not yet up to speed for sufficient fuel delivery.
[Ref: Airframe Handbook H-8083-31A-ATB, Chapter 14 Page 31]

14-25 AMA054
What type of fuel booster pump requires a pressure relief valve?
A. Centrifugal
B. Sliding Vane
C. Concentric

14-28 AMA054
How is the outlet fuel pressure regulated on a submerged, single speed, centrifugal type fuel pump?
A. By the first check valve downstream from the pump.
B. By the pump's design and internal clearances.
C. By the engine driven pump's design and internal clearance.

14-26 AMA054
To prevent vapor lock in fuel lines at high altitude, some aircrafts are equipped with
A. vapor separators.
B. booster pumps.
C. direct injection type carburetors.

14-29 AMA054
Where are flapper valves typically located?
A. In fuel tank partitions.
B. Downstream of fuel filters.
C. Within vane type fuel pumps.

14-27 AMA054
What is used in many aircraft to prevent bubbles in the fuel after it leaves the tank when atmospheric pressure is lower than fuel vapor pressure?
A. Air Fuel Separators
B. Boost Pumps
C. Anti-foaming Additives

14-30 AMA054
Flapper valves are used in fuel tanks to
A. act as check valves.
B. reduce pressure.
C. prevent a negative pressure.

AIRCRAFT FUEL SYSTEM

ANSWERS

14-25 Answer B.
The constant volume of a vane pump can be excessive. To regulate flow, most vane pumps have an adjustable pressure relief feature. It uses pressure built up at the outlet of the pump to lift a valve off its seat, which returns excess fuel to the inlet side of the pump.
[Ref: Airframe Handbook H-8083-31A-ATB, Chapter 14 Page 35]

14-26 Answer B.
Centrifugal boost pumps located in fuel tanks ensure positive pressure throughout the fuel system regardless of temperature, altitude, or flight attitude thus preventing vapor lock.
[Ref: Airframe Handbook H-8083-31A-ATB, Chapter 14 Page 32]

14-27 Answer B.
Centrifugal boost pumps located in fuel tanks ensure positive pressure throughout the fuel system regardless of temperature, altitude, or flight attitude thus preventing vapor lock.
[Ref: Airframe Handbook H-8083-31A-ATB, Chapter 14 Page 32]

14-28 Answer B.
Some centrifugal fuel pumps operate at more than one speed. The outlet fuel flow and pressure are controlled by the speed selected by the pilot depending on the phase of the flight. A single speed pump outlet pressure is only controlled by the pump's design and internal clearances since the speed cannot be changed.
[Ref: Airframe Handbook H-8083-31A-ATB, Chapter 14 Page 32]

14-29 Answer B.
The section of the fuel tank dedicated for pump installation may be partitioned off with baffles that contain check valves, also known as flapper valves. These allow fuel to flow inboard to the pump during maneuvers but does not allow it to flow outboard.
[Ref: Airframe Handbook H-8083-31A-ATB, Chapter 14 Page 32]

14-30 Answer A.
The section of the fuel tank dedicated for pump installation may be partitioned off with baffles that contain check valves, also known as flapper valves. These allow fuel to flow inboard to the pump during maneuvers but does not allow it to flow outboard.
[Ref: Airframe Handbook H-8083-31A-ATB, Chapter 14 Page 32]

14-31 AMA055

Why are centrifugal type boost pumps used in fuel systems of aircraft operating at high altitude?

- A. To permit cooling air to circulate around the motor.
- B. To supply fuel under pressure to engine driven pumps.
- C. Because they are positive displacement pumps.

14-32 AMA054

The purpose of a diaphragm in a vane type fuel pump is to

- A. compensate fuel pressures to altitude changes.
- B. vary fuel pressure according to throttle setting.
- C. equalize fuel pressure at all speeds.

14-33 AMA052

Why is the main fuel strainer located at the lowest point in the fuel system?

- A. It filters and traps all micro organisms that may be present in the fuel system.
- B. It provides a drain for residual fuel.
- C. It traps any small amount of water that may be present in the fuel system.

14-34 AMA053

1. The function of a fuel heater is to protect the engine fuel system from ice formation.
2. An aircraft fuel heater cannot be used to thaw ice in the fuel screen.

Regarding the above statements,

- A. Only No. 1 is true.
- B. Both No. 1 and No. 2 are true.
- C. Only No. 2 is true.

14-35 AMA053

1. Gas turbine engine fuel systems are very susceptible to the formation of ice in the fuel filters.
2. A fuel heater operates as a heat exchanger to warm the fuel.

Regarding the above statements,

- A. Only No. 1 is true.
- B. Only No. 2 is true.
- C. Both No. 1 and No. 2 are true.

14-36 AMA054

What are the four general types of fuel quantity gauges?

1. Sight Glass
2. Mechanical
3. Electrical
4. Electronic
5. Bourdon Tube
6. Vane Type Transmitter
7. Litmus Indicator
8. Direct Reading Static Pressure Type
   A. 2, 3, 5, and 7
   B. 1, 3, 6, and 8
   C. 1, 2, 3, and 4

AIRCRAFT FUEL SYSTEM

ANSWERS

14-31 Answer B.
Centrifugal boost pumps located in fuel tanks ensure positive pressure throughout the fuel system regardless of temperature, altitude, or flight attitude thus preventing vapor lock.
[Ref: Airframe Handbook H-8083-31A-ATB, Chapter 14 Page 32]

14-32 Answer A.
Compensated vane –type pumps are used when the vane pump is the engine-driven primary fuel pump. The relief valve setting varies automatically to provide the correct delivery of the fuel as the air inlet pressure of the fuel metering device changes due to altitude or turbocharger outlet pressure. A vent chamber above the diaphragm attached to the relief valve mechanism is connected to the inlet air pressure source. As air pressure varies, the diaphragm assists or resists the relief valve spring pressure, resulting in proper fuel delivery for the condition at the fuel metering device.
[Ref: Airframe Handbook H-8083-31A-ATB, Chapter 14 Page 36]

14-33 Answer C.
The main fuel strainer is often mounted at a low point on the engine firewall. As with most filters or strainers, fuel is allowed to enter the unit but must travel up through the filtering element to exit.
Water, which is heavier than fuel, becomes trapped and collects in the bottom of the bowl. Other debris too large to pass through the element also settles in the strainer bowl.
[Ref: Airframe Handbook H-8083-31A-ATB, Chapter 14 Page 37]

14-34 Answer A.
Fuel heaters are used to warm the fuel so that ice does not form. These heat exchangers also heat the fuel sufficiently to melt any ice that has already formed.
[Ref: Airframe Handbook H-8083-31A-ATB, Chapter 14 Page 39]

14-35 Answer C.
Turbine powered aircraft operate at high altitude where the temperature is very low. As fuel in the tanks cools, water in the fuel condenses and freezes. It may form ice crystals in the tank or as the fuel/water solution slows and contacts the cool fuel filter element on its way through the fuel filter to the engines. Fuel heaters are used to warm the fuel so that ice does not form. These heat exchangers also heat the fuel sufficiently to melt any ice that has already formed.
[Ref: Airframe Handbook H-8083-31A-ATB, Chapter 14 Page 39]

14-36 Answer C.
A sight glass is a clear glass or plastic tube open to the fuel tank that fills with fuel to the same level as the fuel in the tank. Simple mechanical fuel indicators are used on light aircraft with fuel tanks in close proximity to the flight deck. Electric fuel quantity indicators are more common than mechanical indicators in modern aircraft. Most of these units operate with direct current and use variable resistance in a circuit to drive a ratiometer type indicator. Large and high performance aircraft typically utilize electronic fuel quantity system. They have variable capacitance transmitters in the tanks and thus have no moving parts.
[Ref: Airframe Handbook H-8083-31A-ATB, Chapter 14 Page 40-41]

14-37 AMA054

What is the purpose of a float-operated transmitter installed in a fuel tank?

A. It sends an electric signal to the fuel quantity indicator.
B. It senses the dielectric qualities of fuel and air in the tank.
C. It senses the total amount of fuel density.

14-38 AMA054

What type of remote reading fuel quantity indicating system has several probes installed in each fuel tank?

A. Direct Read In
B. Electromechanical
C. Electronic

14-39 AMA054

One advantage of electrical and electronic fuel quantity indicating systems is that

A. the indicators are calibrated in gallons, therefore, no conversion is necessary.
B. only one transmitter and one indicator are needed regardless of the number of tanks.
C. several fuel tank levels can be read on one indicator.

14-40 AMA054

One advantage of electrical and electronic fuel quantity indicating systems is that the indicator

A. can be located any distance from the tank(s).
B. always measures volume instead of mass.
C. has no movable devices.

14-41 AMA054

The electronic type fuel quantity indicating system consists of a bridge circuit

A. an amplifier, and indicator, and a tank unit.
B. a tank, an amplifier, and an indicator.
C. a tank unit, a tank, and an amplifier.

14-42 AMA054

A probe or a series of probes is used in what kind of fuel quantity indicating system?

A. Capacitor
B. Synchro
C. Selsyn

AIRCRAFT FUEL SYSTEM

ANSWERS

14-37 Answer A.
The movement of a float in the tank moves a connecting arm to the wiper on a variable resistor in the tank unit. The resistor is wired in series with one of the coils of the ratiometer type fuel gauge in the instrument panel. Changes in current flowing through the tank unit resistor change the current flowing through one of the coils in the indicator. This alters the magnetic field in which the indicator pointer pivots across the calibrated dial that indicates the corresponding fuel quantity.
[Ref: Airframe Handbook H-8083-31A-ATB, Chapter 14 Page 41]

14-38 Answer C.
In an electronic fuel quantity indicating system, variable capacitance transmitter are installed in the fuel tanks extending from top to bottom of each tank in the usable fuel. Several of these tank units, or fuel probes as they are sometimes called, may be installed in a large tank.
[Ref: Airframe Handbook H-8083-31A-ATB, Chapter 14 Page 41]

14-39 Answer C.
A fuel summation unit is part of the capacitance- type fuel quantity indication system. It is used to add the tank quantities from all indicators. This total aircraft fuel quantity can be used by the crew and by flight management computers for calculating optimum airspeed and engine performance limits for climb, cruise, descents, etc.
[Ref: Airframe Handbook H-8083-31A-ATB, Chapter 14 Page 43]

14-40 Answer A.
The use of direct reading fuel quantity indicator systems is only possible on light aircraft in which the fuel tanks are in close proximity to the cockpit. Other light aircraft and larger aircraft require remote indicating quantity systems such as electric indicators or electronic capacitance-type indicators.
[Ref: Airframe Handbook H-8083-31A-ATB, Chapter 14 Page 40]

14-41 Answer A.
In an electronic type fuel quantity indication system, the capacitance of the tank units is totaled and compared in a bridge circuit by a microchip computer in the tanks digital fuel quantity indicator on the flight deck. An amplifier is needed in older units to move the servo motor in analog-type indicators.
[Ref: Airframe Handbook H-8083-31A-ATB, Chapter 14 Page 41 & 43]

14-42 Answer A.
Electronic fuel quantity indication systems use variable capacitor-type transmitters in the fuel tanks. These units are also known as probes.
[Ref: Airframe Handbook H-8083-31A-ATB, Chapter 14 Page 41]

14-43 AMA054

What is the dielectric (non-conducting material) in a capacitance type fuel quantity indicating system?

A. Outer shell of the capacitor.
B. Fuel in the tank.
C. Fuel and air in the tank.

14-44 AMA054

A capacitance type fuel quantity indicating system measures fuel in

A. pounds per hour.
B. pounds.
C. gallons.

14-45 AMA054

In a fuel pressure warning circuit, if insufficient fuel pressure occurs,

A. electrical contacts will close.
B. electrical contacts will open.
C. a flapper valve will close.

14-46 AMA054

A fuel totalizer is a component which indicates the

A. total amount of fuel being consumed by all engines.
B. amount of fuel in any given tank.
C. amount of fuel in all tanks.

14-47 AMA054

A transmitter in a fuel pressure warning system serves what function

A. transmits an electrical signal to fluid pressure.
B. transmits fluid pressure directly to the indicator.
C. converts fluid pressure to an electrical signal.

14-48 AMA054

What is indicated when a fuel valve in-transit light illuminates?

A. A fuel valve is currently in motion.
B. Insufficient fuel pressure exists past a fuel valve.
C. Fuel is successfully being transferred to its desired location.

AIRCRAFT FUEL SYSTEM

ANSWERS

14-43 Answer C.
The capacitance of a tank unit can change if the dielectric constant of the material separating the plates varies. The material between the plates is either fuel (if the tank is full), air (if the tank is empty), or some ratio of fuel and air depending on how much fuel remains in the tank.
[Ref: Airframe Handbook H-8083-31A-ATB, Chapter 14 Page 43]

14-46 Answer C.
A summation unit is part of a capacitance-type fuel indication system. It is used to add the fuel quantities from all tanks.
[Ref: Airframe Handbook H-8083-31A-ATB, Chapter 14 Page 43]

14-44 Answer B.
When voltage is induced into the bridge circuit, the capacitive reactance of the tank probes and the reference capacitor can be equal or different. The magnitude of the difference is translated into an indication of the fuel quantity in the tank calibrated in pounds.
[Ref: Airframe Handbook H-8083-31A-ATB, Chapter 14 Page 43]

14-47 Answer C.
Low fuel pressure warning lights can be illuminated through the use of simple pressure switches. The contacts of the switch will close when fuel pressure against the diaphragm is insufficient to hold them open. This allows current to flow to the annunciator or warning light on the flight deck.
[Ref: Airframe Handbook H-8083-31A-ATB, Chapter 14 Page 48]

14-45 Answer A.
Electrical contact points are held open when sufficient fuel pressure exists. If it falls below a preset level, those contacts will close, illuminating a warning light in the cockpit.
[Ref: Airframe Handbook H-8083-31A-ATB, Chapter 14 Page 45]

14-48 Answer A.
An in transit light illuminates when a fuel valve is opening or closing. Contacts in the circuit open and the light goes out when the valve is fully open or fully closed.
[Ref: Airframe Handbook H-8083-31A-ATB, Chapter 14 Page 46]

14-49 AMA055
What unit would be adjusted to change the fuel pressure warning limits
  A. fuel pressure relief valve.
  B. fuel flow meter bypass valve.
  C. pressure sensitive mechanism.

14-50 AMA055
Fuel leaks are usually classified as a stain, a seep, a heavy seep, or a running leak. As a general rule
  A. stains, seeps, and heavy seeps are not flight hazards.
  B. all fuel leaks, regardless of location or severity, are considered a hazard to flight.
  C. stains, seeps, and heavy seeps, (in addition to running leaks) are considered flight hazards when located in unvented areas of the aircraft.

14-51 AMA055
When inspecting a removable rigid fuel tank for leaks, what procedure should be followed?
  A. Pressurize the tank with air and submerge in water to locate leaks.
  B. Pressurize the tank with air and brush with soapy water.
  C. Fill the tank with water and pressurize with air and brush with soapy water.

14-52 AMA055
What is the recommended practice for cleaning a fuel tank before welding?
  A. Steam clean the tank interior.
  B. Flush the inside of the tank with clean cold water.
  C. Purge the tank with ambient air.

14-53 AMA055
What should be used to remove flux from an aluminum tank after welded repair?
  A. Soft brush and warm water.
  B. 5 percent solution of nitric or sulfuric acid.
  C. Mild solution of soap and water.

14-54 AMA052
The absence of particulate contamination of jet fuel in transport aircraft is best maintained by
  A. frequent filter replacements.
  B. frequent sump drains.
  C. attentive fuel temperature control.

AIRCRAFT FUEL SYSTEM

ANSWERS

14-49 Answer C.
When a pressure switch is used to illuminate a low fuel pressure warning light, the switch may have on it an adjustment screw that can be set to illuminate the warning light at the correct pressure.
[Ref: Airframe Handbook H-8083-31A-ATB, Chapter 14 Page 48]

14-50 Answer C.
When fuel leaks into an area where the vapors can collect, the leak must be repaired before flight due to the potential for fire or explosion.
[Ref: Airframe Handbook H-8083-31A-ATB, Chapter 14 Page 49]

14-51 Answer B.
A leak check to ensure a welded repair is sound must follow the repair. This can be done by pressurizing the tank with a specified amount of air pressure and using a soapy solution on all seams and the repaired area. Bubbles form should the air escape. The amount of air pressure used is very low. One half to 3.5 psi is common.
[Ref: Airframe Handbook H-8083-31A-ATB, Chapter 14 Page 51]

14-52 Answer A.
The tank must be treated to remove any fuel vapors that remain in the tank before it is welded. This is critical to avoid serious injury from explosion should the fuel vapor ignite. The manufacturer usually gives a procedure for doing this. Some common methods for purging the tank include steam cleaning, hot water purging, and inert gas purging.
[Ref: Airframe Handbook H-8083-31A-ATB, Chapter 14 Page 51]

14-53 Answer B.
After a seam or damaged area is welded, you must clean the tank of any flux or debris that may have fallen into the tank. Water rinsing and acid solutions are commonly used.
[Ref: Airframe Handbook H-8083-31A-ATB, Chapter 14 Page 51]

14-54 Answer A.
Because of its higher viscosity, particulates are suspended in jet fuel for longer periods of time. Because of this, sumping alone is insufficient. Thus clean and frequently replace filters are the best way to trap particulate contamination.
[Ref: Airframe Handbook H-8083-31A-ATB, Chapter 14 Page 51]

14-55 AMA052
Microbial growth is produced by various forms of micro organisms that live and multiply in the water interfaces of jet fuels. Which of the following could result if microbial growth exists in a jet fuel tank and is not corrected?
1. Interference with fuel flow.
2. Interference with fuel quantity indicators.
3. Engine seizure.
4. Electrolytic corrosive action in a metal tank.
5. Lower grade rating of the fuel.
6. Lectrolytic corrosive action in a rubber tank.
   A. 2, 3, and 5
   B. 1, 5, and 6
   C. 1, 2, and 4

14-56 AMA052
Pressure fueling of aircraft is usually accomplished through
   A. at least one single point connection.
   B. individual fuel tank over wing and/or fuselage access points.
   C. pressure connections on individual fuel tanks.

14-57 AMA055
Which of the following may be used for the repair of fuel leaks on most integral fuel tanks?
   A. Resealing with proper sealing compound.
   B. Brazing
   C. Welding

14-58 AMA052
What can be done to eliminate or minimize the microbial growth problem in an aircraft jet fuel tank?
   A. Use antibacterial additive.
   B. Keep the fuel tank topped off.
   C. Add carbon dioxide as a purgative.

14-59 AMA054
What method is used on turbine powered aircraft to determine when the condition of the fuel is approaching the danger of forming ice crystals?
   A. Fuel Temperature Indicator
   B. Fuel Pressure Gauge
   C. Fuel Pressure Warning

14-60 AMA052
If an aircraft is fueled from a truck or storage tank which is known to be uncontaminated with dirt or water, periodic checks of the aircraft's fuel tank sumps and system strainers?
   A. Are still necessary due to the possibility of contamination from other sources.
   B. Can be eliminated except for the strainer check before the first flight of the day and the fuel tank sump check during 100 hour or annual inspections.
   C. Can be sharply reduced since contamination from other sources is relatively unlikely and of little consequence in modern aircraft fuel systems.

AIRCRAFT FUEL SYSTEM

ANSWERS

14-55 Answer C.
The presence of microorganisms in turbine engine fuel is a critical problem. There are hundreds of varieties of these life forms that live in the free water at the junction of the water and fuel in the fuel tank. They form a visible slime, multiply rapidly, and interfere with proper functioning of filter elements and fuel quantity indicators. The microbe/water layer in contact with fuel tank surfaces provides a medium for electrolytic corrosion or the tank.
[Ref: Airframe Handbook H-8083-31A-ATB, Chapter 14 Page 55-56]

14-56 Answer A.
Pressure refueling occurs at the bottom, front, or rear of the fuel tank. A pressure refueling nozzle locks on to the fueling port at the aircraft fueling station. Normally, all tanks can be fueled from a single point. Valves in the aircraft fuel system are controlled at the fueling station to direct the fuel into the proper tank.
[Ref: Airframe Handbook H-8083-31A-ATB, Chapter 14 Page 58]

14-57 Answer A.
Once the location of the leak has been determined, the tank sealant is removed and new sealant is applied. After cleaning the area with the recommended solvent, apply new sealant as instructed by the manufacturer.
[Ref: Airframe Handbook H-8083-31A-ATB, Chapter 14 Page 52]

14-58 Answer A.
Since microbes live in free water, the most powerful remedy for their presence is to keep water from accumulating in the fuel. The addition of biocides to the fuel when refueling also helps by killing organisms that are present.
[Ref: Airframe Handbook H-8083-31A-ATB, Chapter 14 Page 56]

14-59 Answer A.
Monitoring fuel temperature can inform the pilot when fuel temperature approaches that which could cause ice to form in the fuel system.
[Ref: Airframe Handbook H-8083-31A-ATB, Chapter 14 Page 46]

14-60 Answer A.
A continuous effort must be put forth by all those in the aviation industry to ensure that each aircraft is fueled only with clean fuel of the correct type. Many contaminants, both soluble and insoluble, can contaminate an aircraft's fuel supply. They can be introduced with the fuel during fueling or the contamination may occur after the fuel is on board. Onboard aircraft fuel systems must be maintained and serviced according to manufacturer's specifications.
[Ref: Airframe Handbook H-8083-31A-ATB, Chapter 14 Page 58]

14-61 AMA055
If it is necessary to enter an aircraft's fuel tank, which procedure should be avoided
  A. conduct the defueling and tank purging operation in an air conditioned building.
  B. continue purging the tank during the entire work period.
  C. station an assistant outside the fuel tank access to perform rescue operations if required.

14-62 AMA052
Aircraft defueling should be accomplished
  A. with the aircraft's communication equipment on and in contact with the tower in case of fire.
  B. in a hangar where activities can be controlled.
  C. in the open air for good ventilation.

14-63 AMA052
How may the anti-knock characteristics of a fuel be improved?
  A. By adding a knock enhancer.
  B. By adding a knock inhibitor.
  C. By adding a fungicide agent.

14-64 AMA053
A fuel temperature indicator is located in the fuel tanks on some turbine powered airplanes to tell when the fuel may be
  A. about to form rime ice.
  B. getting cold enough to form hard ice.
  C. in danger of forming ice crystals.

14-65 AMA054
  1. A fuel pressure relief valve is required on an aircraft positive displacement fuel pump.
  2. A fuel pressure relief valve is required on an aircraft centrifugal fuel boost pump.

Regarding the above statements,
  A. Both No. 1 and No. 2 are true.
  B. Only No. 2 is true.
  C. Only No. 1 is true.

14-66 AMA054
Low and mid-wing single reciprocating engine aircraft fuel systems typically consist of an?
  A. Engine driven pump and a primer.
  B. Electric fuel pump and an engine driven fuel pump.
  C. Electric fuel pump, an engine driven fuel pump, and a primer.

AIRCRAFT FUEL SYSTEM

ANSWERS

14-61 Answer A.
Due to the combustible nature of AVGAS and turbine engine fuel, the potential for fire while fueling and defueling aircraft must be addressed. Always fuel and defuel outside, not in a hangar that serves as an enclosed area for vapors to build up to a combustible level.
[Ref: Airframe Handbook H-8083-31A-ATB, Chapter 14 Page 58]

14-62 Answer C.
Due to the combustible nature of AVGAS and turbine engine fuel, the potential for fire while fueling and defueling aircraft must be addressed. Always fuel and defuel outside, not in a hangar that serves as an enclosed area for vapors to build up to a combustible level.
[Ref: Airframe Handbook H-8083-31A-ATB, Chapter 14 Page 58]

14-63 Answer B.
A pinging or knocking sound coming from an engine is a sign of detonation. To increase anti-detonation characteristics of fuel, substances can be added. Adding a substance known to inhibit knocking protects the engine from the damaging effects of detonation.
[Ref: Airframe Handbook H-8083-31A-ATB, Chapter 14 Page 9]

14-64 Answer C.
Monitoring fuel temperature can inform the pilot when fuel temperature approaches that which could cause ice to form in the fuel system.
[Ref: Airframe Handbook H-8083-31A-ATB, Chapter 14 Page 46]

14-65 Answer C.
An aircraft centrifugal fuel boost pump does not require a pressure relief valve since it is a variable displacement pump. A vane type pump is a positive displacement pump. The constant volume can be excessive so, to regulate flow, most vane type pumps have an adjustable pressure relief feature.
[Ref: Airframe Handbook H-8083-31A-ATB, Chapter 14 Page 32-35]

14-66 Answer C.
Fuel from the selector valve flows through the main strainer where it can supply the engine primer. Then, it flows downstream to the fuel pumps. Typically, one electric and one engine-driven fuel pump are arranged in parallel.
[Ref: Airframe Handbook H-8083-31A-ATB, Chapter 14 Page 14]

14-67 AMA054
Some high-wing, high-performance single engine reciprocating engine aircraft have fuel injection systems. In these systems the
A. fuel control delivers fuel to the fuel reservoir tanks.
B. fuel control delivers fuel to the distributor manifold.
C. auxiliary pump must be on to deliver fuel to the fuel control.

14-68 AMA054
A "wobble" pump is
A. an electric primary fuel pump located inside the fuel tank.
B. a hand operated pump used as a fuel primer on older reciprocating aircraft.
C. used to return excess fuel to reservoir tanks on fuel injected aircraft.

14-69 AMA054
The appearance of tan or brown tints on the surface of fuel or in filters is an indication that the fuel has been contaminated by
A. surfactants.
B. microorganisms.
C. moisture.

14-70 AMA054
Most aircraft fuel tanks contain baffling to
A. guide impurities to the sump.
B. provide vent space for the fuel at all attitudes.
C. subdue the fuel from shifting during flight maneuvers.

14-71 AMA054
A fuel selector valve in a single engine or light twin aircraft is likely to be what type of valve?
A. Gate
B. Cone
C. Bypass

14-72 AMA054
At the core of a pulsating electric pump used as an auxiliary fuel pump in light reciprocating engine aircraft is a
A. centrifugal impeller.
B. solenoid.
C. relay controlled rotating vane.

AIRCRAFT FUEL SYSTEM

ANSWERS

14-67 Answer B.
The engine driven fuel pump intakes the pressurized fuel from the electrically driven auxiliary pump or from the reservoir tanks if the electric pump is not running. The fuel control unit meters the fuel according to engine RPM and mixture control inputs from the cockpit. The fuel control delivers the fuel to the distribution manifold, which divides it and provides equal, consistent fuel flow for an individual fuel injector in each cylinder.
[Ref: Airframe Handbook H-8083-31A-ATB, Chapter 14 Page 15]

14-68 Answer B.
A hand-operated wobble pump located upstream of the strainer is used to prime the system for starting on the DC-3 and some other older reciprocating transport aircraft. Electric pumps on later model aircraft replaced the hand-operated wobble pumps.
[Ref: Airframe Handbook H-8083-31A-ATB, Chapter 14 Page 17]

14-69 Answer A.
Surfactants in small quantities naturally occur in fuels. In small quantities they are rarely a problem. Large quantities as indicated by a tan or brown soapy like liquid on the surface or in filters are problematic as they reduce the surface tension between water and fuel, so causing particulates to remain suspended longer.
[Ref: Airframe Handbook H-8083-31A-ATB, Chapter 14 Page 52]

14-70 Answer C.
Most aircraft fuel tanks contain some sort of baffling to subdue the fuel from shifting rapidly during flight maneuvers.
[Ref: Airframe Handbook H-8083-31A-ATB, Chapter 14 Page 22]

14-71 Answer B.
There are three basic types of hand-operated valves used in aircraft fuel systems. The cone-type and the poppet-type are commonly used in light general aviation aircraft as fuel selector valves. Gate valves are used on transport category aircraft as shutoff valves.
[Ref: Airframe Handbook H-8083-31A-ATB, Chapter 14 Page 28]

14-72 Answer B.
The pulsating electric pump uses a plunger to draw fuel in and push fuel out of the pump. It is powered by a solenoid that alternates between being energized and deenergized, which moves the plunger back and forth with a pulsating motion.
[Ref: Airframe Handbook H-8083-31A-ATB, Chapter 14 Page 34]

ORAL EXAM

14-1(O).   Where are fuel strainers located and what purpose do they serve?

14-2(O).   What are the construction characteristics of the three basic types of fuel tanks?

14-3(O).   How is maintenance performed on an integral fuel tank?

14-4(O).   What are some general rules for the installation and routing of fuel lines on an aircraft?

14-5(O).   What are the hazards of fuel system maintenance?

14-6(O).   On many aircraft fuel systems, what is done to ensure positive fuel flow to the engine(s)?

14-7(O).   What is the purpose of a fuel jettison system and what are some characteristics of a typical fuel jettison system?

AIRCRAFT FUEL SYSTEM

ANSWERS

ORAL EXAM

14-1(O).   A fuel strainer is located at the outlet of each fuel tank or there must be a fuel strainer for each boost pump. There must also be a fuel strainer, or filter, between the fuel tank outlet and the inlet of either the fuel metering device or an engine driven positive displacement pump, whichever is nearer to the tank outlet. The purpose of fuel strainers is to prevent the passage of any object that could restrict fuel flow or damage any fuel system component.
[Ref: Airframe Handbook H-8083-31A-ATB, Chapter 14 Page 5-6]

14-2(O).   The three basic types of fuel tanks are the rigid removable tank, the bladder tank, and the integral tank. The rigid removable tank must be strapped into the aircraft. It is typically made from aluminum alloy or stainless steel and is riveted and seam welded to prevent leaks. Many early fuel tanks were made from terneplate which have folded and soldered seams. Some modern rigid removable tanks are made from composite materials. The ability to remove the tank for repair is an important feature of rigid removable tanks. Bladder type fuel tanks are also used. They are constructed out of reinforced flexible material. Bladder tanks are also removable but require a smaller opening in the aircraft structure for installation and removal – a key feature of the bladder tank. Bladder tanks are seamless except where features are installed such as sumps and vents. They are repairable by patching and other techniques in accordance with manufacturer's instructions. Integral fuel tanks are formed when part of the aircraft wing or fuselage is sealed with a fuel resistant, two-part sealant and the cavity is used to contain fuel. The sealed skin and structural members provide the highest volume of space available for fuel storage at the lowest weight. They are repairable by draining, cleaning, and resealing. All fuel tanks share some common characteristics such as being made of non-corrosive materials, and being fitted with means for venting. They all have a sump designed as a place for water and sediment to settle and contain a drain valve. Many tanks have baffles to subdue the fuel from rapid movement during maneuvers and scuppers are often designed into the fill port area to drain away any spilled fuel.
[Ref: Airframe Handbook H-8083-31A-ATB, Chapter 14 Page 22-25]

14-3(O).   Maintenance and repair of an integral fuel tank usually requires that the fuel tank be drained and entered by the technician. When entering and performing maintenance on an integral fuel tank, all fuel must be emptied from the tank and strict safety procedures must be followed. Fuel vapors must be purged from the tank and respiratory equipment must be used by the technician who enters it. A full-time spotter must be positioned just outside of the tank to assist if needed.
[Ref: Airframe Handbook H-8083-31A-ATB, Chapter 14 Page 25]

14-4(O).   Several installation procedures for hoses and rigid fuel lines exist. Hoses should be installed without twisting and separation should be maintained between all hoses and electric wiring. Never clamp a wire to a fuel line. When separation is not possible, always route the fuel line below any wiring. Metal fuel lines and all fuel system components need to be electrically bonded and grounded to the aircraft structure. Special bonded cushion clamps should be used to secure rigid fuel lines in place. All fuel lines should be supported so that there is no strain on the fittings. Specific intervals for clamping are require when securing lines depending on fuel line diameter. Lines should be clamped so that fittings are aligned. Never draw two fittings together by threading. A wrench should be used only for tightening. A straight length of rigid fuel line should not be made between two components or fittings rigidly mounted to the airframe. A small bend should be made to absorb any strain from vibration or expansion and contraction due to temperature changes.
[Ref: Airframe Handbook H-8083-31A-ATB, Chapter 14 Page 26]

ORAL EXAM

14-5(O).   The primary hazard when working with AVGAS or turbine engine fuel is the potential for fire due to the fuel's combustible nature. All precautions taken with combustible liquids must be observed. Another potential hazard is caused by poor practices when handling fuel and when doing maintenance on the fuel system. Fuel contamination can be extremely hazardous and all steps must be taken to only introduce clean, uncontaminated, specified fuel into any aircraft fuel system. Proper inspection, sump draining and filter maintenance procedures should be strictly followed.
[Ref: Airframe Handbook H-8083-31A-ATB, Chapter 14 Page 54-58]

14-6(O).   If an aircraft has fuel tanks located above a carburetor (i.e. high-wing reciprocating aircraft), gravity is used to deliver the fuel to the engine. Vented fuel tanks enable atmospheric pressure to remain on the fuel load forcing it through the lines to the carburetor. Shifting fuel, high temperatures, and reduced atmospheric pressure as the aircraft gains altitude are concerns to avoid vapor lock. On low-wing aircraft, aircraft with fuselage tanks, and transport category aircraft gravity is not able to be used for positive fuel delivery. Often, fuel boost pumps are used. These pumps are located in the tanks (or at the tank outlet). Boost pumps force the fuel through the lines leading to the fuel metering device under positive pressure to ensure no interruption of fuel flow. Similarly, some light aircraft employ pumps that pull the fuel from the tanks in lieu of tank mounted boost pumps.
[Ref: Airframe Handbook H-8083-31A-ATB, Chapter 14 Page 22]

14-7(O).   If an aircraft's design landing weight is less than that of the maximum takeoff weight, a situation could occur in which a landing is desired before sufficient fuel has burned off to lighten the aircraft to or below the acceptable landing weight. Fuel jettisoning systems are required in these aircraft so that fuel can be jettisoned in flight to avoid structural damage cause by landing the aircraft when it is too heavy. Some characteristics of fuel jettisoning systems are required. The rate of fuel jettisoning as well as the various attitudes, speeds, and configurations of the aircraft are taken into consideration. The fuel must discharge clear of any part of the aircraft. The discharge of fuel must not affect the controllability of the aircraft. There must be enough redundancy so that the failure of a single component does not prevent the fuel from being jettisoned. Also, the process of jettisoning fuel must be able to be controlled by a valve and stopped if desired. The amount of fuel able to be jettisoned is also controlled.
[Ref: Airframe Handbook H-8083-31A-ATB, Chapter 14 Page 6-7]

AIRCRAFT FUEL SYSTEM

QUESTIONS

PRACTICAL EXAM

14-1(P).   Given an actual aircraft or mockup and the appropriate documentation, service a fuel system strainer and record maintenance.

14-2(P).   Given an actual aircraft or mockup and the appropriate documentation, install a fuel quantity transmitter and record maintenance.

14-3(P).   Given an actual aircraft or mockup and the appropriate documentation, accomplish an operational check of a fuel quantity transmitter and record maintenance.

14-4(P).   Given an actual aircraft or mockup and the appropriate documentation, install a fuel valve and record maintenance.

14-5(P).   Given an actual aircraft or mockup and the appropriate documentation, accomplish an operational check on a fuel valve and record maintenance.

14-6(P).   Given an actual aircraft or mockup and the appropriate documentation, install a fuel pump and record maintenance.

14-7(P).   Given an actual aircraft or mockup and the appropriate documentation, accomplish an operational check on a fuel pump and record maintenance.

14-8(P).   Given an actual aircraft or mockup and the appropriate documentation for a fuel system with an unknown discrepancy, troubleshoot the system and record your findings.

14-9(P).   Given a specified sized-fuel system leak or seep, determine airworthiness.

14-10(P). Given an actual aircraft or mockup and the appropriate documentation, inspect a fuel system and record your findings.

14-11(P). Given an actual aircraft or mockup and the appropriate documentation, inspect a fuel system component(s) and record your findings.

14-12(P). Given an actual aircraft or mockup and the appropriate documentation, check the operation of one or more fuel system components and record maintenance and any findings.

14-13(P). Given an actual aircraft or mockup and the appropriate documentation, inspect a metal fuel tank and record your findings.

14-14(P). Given an actual aircraft or mockup and the appropriate documentation, inspect a bladder fuel tank and record your findings.

14-15(P). Given an actual aircraft or mockup and the appropriate documentation, locate fuel system operating instructions.

14-16(P). Given an actual aircraft or mockup and the appropriate documentation, locate the procedures to inspect the fuel system.

ICE AND RAIN PROTECTION

Ice Control Systems, Wing and Stabilizer Deicing Systems, Propeller
Deice System, Ground Deicing of Aircraft, and Rain Control Systems

15-1 AMA024
What icing condition may occur when there is no visible
moisture present?
- A. Injector Ice
- B. Carburetor Ice
- C. Inlet Ice

15-2 AMA024
Ice buildup on an aircraft can have which of the
following effects?
1. Reduced control surface movement
2. Reduced radio reception
3. Reduced range
4. Increased fuel consumption
5. Reduced stall speed
6. Increased landing distances
- A. 4 of these 6 effects
- B. 5 of these 6 effects
- C. All of these 6 effects

15-3 AMA024
Some aircraft are protected against airframe icing by heating
the leading edges of the airfoils and intake ducts. When is
this type of anti ice system usually operated?
- A. Whenever icing conditions are first encountered or
  expected to occur.
- B. In symmetric cycles during icing conditions to remove
  ice as it accumulates.
- C. Continuously while the aircraft is in flight.

15-4 AMA024
The standard method of preventing ice buildup on pitot and
static air sensors is with
- A. thermal systems.
- B. chemical systems.
- C. pneumatic systems.

15-5 AMA024
The source of hot air for Wing Anti-Icing (WAI) systems on
turbine aircraft typically comes from
- A. electrically operated heaters powered by the
  engine compressor.
- B. bleed air from the compressor section of the engine.
- C. bleed air from the combustion section of the engine.

15-6 AMA024
What are the maximum operational temperatures on the
wing leading edge produced by a Wing Anti-Ice system on
business and transport jet aircraft?
- A. 140° at the inboard wing sections and 212° at the
  outboard wing sections.
- B. 212° at the inboard wing sections and 350° at the
  outboard wing sections.
- C. 350° at the inboard wing sections and 212° at the
  outboard wing sections.

ICE AND RAIN PROTECTION

ANSWERS

15-1 Answer B.
Carburetor ice can occur during warm weather with no visible moisture present. It is formed inside the carburetor of a reciprocating engine. Water in the fuel is vaporized and freezes when its temperature and pressures is reduced while moving through the venturi.
[Ref: Airframe Handbook H-8083-31A-ATB, Chapter 15 Page 2]

15-4 Answer A.
Thermal electric anti-ice systems are used on most air data probes, such as pitot tubes, static air ports, TAT and AOA probes, ice detectors, engine P2/T2 sensors as well as other small components which do not require a high amperage draw.
[Ref: Airframe Handbook H-8083-31A-ATB, Chapter 15 Page 10]

15-2 Answer B.
Choice 5 is incorrect. Stall speed in increased as ice builds up on the wings and remainder of the aircraft. This is due to both the increase in weight from the ice and because ice buildup will effectively change the shape of the wing thus altering the airflow patterns from its optimum ice free condition.
[Ref: Airframe Handbook H-8083-31A-ATB, Chapter 15 Page 2]

15-5 Answer B.
The engine compressor provides a satisfactory source of anti-icing heat. The bleed air is routed from the compressor section to each leading edge by an ejector in each of the wing's inboard area and then into piccolo tubes for distribution along the entire leading edge.
[Ref: Airframe Handbook H-8083-31A-ATB, Chapter 15 Page 5]

15-3 Answer A.
Electric heat emitting ice prevention systems are turned on before entering icing conditions and are designed to keep ice from forming on critical surfaces.
[Ref: Airframe Handbook H-8083-31A-ATB, Chapter 15 Page 3]

15-6 Answer C.
When the WAI switch is activated and the wing leading edge temperature reaches 140°F, temperature switches turn on the operational light on the WAI control panel. If the temperature in the wing leading edge exceeds approximately +212°F (outboard) or +350°F (inboard), an overheat warning light on the enunciator panel illuminates.
[Ref: Airframe Handbook H-8083-31A-ATB, Chapter 15 Page 5]

15-7 AMA024

Which of the following deactivates the Wing Anti-Ice (WAI) system when the aircraft is on the ground?
- A. System shut down by the crew.
- B. Engine speed sensor.
- C. Weight on wheels sensor.

15-8 AMA024

Which of the following are found in a laminated integral electrically heated windshield system?
1. Autotransformer
2. Heat Control Relay
3. Heat Control Toggle Switch
4. 24v DC Power Supply
5. Indicating Light
- A. 2, 3, 4, and 5
- B. 1, 2, 3, and 5
- C. 1, 2, 4, and 5

15-9 AMA024

Without touching the pitot/static tube, what is one check for proper operation of a pitot/static tube heater after replacement?
- A. Ammeter Reading
- B. Continuity Check Of System
- C. Voltmeter Reading

15-10 AMA024

What is the source of pressure for inflating deicer boots on reciprocating engine aircraft?
- A. Engine driven air pump.
- B. Ram air from engine intake.
- C. Electric pump powered by onboard generator.

15-11 AMA024

Deicer boots help remove ice accumulations by
- A. allowing only a thin layer of ice to build up.
- B. preventing the formation of ice.
- C. breaking up ice formations.

15-12 AMA024

Which if the following regulates the vacuum of the air pump to hold the deicing boots tightly against the wing when the system is shut off?
- A. Distributor Valve
- B. Pressure Regulator
- C. Vacuum Regulator

ICE AND RAIN PROTECTION

ANSWERS

15-7 Answer C.
The WAI system is only used in the air, except for ground tests. Unless overridden for testing, the weight on wheels sensors and/ or airspeed data disarms the WAI system when the aircraft is on the ground.
[Ref: Airframe Handbook H-8083-31A-ATB, Chapter 15 Page 6]

15-8 Answer B.
Whether resistance wires or a laminated conductive film is used, aircraft window heat systems have transformers to supply power and feedback mechanisms, such as thermistors, to provide a window heat control unit with information used to keep operating temperature within acceptable limits. Some systems are automatic while others are controlled by cockpit switches. Separate circuits for pilot and co-pilot are common to ensure visibility in case of a malfunction. Some windshield heating systems can be operated at two heat levels.
[Ref: Airframe Handbook H-8083-31A-ATB, Chapter 15 Page 10]

15-9 Answer A.
Pitot tube, for example, contains an internal electric element that is controlled by a switch in the cockpit. Use caution checking the function of the pitot heat when the aircraft is on the ground. The tube gets extremely hot. An ammeter or load meter in the circuit can be used as a substitute to touching the probe, if so equipped.
[Ref: Airframe Handbook H-8083-31A-ATB, Chapter 15 Page 10]

15-10 Answer A.
Reciprocating-engine aircraft typically use a dedicated engine driven air pump mounted on the accessory drive gearbox of the engine. The suction side of the pump holds the deicer boots tight to the aircraft when not inflated. The pressure side inflates the boots.
[Ref: Airframe Handbook H-8083-31A-ATB, Chapter 15 Page 12]

15-11 Answer C.
Deicer boots remove ice accumulation by breaking up ice formations; during operation, the tubes are inflated and deflated in an alternating cycle. This inflation and deflation causes the ice to crack and break off.
[Ref: Airframe Handbook H-8083-31A-ATB, Chapter 15 Page 3, 12-13]

15-12 Answer C.
A vacuum regulator connected to the suction side of the pressure pump is set to supply the optimum suction sufficient for the aircraft's gyro instruments and to hold the deice boots tightly against the airfoil surfaces when not in use.
[Ref: Airframe Handbook H-8083-31A-ATB, Chapter 15 Page 13]

15-13 AMA024
What controls the inflation sequence in a pneumatic deicer boot system?
  A. Cacuum Pump
  B. Shuttle Valve
  C. Distributor Valve

15-14 AMA024
On a turboprop aircraft, in addition to the wing and stabilizer deice boots, bleed air from a turbine engine is also used for deicing of the
  A. brakes.
  B. water lines and drains.
  C. propeller spinner.

15-15 AMA024
When manually operating a pneumatic wing deicing system, why must inflation of the boots be released after approximately 5 seconds?
  A. Avoid excessive drain of bleed air.
  B. Avoid cooling of the bleed air.
  C. Ice may reform on the inflated boots.

15-16 AMA024
In a deice boot system regulators and relief valves control the pressures on both the positive and suction sides of the deicing boots. Which is true of those pressures?
  A. Inflation pressures are greater than suction pressures.
  B. Suction pressures are greater than inflation pressures.
  C. Suction and inflation pressures are approximately equal.

15-17 AMA024
When installing pneumatic surface bonded type deicer boots?
  A. Apply a solution of glycerin and water between the rubber and the wing skin.
  B. Apply a silastic compound between the boot and the wing skin.
  C. Remove all paint from the area to be covered by the deicer boot.

15-18 AMA024
Why are the tubes of deicer boots alternately inflated?
  A. To minimize the need of bleed air.
  B. To minimize airflow disturbance over the wings.
  C. To minimize the load on the air pumps.

ICE AND RAIN PROTECTION

ANSWERS

15-13 Answer C.
The use of distributor valves is common in pneumatic deicer boots. A distributor valve is a multi-position control valve controlled by the timer. It routes air to different deice boots in a sequence that minimizes aerodynamic disturbances as the ice breaks of the aircraft. Boots are inflated symmetrically on each side of the fuselage to maintain control in flight while deicing occurs. Distributor valves are solenoid operated and incorporate the deflate valve function to reconnect the deice boots with the vacuum side of the pump after all have been inflated.
[Ref: Airframe Handbook H-8083-31A-ATB, Chapter 15 Page 14]

15-14 Answer A.
Besides wing and stabilizer deice books, engine bleed air is used for deicing of the brakes. Water lines, drains, propeller blades and spinners, and pitot tubes are deiced electrically.
[Ref: Airframe Handbook H-8083-31A-ATB, Chapter 15 Page 4 and 14]

15-15 Answer C.
If held inflated for more than 7-10 seconds, ice may reform on the inflated boots. Drain of the bleed air is never a problem. Temperature of the bleed air is not relevant and the boots inflation causes ice to be shed, not its heat.
[Ref: Airframe Handbook H-8083-31A-ATB, Chapter 15 Page 14]

15-16 Answer A.
Typical boot inflation pressures are from 15-20 psi. Suction pressures are limited to the requirements of gyroscopic instruments from 4.5-5.5 "Hg.
[Ref: Airframe Handbook H-8083-31A-ATB, Chapter 15 Page 18]

15-17 Answer C.
When gluing the deice boots to the leading edge of wings and stabilizers, the manufacturer's instruction must be strictly followed. Clean, paint- free surfaces are required for the glue to adhere properly.
[Ref: Airframe Handbook H-8083-31A-ATB, Chapter 15 Page 19]

15-18 Answer B.
In larger turbo prop aircraft, the boots are installed in sections along the wing with the different sections operating alternately and symmetrically about the fuselage. This is done so that any disturbance to airflow caused by an inflated tube is kept to a minimum by inflating only short sections on each wing at a time.
[Ref: Airframe Handbook H-8083-31A-ATB, Chapter 15 Page 13]

15-19 AMA024
Which of the following indications occur during a normal operational check of a pneumatic deicer system?
- A. Pressure and vacuum gauges will fluctuate as the deicer boots inflate and deflate.
- B. Relatively steady readings on the pressure gauge and fluctuating readings on the vacuum gauge.
- C. Fluctuating readings on the pressure gauge and relatively steady readings on the vacuum gauge.

15-20 AMA024
Unless otherwise stated, which is the proper method for removing old deicer boots?
- A. With hot air.
- B. With ethylene glycol.
- C. With solvents.

15-21 AMA024
If the boots of a pneumatic anti-icing system appear to inflate as an aircraft is climbing, the most likely corrective action is to?
- A. Check for loose or disconnected vacuum lines.
- B. Replace the air pump.
- C. Check deflate valves for dirt and debris around the diaphragm.

15-22 AMA024
What mixture should be used to remove frost from an aircraft surface?
- A. Methy Ethyl Ketone (MEK) and ethylene glycol.
- B. Ethylene glycol and isopropyl alcohol.
- C. Isopropyl alcohol and naptha.

15-23 AMA024
What is Hold-Over Time (HOT) as related to aircraft deicing procedures?
- A. Time that deicing fluids prevent the reformation of ice on a surface.
- B. The time needed for deicing fluid to react with and eliminate ice.
- C. Amount of time in which deicing fluid must be cleaned away if accidentally directly sprayed on a sensitive surface such as tires or instrument sensors.

15-24 AMA024
Which of the following is the best means to use when removing wet snow from an aircraft?
- A. Hot Air
- B. Warm Water
- C. A brush or a squeegee.

ICE AND RAIN PROTECTION

ANSWERS

15-19 Answer C.
With the deicer system controls in their proper positions, check the suction and pressure gauges for proper indications. The pressure gauge fluctuates as the deicer tubes inflate and deflate. A relatively steady reading should be maintained on the vacuum gauge.
[Ref: Airframe Handbook H-8083-31A-ATB, Chapter 15 Page 21]

15-20 Answer C.
When removing old deicer boots, use solvents to soften the old cement and peel off.
[Ref: Airframe Handbook H-8083-31A-ATB, Chapter 15 Page 21]

15-21 Answer A.
If the deice boots appear to inflate while climbing, the possible causes could be that the vacuum source for boot holddown is inoperative or the lines running through a pressurized cabin are loose or disconnected. Check the operation of the ball check in the deflate valve, if ok then check for loose or disconnected vacuum lines.
[Ref: Airframe Handbook H-8083-31A-ATB, Chapter 15 Page 22]

15-22 Answer B.
Frost deposits can be removed by placing the aircraft in a warm hangar or by using a frost remover or deicing fluid. These fluids normally contain ethylene glycol and isopropyl alcohol and can be applied either by spray or by hand.
[Ref: Airframe Handbook H-8083-31A-ATB, Chapter 15 Page 25]

15-23 Answer A.
Hold-Over Time (HOT) is the estimated time that deicing/anti-icing fluid prevents the formation of frost or ice and the accumulation of snow on the critical surfaces of an aircraft. HOT begins when the final application of deicing/anti-icing fluid commences and expires when the deicing/anti-icing fluid loses its effectiveness.
[Ref: Airframe Handbook H-8083-31A-ATB, Chapter 15 Page 25]

15-24 Answer C.
Deposits of deep, wet snow when ambient temperatures are slightly above the freezing point can be difficult to remove. This type of deposit should be removed with a soft brush or squeegee. Use care to avoid damage to antennas, vents, stall warning devices, vortex generators, etc., that may be concealed by the snow.
[Ref: Airframe Handbook H-8083-31A-ATB, Chapter 15 Page 27]

15-25 AMA034
Chemical rain repellent should not be used on a dry windshield because it will
- A. cause glass crazing.
- B. etch the glass.
- C. restrict visibility.

15-26 AMA024
Under which condition in below freezing temperatures will deicing fluids have the longest holdover time?
- A. Freezing Drizzle
- B. Snow
- C. Freezing Fog

15-27 AMA024
What is the principle characteristic of a windshield pneumatic rain removal system?
- A. An air blast spreads a liquid rain repellent evenly over the windshield that prevents raindrops from clinging to the glass surface.
- B. A pneumatic rain removal system is simply a mechanical windshield wiper system that is powered by pneumatic system pressure.
- C. An air blast forms a barrier that prevents raindrops from striking the windshield surface.

15-28 AMA024
How many layers of material are pressed together to form a windshield on a modern transport aircraft?
- A. 3
- B. 4
- C. 5

15-29 AMA024
Where are the heat sensors located on most aircraft with electrically heated windshields?
- A. Embedded in the glass.
- B. Around the glass.
- C. Attached to the glass.

15-30 AMA024
What type of anti-icing system is used to prevent the formation of ice in plumbing from lavatories and galleys to waste holding tanks?
- A. Chemical Systems
- B. Hot Air Blowers
- C. Electrical Heater Systems

ICE AND RAIN PROTECTION

ANSWERS

15-25 Answer C.
Chemical rain repellent should only be used in very wet conditions. The rain repellent system should not be operated on dry windows because heavy undiluted repellent restricts window visibility.
[Ref: Airframe Handbook H-8083-31A-ATB, Chapter 15 Page 27]

15-26 Answer C.
The longevity of the effectiveness of deicing fluids varies by the current weather condition. In order from the longest to shortest acceptable holdover times it is: frost, freezing fog, freezing drizzle, snow, and light freezing rain.
[Ref: Airframe Handbook H-8083-31A-ATB, Chapter 15 Page 26]

15-27 Answer C.
Pneumatic windshield rain removal systems direct a flow of heated air over the windshield. This heated air serves two purposes: first, the air breaks the rain drops into small particles that are then blown away; and secondly, the air heats the windshield to prevent the moisture from freezing. The air can be supplied by an electric blower or by bleed air.
[Ref: Airframe Handbook H-8083-31A-ATB, Chapter 15 Page 28]

15-28 Answer C.
Modern high performance windshields are constructed of 5 separate layers including an inner, center, and outer glass ply, with vinyl plies in between each. The vinyl ply contacting the outer glass ply contains a conductive coating to provide electrically generated heat for fog control.
[Ref: Airframe Handbook H-8083-31A-ATB, Chapter 15 Page 31]

15-29 Answer A.
To ensure enough heating is applied to the outside of the windshield, heating elements are placed on the inside of the outer glass ply.
[Ref: Airframe Handbook H-8083-31A-ATB, Chapter 15 Page 29]

15-30 Answer C.
Transport aircraft with water and waste systems on board use heat blankets, heater boots, and in-line electric heaters to prevent the formation of ice in the water supply lines, drain hoses, waste drain lines, and waste tank rinse fittings.
[Ref: Airframe Handbook H-8083-31A-ATB, Chapter 15 Page 32]

ORAL EXAM

15-1(O). What icing condition can occur even when there is no visible moisture present?

15-2(O). What effects does ice buildup have on an aircraft?

15-3(O). What is the most common method to prevent ice buildup on pitot and static air sensors?

15-4(O). What is the source of the hot air used in Wing Anti-Icing (WAI) systems on turbine aircraft and how is this air distributed?

15-5(O). Which aircraft components do ice and rain protection systems protect?

15-6(O). Explain the differences between a deice system and an anti-ice system.

15-7(O). What fluids are most commonly used as deicing fluids to remove frost from an aircraft surface?

15-8(O). Explain how deicer boots work.

15-9(O). What might cause pneumatic deice boots to inflate while climbing?

15-10(O). How would you check for proper operation of a pitot-static tube heater after replacement?

15-11(O). What may be used to clean deicer boots?

15-12(O). Explain how a pneumatic windshield rain removal system works.

15-13(O). Name three anti-ice methods for aircraft windshields.

ICE AND RAIN PROTECTION

ANSWERS

ORAL EXAM

15-1(O). Carburetor ice.
[Ref: Airframe Handbook H-8083-31A-ATB, Chapter 15 Page 2]

15-2(O). Reduced control surface movement, reduced radio reception, reduced range, increased fuel consumption, and increased landing distances.
[Ref: Airframe Handbook H-8083-31A-ATB, Chapter 15 Page 2]

15-3(O). Thermal electric anti-ice systems are the most common.
[Ref: Airframe Handbook H-8083-31A-ATB, Chapter 15 Page 4 & 10]

15-4(O). Bleed air from the compressor section of the engine. The bleed air is routed from the compressor section to each leading edge and distributed along the entire leading edge through piccolo tubes.
[Ref: Airframe Handbook H-8083-31A-ATB, Chapter 15 Page 5]

15-5(O). Wing leading edges, horizontal and vertical stabilizer leading edges, engine cowl leading edges, propellers, propeller spinner, air data probes, flight deck windows, water and waste system lines and drains, and antenna.
[Ref: Airframe Handbook H-8083-31A-ATB, Chapter 15 Page 2-3]

15-6(O). A deice system removes ice after it has formed, while an anti-ice system prevents the formation of ice on an aircraft structure.
[Ref: Airframe Handbook H-8083-31A-ATB, Chapter 15 Page 3, G-3 & G-12]

15-7(O). Ethylene glycol and isopropyl alcohol.
[Ref: Airframe Handbook H-8083-31A-ATB, Chapter 15 Page 25]

15-8(O). Deicer boots remove ice accumulation by breaking up ice formations; during operation, the tubes are inflated and deflated in an alternating cycle. This inflation and deflation causes the ice to crack and break off. [Ref: [Ref: Airframe Handbook H-8083-31A-ATB, Chapter 15 Page 3, 12-13]

15-9(O). The possible causes could be that the vacuum source for boot hold down is inoperative or the lines running through a pressurized cabin are loose or disconnected.
[Ref: Airframe Handbook H-8083-31A-ATB, Chapter 15 Page 22, Figure 15-33]

15-10(O). An ammeter reading.
[Ref: Airframe Handbook H-8083-31A-ATB, Chapter 15 Page 10]

15-11(O). Soap and water.
[Ref: Airframe Handbook H-8083-31A-ATB, Chapter 15 Page 22]

15-12(O). Pneumatic windshield rain removal systems direct a flow of heated air over the windshield. This heated air serves two purposes: first, the air breaks the rain drops into small particles that are then blown away; and secondly, the air heats the windshield to prevent the moisture from freezing.
[Ref: Airframe Handbook H-8083-31A-ATB, Chapter 15 Page 28]

15-13(O). Electrical, pneumatic, and chemical. Although extreme caution should be used with chemical anti-ice fluids.
[Ref: Airframe Handbook H-8083-31A-ATB, Chapter 15 Page 28-31]

PRACTICAL EXAM

15-1(P). Given an actual aircraft or mockup, and the appropriate documentation, and an unknown discrepancy troubleshoot a pitot anti-ice system and record your findings.

15-2(P). Given an actual aircraft or mockup, and the appropriate documentation, check the operation of a pitot-static anti-ice system and record your findings.

15-3(P). Given an actual aircraft or mockup, and the appropriate documentation, inspect a deicer boot and record your findings.

15-4(P). Given an actual aircraft or mockup, and the appropriate documentation, complete an operation check of a deicer boot and record your findings.

15-5(P). Given an actual aircraft or mockup, the appropriate documentation, adjust the tension of a windshield wiper blade to specification and record maintenance.

15-6(P). Given an actual aircraft or mockup, the appropriate documentation, inspect an electrically heated windshield.

15-7(P). Given an actual aircraft or mockup, the appropriate documentation, complete an operation check of an electrically heated windshield and record your findings.

15-8(P). Given an actual aircraft or mockup, the appropriate documentation and an unknown discrepancy troubleshoot a pneumatic deicer boot system and record your findings.

15-9(P). Given an actual aircraft or mockup, and the appropriate documentation, service a pneumatic deicer boot, record maintenance.

15-10(P). Given an actual aircraft or mockup, and the appropriate documentation, repair a pneumatic deicer boot, record maintenance.

PAGE LEFT BLANK INTENTIONALLY

CABIN ENVIRONMENTAL CONTROL SYSTEMS

Aircraft Oxygen Systems, Human Respiration and Circulation, Carbon Monoxide Poisoning, and Composition of the Atmosphere

CHAPTER
16

QUESTIONS

16-1 AMA074

The primary difference between aviation breathing oxygen and other types of commercially available oxygen is that

A. aviation oxygen has all water vapor removed.
B. aviation oxygen has greater purity.
C. aviation oxygen has a higher water vapor content.

16-4 AMA074

Composite oxygen bottles that conform to DOT-E-8162 have a service life of

A. 10 years or 5,000 filling cycles, whichever occurs first.
B. 5 years or 5,000 filling cycles, whichever occurs first.
C. 15 years or 10,000 filling cycles, whichever occurs first.

16-2 AMA074

What causes a sodium chlorate oxygen candle to begin to release oxygen?

A. Breaking a seal exposes it to air.
B. Breaking a seal introduces a catalyst.
C. It is ignited and burns.

16-5 AMA073

How often should standard weight high pressure oxygen cylinders be hydro-statically tested?

A. Every 4 Years
B. Every 3 Years
C. Every 5 Years

16-3 AMA074

What test is used to determine the serviceability of an oxygen cylinder

A. pressure test with water.
B. pressure test with nitrogen.
C. pressure test with manometer.

16-6 AMA074

What type of oxygen system uses the rebreather bag type mask?

A. Demand
B. Diluter Demand
C. Continuous Flow

CABIN ENVIRONMENTAL CONTROL SYSTEMS

ANSWERS

16-1 Answer A.
Aviator's breathing oxygen is tested for the presence of water. This is done to avoid the possibility of it freezing in the small passage ways of valves and regulators which could prevent delivery of the oxygen when needed. The water level should be a maximum of .02ml per liter of oxygen.
[Ref: Airframe Handbook H-8083-31A-ATB, Chapter 16 Page 4]

16-2 Answer C.
An oxygen candle is ignited by a firing pin or electrically. Once lit, it can not be extinguished and provides oxygen through a mask until it burns out.
[Ref: Airframe Handbook H-8083-31A-ATB, Chapter 16 Page 5]

16-3 Answer A.
To ensure serviceability, cylinders must be hydrostatically tested. A hydrostatic test consists of filling the container with water and pressurizing it to 166% (5/3rds) of its certified rating. It should not leak, rupture, or deform beyond an established limit.
[Ref: Airframe Handbook H-8083-31A-ATB, Chapter 16 Page 6]

16-4 Answer C.
Cylinders certified under DOT-E-8162 are tested to the same standard as 3HT cylinders and are now approved under DOT-SP-8162 specifications. They are popular for their light weight as they are constructed with an aluminum core wrapped with Kevlar.
[Ref: Airframe Handbook H-8083-31A-ATB, Chapter 16 Page 7]

16-5 Answer C.
The standard certification time of oxygen cylinders between hydrostatic testing to 5 years (previously 3 years). The manufactured date and certification number is stamped on each cylinder near the neck. Subsequent hydrostatic test dates are also stamped there as well.
[Ref: Airframe Handbook H-8083-31A-ATB, Chapter 16 Page 7]

16-6 Answer C.
Allowing oxygen to continuously flow from the cylinder can be wasteful. Sufficient flow rates are accomplished through the use of rebreather apparatus. Most continuous flow systems include a rebreather bag.
[Ref: Airframe Handbook H-8083-31A-ATB, Chapter 16 Page 7-8]

16-7 AMA072

What controls the amount of oxygen delivered to a mask in a continuous flow oxygen system?
   A. Calibrated Orifice
   B. Pilot's Regulator
   C. Pressure Reducing Valve

16-8 AMA072

In the diluter demand oxygen regulator, when does the demand valve operate?
   A. When the user breathes.
   B. When the user demands 100% oxygen.
   C. When the diluter control is set at normal.

16-9 AMA072

What is used in some oxygen systems to change high cylinder pressure to low system pressure?
   A. Pressure reducer valve.
   B. Calibrated fixed orifice.
   C. Diluter demand regulator.

16-10 AMA051

Tubing containing breathing oxygen for aviation use can be identified by their
   A. green banded tape with the words "BREATHING OXYGEN" and a black rectangle on a white background.
   B. yellow banded tape and the words "BREATHING OXYGEN" and a white rectangle on a green background.
   C. solid green tape with the words "BREATHING OXYGEN" in white over a black rectangle.

16-11 AMA073

How do oxygen system shut-off valves differ from other types of shut-off valves?
   A. They contain a Teflon lining to prevent static electrical build up.
   B. They are designed with finer pitch threads.
   C. They include built in detents to open in increments.

16-12 AMA073

When an aircraft's oxygen system has developed a leak, the lines and fittings should be
   A. removed and replaced.
   B. bubble tested with a special soap solution manufactured specifically for this purpose.
   C. inspected using a special oxygen system dye penetrant.

CABIN ENVIRONMENTAL CONTROL SYSTEMS

ANSWERS

16-7 Answer A.
Built-in continuous-flow gaseous oxygen systems accomplish a final flow rate to individual user stations through the use of a calibrated orifice in each mask.
[Ref: Airframe Handbook H-8083-31A-ATB, Chapter 16 Page 8]

16-8 Answer A.
The diluter-demand type regulator holds back the flow of oxygen until the user inhales. The regulator is a diaphragm operated valve which opens with slight suction and closes when the user exhales.
[Ref: Airframe Handbook H-8083-31A-ATB, Chapter 16 Page 11]

16-9 Answer A.
In a demand-flow oxygen system, the system pressure reducing valve is sometimes called a pressure regulator. This device lowers the oxygen pressure from the storage cylinder(s) to roughly 60-85 psi and delivers it to individual regulators dedicated for each user.
[Ref: Airframe Handbook H-8083-31A-ATB, Chapter 16 Page 11]

16-10 Answer A.
Installed oxygen tubing is usually identified with color coded tape applied to each end of the tubing, and at specified intervals along its length. The tape coding consists of a green band overprinted with the words "BREATHING OXYGEN" and a black rectangular symbol overprinted on a white background border strip.
[Ref: Airframe Handbook H-8083-31A-ATB, Chapter 16 Page 14]

16-11 Answer B.
Oxygen system shutoff valves are designed to open slowly to prevent the oxygen from flowing into obstructions at high velocity which could cause its ignition.
[Ref: Airframe Handbook H-8083-31A-ATB, Chapter 16 Page 15]

16-12 Answer B.
Detection of leaks should be performed with an oxygen-safe leak check fluid. This is a soapy liquid free from elements that might react with pure oxygen. The leak detection solution is applied to the outside of fittings and mating surfaces. The formation of bubbles indicates the location of a leak.
[Ref: Airframe Handbook H-8083-31A-ATB, Chapter 16 Page 16]

16-13 AMA074

The main cause of contamination in gaseous oxygen systems is
  A. moisture.
  B. dust and other airborne particulates.
  C. other atmospheric gasses.

16-16 AMA080

Which section of a turbine engine provides high pressure bleed air to an air cycle machine for pressurization and air conditioning?
  A. C-D inlet compressor duct.
  B. Inlet compressor.
  C. Compressor section of the turbine engine.

16-14 AMA080

The purpose of pressurizing aircraft cabins is to:
  1. Create the proper environment for prevention of hypoxia.
  2. Permit operation at high altitudes.

Regarding the above statements,
  A. Both no. 1 and No. 2 are true.
  B. Only No. 2 is true.
  C. Only no. 1 is true.

16-17 AMA080

Regarding the below statements,
  1. Usually bleed air from a gas-turbine engine compressor can be safely used for cabin pressurization.
  2. Independent cabin condition air machines (air cycle machine) can be powered by bleed air from an aircraft turbine engine compressor.
  A. Only No. 1 is true.
  B. Both No. 1 and No. 2 are true.
  C. Only No. 2 is true.

16-15 AMA080

Which best describes cabin differential pressure?
  A. Difference between the ambient and internal air pressure.
  B. Difference between cabin pressure controller setting and actual cabin pressure.
  C. Difference between cabin flight altitude pressure and Mean Sea Level pressure.

16-18 AMA080

On an turbine aircraft pressurization system, a jet pump multiplier is positioned _____.
  A. at the outflow valve in the aircraft cabin
  B. between the outside air inlet and the bleed air outflow
  C. between the bleed air inlet and the aircraft cabin

CABIN ENVIRONMENTAL CONTROL SYSTEMS

ANSWERS

16-13 Answer A.
The main cause of contamination in an oxygen system is moisture. In cold weather, moisture in the oxygen can condense. With repeated charging, a significant amount may collect. Additionally, systems that are opened contain the moisture from the air that has entered.
[Ref: Airframe Handbook H-8083-31A-ATB, Chapter 16 Page 19]

16-14 Answer A.
A cabin pressurization system must accomplish several functions to ensure passenger safety. It must be capable of maintaining a cabin pressure altitude of 8,000 feet or lower regardless of the altitude of the aircraft in order to ensure that enough oxygen is present at sufficient pressure to facilitate full blood saturation. It must be designed to prevent rapid changes of cabin pressure which can be injurious to passengers and crew. Additionally, it must circulate air from inside the cabin to the outside quickly enough to eliminates odors and to remove stale air.
[Ref: Airframe Handbook H-8083-31A-ATB, Chapter 16 Page 23]

16-15 Answer A.
Cabin differential pressure is the difference between the air pressure inside the cabin and the air pressure outside the cabin. Cabin pressure (psi) - ambient pressure (psi) = cabin differential pressure.
[Ref: Airframe Handbook H-8083-31A-ATB, Chapter 16 Page 23]

16-16 Answer C.
Bleed air from the compressor section of the turbine engine is relatively free of contaminants. As such, it is a great source of air for cabin pressurization.
[Ref: Airframe Handbook H-8083-31A-ATB, Chapter 16 Page 26]

16-17 Answer B.
Bleed air from the compressor section of a turbine engine is relatively free of contaminants. As such, it is a great source of air for cabin pressurization and other cabin air conditioning systems.
[Ref: Airframe Handbook H-8083-31A-ATB, Chapter 16 Page 26]

16-18 Answer C.
The venturi shaped jet pump multiplier creates a low pressure area within the air distribution lines to help draw additional outside air to supplement the airflow from the engine compressor bleed air ports.
[Ref: Airframe Handbook H-8083-31A-ATB, Chapter 16 Page 26-28]

16-19 AMA080
A cabin pressure controller operates by measuring
and comparing
  A. barometric pressure, cabin altitude, and cabin rate
     of change.
  B. bleed air pressure, outside air temperature, and cabin
     rate of climb.
  C. cabin rate of climb, bleed air volume, and
     cabin pressure.

16-20 AMA080
The cabin pressure of an aircraft in flight is maintained at the
selected altitude by
  A. controlling the air inflow rate.
  B. controlling the rate at which air leaves the cabin.
  C. inflating door seals and recirculating conditioned
     cabin air.

16-21 AMA080
What controls the operation of the cabin pressure regulator?
  A. Cabin Altitude
  B. Bleed Air Pressure
  C. Compression Air Pressure

16-22 AMA080
The altitude controller maintains cabin altitude by
modulation of the
  A. outflow valve.
  B. safety valve.
  C. safety and outflow valves.

16-23 AMA080
The cabin pressure control setting has a direct influence
upon the
  A. outflow valve opening.
  B. pneumatic system pressure.
  C. inflow valve opening.

16-24 AMA072
In a high-pressure system, if the pressure reducer fails,
what prevents high pressure oxygen from entering the
system downstream?
  A. Manifold Control Valve
  B. Check Valve
  C. Pressure Relief Valve

CABIN ENVIRONMENTAL CONTROL SYSTEMS

ANSWERS

16-19 Answer A.
With functions and appearance similar to an altimeter the cabin pressure controller is located in the pressurization panel in the cockpit. It may be adjusted for desired cabin pressure with additional options to input barometric pressure and the desired rate of cabin altitude change.
[Ref: Airframe Handbook H-8083-31A-ATB, Chapter 16 Page 28]

16-20 Answer B.
Control of cabin pressure is accomplished through regulating the amount of air that flows out of the cabin. A cabin outflow valve opens and closes to establish the amount of air pressure maintained. The valve operates pneumatically in response to the settings on the cockpit pressurization panel that adjusts the balance between cabin and ambient air pressure.
[Ref: Airframe Handbook H-8083-31A-ATB, Chapter 16 Page 30]

16-21 Answer A.
Cabin air pressure and the pressure regulator is based on a cabin altitude as selected on the pressurization control panel. Once set, no other input is needed from the crew.
[Ref: Airframe Handbook H-8083-31A-ATB, Chapter 16 Page 30]

16-22 Answer A.
Controlling cabin pressurization is accomplished through regulating the amount of air that flows out of the cabin. A cabin outflow valve opens, closes, or modulates to establish the amount of air pressure maintained in the cabin.
[Ref: Airframe Handbook H-8083-31A-ATB, Chapter 16 Page 30]

16-23 Answer A.
A cabin outflow valve opens, closes, or modulates to establish the amount of air pressure maintained in the cabin. They operate pneumatically in response to the settings on the cockpit pressurization panel that balances between cabin and ambient air pressure.
[Ref: Airframe Handbook H-8083-31A-ATB, Chapter 16 Page 30]

16-24 Answer C.
An additional safety valve is a pressure relief valve set to open at a predetermined pressure differential. It allows air to flow from the cabin to prevent internal pressure from exceeding design limitations. Figure 16-56 in the Airframe Textbook • p. 16-32, shows cabin air pressure safety valves on a large transport category aircraft. On most aircraft, safety valves are set to open between 8 and 10 psi.
[Ref: Airframe Handbook H-8083-31A-ATB, Chapter 16 Page 31]

16-25 AMA080

The purpose of the dump valve in a pressurized aircraft is to relieve

    A. a negative pressure differential.

    B. pressure in excess of the maximum differential.

    C. all positive pressure from the cabin.

16-26 AMA080

What component of a pressurization system prevents the cabin altitude from becoming higher than airplane altitude?

    A. Negative pressure relief valve.

    B. Cabin rate of descent control.

    C. Positive pressure relief valve.

16-27 AMA080

If the desired cabin pressure is not being maintained as the aircraft climbs, the control should be adjusted to cause the

    A. cabin compressor speed to decrease.

    B. outflow valve to close slower.

    C. outflow valve to close faster.

16-28 AMA080

On some cabin pressurization systems, pressurization on the ground is restricted by the

    A. main landing gear operated switch.

    B. negative pressure-relief valve.

    C. cabin pressure regulator.

16-29 AMA080

One purpose of a jet pump in a pressurization and air conditioning system is to

    A. produce high pressure for operation of the outflow valve.

    B. provide for augmentation of airflow in some areas of the aircraft.

    C. assist in the circulation of Freon.

16-30 AMA005

What type of oil is suitable for use in a vapor cycle cooling system?

    A. Low viscosity engine oil with the inability to absorb water.

    B. Highly refined synthetic oil, free from impurities with special water absorbing additives.

    C. Special high grade refrigeration oil.

CABIN ENVIRONMENTAL CONTROL SYSTEMS

ANSWERS

16-25 Answer C.
Some aircraft are equipped with pressurization dump valves. These essentially are safety valves that are operated automatically or manually by a switch in the cockpit. They are used to quickly remove air pressure from the cabin, in an abnormal, maintenance, or emergency situation.
[Ref: Airframe Handbook H-8083-31A-ATB, Chapter 16 Page 32]

16-26 Answer A.
A negative pressure relief valve is found on pressurized aircraft to ensure that air pressure outside the aircraft does not exceed cabin air pressure. The spring-loaded relief valve opens inward to allow ambient air to enter the cabin if this situation arises.
[Ref: Airframe Handbook H-8083-31A-ATB, Chapter 16 Page 32]

16-27 Answer C.
Closing the outflow quicker valve causes the cabin to pressurize quicker. Thus, if the outflow valve closes faster, cabin pressure will be more able to keep up with the airplane's climb rate.
[Ref: Airframe Handbook H-8083-31A-ATB, Chapter 16 Page 32-33]

16-28 Answer A.
A weight-on-wheels (WOW) switch attached to the landing gear are integral parts of many pressurization control systems. During ground operations the WOW switch controls the position of the pressurization safety valve, which is held in the open position until the aircraft takes off.
[Ref: Airframe Handbook H-8083-31A-ATB, Chapter 16 Page 33]

16-29 Answer B.
Compressor air is directed through a jet pump venturi creating low pressure. This low pressure area draws outside air which mixes with bleed air from the compressor, and then through a ducting system to various areas of the cabin.
[Ref: Airframe Handbook H-8083-31A-ATB, Chapter 16 Page 34]

16-30 Answer C.
The aircraft or cooling system manufacturer's maintenance manual will state the amount and specific type of oil to be put into the system when filling. These are typically highly refined mineral oils that are free from wax, sulfurs, or moisture.
[Ref: Airframe Handbook H-8083-31A-ATB, Chapter 16 Page 58]

16-31 AMA012
Which is considered a good practice concerning the inspection of heating and exhaust systems of aircraft utilizing a jacket around the engine exhaust as a heat source?
 A. Supplement physical inspections with periodic operational carbon monoxide detection tests.
 B. All exhaust system components should be removed periodically, and their condition determined by the magnetic particle inspection method.
 C. All exhaust system components should be removed and replaced at each 100-hour inspection period.

16-33 AMA006
The Air Cycle Machine (ACM) removes water from the conditioned cool air with a
 A. heat exchanger.
 B. fiberglass sock.
 C. isolation valve.

16-32 AMA002
Which statement is true regarding air-condition vapor cycle system?
 1. There are two sides to a vapor cycle system, low and high.
 2. The low side is at high pressure and temperature.
 3. The low side is at low pressure and temperature.
 A. 1 and 2
 B. 1and 3
 C. 1, 2, and 3

16-34 AMA035
The combustion chamber on a combustion heater uses air from
 A. bleed air from the gas-turbine engine compressor.
 B. ambient air scooped from outside the aircraft.
 C. air-cycle machine.

CABIN ENVIRONMENTAL CONTROL SYSTEMS

ANSWERS

16-31 Answer A.

A major concern of exhaust shroud heat systems is the possibility that exhaust gases could be drawn into the cabin. Even the slightest crack in an exhaust manifold could send enough carbon monoxide into the cabin to be fatal. The use of an in-cabin Carbon Monoxide detector as well as strict inspection procedures of all related components must be routinely carried out to minimize this threat.

[Ref: Airframe Handbook H-8083-31A-ATB, Chapter 16 Page 59]

16-32 Answer B.

There are two sides to the vapor cycle air-conditioning system. One accepts heat and is known as the low side. The other gives up heat and is known as the high side. Refrigerant on the low side is characterized as having low pressure and temperature. Refrigerant on the high side has high pressure and temperature.

[Ref: Airframe Handbook H-8083-31A-ATB, Chapter 16 Page 45]

16-33 Answer A

A water separator is used to remove the water from the saturated air before it is sent to the aircraft cabin. The separator operates with no moving parts. Foggy air from the Air Cycle Machine (ACM) enters and is forced through a fiberglass sock that condenses and coalesces the mist into larger water drops. The water collects on the sides of the separator and drains down and out of the unit, while the dry air passes through. A bypass valve is incorporated in case of a blockage.

[Ref: Airframe Handbook H-8083-31A-ATB, Chapter 16 Page 39]

16-34 Answer B.

The air used in the combustion process is ambient air scooped from outside the aircraft, or from the compartment in which the combustion heater is mounted.

[Ref: Airframe Handbook H-8083-31A-ATB, Chapter 16 Page 60]

ORAL EXAM

16-1(O).   How does an exhaust heat exchanger function to heat the cabin of an aircraft and what are the major concerns with this system during inspection?

16-2(O).   What is a combustion heater and describe any criterion for inspection of a combustion heater that may be particularly important?

16-3(O).   Briefly describe the vapor cycle of a vapor cycle air conditioning system.

16-4(O).   Briefly describe how an air cycle air conditioning system provides cool air to the aircraft cabin.

16-5(O).   Explain the two basic modes of cabin pressurization and name the single component that modulates to control the pressure of the air in the cabin during both modes of operation.

16-6(O).   What type(s) of oxygen system is typically used on light, general aviation aircraft and what type(s) is used on transport category aircraft?

16-7(O).   Name some precautions to be taken when performing maintenance on aircraft oxygen systems.

CABIN ENVIRONMENTAL CONTROL SYSTEMS

ANSWERS

ORAL EXAM

16-1(O). Used mostly on single-engine light aircraft, the exhaust shroud heater system directs ambient air into a metal shroud that encases part of the engine's exhaust system. The air is warmed by the exhaust pipes or muffler and is ducted through a firewall heater valve into the cabin. The major concern during inspection of this type of system is that the air routed to the cabin could be contaminated by exhaust gases. Even a small crack in the exhaust system could send enough carbon dioxide into the cabin air to be fatal. Typically during inspection, the exhaust system is pressurized and checked for leaks to ensure that there are no cracks.
[Ref: Airframe Handbook H-8083-31A-ATB, Chapter 16 Page 59]

16-2(O). A combustion heater is an independent heat source from the aircraft's engine(s). It is used on small to medium sized aircraft. The combustion heater is similar to an exhaust shroud heater in that ambient air is heated and ducted into the cabin. The source of heat is an independent combustion chamber located inside the cylindrical outer shroud of the heater unit. The correct amount of aircraft fuel and air are ignited in the air-tight inner chamber. The exhaust from this combustion is directed overboard. The ambient air is directed between the combustion chamber and the outer shroud. It absorbs the combustion heat by convection and is ducted into the cabin. Since the source of heat of a combustion heater is burning fuel, it is essential during inspection that close observation for fuel leaks or cracks in the combustion chamber be made so the warmed ambient air is not contaminated by fuel vapor or carbon monoxide.
[Ref: Airframe Handbook H-8083-31A-ATB, Chapter 16 Page 60-62]

16-3(O). Vapor cycle air conditioning is a closed system used solely for the transfer of heat from inside the cabin to outside of the cabin. Heat energy is moved from the cabin air into a liquid refrigerant by blowing the cabin air over a heat exchanger containing the refrigerant. Due to the additional energy, the liquid changes into a vapor. The vapor is then compressed and becomes very hot. The very hot vapor refrigerant is routed into a different heat exchanger where the heat from the refrigerant is transferred to the outside air. In doing so, the refrigerant cools and condenses back into a liquid where it is used to begin the cycle described again. The routing of refrigerant through the vapor cycle air conditioning components is as follows: Evaporator ? compressor ? condenser ? receiver dryer ? expansion valve ? evaporator. Be prepared to discuss the function of each component with the examiner. See the referenced pages for this information.
[Ref: Airframe Handbook H-8083-31A-ATB, Chapter 16 Page 40-51]

16-4(O). Turbine engine bleed air is conditioned for use in the cabin during air cycle air conditioning. It is let into the system where it is routed to a heat exchanger that cools the bleed air with ambient air. The cooled bleed air is directed into the compressor of the air cycle machine (ACM). There, it is compressed before flowing through a secondary heat exchanger that again cools the bleed air with ambient air. The bleed air flows back into the ACM where it drives an expansion turbine. This cools the bleed air even further. Water is then removed and the bleed air is mixed with bypassed hot bleed air and sent to the cabin at the temperature requested by the crew. Be prepared to discuss the function of each component of the air cycle air conditioning system with the examiner. See the referenced pages for this information.
[Ref: Airframe Handbook H-8083-31A-ATB, Chapter 16 Page 36-40]

16-5(O). The two modes of pressurization are the isobaric mode and the differential pressure mode. In the isobaric mode, the pressurization system works to maintain a single pressure inside the cabin, known as cabin altitude, despite the altitude of the aircraft or the pressure of the ambient air outside of the aircraft. In the differential pressure mode, the system controls the cabin pressure to maintain a constant pressure difference between the air inside the cabin and the air outside of the aircraft regardless of altitude changes. The single device that opens, closes, or modulates to control the air exiting the cabin, and thus, the air pressure in the cabin is the outflow valve.
[Ref: Airframe Handbook H-8083-31A-ATB, Chapter 16 Page 27-30]

ORAL EXAM

16-6(O). Many light general aviation aircraft may not have an oxygen system if the aircraft is not designed to fly at altitudes where oxygen is required. For those that carry oxygen, general aviation aircraft may have simply a portable oxygen bottle to be used by the crew when desired. Or, a built in system may exist that uses approved containers of pressurized, gaseous oxygen. Both are typically delivered through regulated, continuous flow systems where oxygen is supplied at a steady rate when the valve of the oxygen container is opened. However, electronic pulse demand oxygen delivery systems are currently available for general aviation aircraft. These deliver timed pulses of oxygen, essentially creating a demand-type system where oxygen is only delivered when the crew inhales. Oxygen is carried on transport category aircraft for emergency purposes only. The pressurization of the cabin provides enough oxygen for the passengers and crew under normal circumstances. Gaseous and solid oxygen are used. The gaseous oxygen is stored in remote, pressurized tanks and routed to the users through a system of tubes. Solid oxygen generators produce gaseous oxygen for use when ignited. Passengers receive the oxygen from either source through a continuous flow delivery system. Most crew oxygen is delivered via demand flow or pressure-demand flow type regulators.

[Ref: Airframe Handbook H-8083-31A-ATB, Chapter 16 Page 16]

16-7(O). When working around oxygen and oxygen systems, cleanliness enhances safety. Clean, grease-free hands, clothes, and tools are essential. A good practice is to use only tools dedicated for work on oxygen systems. There should be absolutely no smoking or open flames within a minimum of 50 feet of the work area. Always use protective caps and plugs when working with oxygen cylinders, systems components, or plumbing. Do not use any kind of adhesive tape. Oxygen cylinders should be stored in a designated, cool, ventilated area in the hangar away from petroleum products or heat sources. Oxygen system maintenance should not be accomplished until the valve on the oxygen supply cylinder is closed and pressure is released from the system. Fittings should be unscrewed slowly to allow any residual pressure to dissipate. All oxygen lines should be marked and should have at least 2 inches of clearance from moving parts, electrical wiring, and all fluid lines. Adequate clearance must also be provided from hot ducts and other sources that might heat the oxygen. A pressure and leak check must be performed each time the system is opened for maintenance. Do not use any lubricants, sealers, cleaners, etc., unless specifically approved for oxygen system use.

[Ref: Airframe Handbook H-8083-31A-ATB, Chapter 16 Page 20-21]

CABIN ENVIRONMENTAL CONTROL SYSTEMS

PRACTICAL EXAM

16-1(P). Given an actual aircraft or mockup, the appropriate documentation, and an unknown discrepancy troubleshoot an exhaust heat exchanger cabin heat and record your findings.

16-2(P). Given an actual aircraft or mockup, and the appropriate documentation, inspect an exhaust heat exchanger cabin heat system and record your findings.

16-3(P). Given an actual aircraft or mockup, the appropriate documentation, and an unknown discrepancy troubleshoot an exhaust heat exchanger cabin heat component and record your findings.

16-4(P). Given an actual aircraft or mockup, and the appropriate documentation, inspect an exhaust heat exchanger cabin heat component and record your findings.

16-5(P). Given an actual aircraft or mockup, the appropriate documentation, and an unknown discrepancy troubleshoot a combustion air heater system and record your findings.

16-6(P). Given an actual aircraft or mockup, and the appropriate documentation, inspect a combustion air heater system and record your findings.

16-7(P). Given an actual aircraft or mockup, the appropriate documentation, and an unknown discrepancy troubleshoot a combustion air heater component and record your findings.

16-8(P). Given an actual aircraft or mockup, and the appropriate documentation, inspect a combustion air heater component and record your findings.

16-9(P). Given an actual aircraft or mockup, and the appropriate documentation, select proper solution and leak test oxygen system component and record your findings.

16-10(P). Given an actual aircraft or mockup, the appropriate documentation, and an unknown discrepancy troubleshoot an oxygen system and record your findings.

16-11(P). Given an actual aircraft or mockup, and the appropriate documentation, inspect an oxygen system component and record your findings.

16-12(P). Given an actual aircraft or mockup, the appropriate documentation, and an unknown discrepancy troubleshoot an oxygen system component and record your findings.

16-13(P). Given an actual aircraft or mockup, and the appropriate documentation, complete an operation check of an oxygen system and record your findings.

16-14(P). Given an actual aircraft or mockup, and the appropriate documentation, service an oxygen system and record maintenance.

16-15(P). Given an actual aircraft or mockup, and the appropriate documentation, purge an oxygen system and record maintenance.

16-16(P). Given an actual aircraft or mockup, the appropriate documentation, and an unknown discrepancy troubleshoot a vapor cycle cooling system and record your findings.

PRACTICAL EXAM

16-17(P). Given an actual aircraft or mockup, and the appropriate documentation, inspect a vapor cycle cooling system and record your findings.

16-18(P). Given an actual aircraft or mockup, the appropriate documentation, and an unknown discrepancy troubleshoot a vapor cycle cooling component and record your findings.

16-19(P). Given an actual aircraft or mockup, and the appropriate documentation, inspect a vapor cycle cooling component and record your findings.

16-20(P). Given an actual aircraft or mockup, the appropriate documentation, and an unknown discrepancy troubleshoot a cabin pressurization system and record your findings.

16-21(P). Given an actual aircraft or mockup, and the appropriate documentation, inspect a cabin pressurization system and record your findings.

16-22(P). Given an actual aircraft or mockup, the appropriate documentation, and an unknown discrepancy troubleshoot a cabin pressurization system component and record your findings.

16-23(P). Given an actual aircraft or mockup, and the appropriate documentation, inspect a cabin pressurization system component and record your findings.

16-24(P). Given an actual aircraft or mockup, the appropriate documentation, and an unknown discrepancy troubleshoot an air cycle machine system and record your findings.

16-25(P). Given an actual aircraft or mockup, and the appropriate documentation, inspect an air cycle machine system and record your findings.

16-26(P). Given an actual aircraft or mockup, the appropriate documentation, and an unknown discrepancy troubleshoot an air cycle machine system component and record your findings.

16-27(P). Given an actual aircraft or mockup, and the appropriate documentation, inspect an air cycle machine system component and record your findings.

16-28(P). Given an actual aircraft or mockup, and the appropriate documentation, locate the procedures for protecting a vapor-cycle system from contamination during component replacement.

16-29(P). Given an actual aircraft or mockup, and the appropriate documentation, locate the procedures for servicing a vapor-cycle cooling system.

16-30(P). Given an actual aircraft or mockup, and the appropriate documentation, locate the procedures for inspecting a cabin outflow valve.

PAGE LEFT BLANK INTENTIONALLY

FIRE PROTECTION SYSTEMS

Fire Detection and Overheat Systems, Smoke, Flame, and Carbon Monoxide Systems, Extinguishers, Cargo Fire Detection, and Maintenance

CHAPTER
17

QUESTIONS

17-1 AMA048
Which class of fire requires an electrically non-conductive extinguishing agent?
A. Class A
B. Class B
C. Class C

17-2 AMA046
Which fire detection system measures temperature rate of rise compared to a reference temperature?
A. Lindberg Continuous Element
B. Fenwall Continuous Loop
C. Thermocouple

17-3 AMA046
A thermocouple fire warning system is activated by
A. certain temperature.
B. core resistance drop.
C. rate of temperature rise.

17-4 AMA046
When used in fire detection systems having a single indicator light, thermal switches are wired in
A. series with each other and parallel with the light.
B. parallel with each other and in series with the light.
C. series with each other and the light.

17-5 AMA046
As a metal's temperature increases, its resistance to electric current decreases. This is the basic principle behind which of the below fire detection system(s).
1. Fenwal system
2. Kidde system
3. Meggitt Safety system
4. Thermocouple system
5. Thermal switch system
6. Lindberg System
A. 1, 2, 4, and 5
B. 1, 2, 3, and 6
C. All of the above systems.

17-6 AMA046
When a fire has been extinguished, a Fenwall fire detection system
A. automatically returns to standby status.
B. must be reset by an operator to continue service.
C. must have the sensing element replaced before returning to service.

FIRE PROTECTION SYSTEMS

ANSWERS

17-1 Answer C.
Class C fires involve energized electrical equipment where a non-conductive extinguishing agent is important such as carbon dioxide, dry chemicals or Halon. Water or specialized Class D dry powders are not appropriate for an electrical fire.
[Ref: Airframe Handbook H-8083-31A-ATB, Chapter 17 Page 2]

17-2 Answer C.
On a thermocouple system several active thermocouples are placed around the potential fire zone to be monitored and are connected to each other in series and with an additional referenced thermocouple outside the fire zone. When an active thermocouple sharply increases in temperature over the reference thermocouple, that change creates a voltage which completes the circuit to a warning light giving a visual fire warning in the cockpit.
[Ref: Airframe Handbook H-8083-31A-ATB, Chapter 17 Page 3]]

17-3 Answer C.
A thermocouple depends on the rate of temperature rise and does not give a warning of a gradual overheating condition when temperatures rise rapidly, the thermocouple produces a voltage because of the temperature difference between the reference junction and the hot junction. If both junctions are heated at the same rate, no voltage results.
[Ref: Airframe Handbook H-8083-31A-ATB, Chapter 17 Page 3]

17-4 Answer B.
As used in many older model aircraft, thermal switches are heat sensitive units that complete electrical circuits at a certain temperature. They are connected in parallel with each other but in series with the indicator lights. If the temperature rises above a set value the thermal switch closes, completing the light circuit to indicate a fire or overheat condition.
[Ref: Airframe Handbook H-8083-31A-ATB, Chapter 17 Page 3]

17-5 Answer A.
Each of these are thermo electric systems which read the current variation which occur when metals increase in temperature. Numbers 3 and 4 are pressure sensitive which measure the expansion of a gas as it heats up.
[Ref: Airframe Handbook H-8083-31A-ATB, Chapter 17 Page 3-6]

17-6 Answer A.
When the fire has been extinguished and the critical temperature lowered below the set point, the electrical resistance of the sensor returns to normal and reduces current flow. The Fenwal system then automatically returns to standby alert, ready to detect any subsequent fire or overheat condition.
[Ref: Airframe Handbook H-8083-31A-ATB, Chapter 17 Page 4]

17-7 AMA047

When performing a system test of a continuous loop fire detection system, a test switch switches one end of the sensing loop from its control circuit to
  A. ground.
  B. a power source.
  C. a test circuit built into the control unit.

17-8 AMA047

Maintenance of fire detection systems includes the
  A. repair of damaged sensing elements.
  B. removal of excessive loop or element material.
  C. replacement of damaged sensing elements.

17-9 AMA046

In a pneumatic type continuous loop fire detection system
  A. expanding hydrogen gas measures average temperatures; quantities of released helium gas indicate when a localized area is heated.
  B. expanding helium gas measures average temperatures; quantities of released hydrogen gas indicate when a localized area is heated.
  C. average measurement of both gasses provide for system redundancy and reduce false warnings.

17-10 AMA046

Class B fire zones in powerplant compartments are
  A. areas of no airflow such as wheel wells.
  B. areas of low airflow such as an accessory compartment.
  C. area of heavy airflow past aerodynamically clean obstructions.

17-11 AMA095

An ionization type lavatory smoke detector
  A. is powered by the aircraft's DC electrical system.
  B. is powered by the aircraft's AC electrical system.
  C. is powered with its own battery.

17-12 AMA095

What occurs when a light refraction type smoke detector is activated?
  A. A lamp within the indicator illuminates automatically.
  B. The test lamp illuminates and an alarm is provided automatically.
  C. A warning bell within the indicator alarms automatically.

FIRE PROTECTION SYSTEMS

ANSWERS

17-7 Answer C.
Actuating a test switch from the flight deck switches one end of the sensing element loop from its control circuit to a test circuit built into the control unit which simulates the resistance change due to heat. The other end of the loop stays in place.
[Ref: Airframe Handbook H-8083-31A-ATB, Chapter 17 Page 5]

17-8 Answer C.
Continuous loop sensing elements come in pre- made lengths and calibrations and cannot be altered in any way. Sensing elements are easy to replace. Do not attempt to repair them.
[Ref: Airframe Handbook H-8083-31A-ATB, Chapter 17 Page 6]

17-9 Answer B.
In a pneumatic fire detection system helium gas inside a sensing element expands when heated and increases pressure on an activation switch thus measuring average temperature within an observed area. Hydrogen gas within the core of the sensor is released in large quantities when a small section of the tube reaches a preset temperature. The outgassing increases pressure further inside the sensor and activates the alarm.
[Ref: Airframe Handbook H-8083-31A-ATB, Chapter 17 Page 7]

17-10 Answer C.
Included in class B zones are heat exchanger ducts, exhaust manifold shrouds, and areas where the inside of the enclosing cowling or other closure is smooth, free of pockets, and adequately drained so leaking flammables cannot puddle.
[Ref: Airframe Handbook H-8083-31A-ATB, Chapter 17 Page 8]

17-11 Answer A.
Both the sensing device and warning horn of an ionization smoke detector is connected to the aircraft's 28 volt DC electrical supply.
[Ref: Airframe Handbook H-8083-31A-ATB, Chapter 17 Page 8]

17-12 Answer A.
The light refraction type of smoke detector contains a photoelectric cell that detects light refracted by smoke particles. Smoke particles refract the light to the photoelectric cell and, when it senses enough of this light, it creates an electrical current that sets off a light.
[Ref: Airframe Handbook H-8083-31A-ATB, Chapter 17 Page 8-16]

17-13 AMA046
What causes the fire extinguishing system in the waste compartment of an aircraft lavatory to discharge?
 A. An optical sensor detects flames.
 B. Excess temperature.
 C. Smoke is detected.

17-14 AMA046
When air samples contain carbon monoxide, portable carbon monoxide detectors containing yellow silica gel will turn what color?
 A. Blue
 B. Dark Gray
 C. Red

17-15 AMA048
Halon (halogenated hydrocarbon) type fire extinguishing agents are recommended only for which of the following fire types?
 1. Class A
 2. Class B
 3. Class C
 4. Class D
 A. All of the above
 B. Type A&B only
 C. Type A, B, and C only

17-16 AMA048
The proper fire extinguishing agent to use on an aircraft brake fire is
 A. dry powder chemical.
 B. water.
 C. carbon dioxide.

17-17 AMA048
The types of fire extinguishing agents for aircraft interior fires are
 A. water and halon 1211.
 B. water and chlorobromomethane.
 C. water, carbon dioxide, and dry chemical.

17-18 AMA048
Which fire extinguishing agent is considered to be the least toxic?
 A. Bromochloromethsane (Halon 1011)
 B. Carbon dioxide
 C. Bromotrifluoromethane (Halon 1301)

FIRE PROTECTION SYSTEMS

ANSWERS

17-13 Answer B.
A Halon type fire extinguisher system is located in the waste compartment of aircraft lavatories. It is designed to discharge at approximately 170°F when a solder seal enclosing the extinguisher bottle melts.
[Ref: Airframe Handbook H-8083-31A-ATB, Chapter 17 Page 18]

17-14 Answer B.
On portable carbon monoxide detectors, the presence of carbon monoxide will turn the yellow or tan colored silica gel into darker shades of gray, or in extreme cases, even black. The speed and the intensity of this color change is an indication of the concentration and duration of exposure.
[Ref: Airframe Handbook H-8083-31A-ATB, Chapter 17 Page 9]

17-15 Answer C.
Do not use Halon extinguishers on class D fires as Halon agents react vigorously with burning metal.
[Ref: Airframe Handbook H-8083-31A-ATB, Chapter 17 Page 10]

17-16 Answer A.
Brake components are often constructed with magnesium which cannot be extinguished with water or carbon dioxide type extinguishers.
Burning magnesium is considered a class D fire which must be extinguished with special dry power chemicals.
[Ref: Airframe Handbook H-8083-31A-ATB, Chapter 17 Page 10-11]

17-17 Answer A.
All materials used in the cockpit and cabin must conform to strict standards to prevent fire. In case of a fire, several types of portable fire extinguishers are available to fight the fire. The most common types for this purpose are Halon 1211 water.
[Ref: Airframe Handbook H-8083-31A-ATB, Chapter 17 Page 11]

17-18 Answer C.
The most common agent used today is Halon 1301 because of its relatively low toxicity. Noncorrosive Halon 1301 does not affect material it contacts and requires no cleanup when discharged. Halon 1301 cannot be produced anymore because it depletes the ozone layer. It will be used until a suitable replacement is developed.
[Ref: Airframe Handbook H-8083-31A-ATB, Chapter 17 Page 12]

17-19 AMA048
Built in aircraft fire extinguishing systems are ordinarily charged with
A. sodium bicarbonate and nitrogen.
B. carbon dioxide and nitrogen.
C. halogenated hydrocarbons and nitrogen.

17-20 AMA048
What method is used to detect the thermal discharge of a built in fire extinguishing system?
A. A discoloring of the yellow plastic disk in the thermal discharge line.
B. A rupture of the red plastic disk in the thermal discharge line.
C. The thermal plug missing from the side of the bottle.

17-21 AMA048
In some fire extinguishing systems, evidence that the system has been intentionally discharged is indicated by the absence of a
A. red disk on the side of the fuselage.
B. yellow disk on the side of the fuselage.
C. green disk on the side of the fuselage.

17-22 AMA048
When the engine fire switch is activated. The engine shuts down due to
A. fuel flow being cut off.
B. ignition being cut off.
C. fire retardant agent displacing air (oxygen) flow.

17-23 AMA048
Which of the following are true regarding the complete requirements for a fire detection system within a cargo or baggage compartments on transport category aircraft?
1. Fire must be detected at a temperature less than what would cause structural damage to the aircraft.
2. Fire must be visually indicated to the flight crew within 1 minute of its start.
3. The flight crew must be able to check prior to flight for the proper functioning of each fire detector circuit.
A. 1 and 2
B. 1 and 3
C. All three requirements exist on the fire detection system of transport aircraft and are applicable to each individual cargo and baggage compartment on board.

17-24 AMA048
Cargo compartments are classified by their accessibility for flight crew members to detect and extinguish the fire. The classification of a cargo compartment on an aircraft used only for cargo in which cockpit displays and controls provide the flight crew with the means to detect and extinguish a fire is
A. Class E.
B. Class B.
C. Class C.

FIRE PROTECTION SYSTEMS

ANSWERS

17-19 Answer C.
Fire extinguisher containers store a liquid halogenated extinguishing agent, also known as Halon along with nitrogen as a pressurizing gas. Nitrogen which is both inert and non-corrosive pushes the Halon through the discharge port.
[Ref: Airframe Handbook H-8083-31A-ATB, Chapter 17 Page 12-16]

17-20 Answer B.
The thermal discharge indicator is connected to the fire container relief fitting and ejects a red disk to show when container contents have discharged due to excessive heat. This gives an indication that the fire extinguisher container needs to be replaced before next flight.
[Ref: Airframe Handbook H-8083-31A-ATB, Chapter 17 Page 13]

17-21 Answer B.
If the flight crew activates the fire extinguisher system, a yellow disk is ejected from the skin of the aircraft fuselage. This is an indication for the maintenance crew that the fire extinguishing system was activated and the fire extinguishing container needs to be replaced before next flight.
[Ref: Airframe Handbook H-8083-31A-ATB, Chapter 17 Page 14]

17-22 Answer A.
When an engine fire switch is activated;
1. the engine stops because the fuel control shuts off,
2. the engine is isolated from the rest of the aircraft and,
3. the fire extinguishing system is activated.
[Ref: Airframe Handbook H-8083-31A-ATB, Chapter 17 Page 14]

17-23 Answer C.
While choice 3 is in fact correct, the complete requirement is that the flight crew also have the ability to check the function of each fire detector circuit while in the aircraft is in flight.
[Ref: Airframe Handbook H-8083-31A-ATB, Chapter 17 Page 14-15]

17-24 Answer A.
Additional class E requirements are that controls to shut off ventilated air to the compartment are accessible to the flight crew, that means exist to exclude flame and hazardous smoke from the crew compartment, and that emergency exits exist for the crew under any cargo loading condition. Class B compartments are those in which a crew member while in flight may reach the fire with a hand held extinguisher. Class C compartments are similar in requirements to Class E, except on passenger configured transport aircraft.
[Ref: Airframe Handbook H-8083-31A-ATB, Chapter 17 Page 15]

17-25 AMA048

A cargo bay smoke detector system works through the principle of

A. "sniffing" for the chemical presence of smoke.
B. measuring an increase in light intensity due to the reflectivity of smoke particles.
C. measuring a decrease in light intensity due to the absorption of light by smoke particles.

17-26 AMA048

What type of fire extinguishing agent is used in built in cargo compartment extinguishing systems?

A. Halon 1301 or equivalent.
B. Carbon dioxide or equivalent.
C. Dry Powder chemicals or equivalent.

17-27 AMA095

When a lavatory smoke detector senses smoke on aircraft with passenger capacity of 20 or more, it

1. provides a visual or audible warning to the pilot.
2. may provide a visual or audible warning at the lavatory and flight attendant station.
3. may automatically discharges a built in fire extinguisher.
A. 1
B. Both 1 and 2
C. 1 or 2, plus 3

17-28 AMA047

When inspecting the sensing elements of a continuous loop fire detection system, you find a section of tubing which has been dented. The proper corrective action is to

A. repair the section with a bullet tool or splice in a new section.
B. fabricate a new section.
C. replace the section.

17-29 AMA047

On a periodic check of a fire extinguisher container, the pressure was not between minimum and maximum limits. What procedure should be followed?

A. Release pressure if above limits.
B. Replace the extinguisher container.
C. Increase pressure if below limits.

17-30 AMA047

If a fire extinguisher cartridge is removed from a discharge valve for any reason, it

A. cannot be used again.
B. must be pressure checked.
C. may be used only on the original discharge valve assembly.

FIRE PROTECTION SYSTEMS

ANSWERS

17-25 Answer B.
Inside the smoke detection chamber, air flows between a source (LED) and a detector photodiode. If the air has smoke in it, the smoke particles reflect more light on the scatter detector. This causes an alarm signal.
[Ref: Airframe Handbook H-8083-31A-ATB, Chapter 17 Page 16]

17-26 Answer A.
The fire extinguishing bottles contain Halon 1301 or equivalent fire extinguishing agent pressurized with nitrogen, which is suitable for class A, B, and C type fires.
    A = Common combustible material
    B = Petroleum based fires
    C = Electrical fires
[Ref: Airframe Handbook H-8083-31A-ATB, Chapter 17 Page 16]

17-27 Answer C.
Airplanes with a passenger capacity of 20 or more are equipped with a smoke detector system that monitors the lavatories. Smoke indications provide a warning light in the cockpit or provide a light or audible warning at the lavatory and flight attendant stations. Each lavatory also has a built-in fire extinguisher that discharges automatically.
[Ref: Airframe Handbook H-8083-31A-ATB, Chapter 17 Page 17]

17-28 Answer C
If dents or kinks in sensing element sections are found which are beyond the manufacturer's stated tolerance, the section should be replaced with a preformed section from the manufacturer. No attempt should be made to straighten any acceptable dent or kink, since stresses may be set up that could cause tubing failure.
[Ref: Airframe Handbook H-8083-31A-ATB, Chapter 17 Page 19]

17-29 Answer B.
Fire extinguisher containers are checked periodically to determine that the pressure at ambient temperatures fall within prescribed limits. Service manuals provide acceptable readings. If the pressure does not fall within limits, the container is replaced.
[Ref: Airframe Handbook H-8083-31A-ATB, Chapter 17 Page 20]

17-30 Answer C.
If a cartridge is removed from a discharge valve it should not be used in another discharge valve assembly, since the distance the contact point protrudes may vary with each unit. Continuity might not exist if a used plug that had been indented with a long contact point were installed in a discharge valve with a shorter contact point.
[Ref: Airframe Handbook H-8083-31A-ATB, Chapter 17 Page 21]

ORAL EXAM

17-1(O).   What types of fire detection systems may be found on a large turbine powered aircraft?

17-2(O).   What fire extinguishing agents are used in aviation?

17-3(O).   Compare thermal switch type fire detection operational characteristics to those of a continuous loop type fire detection systems.

17-4(O).   Compare the operating characteristics of a halogenated hydrocarbon type fire extinguisher to that of an inert cold gas fire extinguisher.

17-5(O).   How does one determine the proper container pressure for an installed fire extinguisher system?

17-6(O).   What are some maintenance procedures for fire extinguishing systems?

17-7(O).   For what items should a continuous loop fire detection system be periodically inspected?

17-8(O).   How does a carbon monoxide detector indicate the presence of CO?

17-9(O).   What are some common faults and troubleshooting techniques used on a fire detection system?

FIRE PROTECTION SYSTEMS

ANSWERS

ORAL EXAM

17-1(O).   Rate of temperature rise detectors; radiation sensing detectors; smoke detectors, overheat detectors; carbon monoxide detectors; combustible mixture detectors; optical detectors; observation of crew and passengers.
[Ref: Airframe Handbook H-8083-31A-ATB, Chapter 17 Page 2]

17-2(O).   Halogenated hydrocarbons; inert cold gases; dry powders; Water.
[Ref: Airframe Handbook H-8083-31A-ATB, Chapter 17 Page 10-11]

17-3(O).   Thermal switches are heat sensitive units that complete electric circuits at a certain temperature. These circuits warn the crew of a fire hazard by illuminating a light or creating an aural tone. A thermal switch is spot detector that only responds to temperature in the specific location of the switch. Continuous loop fire detectors also close an indicating electric circuit at a certain temperature. However, lengths of the sensing loop provide superior detection coverage over a wide area. Anywhere the loop is run, a rise in temperature can cause the electric warning circuit to close and provide an indication to the crew.
[Ref: Airframe Handbook H-8083-31A-ATB, Chapter 17 Page 2-4]

17-4(O).   A halogenated hydrocarbon (Halon) type fire extinguisher is designed to dilute the atmosphere with an inert agent that does not support combustion. It is forced out of the container by pressurized nitrogen. An inert cold gas type fire extinguisher, primarily CO_2, provides its own pressure for discharge from the storage vessel. The agent is heavier than air and non-combustible. It replaces the air above burning surfaces and maintains a smothering atmosphere. It dilutes the air and reduces oxygen content so that combustion is no longer supported.
[Ref: Airframe Handbook H-8083-31A-ATB, Chapter 17 Page 10, 11, 16]

17-5(O).   Determining the proper pressure for an installed fire extinguisher system container involves reading the gauge mounted on the container. Since pressure varies with atmospheric temperature, the gauge indication must be compared to values presented on a temperature compensation graph to ensure it is within serviceable limits.
[Ref: Airframe Handbook H-8083-31A-ATB, Chapter 17 Page 13, 20]

17-6(O).   Regular maintenance of fire extinguisher systems typically includes the inspection and servicing of the extinguisher containers and removal and installation of discharge cartridges which have a limited service life. Discharge tubing is tested for routing and leakage and electrical wiring continuity tests may be performed.
[Ref: Airframe Handbook H-8083-31A-ATB, Chapter 17 Page 20]

17-7(O).   Cracked, broken, or crushed sections; abraded sections; condition of rubber grommets and clamps; dents and kinks in the detection element; security and safety of connection joint nuts; integrity of braided wire shielding; routing and clamping security of sensing element – proper support and bend radius; interference with cowling; proper grommet installation.
[Ref: Airframe Handbook H-8083-31A-ATB, Chapter 17 Page 18-19]

17-8(O).   Chemical color-change types of CO detectors are common. The chemical is applied to the visible surface of the detector. Normally, the color is tan but in the presence of carbon monoxide, the color of the chemical turns gray. A higher concentration of CO will turn the chemical dark gray or black.
[Ref: Airframe Handbook H-8083-31A-ATB, Chapter 17 Page 9]

ORAL EXAM

17-9(O).   Intermittent alarms most often caused by loose wires can often be found by moving the wires to recreate the fault. Alarms and warnings of a fire when there is no fire present can be located by disconnecting the sensors from the control unit. If the alarm stops when a sensor is disconnected, the problem is in that sensor. If all sensors are disconnected and the alarm continues, the problem is likely in the control unit. Kinks and sharp bends in a sensing element can cause a short inside the sensing element. The fault can be located by checking the sensing element with an ohm-meter while tapping the suspected areas to produce the short. Failure to obtain an alarm when a detection system is tested is often caused by a defective test switch or control unit, lack of electric power, inoperative indicator lamp, or an opening in a sensing element or connecting wire. Check for power to the test circuit and replace the lamp. The continuity of sensing loop can be determined by opening the loop and measuring the resistance. Replacement of the test switch or control unit may be required if no other faults are discovered. Occasionally moisture can cause a false alarm. This is detected in a sensor loop when disconnected from the control unit. Replacement of the sensor solves the problem.
[Ref: Airframe Handbook H-8083-31A-ATB, Chapter 17 Page 19-20]

FIRE PROTECTION SYSTEMS

QUESTIONS

PRACTICAL EXAM

17-1(P). Given a fire extinguisher container and the appropriate documentation inspect and determine if the pressure is within limits and record your findings.

17-2(P). Given a fire extinguisher, determine the hydrostatic test date of a fire extinguisher container and record your findings.

17-3(P). Given an actual aircraft or mockup, the appropriate documentation, and an unknown discrepancy troubleshoot a fire detection system and record your findings.

17-4(P). Given an actual aircraft or mockup, the appropriate documentation, install or replace a smoke detection system component and record maintenance.

17-5(P). Given an actual aircraft or mockup, the appropriate documentation, install or replace a fire detection system component and record maintenance.

17-6(P). Given an actual aircraft or mockup, the appropriate documentation install or replace a fire extinguishing system component and record maintenance.

17-7(P). Given an actual aircraft or mockup and the appropriate documentation, inspect a smoke detection system and record findings.

17-8(P). Given an actual aircraft or mockup and the appropriate documentation, inspect fire extinguishing system and record findings.

17-9(P). Given an actual aircraft or mockup and the appropriate documentation, inspect a fire detection system and record findings.

17-10(P). Given an actual aircraft or mockup and the appropriate documentation, inspect a smoke detection system component and record findings.

17-11(P). Given an actual aircraft or mockup and the appropriate documentation, inspect fire extinguishing system component and record findings.

17-13(P). Given an actual aircraft or mockup and the appropriate documentation, inspect a fire detection system component and record findings.

17-14(P). Given an actual aircraft or mockup and the appropriate documentation, locate the inspection procedures for the carbon monoxide detectors.

17-15(P). Given an actual aircraft or mockup and the appropriate documentation, locate the procedures for checking a smoke detection system.